Johnson's
England

DR. JOHNSON

From the portrait by J. Opie in the possession of Dr. Rosenbach

Johnson's England

An Account of the *Life & Manners* of his AGE

Edited by

A. S. TURBERVILLE

*Professor of Modern History in the
University of Leeds*

VOL. I

Clarendon Press Oxford

1933

OXFORD
UNIVERSITY PRESS
AMEN HOUSE, E.C. 4
London Edinburgh Glasgow
Leipzig New York Toronto
Melbourne Capetown Bombay
Calcutta Madras Shanghai
HUMPHREY MILFORD
PUBLISHER TO THE
UNIVERSITY

PREFACE

THE object of this work is to depict the life of the period in English history which may legitimately be described as the Age of Johnson. Johnson lived from 1709 to 1784; as a small child he was 'touched for the evil' by Queen Anne, and he lived into the third decade of the reign of George III, to see, a few months before his death, the triumphal election which established the Younger Pitt in power. It is clear that the term the Age of Johnson cannot properly be applied to the whole of the Doctor's lifetime: no one in using it has in mind the period which may be appropriately designated the Age of Addison or of Pope; nor yet the Doctor's early years, when he was an undergraduate at Oxford or an unsuccessful school-master at Edial. It was not until the spring of 1737 that, accompanied by his former pupil, David Garrick, he went up from Lichfield to London in order to try his fortunes in the city with which he is perhaps more closely associated than any other Englishman; and not till ten years after that did he start upon the Dictionary, which brought the fame that his play, his poems, and even *The Rambler* had failed to win. It seems proper to characterize as the Age of Johnson the last fifty years of his lifetime, though it would obviously be pedantic to tie oneself down to any particular year for its commencement, and it is sometimes necessary for a full appreciation of the aspects of the national life portrayed in the following pages to refer back to the earlier decades of the eighteenth century.

The purpose of the book is descriptive rather than critical or expository. Perhaps the commonest temptation to one surveying a past epoch is to view it too much from the stand-point of present conditions and in the light of later know-ledge, to judge it by modern standards—not so much ethical and aesthetic standards as the mere criterion of modern notions of comfort and convenience—and so to bring out unduly the strangeness, the oddity, or even the uncouthness of the habits and arrangements of our ancestors. Were we to be suddenly whirled back into the middle of the eighteenth century we should no doubt discover a good deal that was jarring and disagreeable to us. Those who have become habituated to the noise, bustle, and speed of the twentieth century, and to its facilities for inexpensive and ubiquitous entertainment, might find England as it was two hundred years ago (outside the capital at all events) both slow and dull; and, the nose being the most sensitive of organs, probably we should all of us find something offensive in days when standards of cleanliness were much less high than they are to-day, and sanitation was still rather rudimentary. But this book has not been written for those who seem to concern themselves with the past mainly that they may extol the superior amenities of the present; nor yet for those whose sole conception of history is teleological, to whom the significance of a period lies entirely in its contribution to an evolutionary process. It is intended rather for those who study a past epoch for the sheer pleasure it gives them, who enjoy wandering in an England at once so familiar and so strange, anxious rather to explore and to learn to understand than to be for ever apportioning praise or blame. Just as it is an impertinence to criticize a foreign country when one possesses as yet only a tourist's knowledge of it, before one has learnt to know its people, to speak their language, and to become at home in their surroundings; so, we must in imagination become the friends and neighbours of our forefathers before we are entitled to dogmatize about them. The intelligent visitor to the foreign country will at once be struck by the differences between its mode of life and his own; the benefit he derives from his visit will depend partly upon his own powers of observation, but partly also upon the questions he asks and the people to whom he puts them. It is hoped that in these volumes there have been propounded some of the problems which would assail some twentieth-century Gulliver who should suddenly find himself brought to the shores of Johnson's England, and, still more important, that they contain some of the explanations which would be given by Englishmen who knew no later England than Johnson's.

In short, the whole intention of the work could hardly be better expressed than in the words of Mr. Charles Morgan in his novel, *The Fountain*: 'A student of history must beware of supposing that the men of the past are arraigned before him for his approval or condemnation; he is not their judge. Nor is he what many historians are content, and even eager, to remain—a visitor with a cloak of darkness, a note-book, and a curious eye, loving facts, as avarice loves diamonds, for the value given them by their rarity. The historian has much in common with the artist; he must yield himself to his subject and become a creature of the time he investigates, standing apart from it only now and then, as a traveller, wishing to examine a map which he alone possesses, may for a little while leave his companions, soon to rejoin them. He must be able to accept the limitations of contemporary vision that he may experience its intensity.'[1]

To present at all a living picture of the life of a past age in all its varied aspects is always a difficult task; indeed it demands so much specialized knowledge that it is perhaps only by the method of collaboration in a composite work that it can be accurately accomplished. The method has its obvious drawbacks, but provided that unity of aim and design are secured, its advantages greatly outnumber its defects. What is known as social history is nowadays generally found more attractive than political history; but it is a fallacy to suppose that it is easier. People commonly find the politics of their own day extremely interesting and therefore narrate them fully and comment upon them lavishly, however dull they may appear to a later generation; while, upon the other hand, the details of their everyday existence, which pique the curiosity of posterity, seem to them too trivial and are too much taken for granted to be recorded. Occasionally there is to be found a Pepys or a Woodforde, who provides a chronicle of daily routine; but such minute annals are rare. And, in any case, rich as the eighteenth century is in diaries, letters, and memoirs, there are many questions to which they afford no answers, and for which it is necessary to consult materials of a very different, and a more recondite, type.

An attempt has been made in the present work, so far as the limits of reasonable space permit, to furnish something more precise and more valuable than merely general impressions. A few illustrations may be given at random. Pluralism in the Anglican Church of the eighteenth century is a byword, but why was it necessary? The clergy are supposed to have been lax and indifferent, but how many services were held in parish churches and how often were the sacraments administered? Every one has heard of the press-gang, but how was the class of naval officers recruited? The

[1] Quoted by kind permission of the author and Messrs. Macmillan & Co.

stage-coach is very familiar, but how frequent were its
services, and what were the fares? The industrial changes
of the period are notorious, but how were they financed in
the absence of joint-stock banks and when banking facilities
were concentrated in London? The Georgian house we all
know, but to what building regulations had it to conform?
Every one has heard of Capability Brown and his landscape
gardening, but what sort of trees and flowers were to be
found in the gardens? Grub Street has become a legend, but
how did authors get their books published and what was the
system of remuneration? Cricket was played, but what was
the shape of the bat, and what was the height of the wickets?
Such hospitals as St. Bartholomew's and St. Thomas's existed,
but how did a patient obtain admission to them, and what
sort of training had been received by the surgeons and nurses
whom he found there? The judges' circuits were much as they
are to-day, but what rules of procedure did the judges apply?
Divorce was possible, but in the absence of a Divorce Court,
how was it obtained?

The visitor to Johnson's England can have no better guide
than the Doctor himself. When due allowance has been
made for the 'pleasure in contradiction' taken by one who,
when he talked, was apt to talk for victory, the outlook of
Johnson upon the men and the institutions of his time was
extraordinarily sane and well balanced. If he had strong
prejudices, he had an even stronger sense of humour, and his
sympathies were as wide as his charity was deep. He was
very tolerant of human failings, though not indeed of cruelty,
insincerity, make-believe, irreverence, and profanity. He
was no cynic and equally he was no 'enthusiast'. He was
English to the backbone, but to utter dithyrambs about his
country's greatness would have been abhorrent to him; he
preferred rather to tease the Scots. When he spoke about
patriotism it was but to castigate an obnoxious type of
politician. He had a great objection to exaggeration (save
when it was playfully adopted by himself for the sake of
argument!). There were plenty of morose people in Johnson's day, as there have been in all periods of our history—
even in those of Elizabeth, Anne, and Victoria—who perceived around them the clear evidences of racial degeneracy.
There was a popular theory—Goldsmith, for example, held
it—that the English people were being enervated by luxury.

With robust good sense Johnson roundly declared: 'I believe there are as many tall men in England now, as ever there were'; and he added: 'Our soldiery, surely, are not luxurious, who live on sixpence a day; and the same remark will apply to almost all the other classes. Luxury, so far as it reaches the poor, will do good for the race of people; it will strengthen and multiply them.' Similarly with politics. He indeed confessed that he had 'no delight in public affairs'; he was, like the majority of his fellow countrymen, opposed to the American colonies on the most burning political question of his lifetime, and was 'against the Ministry; but it is for having too little of that, of which opposition thinks they have too much'. On the other hand, when Boswell asked him whether he was not vexed by the adoption of Dunning's famous motion: 'The power of the Crown has increased, is increasing, and ought to be diminished,' Johnson, sturdy Tory and monarchist as he was, retorted: 'Sir, Public affairs vex no man . . . I never 'slept an hour less, nor ate one ounce less meat. I would have knocked the factious dogs on the head to be sure; but I was not vexed'—a statement which was followed by the famous adjuration, 'Clear your *mind* of cant'.

If there was any contemporary tendency that Johnson bewailed it was the lack of subordination. No man, he remarked, has nowadays the same authority that his father had—except a jailer; and, as he said on another occasion, 'Order cannot be had but by subordination'. All boys loved liberty till they made the discovery that they were not as fit to govern themselves as they imagined, and as for the liberty of the mob to govern—'when that was the case some time ago, no man was at liberty not to have candles in his windows'. On the other hand, he professed himself on the side of youth. 'I am always on the young people's side', he said, 'when there is a dispute between them and the old ones.' And in his 'Essay on the Bravery of the English Common Soldier', he ascribed this courage ultimately to the independence shown by the man in the street and his dislike of restraint. Inconveniences might from time to time proceed from it, 'but good and evil will grow up in this world together; and they who complain in peace of the insolence of the populace, must remember that their insolence is bravery in war'.

One other illustration must suffice. The deficiencies of the English universities in the eighteenth century are an oft-repeated theme, and no one will deny that their defects were glaring, and the general standard of teaching deplorable: yet a century which produced such men of learning as Hearne, Tyrwhitt, Lowth, and Thomas Warton at Oxford; Bentley, Porson, and Thomas Twining at Cambridge, has a far from negligible record in university scholarship. The origin of most people's impression of eighteenth-century Oxford can be traced to the famous passage in Gibbon's *Autobiography*. But why should the evidence of one who when he went up to Oxford was only a boy of fifteen, and who spent only a little over a year there, be preferred to that of Johnson, who knew Oxford a great deal better? It is worthy of note that the patient and minute investigations of Mr. Lyell Reade into Johnson's Oxford career seem to show that there were undergraduates who lived frugally and worked hard and who derived from their university course the kind of benefit the pious acknowledgement of which by Bishop Lowth Gibbon so scornfully derided. At all events Johnson, like Lowth, 'delighted in his own partiality for Oxford'. He praised the 'progressive emulation', the desire of the student to appear well with the tutor, of the tutor to appear well with the College, of the College to appear well with the University. He praised, too, the College discipline. He admitted that it might sometimes be ill observed, but he was arguing (as he said) 'for the excellence of the institution'. It was alleged that the Universities were too rich: Johnson, on the contrary, maintained that they were not rich enough. The most learned men in England were not always to be found at the Universities, as was the case abroad, simply because professorships on the Continent were sufficiently well paid to attract the first-rate men, whereas at Oxford and Cambridge they were not.

No doubt there was in the period which the late Professor Dicey described as that of 'Blackstonian optimism' too comfortable a disposition to assume that because we possessed the best of all possible constitutions, we enjoyed the best of all possible worlds in all respects. But to think of the age of Johnson as purely static and self-satisfied is clearly to go wide of the mark: it was in all manner of ways extraordinarily energetic and progressive. The very fact that we hear so much of its abuses is in truth a sign of this. Once practices and institutions which have been accepted without criticism for generations come to be so spoken of, there is evidence that the national conscience is being aroused. Before the death of Johnson there had begun the crusades for parliamentary reform, for prison reform, and for the abolition of the slave trade. Like many other high Tories, Johnson was a great philanthropist. He was as unequivocal as Granville Sharp and Wilberforce themselves in his condemnation of slavery—wherein Boswell, it will be remembered, proved to his own satisfaction that his oracle was egregiously mistaken. Johnson, whose own private generosity to the poor was boundless, made one great claim for his generation. 'The present age,' he wrote in 1758, 'though not likely to shine hereafter among the most splendid periods of history, has yet given examples of charity, which may be very properly commended to imitation.' The researches of Mrs. George and others in the same field have shown that despite the prevalent persuasion that the late decades of the eighteenth century were an exceptionally unhappy period, actually there was a definite amelioration in social and hygienic conditions during the century.

The very year after Johnson wrote the words just quoted was the year of Minden, of Quiberon Bay, Lagos, and the taking of Quebec, a series of victories to which there is no parallel in our annals save in 1918. The age which was that not only of Johnson but also of Chatham, Clive, Warren Hastings, Hawke, Cook, Wolfe, Burke, Fox, Hardwicke, Mansfield, Gibbon, Fielding, Reynolds, Gainsborough, the Adams, Garrick, Cavendish, Priestley, the Hunters, Watt and Brindley, Tull and Bakewell, is surely to be reckoned among the splendid periods of history. It is strange it should sometimes be thought of as rather dull and placid when it was so full of intense activity and creative energy.

The Editor wishes to express his very sincere thanks to all those who have assisted in the production of the book. The Hon. Andrew Shirley has not only edited the chapter on Painting and Engraving but has also undertaken editorial work in connexion with the other four chapters on Art. The Editor owes a great deal to the unstinted help of Dr. R. W. Chapman, Professor Nichol Smith, and Mr. L. F.

Powell, who have all three most generously and constantly put their great knowledge of the period at his disposal; and he cannot exaggerate his debt also to the officers of the Clarendon Press, who have at different times been in charge of the work, for their assiduous devotion to it. They have been largely responsible for collecting such of the illustrations as have not been furnished by the contributors themselves. The Editor would like to express his appreciation of the kindness of all the contributors in so readily acceding to suggestions, and especially to Mr. Justice MacKinnon in undertaking to write a chapter at short notice. The Law was not originally included in the plan of the book, as it did not appear to come within its scheme—how mistakenly readers of the chapter will appreciate. The consequence of its late incorporation is that it perforce appears in Volume II instead of in its proper place, near the beginning of Volume I. Thanks are also due to Mr. A. B. Emden, Mr. L. G. Malcolm, and Dr. E. A. Sadler of Ashbourne for advice or information on particular points: to the authorities of the Department of Prints and Drawings at the British Museum, and Mr. J. L. Douthwaite, Librarian of the Guildhall Library, for much invaluable assistance in connexion with the illustrations; and to Mr. R. H. New, who has compiled the Index.

Acknowledgements for permission to reproduce prints and pictures are due to many institutions and corporate bodies, and in the first place to the Directors of the British Museum and the Victoria and Albert Museum, from whose collections have been drawn a large proportion of the illustrations in this book; to the Ashmolean Museum, for the engravings in the Hope Collection of the portraits of Lord Tavistock and Charles Towneley; the Governors of Dulwich College, for the paintings of A Fishing Party by William Hogarth, and a landscape by an unknown English artist; the Guildhall Library, for the prints of A Racecourse and The Dog and Duck; The London Museum, for the prints of London Bridge in 1757, The Battle of Umbrellas, Refreshment at St. James's, Black-friars Bridge, and the Hyde Park Corner Turnpike; the National Gallery, for the pictures of a Gentleman driving a Phaeton by George Stubbs, and Marriage à la Mode, Plate IV, by William Hogarth; the Royal Academy, for the paintings of the Life School in St. Martin's Lane, the Antique School of the Royal Academy at Somerset House, and the Life Class of the Royal Academy; the Royal Agricultural Society, for the picture of Robert Bakewell; the Royal Artillery Institution, Woolwich, for the drawing of a soldier of the 29th Regiment of Foot; the Royal College of Surgeons, for the print of an eighteenth-century hospital; the Royal Geographical Society, for A New Map of the Terraqueous Globe and A Map of the World, 1771; the Science Museum, South Kensington, for the model of an 18-gun sloop and for the painting of the *Barfleur* by Joshua Marshall; the President of Corpus Christi College, Oxford, for the map of the Parish of Tackley before inclosure; the Mayor and Corporation of Stratford-upon-Avon, for the painting of David Garrick by Thomas Gainsborough; and the Curator of the Theatre Collection, Harvard College Library, for the print of a Scene from 'The Duenna'.

His Majesty the King has graciously permitted the reproduction of the painting of Regulus by Benjamin West, in Kensington Palace, and the drawing of a trooper of the King's Carabineers in the Royal Library at Windsor Castle.

Many private persons have kindly given permission for the reproduction of prints and pictures in this book: the Most Honourable the Marquis of Bristol, the picture of Captain John Augustus Hervey taking leave of his family; the Right Honourable the Earl of Durham, the picture of Mr. and Mrs. Thrale entertaining Dr. Johnson to tea; Miss Olive Lloyd-Baker, the picture of a Music Party on the Thames at Fulham; Mr. George H. Drummond, the picture of the Drummond Family; Mr. Gaston Boudou, the picture by J. Collett; Mr. C. R. M. F. Cruttwell, the engraving of the Exhibition of the Royal Academy in 1787; Mr. J. L. Douthwaite, the engraving after William Mason of a Scene in a Country Town at the time of a Race; Sir Charles Firth, the broadside commemorating Dick Turpin; Mr. J. H. Hallam, the picture of Doctors' Commons; Sir Ambrose Heal, the engraved trade card of John Flude and advertisement of Dr. James's Powder; Major H. Howard, the picture of the Thomlinson family by A. Devis; the Right Honourable Lord Huntingfield and the Hon. A. Vanneck, Lancelot Brown's Plan for Heveningham Hall, Norfolk; Mr. L. F. Powell, the print of Eton College from the Playing

Fields; and Dr. A. S. W. Rosenbach, the picture of Dr. Johnson by J. Opie.

Sir Philip Sassoon, Dr. G. C. Williamson, and Messrs. B. T. Batsford have kindly given permission for the use of the photographs of the pictures belonging to the Marquis of Bristol, the Earl of Durham, Miss Lloyd-Baker, and Mr. Drummond, which were reproduced in *English Conversation Pieces* (Batsford, 1931); and acknowledgements are also due to Messrs. Arthur Ackermann, for the picture of Shooting in 1769 by George Stubbs; Messrs. Cassell, for that of Brushing into Cover; Messrs. B. T. Batsford, for the photograph of a Parson's School about 1750, from *Life and Work of the English People*, by Dorothy Hartley and Margaret M. Elliot, vol. vi.

CONTENTS

VOLUME I

VOLUME II

LIST OF ILLUSTRATIONS
VOLUME I

VOLUME II

I

THE AGE OF JOHNSON

By G. M. TREVELYAN

It is often the custom to think of the eighteenth century, prior to the French Revolution, as a period of effete politeness and intelligence, of cultured and artificial decadence, of scepticism, atrophy, and want of enterprise—like the figure in Max Beerbohm's famous cartoons of the three centuries. The first reaction of many minds to the words 'eighteenth century' is a vision of beaux in coloured silk garments, drinking coffee out of small cups, while engaging in elegant philosophic small talk with ladies with towering powdered head-dresses and patched cheeks.

With regard to the continent of Europe, there is a certain amount of symbolical truth in this popular impression, but, for Britain, a more illuminating picture of the eighteenth century would be supplied by a vision of something more robust—Clive planted four-square across the breach of Arcot; Wolfe and his men scrambling up the precipitous forest track towards Quebec; Captain Cook's sails sweeping into Botany Bay; Wesley's lean face and long white hair, as he preaches to mass meetings of miners and throws powerful men into fits of hysteria; James Watt working in the instrument maker's shop, with thoughts in him that shall have their consequences in the history of mankind.

England, indeed, had also its Lord Chesterfields and its Beau Nashes, but they occupied a relatively small part of the scene. The eighteenth-century English, on the average, were an earnest, virile, original, unconventional, and energetic race. They practised self-help and individualism before the Victorians, but without bothering to write books about those virtues. That a man must help himself, seemed to them too natural to remark upon. If he did not, who else was to help him? Unless, indeed, he were cousin to a lord, or had a vote in a rotten borough, in which case the lord would provide. If they were to meet us, our eighteenth-century forefathers would, I shrewdly suspect, regard us as the decadents, with our grandmother, the State, running about after us all day long. If a man could not find honest

employment, they expected him to be man enough to go
to the Colonies or take to the Highway, in which latter case
the State would sooner or later do its one useful office by
him at Tyburn Gallows—and the admiring public would
turn him into a ballad hero. Dr. Johnson's English were
a sturdy crew.

With regard to the continent of Europe, the popular impression that the eighteenth century was effete and conventional has at least a certain relation to truth. The France
that staggered on from the defeat of the ambitions of the
Grand Monarch at Blenheim in 1704, to the final gulf of
bankruptcy and revolution in 1789—that phoenix fire of an
appalling rebirth—eighteenth-century France was in some
senses effete. So, too, was Germany, with the exception of
Frederick the Great's little Prussia; Germany, bled white by
the Thirty Years War, was no longer the Germany of Luther,
Albert Dürer, and the great merchant cities. Italy, too, the
Italy of Piranesi's prints, was peaceful and stagnant—a land
of hard-working, ragged, submissive peasants, of idle beggars,
and of cultured dilettante nobles and clergy with few interests
in life beyond the innocent occupation of reading to each
other insipid compositions in verse, and disquisitions, learned
and sentimental, on the monuments of antiquity—a land
strangely different from the fierce and passionate Italy of
the Middle Ages, of the later Risorgimento, or of modern
Fascism.

A lethargic peace, not unfavourable to thought and culture as distinct from action, did in fact brood over much of
eighteenth-century Europe. Until 1789 Europe, outside the
small dominions of Frederick the Great, was energetic and
creative only in thought, hardly at all in deed. It made no
great industrial, social, or political change inside its own
borders. And, except for the unsuccessful attempt of the
French to drive us from India, continental Europe in that
epoch made no great outward push at colonization in
America, Africa, and the East, as the French, Spaniards,
and Dutch had done in previous centuries, and as all
European countries were destined to do in the nineteenth
century.

But when we turn to the Britain of the period we have
a different story to tell. This was the time when our fathers
conquered Canada and half India, rediscovered and began

to settle Australia, and traded on an ever-increasing scale all over the inhabited globe; reorganized British agriculture on modern methods; began the Industrial Revolution in our island, thence in later times to spread over the whole world; and if the thirteen American colonies were at the same time lost to the British Empire, it was the result less of decadence in Great Britain than of young and mutinous energies in English America.

And on this side of the Atlantic, Great Britain, over and above her efforts in the material sphere of war, industry, and commerce, could show no less wonderful achievements in the sphere of intellect and of culture. England produced not only the classical perfection of Johnson's conversations and Gray's and Goldsmith's writings, but the intellectual originality of men like Adam Smith, Bentham, and Blake, breaking up new soil of the mind and of the spirit. The historical genius of Gibbon was the perfect fruit borne by the widespread antiquarian learning common in the leisured class of the period, whence modern historical study emerged.

Indeed, Johnson's England was full of creative intellectual power both in the sciences and in the arts. In the country at large, the physical science of the Newtonian school—originated at the universities in the former age—was being applied by men of business to the processes of industry. It was in the later eighteenth century that Englishmen, taught by White of Selborne and Bewick of Tyneside, first learnt that peculiar interest in the bird life and natural history of their own land that has ever since distinguished them. It was the first great age of native English painting, with Reynolds and Gainsborough. The novel was being evolved by Defoe, Fielding, Richardson, Smollett, and Miss Burney, to be the principal instrument of literature in coming ages.

Whether or not I am right in supposing that the England of the eighteenth century had an energy of spirit that was lacking elsewhere in the Europe of that day, it is at least certain that this view was then generally held upon the Continent. After the Marlborough wars with which the century opened, and, still more after the great victories of Chatham in two hemispheres in the Seven Years War, foreigners were always asking each other what was the secret of English success, and the answer they found was that the secret lay in our free institutions. In the days of Charles I and II our Parliament had been regarded abroad as a source of confusion and weakness to England. But the course of William III's and Marlborough's wars had changed that view completely. For the British Parliament had defeated the all-worshipped despotism of Louis XIV in a long-drawn contest, in which England had proved supreme alike in land warfare, in sea warfare, in diplomacy, and in financial strength. This unexpected event gave a prestige to our institutions which coloured European thought from the time of Marlborough right down to the French Revolution. The prosperity of England under Walpole, the constant increase of her trade and maritime power, her victories under Chatham in Canada and India, all confirmed the same impression. Even our great catastrophe—the loss of the American Colonies—was read in France as another demonstration of the power that freedom gives. It was not only our Parliament that was admired, but freedom of speech, press, person, and religious toleration. The England of the Revolution settlement stood for all these things, and in their strength it had triumphed over the despotic and intolerant institutions of France. Frenchmen were as eager as we ourselves to draw the lesson. They observed that whereas their own decline might be dated from the renewed persecution of the Huguenots by the revocation of the Edict of Nantes, England had never looked back since she had given peace to her own religious discords by the Act of Toleration of 1689.

The criticisms passed by Montesquieu, Voltaire, and the Encyclopaedists on French and continental institutions in Church and State, would have received little attention if Louis XIV had triumphed at Blenheim, and if his descendants had dominated Europe, Canada, and India.

In our own day, men are somewhat confused in trying to draw general conclusions from contemporary events. The fall of the autocratic principle in Russia, Germany, and Austria, on the one hand, is countered by the fall of parliamentary government in Italy and its failure to fill the gap left in Russia by the disappearance of the Czardom. These signal failures, almost at the same moment, of despotic and of free government, render it difficult for men in our day to draw conclusions of universal applicability. We are, moreover, better aware than the Encyclopaedists of the diversities of men and things; but in the eyes of the eighteenth-century philosophers, human beings were thought of in the abstract. National differences were little understood. One panacea, it was held, would suit the whole human race, or at least all white men; and that panacea must clearly be parliamentary government and personal freedom, for it had been tried in England and had succeeded there. It had not yet been tried anywhere else—unless, indeed, in Holland, where also freedom had made a great nation out of a little clan.

Voltaire, in his *Lettres sur les Anglais,* told his countrymen:

The English nation is the only one on earth which has managed to regulate the power of its kings while resisting them; where the lords are great without insolence and without vassals, and where the people takes part in the government without confusion. In England it is common to think (*communément on pense*); and literature has more honour than with us French. This advantage is a necessary outcome of their form of government.

Nothing is more touching and admirable than the personal relations of the French and English educated classes during this century of reason and good manners, in spite of the fact that two-fifths of its hundred years was spent in war between France and Britain. We breathe a harsher air in the international contests and alliances of our own era. Chatham was the admired man in the country on which he had heaped the disasters of the Seven Years War. To be a fellow countryman of Chatham, of Hume, of 'le grand Newton', opened every salon in Paris to the travelling Englishman. Gibbon was almost as much at home in the society of Paris as in that of London.

In those days, the English gentleman, once or oftener in his life, made the Grand Tour of France and Italy (hardly ever of Germany, and practically never of the English Colonies in America, which was one reason why we lost them). On the Grand Tour the English gentleman was received into the society of French salons and Italian petty Courts, mingling there with the foreign nobles and with the artists and men of letters whom they patronized. English tourists were not in those days isolated in cosmopolitan hotels from all contact with the life of the peoples in whose lands they travelled. This was partly because the travellers were in those days fewer and their Grand Tours more protracted. The Continent was visited not once in twelve months, but once in a lifetime, and then for a year or more on end. Moreover, there was a social freemasonry between the upper classes of all continental Europe that no longer exists. The noblesse of France and Italy and the gentry of England felt a mutual obligation and camaraderie that has no place in our busy world, where society is more mixed and classes are less distinguishable from one another in dress, education, and manners. At the present day, indeed, there seems, in theory at least, to be a greater camaraderie between the working classes of different countries. Cosmopolitanism was then upper class, it is now lower class. In the eighteenth century the English working man—then called the jolly yeoman or the industrious 'prentice—was intensely British, boasted himself a free-born Briton, and had no use for the frog-eating, priest-ridden Frenchman of his imagination. The average Englishman had not made the Grand Tour, and had no information about foreigners such as is being constantly poured in upon us to-day through newspapers, cinemas, books, pamphlets, and photographs. What the common English thought of the French you can see in Hogarth's uncomplimentary picture, entitled 'Calais Gate', in the National Gallery. This contempt for, and ignorance of, foreigners was extended not only to the Irish, but even to the Scots—who only became understood and admired in England in the age of Walter Scott, partly through the powerful influence of his pen.

Nor must it be supposed that even the gentry who had made the Grand Tour had been cosmopolitanized to a serious extent. Their portraits were painted not by foreign hands but by Gainsborough and Reynolds; their library shelves were weighted with luxurious editions of English history, poetry, and novels; their literary oracle was Dr. Johnson, the most abnormally English creature God ever made. The life that the English gentry lived was as different as possible from that of their continental friends. The nobles of France and Italy thought little of existence away from the Court of their master, the King or reigning Duke. But the English gentry, when they came to town, came first and foremost to their own Parliament, only secondarily to the King's Court—a place of dull ceremony, no longer the true heart of the land's activities as it had been under the

Plantagenets and the Tudors. But the bulk of their lives the English gentlemen spent neither at Court nor yet in the purlieus of Parliament, nor in London at all; but in the country, among their neighbours of all classes whom they led, entertained, bullied, and at election time courted and bribed. It was to their country houses that they brought back the art treasures they had collected on the Grand Tour—treasures in our day being scattered oversea by the auctioneer's hammer. They lived among their neighbours, hunting foxes, shooting partridges, inclosing and draining land, improving breeds of sheep and cattle, governing the countryside as Justices of the Peace. Their whole manner of life and way of thought was English, and though every English gentleman was recognized as belonging to the same social level as the continental nobleman, he was also recognized as belonging to a separate and unique island species of the genus European gentleman.

There was therefore in eighteenth-century England, prior to the changes gradually made manifest by the Industrial Revolution, a national solidarity and unity of idea which bound Englishmen of all classes together and separated them from foreigners. Power, as we think looking back, was unduly concentrated in the hands of one class, the country gentry, but their monopoly was not popularly regarded as a grievance. The novelist Fielding is one of the very few contemporary critics of squirarchical power in the mid-eighteenth century. Classes were distinct in England—less distinct and rigid, indeed, than on the Continent at that time, but much more distinct and rigid than they are to-day. Wealth was very unevenly distributed. But there was little or no social discontent, and the national idea made every one proud of being a free-born Englishman.

> To glory we call you as freemen not slaves,
> For who are so free as the sons of the waves?

That song is the authentic popular voice of the England of Chatham. And therefore, when the French Revolution raised new issues between classes, and Tom Paine attacked the upper class monopoly of power, the first response of Englishmen to it was a decided rally to the English idea of national solidarity as distinct from the new French idea of equality and class war. But the Industrial Revolution was by that time busily at work sapping the old order in society; and therefore, early in the next century, at the time of Peterloo, we find an amount of conscious discontent and the arraying of class against class, from which the age of Johnson had been immune.

It is, indeed, arguable that a little more social discontent in the time of Walpole and Chatham might have prevented the Industrial Revolution, when it came, from developing on lines chosen with so little regard to the masses. In that case we might have avoided some at least of the dangerous class cleavages of the nineteenth and twentieth centuries. But that, like all the might-have-beens of history, is the merest speculation. Things were what they were, and the consequences will be what they will be.

If Johnson's England differed from Voltaire's France in her parliamentary constitution, in the greater amount of freedom secured to the individual citizen in speech, press, and person, and in the superior energies of the individual at home and overseas—England nevertheless shares with the rest of Europe one marked characteristic of the eighteenth century civilization, the lethargy of all established and chartered corporations. In England it was a great age for the energies of the private person—the adventurer, the merchant, the author—acting freely in a free community. But the chartered institutions were antiquated and corrupt. The universities, the endowed schools, the municipalities, the electoral bodies, had lost their old vigour and had not yet acquired the modern energies that gave them a fresh life in the following century. It was characteristic of the time that the established Church, just because it was established, was unable to accommodate itself to the new life brought to its service by Wesley; that the vast increase of British industry took place no longer, as in the Middle Ages, under cover of municipal protection, but for the most part outside the old municipal boundaries; that thought and learning were at a low ebb in the Oxford known to Gibbon and the Cambridge known to Wordsworth, although in every corner of the land private scholars were devoting their lives to antiquarian and classical lore.

It would appear that the chartered institutions and corporations—Church, universities, municipal bodies—were too secure; they had no fear of reform, and therefore they settled comfortably down to sleep. The undisturbed security of the chartered corporations is characteristic of the eighteenth century. But if privilege was immune from attack in England, it was partly because of the toleration which the privileged orders extended to those outside their own limits. The town municipalities and guilds no longer, as in the Middle Ages, pretended to control and direct all the industry and trade of the land. If the rotten municipalities of the eighteenth century had attempted to prevent the cloth and cotton manufacturers from spreading outside their jurisdiction, there would have been a sharp crisis, ending in a reform of the municipalities long before 1835. If the Church, after 1689, had continued to persecute Dissenters, the Wesleyans must have striven, like the Puritans before them, to annex or to overthrow the Church instead of leaving it on one side.

But the security of all chartered corporations from attack was based not merely on their tolerant practice towards outsiders, but also on the unreforming spirit of the age. The religious and political storms of the seventeenth century had spent their fury; the social and political storms of the modern era had not yet begun to blow. The intervening century of reason and toleration had the merits and defects of an era when existing institutions are taken for granted. It was therefore much sneered at in the retrospect by the more earnest and restless nineteenth century. We in the twentieth century are perhaps more nearly tempted to give a sigh of helpless envy in contemplating so fair and peaceful a field for individual thought and energy as was presented by the age of Johnson, Wedgwood, and Reynolds.

'Let sleeping dogs lie' was Walpole's motto. 'Rejoice in our matchless constitution' was the lesson Blackstone taught to his contemporaries. According to the optimistic political philosophy of Blackstone and Burke, our British freedom was held to be based on the security of chartered corporations, and on the impotence of the central government to interfere with those rights and privileges. James II had attacked the chartered privileges of Parliament, Municipalities, Church, Universities, and the rights of freehold property. The attempt had cost him his throne, and the consequence was that for a hundred years after the Revolution

no one ventured to attack chartered rights again, or even
seriously to criticize their abuse. A habit of mind was
formed which thought that 'whatever is is right', provided
it can show a charter. The formidable Conservatism with
which the eighteenth century ended, the anti-Jacobin Conservatism of the later Burke, Pitt, and Eldon, was based on
a retrospective enthusiasm for the Revolution that had
dethroned James II. That memorable event, so far from
being merely a Whig shibboleth, was pleaded by the anti-
Jacobin Tories a hundred years later as the palladium of our
Constitution, henceforth unalterable. They held up the
Conservative Revolution of 1689 as the touchstone which
should render immune for all time all those institutions
which James had illegally attacked, which the Radicals of a
later age were proposing to alter in another direction and for
a different purpose.

But long before the days of anti-Jacobins, in the mid-
eighteenth century period of Walpole and Chatham, the
holders of property and privilege, particularly of corporate
rights, had felt so secure from criticism and reform that
many abuses had grown up in Boroughs, Church, Universities, Civil Service, Army, and Parliament.

Before the Industrial Revolution, the mass of the people
of all classes, though they worked for longer hours than now
(eleven to thirteen hours normal) and for less pay, had the
great advantage of living in the country instead of in the
city; and even the dwellers in the moderate-sized cities of that
time were not far removed from rural influence and tradition.
The Tudor, Stuart, and early Hanoverian period, culminat-
ing in the eighteenth century, was the great period of
English village life. In the Middle Ages the village had indeed been the normal scene of English life, but the medieval
village was poverty-stricken and often famine- and plague-
stricken; its inhabitants, even when not actually serfs,
were nearly all of them engaged in a struggle with nature
under harsh and difficult conditions. The medieval villagers
were engaged in agriculture or in the simpler crafts immediately subsidiary to agriculture; the finer crafts, industry, and
commerce of the Middle Ages had been centred in the walled
cities for the most part. But, from the time of the rise of English cloth manufacture, many industries and crafts moved

into the countryside, increasingly in Tudor and Stuart times. Workshops were more and more set up in the villages, which had become safe enough and civilized enough to be the scene of the most elaborate manufactures and, in particular, of the great weaving industry. The move back to the cities came with the Industrial Revolution, when industry from the end of the eighteenth century until our own day migrated back to urban areas, carrying with it far the greater part of the population.

But in the fortunate eighteenth century, many villages were centres of industry as well as of agriculture. The typical Englishman was a villager, but a villager accustomed to meet men of various crafts and occupations and classes— by no means, therefore, a mere rustic boor, ignorant of all save the plough handle. Moreover, some people are inclined to forget that ploughing and agricultural operations generally are an extremely skilled trade. But the village was alive with the activities of all sorts and conditions of men.

This, according to my fancy at least, was a more wholesome state of society than the village of the medieval serf on the one hand, or the present-day city and urban district, where dwell the millions divorced from nature and only very partially redeemed by education.

But the old system of village life and handicraft that culminated and began to decline in the eighteenth century, excellent as it was in many respects, could only maintain some 7 millions alive in this island, and then at a much lower standard of material comfort than that enjoyed by 42 millions in our own day. Indeed, it may be doubted whether English prosperity, such as it was in the time of Chatham, could have gone on much beyond the middle of the eighteenth century if it had not been for the great inventions and the Industrial Revolution. Already there was a fuel famine, due to the using up of the forests—a fuel famine that was killing our old timber-fed iron industry, and was rendering warmth and cooked food unattainable in the cottages of the poor in many districts. No fuel in the cottage meant a bread and cheese diet. The canals that brought coal to all parts of the island were the first great step towards the new era.

In the east and midlands the typical village was, as it is to-day, a large collection of houses round the parish church.

But in the west and north the church stood with only
a few houses near it, and the parish consisted of a number
of scattered hamlets or scattered farms, looking to the
parish church as their centre so far as they had any
definite unity at all. The land of scattered hamlets in the
west, and of scattered farmsteads in the north, generally
meant inclosed fields round every farm. But in the east
midlands, round the large centralized villages, the uninclosed open fields were still the prevailing method of cultivation until the great inclosures of the reign of George III.

There was great diversity of agricultural method, of
tenure, and of social type in the various parts of England.
Even in the same district one village differed from another
in its social groupings and economic arrangements, much
more than in the nineteenth century, when the village scene
became more nearly monopolized by the tenant farmer and
his employee, the landless agricultural labourer. But in the
eighteenth century there was a great variety of craftsmen
and manufacturers in or near the village, some supplying
the needs of the village, others supplying the world market.
There were large and small squires, large and small freehold
yeomen, besides tenant farmers large and small. There
were hired labourers who had no land, there were hired
labourers who had also a little land or a garden of their own,
there were men camped on or round the common, some
making a respectable and hardy struggle with poverty,
others little distinguishable from gipsies, thieves, or professional poachers. Amateur poaching, as a by-occupation,
was one of the chief incidents of village life—an endless
subject of talk and dispute, of tragedy and comedy. In
most cottages and farmhouses the women and children
engaged their spare time in spinning or minor handicrafts.
And then there were the parish paupers, a terrible problem.
Over this multiform and vigorous society, part agricultural,
part industrial, the power of the squire loomed large, beneficent or tyrannical as the case might be—Sir Roger de
Coverley or Squire Western—but always patriarchal.

There was no elective local government—no county
councils or rural district councils, or even parish councils.
Administration as well as justice, therefore, lay in the hands
of the Justice of the Peace, who was usually a local squire,
occasionally a parson. When the squire was also, like Coke

of Norfolk, a successful agricultural improver and the maker of the well-being of the whole countryside, he commanded the affection as well as the obedience of his neighbours.

But apart from the power and influence of the squire, the village that lay in the shadow of the Hall had a life of its own, far more varied, independent, and energetic than the life of the village of serfs in the shadow of the medieval castle or manor-house. It was because of this greater freedom, variety, and energy that the English village of Stuart and early Hanoverian times proved capable of founding English-speaking America and beginning the Industrial Revolution. And in so doing it put a term to its own existence.

In this volume are portrayed, with the full knowledge of the expert, various aspects of the mature and vigorous civilization of Johnson's England, of which we may say 'Here is God's plenty'.

II
THE CHURCH

By THE REV. N. SYKES

On Friday, April 13, being Good-Friday, I went to St. Clement's church
with him as usual. There I saw again his old fellow-collegian, Edwards, to
whom I said, 'I think, Sir, Dr. Johnson and you meet only at Church'. 'Sir,
(said he,) it is the best place we can meet in, except Heaven, and I hope we
shall meet there too.'—*Life of Johnson* (13 April 1781).

THE emphatic verdict of the author of *The Extraordinary
Black Book* of 1831 that 'although the Church of England is
ostentatiously styled the *reformed* Church, it is, in truth, the
most unreformed of all the churches', would doubtless have
provoked an indignant rejoinder from Dr. Samuel Johnson,
had he lived to read so unsparing a denunciation of the Church
of the Georgian era. The majority of the clerical and lay
churchmen of his day would have repeated rather the confident
eulogy pronounced at the beginning of the century by Archbishop Sharp of York that 'the Church of England is undoubtedly both as to doctrine and worship the purest church
that is at this day in the world: the most orthodox in faith,
the freest on the one hand from idolatry and superstition,
and on the other hand from freakishness and enthusiasm,
of any now extant'. The complacency of the Hanoverian
divines concerning their religious settlement and their praise
of its moderation and reasonableness have been requited in
full by the censure of their successors. The Church establishment, which to the eye of Warburton was so perfect that it
might have been derived 'solely from the contemplation of
nature and the unvariable reason of things', appeared to a
later generation as 'an immense waste which wanted surveying and enclosing, if not by act of parliament then by the
act of the people'. The *epigoni* of the age of enlightenment
not only disavowed its theological shibboleths, but blushed
at the exposure of the abuses of its administration by the
profane hands of radicals of the reform epoch. To understand the ethos of the Georgian Church, however, it is
necessary to regard it from the standpoint of the pre-reform
age to which, alike in constitution and temper, it belonged.
The survival of its medieval administrative machinery accompanied by privilege and inequality occasioned little

scandal to the eighteenth-century society which accepted the
existence of similar anomalies in the body politic and knew
not the ideas of equality and democracy accepted by a later
age. In truth the Hanoverian Church was both reformed and
unreformed; for the Reformation which had remodelled its
doctrine and liturgy had effected comparatively few changes
in its internal administration.

The episcopate itself was not only the keystone of the
ecclesiastical constitution but the best illustration of the
character of the establishment of Georgian England. Tradi-
tionally the English bishop was a royal counsellor in matters
of state, upon occasion holding offices of state, no less than
a prelate of the Church. Even as late as the beginning of the
eighteenth century, during the early years of Johnson's life,
Bishop John Robinson of Bristol was accredited as British
plenipotentiary at Utrecht; and the reward of his diplomatic
services there took the form in the ecclesiastical sphere of
translation to the rich see of London and in the political of
his appointment as Lord Privy Seal in the Administration
of Oxford. The elevation of a divine to secular office was an
exception at this date, but the political influence of prelates
had suffered a change of form rather than of principle since
the Reformation. The eighteenth century indeed witnessed
a development in the parliamentary importance of the episcopate which provoked much criticism, especially of the
method of its recruitment. 'No man, for instance, can now
be made a bishop for his learning and piety,' complained
Johnson on Good Friday 1775; 'his only chance for
promotion is his being connected with somebody who has
parliamentary interest.' Nor did learning seem a surer pass-
port to preferment. 'Few bishops are now made for their
learning,' observed the Doctor upon another occasion; 'to be
a bishop, a man must be learned in a learned age, factious
in a factious age, but always of eminence. Warburton is an
exception, though his learning alone did not raise him . . .
Pope introduced him to Allen, Allen married him to his
niece; so by Allen's interest and his own, he was made a
bishop.' It would be as incorrect to interpret the sentiments
of Johnson as implying that Georgian bishops were eminent
for factiousness alone, as to infer that piety and learning
were unrepresented among their virtues; but the growth of
the organization of political parties, which seemed to him

the quality of a factious age, introduced important modifications in the relations of the episcopate to the Crown and to its ministers of state.

The political consequences of the Revolution settlement led to a considerable appreciation of the power of Parliament, and, combined with the stabilization of the parties of Whig and Tory, necessarily affected the position of the bench. In particular the establishment of the custom of homogeneous party Administrations resulted in the virtual appropriation of the ecclesiastical patronage of the Crown by the political leaders, and the consequent nomination to the episcopate of divines of their own allegiance, whether Whig or Tory. Imperceptibly the bishops became the friends and allies of the rival Whig and Tory ministers rather than direct counsellors of the ruling prince. In this capacity they not infrequently employed their talents, both of voice and pen, in support of their own party, so that it seemed natural to Lord Shelburne, in nominating Dr. Richard Watson in 1782 to the see of Llandaff, to express 'to the duke of Grafton his expectation that he [Watson] would occasionally write a pamphlet for their administration'.[1] Within the House of Lords itself the control of a solid phalanx of twenty-six votes of the episcopal bench was of obvious importance to ministers to whom the art of parliamentary management was an essential element of statecraft. The acme of episcopal loyalty was enjoyed by Sir Robert Walpole in 1733 when in two critical divisions in the Upper House on May 24 and June 1 of that year he was saved from defeat by the fact that 'out of the twenty-six bishops, twenty-five were present or voted by proxy, of which twenty-four were for the court'; a result, the moral of which was pressed home in a popular ballad bidding him to

> Consider the church is your rock of defence,
> Your South Sea escape in your memory cherish,
> When sinking, you cry'd, 'Help, lords, or I perish'.

The close alliance between the episcopate and the Ministry provoked much criticism, which proceeded generally from opponents who, like Johnson, believed that Whiggism 'as a mere party distinction under Walpole and the Pelhams, was no better than the politics of stock-jobbers and the religion

---

[1] *Anecdotes of the Life of Richard Watson* (2 vols. 1818), vol. i, p. 153.

of infidels'. But the only solution of the problem, that of
depriving the bishops of their seats in Parliament, was
repudiated with equal indignation by the critics, as by Johnson himself in his reply to Sir Adam Ferguson: 'Who is
more proper for having the dignity of a peer than a bishop,
provided a bishop be what he ought to be; and if improper
bishops be made, that is not the fault of the bishops, but of
those who make them.'

Another circumstance which cemented the alliance between prelates and ministers was the great inequality in
revenue of the several sees. A list of the ecclesiastical
dignities in the gift of the Crown with their estimated annual
value, drawn up for George III about 1762, revealed a wide
disparity between such sees as Canterbury with £7,000, York
with £4,500, Durham with £6,000, and Winchester with
£5,000 a year, and those of Bristol with £450, Oxford and
Llandaff with £500 each.[1] When Secker became bishop of
Bristol in 1735 he computed the revenues to be 'no more
than £360 a year, out of which he was to pay £27 a year
tenths, and maintain a steward, so that the true profits
were but £300 per annum, and there was £900 to be paid in
first fruits'.[2] Twenty-five years later Bishop Newton complained that its net profits were still only £300; yet the
expenses of living in London for the greater part of the year
in attendance upon the Court and Parliament, together
with the maintenance of a sufficient hospitality in both the
capital and the diocese, were the same for all bishops whether
rich or poor. Accordingly, the prelates of Bristol or Oxford
were compensated by the addition of other Church preferment to eke out the scanty substance of their sees; for
example, both Butler and Newton at Bristol held the
deanery of St. Paul's *in commendam*, whilst that of Westminster was joined generally to the see of Rochester. Occasional protests were raised against this practice of episcopal
commendams, but the protesters, as in the case of Bishop
Watson of Llandaff, earned no gratitude from either Ministers of State or Primates to whom they urged the adoption
of schemes for equalizing the revenues of bishoprics and
for raising the value of the benefices of the inferior clergy

[1] *Correspondence of George III* (ed. J. Fortescue), vol. i, pp. 33–43.
[2] *Diary of Viscount Perceval* in *Egmont MSS.* (Hist. MSS. Comm.), vol. ii,
p. 137.

at the expense of cathedral dignities. Even to their holders, commendams were but a temporary expedient, and the prelates of 'the little bishoprics' hoped always for translation to a lucrative see, a desire which naturally ensured their loyalty to the Administration which had appointed them and to which they looked for further rewards of service. There can be no doubt that the expectation of translation to a rich diocese curtailed the independence of many bishops; for the prediction of Bishop Watson on his own nomination to Llandaff that 'he had hitherto followed and would continue to follow his own judgement in all public transactions, that all parties understood this, and it was probable that he might continue to be bishop of Llandaff as long as he lived', indicated the fate which he anticipated as the result of his sturdy individualism. His elevation, indeed, had been more the effect of accident than design on his part, for having written against 'the supporters of the American war because he thought that war not only to be inexpedient but unjust', he happened thereby 'to please a party and they made him a bishop', only to leave him in distant Wales for the remaining thirty-three years of his life.[1] The degree of political fidelity expected of clerics promoted by a party minister found apt illustration in the nomination of Dr. Zachary Pearce by Sir Robert Walpole to the deanery of Winchester in 1739. Hitherto Pearce had been accounted a friend of Walpole's rival, Pulteney, who therefore released him from the political consequences of that friendship by declaring to him:

Dr. Pearce, though you may think that others besides Sir Robert have contributed to get you this dignity, yet you may depend upon it, that he is all in all and that you owe it entirely to his goodwill towards you. And therefore as I am now so engaged in opposition to him, it may happen that some who are of our party, may, if there should be any opposition for members of parliament at Winchester, prevail upon me to desire you to act there in assistance of some friend of ours: and Sir Robert at the same time may ask your assistance in the election for a friend of his own against the one whom we recommend. I tell you therefore beforehand that if you comply with my request rather than with Sir Robert's, to whom you are so very much obliged, I shall have the worse opinion of you.[2]

---

[1] *Anecdotes of the Life of Richard Watson*, vol. i, pp. 153–4.
[2] Life of Bishop Zachary Pearce in *Lives of Dr. E. Pocock, Dr. Z. Pearce, Dr. T. Newton, and the Rev. P. Skelton* (2 vols., 1816), vol. i, p. 392.

In an essay contributed to *The Spectator* of March 24, 1710/11, Addison, lamenting the overcrowding of the clerical profession, observed that

we may divide the clergy into generals, field officers, and subalterns. Among the first we may reckon bishops, deans, and archdeacons. Among the second are doctors of divinity, prebendaries, and all that wear scarfs. The rest are comprehended under the subalterns. As for the first class, our constitution prevents it from any redundancy of incumbents, notwithstanding competitors are numberless. Upon a strict calculation it is found that there has been a great exceeding of late years in the second division, several brevets having been granted for the converting of subalterns into scarf-officers. As for the subalterns, they are not to be numbered.

The cleavage between the positions of the higher and lower clergy thus noted by Addison, and particularly the sharp contrast between the plurality of preferments enjoyed by the former and the poverty of the latter, continued throughout the age of Johnson. From the Reformation to the nineteenth century the practice of pluralism was regulated by the statute of 21 Henry VIII, c. 13, entitled *Spiritual Persons abridged from having Pluralities of Livings*. The Act, having laid down the general rule that no person possessing a benefice with cure of souls of the value of £8 or above should be suffered to hold any other benefice with cure, proceeded to recite a long list of exceptions to this rule, embracing the chaplains of all peers, temporal and spiritual, and divers other persons there specified. To cathedral dignities, being benefices without cure of souls, the statute of course did not apply; and since the number of chaplains allowed to the several ranks of the peerage varied from the six of dukes and archbishops to the single chaplain allotted to the Lord Chief Justice and to the Warden of the Cinque Ports, the number of preferments necessary to satisfy the dignity of the nobility was very considerable. It was indeed a point of honour on the part of noblemen to secure a proper reward for their spiritual attendants, and the profession of Orders was regarded further as a fit sphere for the talents of the younger sons of noble families who might hope to find relief from their financial necessities by the provision of cathedral dignities. The correspondence of the Duke of Newcastle abounds in embarrassing instances of peers cajoling, threatening, or rebuking his grace for the neglect of their relatives and chaplains in the disposition of Church preferment. The competition for prebends of the churches of Canterbury, St. Paul's, Westminster, and Windsor was so great that Newcastle confessed in 1757 that they were 'sometimes more difficult to be had than a deanery', whilst Archbishop Herring teased him in 1755 by the observation that 'he could not help smiling to see with how much more ease his grace filled up a bishopric than a prebend'. The chief cause of the zeal for the office of prebendary was that, whilst at Windsor the prebends were worth £450, at Canterbury £350, and at Westminster £300, according to George III's list, in the great majority of cases their duties were nominal, the discharge of the obligation to preach twice each year in the cathedral *aut per se aut per alium.*

To the aspiring cleric the way to preferment was clear, by the means of the favour of some influential patron. Prelates of noble birth such as Archbishop Cornwallis, and Bishops Trevor, Keppel, Barrington, and North supplied the condition in their own families. But clergy lacking this initial advantage strove to recommend themselves to the notice of some temporal peer or bishop, either by dedicating to them the literary fruits of their genius or by rendering some political service to their family in elections or otherwise. Despite the aristocratic character of eighteenth-century society several divines of humble birth rose to the highest offices of the Church. Archbishop Potter, the son of a Wakefield linen-draper, dedicated one of his early works of classical scholarship to Robert Harley, but being appointed two years later a chaplain to Tenison, he laid the foundations of his future preferment upon a Whig basis, securing the support of the Duke of Marlborough for his candidature for the Regius Professorship of Divinity at Oxford. His successor at Canterbury, Thomas Herring, was the friend of Lord Chancellor Hardwicke, whose influence had paved the way for his elevation to the primacy through the sees of Bangor and York. Archbishop Secker entered into Anglican Orders upon a promise of Bishop Talbot to provide for him in his family, and after the Bishop's death his son, Lord Chancellor Talbot, made Secker his chaplain, thereby bringing him into closer contact with the Queen and Court circles. Archbishop John Moore became tutor to Lord Blandford, son of the Duke of Marlborough, and made a prudent second marriage with the sister of Sir William Eden, first Lord Auckland, by whose influence he rose to the primacy. Very few clergy lacking influence or money at the outset of their career would have achieved the distinction of Richard Watson, who, being offered at the age of twenty-three by the Vice-Chancellor of Cambridge University 'the curacy of Clermont, and advised to accept it, as it would give him an opportunity of recommending himself to the Duke of Newcastle', the archdispenser of patronage, refused because he prized 'his independence above all prospects'.[1] The surest road to success lay through the office of royal chaplain, and the number of candidates for that duty was inexhaustible because of the prospects of preferment. George III, indeed, created consternation amongst the ranks of the clerical body by appointing at his accession an entirely new rota of royal chaplains, from which he might replenish the sees and cathedral dignities as occasion arose. Tradition has recognized fully his personal interest in the distribution of the ecclesiastical patronage of the Crown, from the first year of his reign when he translated Bishop Hayter to London, despite the protests of Newcastle, and nominated Dr. Thomas Newton to Bristol; and throughout the period of his friendship with Warburton and with Hurd, whom he offered the primacy in 1783, down to the famous incident of 1805 when in order to forestall the intention of Pitt to recommend Bishop Pretyman to Canterbury, the King took horse himself to secure Bishop Manners Sutton's acceptance of that see.

The determination of George III to assert his will in the bestowal of preferments differed from that of his predecessor rather in the personnel of his clerical entourage than in the strength of resolve not to be ignored. The Duke of Newcastle not infrequently found that even his most long-standing promises and his closest dependants were put aside by the fidelity of George II to his own chaplains. The rewards of chaplains, both of the King and of temporal lords, were indeed regarded by Bishop Hurd as necessary satisfactions for services rendered; for he argued that 'preferments, when conferred by the great on their dependants, are not so properly favours as debts; that a course of years spent in servitude is the price they pay for such things; and that when promotion comes at last, it comes in the way of recom-

[1] *Anecdotes of the Life of Richard Watson*, vol. i, pp. 33–4.

pense and not of obligation'.[1] Notwithstanding, it must be allowed that in many cases the remuneration was adequate to the duty done. Dr. Edmund Pyle, whose *Memoirs of a Royal Chaplain* illustrate the lighter side of Georgian divinity and churchcraft, received ample returns for his moderate abilities and services. Introduced into the royal favour by his friendship with Bishop Hoadly, he received in addition to his preferments at Lynn and Gedney, cathedral dignities. In 1751 he became Archdeacon of York, where he nearly lost his heart to the ladies of that city. 'Nothing but ladies by dozens (and very pretty ones) on the right hand or the left or in front of my stall,' he wrote in his account of his installation; 'but through mercy, having the service to read I was forced to look at least as much on the rubric of the book as upon that of their cheeks.'[2] In 1752 he settled in the household of Hoadly at Chelsea as companion, and in 1756 was made prebendary of the first stall at Winchester. There he learned that 'the life of a prebendary is a pretty easy way of dawdling away one's time: praying, walking, and visiting; and as little study as your heart would wish'; whilst in anticipation that he would outlive his patron, he proposed thereafter to spend of each year, 'May, June, July, August at York and his living: thence to the end of January at Winchester, and the other three months at London'.[3] Greater rewards might be expected by the chaplain chosen for the duty of accompanying George II on his visits to Hanover. When that King wished to find preferment for Dr. John Thomas, chaplain at Hamburg, he resolved to make him one of his chaplains; 'and the next time I come to Hanover,' he promised, 'you shall come over with me, and then if a prebend or deanery should happen to fall, you will have a good chance of succeeding to it.' The royal word was a faithful bond; for in 1740 Dr. Thomas, already a chaplain, accompanied his master to Hanover, where fortune so favoured him that, the deanery of Peterborough falling vacant during his attendance, he was nominated straightaway to it.[4] His case became a precedent quoted by the Duke of Newcastle in 1748, that 'the king's chaplain at Hanover

[1] F. Kilvert, *Memoirs of the Life and Writings of Bishop Hurd* (1860), p. 82.
[2] E. Pyle, *Memoirs of a Royal Chaplain* (ed. A. Hartshorne, 1905), p. 168.
[3] Ibid., pp. 263, 266.
[4] *Some Account of the Life of Dr. Thomas Newton, Bishop of Bristol. Written by Himself.* In *Lives of Pocock, Pearce, Newton, Skelton*, vol. ii, p. 83.

has always set aside at all times all other promises', when he wished to secure the nomination of his friend Dr. James Johnson, then in attendance upon the King abroad, to a residentiaryship of St. Paul's, and again in 1752 when Johnson, now on his third visit to Hanover in the company of Newcastle and their sovereign, was rewarded by the see of Gloucester.

The multiplication of preferments bestowed upon royal and other chaplains led to the widespread pluralism which became the butt of all satirists. In painful contrast also to the wealth of the pluralists was the miserable lot of the inferior clergy whose merits had failed to attract the attention of some powerful patron. To the over-large number of poor scholars of the universities who entered into Orders, their choice of the clerical profession was of the nature of a lottery. The few achieved the prizes, as did Bishop Hurd, born the second son of parents whom he described as 'very plain people, for they were farmers'; but the many continued in poverty. Not only was there a wide disparity between the value of the several benefices with cure of souls, but the number of ordinations was in no wise related to the prospects of promotion to a benefice. From the prevalence of pluralism there followed the natural consequence of non-residence. The cleric without influence or friends, ordained to the diaconate and licensed to serve the cure of a non-resident incumbent, languished often for a long period of years in the obscurity of his country parish. Not infrequently he served an equally prolonged diaconate, for the expenses attendant upon ordination to the priesthood discouraged him from receiving that further status until the presentation to a benefice provided both the occasion and the means for taking this step. Nor even when the hopeful curate added the qualification of priesthood did promotion to a vicarage or rectory follow with any rapidity. The circumstances of Mr. Robert Robson, son of a yeoman farmer of Sebergham in Cumberland and a graduate of Queen's College, Oxford, were typical of many clergy of his time. He received deacon's orders at the hands of Bishop Mawson of Chichester in September 1745, a licence to serve the curacy of Pulborough, and ordination to the priesthood from the same bishop in October 1748. In 1751 he married and removed to act as curate of Cocking, whose rector, Dr. Thomas Hutchinson, was also vicar of Horsham.

A JOURNEYMAN PARSON GOING ON DUTY.

A MASTER PARSON RETURNING FROM DUTY.

From engravings by R. Dighton, about 1780

Thus he continued for a full quarter of a century despite the efforts of relatives to rescue him from what they feared might be the perpetual inferiority of an unbeneficed clergyman. In 1767 his brother John Robson, steward to the Bishop of Durham, wrote that 'it would give him inexpressible satisfaction to hear of his better success at that time of life after the toil of so many years in the curatical state: nothing but drudgery and patience for many in his situation, while many a worthless rector was as hard put to it to live on £5 or £600 per annum as his honest worthy curate upon £50'. Not until 1778 did the influence of another brother with Sir James Peachey secure for him the presentation to the living of Stedham, which he enjoyed until his death in 1783.

Of the conditions of service of the numberless army of curates no alluring picture can be drawn. The general salary varied between £30 and £40 per year, the latter figure being attained in large towns or in wealthy parishes. In 1763 Parson Woodforde had the option of two curacies worth £28 plus surplice fees and £40 respectively at Newton Purcell in Oxon. and Thurloxton in Somerset; having chosen the latter he left Oxford for Somerset, transferring shortly to the curacy of Babcary for £30 plus 'the house, stable, gardens and Easter offerings'. After a further brief interval he added to this the curacy of Castle Cary for £20 a year, which meant that he could serve Babcary only once per Sunday. Upon the death of his father new arrangements had to be made, which resulted in his serving Castle Cary for £30 a year plus surplice fees and combining with it the curacy of Ansford. Thirty years earlier, in 1730, John Wesley had informed his mother of his acceptance of a curacy, possibly that of Stanton Harcourt, eight miles from Oxford, and 'the salary £30 per year'. In 1782 Woodforde, in discharging the financial business of his friend Dr. Bathurst, recorded the payment of his curate at the rate of £50 per annum; and throughout the greater part of the age of Johnson the salaries of curates averaged between £30 and £40 per annum, though in the later years of the eighteenth century the standard showed a steady rise towards double that sum.[1]

[1] The addition of the office of schoolmaster to that of curate or parish priest was a recognized means of eking out the inadequate stipends of curacies and poor benefices. The 78th canon ('Curates desirous to teach to be licensed before

In addition to the meagre stipend the office of curate involved other difficulties. In most cases it was attended by insecurity of tenure, and curates were often dismissed with the shortest of notice, as when Woodforde himself on July 19, 1773, being a Monday, was informed by the incumbent of Ansford 'that he intended serving Ansford next Sunday himself, which notice of his leaving the curacy' the diarist thought 'not only very unkind but very ungentlemanlike'. Such insecurity led to the existence of a class of vagabond clergy, whose habits of frequent change of curacy and consequent itinerancy presented to contemporary bishops an insoluble problem of clerical discipline. In many villages also no proper accommodation for the lodging of a curate could be found, if the non-residence of the incumbent had been occasioned or followed by the dilapidation of the parsonage. Woodforde himself on arrival at Thurloxton found no house suitable to receive him, until good fortune secured his admission to the squire's house on the terms: 'that I should live as he does, (which is very well I am sure), that I should have my linnen washed by him, and that he should keep my horse (corn excepted): £21; and that for every day that I was absent I should be allowed each day 1s. 1½d.'

In estimating the status of curates, however, the extreme poverty of many benefices should be remembered, for in several cases the transition from the position of unbeneficed to that of beneficed cleric brought little financial advantage. On the establishment of Queen Anne's Bounty at the beginning of the century, there were 5,597 livings, amounting to more than half of the total number, whose income did not exceed £50 per annum; whilst after the lapse of a full century with its changes in the value of money, the diocesan returns of 1809 reckoned 3,998 benefices still under £150 per annum. The practice of pluralism spread, therefore, not only among the wealthy clergy of the Court and cathedrals, but among the poor incumbents of small livings, whose necessities compelled the addition of more than one benefice to furnish means of subsistence. Non-residence also was

others') specifically provided for this, in parishes lacking a public school, by decreeing that curates of the degree of M.A. or B.A. who were willing to teach children 'for the better increase of their living and training up children in principles of true religion', should receive licence thereto from the Ordinary, in preference to any other person.

allowed for other reasons than plurality of cures, for example the ruinous condition of many vicarage houses, the unhealthiness of the locality (a misfortune which had to be borne by the unhappy curate), and the urgent avocation elsewhere of the incumbent. The returns to the Articles of Visitation of Archbishop Herring in the large diocese of York in 1743 revealed that of the 836 parishes making replies to the queries, 393 had non-resident incumbents, and of the 711 clergy officiating in the diocese 335 were pluralists; and in these respects York was typical generally of the dioceses of the kingdom.[1] The existence of such wide disparity between the emoluments and services of the higher and lower clergy afforded both a ready target for the wit of anti-clerical writers and a constant provocation to reforming prelates of the calibre of Richard Watson. To the majority of churchmen, however, it afforded no occasion of scandal. Twice Boswell complained to Johnson of the inequality of livings and the poverty of curates. On the first mention of the subject Johnson replied: 'Why yes, Sir; but it cannot be helped. You must consider, that the revenues of the clergy are not at the disposal of the State, like the pay of the army. Different men have founded different churches; and some are better endowed, some worse. The State cannot interfere and make an equal division of what has been particularly appropriated.' Boswell returned to the attack with the contention that no vicar or rector should be allowed to have a curate unless he paid a salary of £100 a year, but Johnson again rejoined:

To be sure, Sir, it is wrong that any clergyman should be without a reasonable income; but as the church revenues were sadly diminished at the Reformation, the clergy who have livings cannot afford, in many instances, to give good salaries to curates, without leaving themselves too little; and, if no curate were to be permitted unless he had a hundred pounds a year, their number would be very small, which would be a disadvantage, as then there would not be such choice in the nursery for the church, curates being candidates for the higher ecclesiastical offices, according to their merit and good behaviour. ... It is not thought fit to trust a man with the care of a parish, till he has given proof as a curate that he shall deserve such a trust.

Upon which comfortable defence of the régime of privilege

[1] *Archbishop Herring's Visitation Returns, 1743* (ed. S. L. Ollard and P. C. Walker, Yorkshire Archaeological Soc., 5 vols., 1928–31).

and inequality, the faithful biographer made the apt comment: 'This is an excellent *theory*; and if the *practice* were according to it, the Church of England would be admirable indeed'.

That practice should lag far behind the virtues of such theory was inevitable in the unreformed state of the Georgian Church. The survival of many obsolete medieval elements in its constitution made difficult the problem of administration even to the most energetic prelates. The obstacles in the way of episcopal oversight were indeed virtually insuperable, and from the lack of careful supervision on the part of the episcopate followed many of the shortcomings of parochial organization. At the outset, the convention requiring the residence of bishops in London for the greater part of the year, to fulfil their attendance upon the Court and Parliament, withdrew them from the active work of their dioceses except during the interval of the summer recess of Parliament. Viscount Perceval represented contemporary opinion in his commendation of Bishop Wilcocks of Gloucester in 1730 that 'he resides as much as any bishop in his diocese, at least four months in the year, and keeps a very generous and hospitable table, which makes amends for the learning he is deficient in'.[1] To this shortness of time available for diocesan duties, there were added the problems of distance and of the large size of some dioceses. The Reformation had contributed comparatively little to the efficient administration of the *Ecclesia Anglicana* apart from the abolition of the protracted commerce with Rome; for, though it added five permanent bishoprics to the Church, only one of these, Chester, fell in the northern province; that of Bristol presented the difficult problem of the isolation of the episcopal city from its diocese, the county of Dorset; and the creation of Oxford and Peterborough while reducing the extent of the old diocese of Lincoln, had added to the difficulty of its administration by severing it into two isolated parts. Furthermore, by an unhappy accident the provision of suffragan bishops was discontinued after the reign of Mary Tudor, so that the post-Reformation bishops inherited most of the administrative problems of their medieval predecessors without that agency which had made possible the provision of episcopal offices for their dioceses. The largest diocese of

---

[1] *Diary of Viscount Perceval* in *Egmont MSS.* (Hist. MSS. Comm.), p. 100.

Georgian England was that of Lincoln with 1,312 parishes, whilst in the northern province the diocese of York, albeit relieved of a large extent of its jurisdiction by the new and straggling diocese of Chester, yet retained 903 parishes, in striking contrast to the small border diocese of Carlisle with only four deaneries and about 100 parishes, where Bishop Nicolson had made it his boast that his visitation 'seldom kept him above two nights from his own bed'. In the majority of dioceses it was manifestly impossible for prelates resident in the capital during the greater part of each year to exercise an efficient supervision. The episcopal offices of ordination and institution of incumbents to benefices might, indeed, be discharged generally by requiring the candidates to wait upon the bishop in London, as Woodforde did for his institution to Weston rectory, or, alternatively, in the case of ordinands, by the issue of letters dimissory to neighbouring bishops holding an ordination in their diocese. Even so the intercourse of prelates with their clergy was occasional and infrequent, as the diary of Woodforde testifies, for the appearances of the bishop were generally confined to formal visitations with the attendant office of confirmation of the laity.

In regard to confirmation, the 60th canon of the Canons of 1604, reciting the tradition by which 'this holy action hath been accustomed in the church in former ages to be performed in the bishop's visitation every third year', required every prelate in his own person to observe the said custom in his visitation. Accordingly, the bishops held triennial visitations and confirmations in their dioceses, usually during the summer months when Parliament was not sitting, and conditions of weather and daylight facilitated travel. Having mapped out, in consultation with their archdeacons, the centres at which they proposed to call, their lordships customarily held the visitation of their clergy in the morning and the confirmation of the laity in the afternoon. To modern eyes the numbers of persons confirmed triennially are almost incredibly large. Thus Archbishop Drummond of York during the years 1768–71 confirmed in his diocese no fewer than 41,600 candidates, whilst in the diocese of Exeter Bishop Keppel confirmed in 1764 in Devon and in 1765 in Cornwall a total of 41,642, and his successor Bishop Ross confirmed at his triennial visitations of 1779,

1782, and 1785-6, the gross numbers of 26,671, 14,938, and 22,289 persons respectively. The figures of Keppel and Ross are particularly noteworthy as a caution against inferring from the large returns of one bishop any remissness on the part of his predecessor. The task of the laying of hands upon so many people was one involving severe physical exhaustion, and the office of bishop was no easy one in such cases as that of Bishop Benson of Gloucester who confirmed for Archbishop Blackburne of York on 9, 10, and 11 September 1737 at Halifax and Ripponden. At the latter place on the first day he consecrated a new church, following that by the confirmation of about 1,500 persons, whilst on the succeeding days at Halifax 'he was in church from about nine in the morning till near seven at night'. It was noted especially of him that he confirmed in all 8,922 candidates 'by only two at a time, with great devotion and solemnity'. The discovery of the best method of discharging the office of confirmation with so many persons was itself a problem of difficulty to bishops; and Archbishop Gilbert of York gained the credit of introducing a new solution. 'This was, instead of going round the rail of the Communion table and laying his hands upon the heads of two or four persons held close together, and in a low voice repeating the form of prayer over them, he went round the whole rail at once, laid his hand upon the head of every person severally, and when he had gone through the whole, then he drew back to the Communion table, and in as audible and solemn a manner as he could, pronounced the prayer over them all.' Dr. Newton, afterwards Bishop of Bristol, who accompanied his grace on many of his tours, since he had received from him the precentorship of York, averred that 'the clergy and people were struck with the decency as much as with the novelty of the ceremony. The confirmations were performed in less time and with less trouble, with more silence and solemnity, and with more regularity and order'.[1] Throughout the century there are evidences of quiet improvement in the administration of the rite. At the confirmation by Bishop Manners Sutton which Parson Woodforde attended at Reepham church on October 7, 1794, only 200 candidates were presented, but three clergy 'were with the bishop in

[1] *Some Account of the Life of Dr. Thomas Newton, Bishop of Bristol*, op. cit., vol. ii, p. 105.

the church, arranging the people in order as they came, and the chaplain received the tickets at the church gates'.

Similar difficulties to those besetting the bishops in the discharge of the spiritual duties of their office hindered the parish clergy from fulfilling the ideal of a pastoral ministry. Of these the chief were the results of pluralism and non-residence, for a vicar charged with the cure of two small livings the stipends of which were insufficient to maintain a curate, or a curate struggling to serve the parishes of a non-resident incumbent, could not give full services and attention to each of his churches. In parishes where the incumbent was resident and had no other duty, divine service was celebrated twice each Sunday, with one sermon, often delivered alternately in the morning and afternoon. Such, manifestly, was the case with Parson Woodforde, whose diary affords evidence of the alternation of his discourses, whilst the Blecheley Diary of William Cole takes note of one particular September Sunday as 'the only time when there are two sermons'. Not unnaturally the congregation gathered to hear the sermon; and when prayers only were read few parishioners troubled to attend. It was, therefore, a mark of unusual piety in Johnson that 'he went more frequently to church when there were prayers only, than when there was also a sermon, as the people required more an example for one than the other; it being much easier for them to hear a sermon than to fix their minds on prayer'. Where the incumbent or curate had to serve more than one parish divine service was performed only once a Sunday in each of his churches. Thus of the 836 churches represented in the York Visitation Returns of 1743 only 383 maintained two services on Sunday all the year round; whilst in similar returns for the diocese of London in 1741–2, of 436 churches only 236 held divine service twice. Practical considerations compelled the episcopate to acquiesce in this state of affairs, and to limit their prohibitions to the undertaking of services in as many as three different churches by any of their clergy. The Holy Communion was celebrated with varying frequency in different parishes. In large towns some churches attained the standard of a monthly sacrament, and in certain London parishes even weekly; but the great majority of country parishes, as in the days of Woodforde at Weston and also of the High Churchman Cole at Blecheley, had three or four sacraments each year, at Easter, Christmas, Whit-Sunday, and at Michaelmas.

The infrequency of the celebration of the Communion, however, should not be interpreted as a sign of neglect or irregularity of religious life on the part of either clergy or laity. George Herbert had written in the preceding century, 'touching the frequency of the Communion, the parson celebrates it, if not duly once a month, yet at least five or six times in the year'; and before the effects of the Methodist revival were felt on the Established Church the proportion of communicants to the adult population of parishes was remarkably high in most parts of the kingdom. The diocese of York in 1743 was characterized by the large number of communicants which were 'often startling in their size', whilst in the remote diocese of Bangor, the visitation returns of Bishop Pearce in 1749 indicated that 'the number of communicants at Easter was very remarkable, . . . and seemed to show that . . . the main body of adults were communicants'.[1] Preparation for the Easter Communion appears to have been a serious exercise both with clergy and laity; for on Good Friday 1777 Woodforde fasted 'till five in the afternoon and then eat only a few apple fritters and some bread and cheese', whilst Johnson on that day in 1775 'fasted so very strictly that he did not even taste bread, and took no milk with his tea'. The Doctor attended church twice, remarking that the holy day 'was upon the whole very well observed, even in London', and after the departure of Boswell he directed his servant's preparation for communion, and spent the eve of Easter Day in private meditation to that end. His diary contains several references to his careful preparation for and reception of the Easter Eucharist, especially in 1773 when he attended Matins and Litany followed by the Communion, at which he recited his special prayer, and again in 1777; whilst the importance which he attached to that preparation was testified further when on June 3, 1781, at Southill church, 'it being the first Sunday of the month, the holy sacrament was administered', and Boswell stayed to partake, whereon Johnson observed afterwards, 'You did right to stay and receive the communion; I had not thought of it'. No estimate of English piety in the eighteenth century is adequate which fails

[1] A. I. Price, *The Diocese of Bangor during Three Centuries* (Cardiff, 1929), p. lxii.

THE INTERIOR OF ST. CLEMENT DANES CHURCH

From an engraving by J. Boydell, 1751

to take account of the religious exercises of such devout laity as Johnson, who was zealous for the proper observance of Sunday, believed that 'the holydays observed by our church are of great use in religion', commended Law's *Serious Call* as 'the finest piece of hortatory theology in any language', and stoutly defended the English clergy as having 'produced the most valuable books in support of religion both in theory and practice'.

Apart from the performance of divine service on Sundays and the quarterly Sacrament, the generality of the clergy fulfilled their other duties as special occasions demanded. Public prayers on weekdays were maintained in large town churches, but not in the majority of country parishes, though Mr. Cole read public prayers on the holydays and saints' days; the clergy catechized the youth in the season of Lent, with additional attention to the instruction of children upon receipt of notice of the bishop's triennial visitation and confirmation. The diary of Woodforde contains a pleasing and homely picture in the autumn of 1794 of his activities in such circumstance; his preaching 'on the benefits and use of confirmation', and the receiving of companies of young people 'come to be examined against confirmation', to whom after due instruction he gave 'cake and a glass of wine'.

Of the ordinary divine service performed on Sundays many accounts have been given; but perhaps that of a hostile witness, whose criticism was sharpened by religious rivalry, may be relied upon to afford the maximum of unfavourable comment. In 1757 John Wesley wrote to a correspondent setting forth the superiority of Methodist public worship to that of the Church.

It is no small advantage that the person who reads prayers, though not always the same, yet is one who may be supposed to speak from his heart, one whose life is no reproach to his profession, and one who performs that solemn part of divine service, not in a careless, hurrying, slovenly manner, but seriously and slowly, as becomes him who is transacting so high an affair between God and man. Nor are their solemn addresses to God interrupted by the formal drawl of a parish clerk, the screaming of boys who bawl out what they neither feel nor understand, or the unseasonable and unmeaning impertinence of a voluntary on the organ. When it is seasonable to sing praise to God, they do it with the spirit and with the understanding also; not in the

F

miserable, scandalous doggerel of Hopkins and Sternhold, but in psalms and hymns which are both sense and poetry. . . . What they sing is therefore a proper continuation of the spiritual and reasonable service; being selected for that end, not by a poor humdrum wretch who can scarce read what he drones out with such an air of importance, but by one who knows what he is about and how to connect the preceding with the following part of the service.[1]

This caricature touches upon the familiar features of the Anglican service: the metrical psalms, the regular and unvarying form of prayers, the intonation of parish clerk and rustic choir; but the same combination of ingredients produced in many churches an office no less worthy in content and devout in utterance than the less restrained and formal inventions of extemporaneous lay preachers.

The survival of obsolete medieval machinery in the constitution of the Established Church may explain many of the anomalies which hindered the efficient discharge of episcopal and parochial duties in Johnson's England; but to account for the particular kind of religious belief and practice characteristic of that age recourse must be had rather to the intellectual temper of the time. Until the effect of the Methodist revival produced a resuscitation of Calvinist preaching amongst Evangelical clergy within the Church, the prevailing tradition of theology and of preaching was strongly Latitudinarian. Partly in reaction against the theological disputes of the seventeenth century upon abstruse points of divine election and reprobation, and partly under the influence of the new scientific movement which was devoted in particular to the study of astronomy, the intellectual temper of the Hanoverian age was indifferent to matters of church government and to confessional creeds which severed church from church. Revelation even in the discourses of orthodox divines passed imperceptibly into the fashionable vogue of natural religion; sermons were sparing of emotional appeal and dogmatic claims; and the generality of preachers desired to inculcate lessons of morality or to establish belief in Christianity upon the grounds of reasonable evidences. When in 1771 Richard Watson was elected to the Regius Professorship of Divinity in the University of Cambridge, he declared the principles of his religious persuasion.

I reduced the study of divinity into as narrow a compass as I could,

---

[1] *The Letters of John Wesley* (ed. J. Telford, 8 vols., 1931), vol. iii, p. 227.

for I determined to study nothing but my Bible, being much un-
concerned about the opinions of councils, fathers, churches, bishops
and other men as little inspired as myself. . . . My mind was wholly
unbiassed; I had no prejudice against, no predilection for, the Church
of England; but a sincere regard for the Church of Christ, and an
insuperable objection to every degree of dogmatical intolerance. I
never troubled myself with answering any arguments which the
opponents in the divinity school brought against the articles of the
church, nor ever admitted their authority as decisive of a difficulty;
but I used on such occasions to say to them, holding the New Testa-
ment in my hand, *En sacrum codicem.*[1]

Such a scheme of divinity tended naturally to the dissolution
of the differences alike of creed and polity which divided
churches from each other. In its positive tenets Latitudinarian theology laid much stress upon the Fatherhood of God
and upon the consequent necessity of benevolence in men.
Parish clergy even in country cures (if one may judge from
the incumbency during the first generation of the nineteenth
century at Camerton, Somerset, of Mr. John Skinner who
represented the last strain of Latitudinarianism amidst the
hostile environment of Methodism) delivered courses of
sermons upon Christian evidences, the Apostles' Creed, and
the Lord's Prayer, and endeavoured to expound Christianity
in a rational manner against the extremes of superstition
and fanaticism. The one criticism which Johnson allowed
against Anglican sermons was that 'the established clergy
in general did not preach plain enough; and that polished
periods and glittering sentences flew over the heads of the
common people, without any impression upon their hearts.
Something might be necessary,' he observed, 'to excite the
affections of the common people, who were sunk in languor
and lethargy, and therefore he supposed that the new
concomitants of Methodism might probably produce so
desirable an effect.' In the sphere of practice the Latitudinarian tradition emphasized the importance of good works of
charity and benevolence. The Georgian period was the age
of hospitals alike in London, in the university towns, and in
the widespread foundation of county hospitals; and in the
rural life of the parish this solicitude found its counterpart
in such ubiquitous charitable gifts as those of Parson Woodforde. That there could be found clergy of scandalous life

[1] *Anecdotes of the Life of Richard Watson*, vol. i, pp. 62–3.

was true in the eighteenth as in all centuries; that there were also devout parish clergy of the type of Johnson's ideal, Prebendary Zachariah Mudge, vicar of St. Andrew's, Plymouth, and prebendary of Exeter, is evident; and between them stood the host of ordinary country clergy of whom James Woodforde is probably a typical example. The verdict of the editors of Archbishop Herring's Visitation Returns upon the clergy of the York diocese, that they were 'a body of dutiful and conscientious men, trying to do their work according to the standards of their day', may be accepted as true of the majority of their brethren in other parts of the kingdom.

The standards of their day were in process of change during the lifetime of Johnson largely as a result of the Methodist revival. The story of the development of that movement from its high-church sacramentarian beginnings at Oxford to its separation from the Established Church and the creation of a new religious society has been told too often to bear repetition here. Both the theology and preaching of John Wesley were an avowed contradiction of the Latitudinarian tradition, and reconciliation between them was not to be expected. More important was the circumstance of Wesley's genius in the organization of a new church polity to minister to the needs of the new populations in the growing industrial areas of Britain. The cumbrous machinery of the Church of England was no more able to adapt itself to the changes of the Industrial Revolution than the antiquated unreformed parliamentary system, and the creation of new parishes lagged as far behind the needs of the times as the formation of new parliamentary constituencies. The ultimate severance of the Methodist societies from the formal communion of the Church was the natural consequence of Wesley's discharge of the apostolate of the mining and industrial classes who had scarcely come within the ambit of Anglican ministrations. John Wesley himself remained attached to the church of his ordination rather by ties of affection than by bonds of reason; the perusal of Bishop Stillingfleet's *Irenicon* had convinced him of the validity of presbyterian ordination; and so early as 1755 he could write that 'his conclusion (which he could not yet give up) that it was lawful to continue in the Church, stood (he knew not how) almost without any premises that were able to bear its weight'. Converts who were unhampered by his sentimental regard for the Established Church inevitably repudiated a connexion so feebly supported, and in particular the problem of providing for the Communion of members who were indifferent whether the Sacrament were administered by ministers episcopally ordained or not, emphasized the chief point of divergence. The influence of Methodism on the Established Church was reflected rather in the Evangelical revival stimulated within its borders. In theology the revival was strongly Calvinist, forsaking the Arminianism of John Wesley in favour of the sterner creed of Whitefield; but in Cowper it found a poet and hymn-writer who gave classic expression to its religious aspirations and ideals, and in such divines as Grimshaw, Berridge, Romaine, and Venn there was reproduced much of the fervid emotional preaching of the Methodists, accompanied in some cases by imitation of the itinerant method of evangelism.

But although the lifetime of Johnson himself witnessed the growth of the Methodist movement which changed the religious complexion of Great Britain and the New World, and evoked within the communion of the Established Church the new evangelical revival which challenged the long dominance of the Latitudinarian school, yet the Church of his age was essentially the Georgian Church unreformed in constitution and Latitudinarian in temper. The proclamation of the need of administrative reform, by the voice of Richard Watson immediately upon his elevation to the episcopate, fell upon deaf ears, and the lapse of a full half-century was needed before the Whig reforms of the early nineteenth century swept away the medieval survivals in Church and State. When the horrors of the Reign of Terror and the enthronement of the goddess of reason in France had enlisted the clergy of the Established Church in England as officers in the war against regicide and atheism, the venerable abuses of the unreformed Church and Parliament seemed to the majority of Englishmen a matter of praise rather than of denunciation. Encumbered thus by many obstacles, the Church of Johnson's England strove, not unworthily upon the whole, to work out its own salvation and to minister to the needs of the times according to the standards of the age. In religion there were many who agreed with Archbishop Herring's confession that he found 'something comfortable in addressing the Deity as the Father, not the Tyrant, of the creation', and in the practice of human benevolence deduced by preachers from that doctrine; and in politics there seemed to contemporaries, whose lot was cast in the interval of tranquillity and recovery between the wars of religion of the preceding and the revolutionary wars of a succeeding age, much wisdom in the resolve of the Georgian Church and State *quieta non movere*.

BIBLIOGRAPHY.—The best general histories of the Church of England in the eighteenth century are still those of Abbey and Overton: *The English Church in the Eighteenth Century* (2 vols., 1878), by C. J. ABBEY and J. H. OVERTON; and *The English Church and its Bishops, 1700–1800* (2 vols., 1887), by C. J. ABBEY. Both histories are essential for the general history of the period. The most important autobiographies of prelates of the age should certainly be read: *Some Account of the Life of Dr. Thomas Newton, late lord Bishop of Bristol: written by himself*; and *The Life of Dr. Zachary Pearce, Bishop of Rochester* (largely autobiographical); both of which are conveniently printed together in *The Lives of Dr. Edward Pocock, Dr. Zachary Pearce, Dr. Thomas Newton, and the Rev. Philip Skelton* (2 vols., 1816); *Anecdotes of the Life of Richard Watson, Bishop of Llandaff, written by himself*, published by his son, Richard Watson (2 vols., 1818). To these may be added F. KILVERT, *Memoirs of the Life and Writings of Bishop Hurd* (1860); and the amusing *Memoirs of a Royal Chaplain*, by EDMUND PYLE, edited by Albert Hartshorne (1905). Among modern biographies of Georgian divines, may be consulted N. SYKES, *Edmund Gibson, Bishop of London, 1669–1748* (Oxford, 1926).

Much useful statistical information and many sidelights on the clerical standards of the century will be found in *Archbishop Herring's Visitation Returns, 1743*, edited by Canon S. L. Ollard and P. C. Walker for the Yorkshire Archaeological Society (5 vols., 1928–31); and in *The Diocese of Bangor during Three Centuries*, by A. I. PRICE (Cardiff, 1929). Of clerical diarists *The Diary of a Country Parson*, JAMES WOODFORDE, edited by J. Beresford, 5 vols. (Oxford, 1926–31), has established itself as an easy favourite; The *Blecheley Diary* of William Cole, edited by F. G. Stokes and Miss Helen Waddell (1931), illustrates the standards of a High Churchman of the Georgian era; and *The Journal of a Somerset Rector*, JOHN SKINNER, edited by H. Coombs and A. N. Bax, 1930, though later in date, should be consulted for its picture of a Latitudinarian rector surviving into the reform age. BOSWELL'S *Life of Johnson* affords many incidental illustrations of church life and matters. In addition to the numerous Lives of John Wesley, and the standard edition of his *Journals*, the Epworth press have published in 1931 the standard edition of *The Letters of John Wesley*, edited by J. Telford (8 vols.). Curious details of ceremonial and worship in the Church are recorded in J. WICKHAM LEGG, *English Church Life from the Restoration to the Tractarian Movement* (1914); whilst much useful information is found in A. W. ROWDEN, *The Primates of the four Georges* (1916), though the accuracy of the book is not unimpeachable. The realization of the extent of anomalies and abuses in the unreformed church can be obtained best from *The Extraordinary Black Book of 1831*; whilst the religious and pastoral ideals of the best clergy of the age may be read in *The Works of Archbishop Secker*, with his *Life* by BEILBY PORTEOUS (6 vols., 1811). *The Diary of Viscount Perceval*, in the *Egmont MSS*. (Historical Manuscripts Commission, 3 vols., 1920–4), affords sidelights on the religion of an orthodox layman and upon his relations with eminent prelates, during the reign of George II. There is an essay of particular value on *Confirmation in the Anglican Communion* by S. L. OLLARD, in *Confirmation* (vol. i, S.P.C.K., 1926).

III

THE NAVY

By ADMIRAL SIR HERBERT RICHMOND

No man will be a sailor, who has contrivance enough to get himself into
a jail; for, being in a ship is being in a jail, with the chance of being drowned.
The man in a jail has more room, better food, and commonly better company.—*Tour to the Hebrides* (31 Aug. and 23 Sept. 1773).

Every man thinks meanly of himself for not having been a soldier, or not
having been at sea. *Boswell*: Lord Mansfield does not. *Johnson*: Sir, if Lord
Mansfield were in a company of General Officers and Admirals who have been
in service, he would shrink; he'd wish to creep under the table.—*Life of
Johnson* (10 April 1778).

THE Navy of 'Johnson's England' was the principal instrument of British policy in that series of three wars[1] which
decided whether England or France should possess the
New World and the Indies. In each of these wars the Navy
was slow to get into its stride, its power was but tardily
brought into effective use. This was due partly to uncertainty on the part of the statesmen as to how to use the
weapon they possessed: it took them nine months in 1739
to decide how they should conduct the war, and a like
delay took place from 1756 to 1758, and from 1778 to 1780.

But though a want of clear objective vision in the main
strategy hampered and delayed the march of success, there
was also an administrative reason. A navy cannot spring
into existence, Minerva-like, when an emergency arises.
Ships take long to build, and therefore must exist when their
services are needed. But as they cost great sums in wages,
stores, and provisions if kept ready and manned, the smallest
number compatible with the police and political duties
needed was maintained in commission in time of peace. Of
the four-score ships of the line required in war, none were
kept fully prepared in peace; a few frigates and smaller craft
afforded all the security needed. Some twenty great ships,
kept partly manned, could be completed for sea within a
short time; and security was assured because this force could
be prepared more quickly than an equal force of our neighbours. In accordance with these principles the establishment of seamen maintained in peace was fixed at a figure of

[1] Viz.: The War of the Austrian Succession, 1741–9; The Seven Years War,
1755–62; The War of American Independence, 1775–82.

16,000 men. Parliament voted this money, the Admiralty disposed the men according to the needs, and the number was only exceeded when a risk of war arose and more ships were put into commission.

Thus, before the Navy could begin its work in war its ships had to be manned and fitted out for sea. It was slow to get into its stride because the machinery for manning was defective, and because the ships laid up 'in ordinary' were in want of repairs, or stores for fitting them out were lacking. Parsimony and peculation played their parts. For the wise spending upon upkeep—that stitch in time which is the essence of good economy—there was substituted the false economy of not spending when it was needed; and, in the spending, the country failed to obtain twenty shillings of value for every pound that Parliament voted. The corruption in the dockyards in Johnson's time was assuredly not less than it was later, when old St. Vincent, making his heroic but unsuccessful cleansing of the Dockyard Administration, wrote, 'You may rest assured that the Civil Branch of the Navy is rotten to the core'.[1]

The want of sufficient great ships of the line *in readiness* was one of the causes ('Command' being the other) of those indecisive actions which ushered in each war. But navies do not consist, even in the material sense, of ships of the line alone. Light forces—frigates, sloops, brigs, and cutters are no less indispensable. The great ships could afford security against invasion: they could sanction the passage of British soldiers across the sea to defend the colonies; but they were too few to protect our ubiquitous trade. At the beginning of each war the trade suffered severely, for the false economies of peace of this period cut deep into the numbers of the essential lesser vessels, and not all the plain warnings of experience served to ensure that another war should not again find the country's trade exposed to grievous injury. Although the losses at sea in the wars of Queen Anne had shown the need of frigates, the outbreak of war in 1739–40 found the nation's trade ravaged successfully by petty privateers from Spain, ranging the sea from Gibraltar to Dungeness. Bitter complaints from the merchants poured in, but the Admiralty could give no more satisfying a reply

---

[1] Memoirs of the Administration of the Board of Admiralty. Reprinted in *Letters of Lord St. Vincent*, Navy Records Society, vol. lxi, p. 429.

to their tales than that there were not enough vessels to meet the many demands. Partly by purchase of merchant ships, partly by the slower process of building, fighting ships were added to the Navy: yet never were there enough to do all that was needed. Every flag officer at sea from the Channel to the Mediterranean, from the Caribbean to the Coromandel Coast, pointed out with chapter and verse the injury done to British interests from the want of small ships. Three thousand two hundred merchant ships were lost in that first war, the Western Squadron had not scouts enough, and the Mediterranean fleet was without an adequate frigate force to conduct the military operations in which it was engaged with our allies on the Riviera.

The recollection of the lessons thus dearly learnt was obliterated by the desire for an immediate economy when peace came. When the next—the Seven Years—war began, there was again an insufficiency of ships to defend the trade; and the merchants, for fear of capture, largely suspended their freighting business. But things were not as bad as they had been in the earlier war, for owing to the efforts of that great seaman First Lord, Anson, the fleet had been largely remodelled. Nevertheless, it proved necessary to increase the frigate forces by fifty per cent.—from 82 to 120. The trade, organized in great escorted convoys, sailed eventually in safety, under the cover of the battle fleets.

The end of the Seven Years War found the country a triumphant victor but at the same time deeply in debt; for the war had cost some 112 millions. Economy was again essential and it was insisted upon by Parliament. To combine economy with good husbandry required great administrative skill, efficiency, and perseverance. Anson was dead, and his successors were not men of his calibre: they lacked his power and his wide grasp of naval policy. When, later, Hawke became First Lord, he found that the establishment would not maintain the eighty ships of the line which the Two Power Standard required in war. To Hawke, indeed, we owe the first definite expression of that principle of British naval policy. 'Our fleet', he said, 'could only be termed considerable in the proportion that it bore to that of the House of Bourbon.'[1] But the money voted not only would not maintain that relative strength in ships of the line; it could not

[1] M. Burrows, *Life of Hawke* (1883), pp. 455–6.

provide for the absolute requirements in cruiser forces. The Navy, though it remained imposing on paper, steadily dwindled, and the result was experienced between 1778 and 1782.

Lord Sandwich, Hawke's successor, was an able and shrewd, but an easy-going, man. Lord North made constant demands upon him for economy, on the grounds that the Court of France was so pacifically inclined, and peace would last so long, that naval expenditure was unnecessary. In this expectation he was disappointed, and when war came in 1775 few ships of the line could be fitted out and manned. It was owing to the unreadiness of the ships of the line that Keppel, in 1779, could not meet d'Orvilliers with even equal force, and that a squadron could not be sent to intercept d'Estaing: while, to meet the lack of frigates, the great ships had to be used instead, thereby wearing themselves out. So the trade suffered. Between 1776 and 1783 the enemy captured 3,386 sail of merchants' ships. America was lost because the British fleet could not control the communications. A further difficulty was the shortage of timber. In order to release the country from its dependence on the Northern Powers in war the policy of procuring our naval timber supplies from the Colonies had been adopted. Owing to their anxiety especially regarding the supply of oak for the dockyards, the Navy Board in 1769 expressed a desire that no more oak should be felled and sold for private use, but that the Navy Board should be allowed the pre-emption of whatever quantity it required.[1] Hemp, flax, and tar were no less important, and colonial trade in them was similarly encouraged.

Hemp being absolutely necessary for shipping, England is at Russia's mercy, and also that of Denmark, whose forts command the Sound. When Sweden in 1703 refused to let us have any more naval stores save in her own ships, Parliament granted a bounty on the importation of such stores from the Colonies, with the result that tar, pitch, and turpentine were presently brought thence in such quantities as almost wholly to supply the demand, and were sold at one third of the price formerly paid to Sweden.[2]

Unreadiness in the ships and want of supplies, severely as

[1] Cf. *Eighteenth-century Documents relating to the Forests, &c.* (ed. A. L. Cross, Univ. of Michigan, 1928), pp. 108-9.
[2] *Papers of Captain H.V. Knox* (Hist. MSS. Comm.), vol. vi, p. 293 (c. 1780-90).

18-GUN SLOOP, *c.* 1780

From a model in the Science Museum, South Kensington

THE BARFLEUR, 1768

From a painting by Joshua Marshall, 1774, in the Science Museum, South Kensington

they crippled England in this great naval struggle, were not, however, the determining reasons for her failure at sea. That failure was due to the manner in which the operations were directed. The war, said Lord Howe, could have been won in the Bay of Biscay. The failures were failures of strategy and command.

THE ADMIRALTY

Throughout this period of Johnson's England, and for another fifty years afterwards, the general direction of the Navy was in the hands of the Admiralty Board, with its subordinate administrative boards. The Admiralty Board corresponded with the Board of Directors of any great business of to-day. It conducted the policy, decided the entry, selection, appointment, and advancement of the officers, collected and considered information concerning their rival firms—the foreign navies. It made the distribution of the instruments which policy demanded. But it was not concerned with matters of supply. The business of supply was conducted by those lower organizations, the boards of the Navy, of victualling, and of the sick and hurt. These corresponded to the managing directors. The Admiralty Board determined what ships were needed. The Navy Board designed, built, rigged, and maintained them: it administered the Dockyards—subject to visitations by the higher board—it provided the needed stores. The Victualling Board, and the Sick and Hurt Board, as their names imply, provided food and the needs of the sick. One department was lacking—a department which should provide, and provide for, the men. Such a Board, capable of devoting its attention to the problem, might have developed systems of recruitment and reward, which would not only have been of the highest value both to the fighting and commercial services in war, but would also have spared the seamen of the country many cruel hardships and much injustice.

The distinction, essential to well-regulated business, between command and supply was so clearly understood that no necessity was either felt or experienced for the Boards to be under the same roof. The Admiralty sat, where it now sits, in Whitehall. The Navy Board had its offices, first on Tower Hill and later in Seething Lane: an arrangement handed down in direct succession from Tudor times and excellently contrived for the execution of its tasks. The system stood the test of the three great wars of this period, and the still severer one of the subsequent twenty years' war with France.

The Admiralty Board represented the Lord High Admiral, whose office was thus put into commission. The Commissioners were in part 'gentlemen of Parliamentary interest' and in part sea-officers, sometimes of distinction, but not always; for interest played its part in the selection of the officers, factions had their sway. The Board consisted usually of seven members, but in no fixed proportions of civilians and seamen. Thus, in 1759, three of the seven were seamen, with Anson at the head. In 1744, two only were seamen, and in 1775 there was but one; and in each of those years the head of the Board was a landsman. It was, in fact, not regarded as necessary that the sea element should be strongly represented; and when, after the Peace of Aix-la-Chapelle, Anson took the place of Lord Sandwich, and two other seats were filled by Admirals Rowley and Boscawen, the comment was made, 'How three Admirals will agree, only time will show'.

The First Commissioner, at the beginning of our period (1740), was Sir Charles Wager, a veteran of the previous war, who had shown spirit and energy in the capture of Spanish galleons. He was the successor of a long line of seamen as First Lord—Berkeley, Byng, Russell among them. 'Your Majesty knows very well', wrote Sir John Norris to the King in 1742, when Wager retired, 'that ever since you have been in the Kingdom the chief direction of sea affairs has been in the hands of seamen.' But the line of maritime succession was broken when Walpole fell. Lord Winchilsea was placed in this important post, a man who lent a deaf ear to professional advice, and of whose methods one of his colleagues wrote that 'the only method left of showing his dislike of the absurd and ridiculous orders which were issued from that Board was to refuse signing them'.

The Navy Board was likewise composed partly of seamen, partly of landsmen. Under the 'Comptroller' it had charge of the material of the fleet. Its duty was to take care that the ships and stores were kept up to their proper establishments, and the Navy in such a state as to be ready for immediate war. Its efficiency would seem to have varied almost directly with the proportions of its members. When the majority was composed of persons 'bred from their infancy to a quill'—as Admiral Mathews described them—the business of supply was conducted with all the inefficiency that red tape and officialdom produce in such luxurious crops in all ages. But when its record in these forty years is considered as a whole, through those three great wars and many rumours and risks of wars, it stands comparison with any contemporary organization and with others of much later dates. Neglect and corruption, however, there were in plenty. Sir John Laughton has said that there is the strongest reason to believe that the loss of the *Royal George*, 'when Kempenfelt went down', was due to serious neglect on the part of some highly placed official.[1]

THE SHIPS

In the ships, many important changes took place during these forty years. The fleet, at the beginning of that period, consisted of a mass of ships of various sizes, or 'rates', which bore no relation to any governing strategical or tactical ideas. Like Topsy, 'they growed'. As the man-of-war had gradually developed during the previous century and a half, so she had been built in many sizes from the first rate of 100 guns to the sixth of 20. There were ships of 100, 90, 80, 70, 60, 50, 44, 40, and 20 guns. But when that great thinking seaman Anson became First Lord rules of thumb were discarded, and a more scientific classification came into being. Three distinct classes of ships become recognizable—those intended to fight in the mass, those needed for scouting and detached services, and the small craft, or 'flotilla', required for that infinite variety of services that arise in the course of every war of all times, yet are so consistently forgotten in peace. Under Anson the great mass of the 140 ships 'of the line' were medium-sized vessels of 74 and 64 guns, with a small number only of exceptionally powerful ships of 100, 90, or 80 guns, used mainly, though not wholly, as flagships. The intermediate class of ships, neither of the line-of-

[1] The conscious guilt of influential persons of the Navy Board is indicated plainly by the universal acceptance of the rumours that all efforts to raise the ship were frustrated and that evidence given at the Court Martial was suppressed. See *Recollections of J. A. Gardner* (Navy Records Society, vol. xxxi), Introduction, p. 24 *n*.

battle nor the cruising classes, of 50 and 40 guns, tended to die out, and in their place arose the true frigate of 38 to 30 guns. What remained of the larger 'intermediates' served as frigate-flagships or might, on occasion, be posted *in* the line of battle, though they were not *of* the line.

One complaint runs continuously throughout this period: the inferiority of the British ships of the line to those of our enemies. Though England had produced the great ship-builders of the Pett family in the previous century, she failed to maintain her ascendancy in naval architecture. The French built better sailing ships, stiffer in a breeze, more heavily armed.

The unthinking populace [wrote Sir Charles Knowles in 1745] are too free to censure without examining into the reason of things, and imagine it strange that an English ship of war of 70 guns cannot take a French or Spanish ship of the same force, whereas it is pretty apparent that our 70-gun ships are little superior to their ships of 52 guns.

In confirmation of this, Admiral Medley in the same year gave the weights of general discharge of British and French ships, thus:[1]

English.		French.	
90-gun ship fires 1,606 lb.		74-gun ship fires 1,705 lb.	
80 ,,	,, 1,312 ,,		
70 ,,	,, 1,044 ,,	64 ,,	,, 1,103 lb.
60 ,,	,, 918 ,,		

Even in a light breeze the English ships heeled so much— 'lay along' was the contemporary phrase—that they could not open their lower deck ports where their heaviest guns, 32 and 24 pounders, were mounted. Deprived of these they were left to fight the 32 and 40 pounders of their opponents with the 18 and 12 pounders of their higher tiers. These conditions were improved after an inquiry by a committee, but the better sailing qualities of the Frenchmen were for long the envy of the British captains. The introduction of the practice of coppering the ships' bottoms, of which trials were made in 1761, gave a temporary advantage until our enemies did the same. Fortunately, neither wars nor battles are won merely by the possession of heavier metal or greater

---

[1] *Papers of Lady Du Cane* (Hist. MSS. Comm.), vol. i, p. 64; *Despatches of Admiral Mathews,* 1744; Report from Admiral Knowles, B.M. Add. MSS. 15956, † 119, 1745.

speed, important as they are, but by men, and the British Navy came into possession of several excellent ships which served as models for our constructors and as units in the fleet.

THE SEAMEN

The ancient and recognized source of supply of the seamen for the Navy was the seafaring population of the country; but when recruiting was bad, and volunteers did not offer themselves, recourse was had to 'the Press': a right summarized by the great Lord Mansfield as 'founded upon immemorial usage allowed for ages. If not it can have no ground to stand upon. The practice is deduced from that trite maxim of the constitutional law of England that private mischief had better be submitted to than public detriment should ensue'. Private mischief there was indeed in plenty, for the press-gangs were neither over-particular as to whom they took nor sparing of the feelings of those whom they might legitimately seize.

The fundamental difficulty of manning the fleet on the outbreak of war arose from the fact, already referred to, that the number of men kept in employment in peace was but a bare fifth of what was needed in war. The mere administrative problem of expanding the number of seamen from 16,000 to 80,000 was serious enough, as it involved withdrawing this great number of skilled men from their normal profession and disturbing seriously the trade of the country. The actual business of obtaining the men was made difficult by the dislike of the seamen to service in the Royal Navy. Hard as his life was in a merchant ship, brutal his treatment and bad his food, the existence was more bearable than it was as a general rule—though exceptions there were, and not a few of them—in the Navy. The merchant paid his men better wages and with greater regularity; the privateer offered also higher rewards. Absences from home in the trading ships were long; in the Navy they were longer, service was more capricious, discipline more harsh. Injustice and ill-treatment were the prime causes of an aversion which drove the seaman to attempt by every possible means to evade serving in the King's ships, and in this he was often abetted by the Civil magistrates and by the mercantile community.

When the fleet was fitting out, attractions were offered to seamen to join. A bounty of £2 was offered to all seamen and able-bodied landsmen who should join within a stated period, and two months' wages in advance, together with conduct money, were paid. But at the same time, since these inducements never proved sufficient to provide the needs of the fleet, the Press was put into operation. Warrants to 'press' men were issued, and the gangs to whom the duty fell to execute them were scattered wherever the seafaring man might be found. They haunted the seaport towns, they lay in wait in the approaches by road, they cruised in 'tenders' to intercept the home-coming merchant ship, either off the harbour mouth or even farther out at sea. The seaman in the outward-bound ship was immune, though he might be snapped up at the other end of his voyage to feed the foreign squadron, but the wretched fellow returning from a voyage, however long his absence, might be wrenched from his ship when in sight of the very shores of England, to be embarked, without seeing his home, for service abroad, in the East Indies or the West, in the Mediterranean or off Brest, from whence he might not return for years—if at all.

Vernon, that great and kindly Admiral, whose habit of freely speaking his mind led to his being unjustly removed from the Navy, was a constant advocate of the seamen. One of the earliest reformers, he urged unceasingly that better treatment should be given them. 'Our fleets,' he said, 'which are defrauded by injustice are first manned by violence and maintained by cruelty.' From the time the men were forced on board, they were, he said, 'in effect condemned to death, since they are never allowed again to set foot on shore, but turned over from ship to ship; and when they have finished one expedition, hurried into another without any regard for the hardships they have undergone, or for the length of the voyage'. Men would run great risks to avoid the service. Thus, the captain of a sloop in 1743 reported that four men recently impressed 'swam away from the ship in the night when it blowed so hard that a boat could not row ahead', and this in spite of the fact that two men had been drowned in making a similar attempt shortly before.[1] It showed, he

---

[1] Captain James Douglas, H.M.S. *Ferret*, Dec. 1747. P.R.O. *Ad. Sec. Captains' Letters*. Douglas had obtained only eight men in a whole cruise.

The Press Gang or English Liberty Display'd

From the Oxford Magazine, 1770

said in his letter to the Admiralty, the aversion the men had for the service.

Only too often the men thus raised were but poor creatures, the very sweepings of the streets. Hawke, when fitting out the *Berwick* in 1743, reported that several of the men who had joined were 'poor little sickly fellows that are of no service . . . a great number of them distress a large ship like this greatly, and what is worse most of these poor creatures are now sick'. On reaching the Mediterranean he had 123 men ill, for which great number he could only account by the fact that many of them had only recently returned from the East Indies and had had no time at home to recover from the double effects of the climate and the long voyage, while others 'are raw men, picked up by the press-gangs in London, and are poor, puny fellows'. The story, indeed, as told in many a letter from captains of ships, of the wretched quality of the men makes the wonder the greater that they acquitted themselves so nobly in battle. The 'poor puny fellows' of the *Berwick* reduced the Spanish *Poder*, of her own size, in a very short time in the battle off Toulon a bare year later.

With the Government, the Admiralty, and the officers lay a choice of method in procuring men. They could give the men better and more regular pay, better treatment, and better food on board, a fairer distribution of rewards, and thus get more volunteers: or, paying and treating them badly, get their men by force. Blindly they chose the latter course, denying the possibility of the other. Yet prize money could have been more equitably distributed, and there can be but little doubt that much hardship, much ill-treatment, would have been cheerfully accepted in the certainty of that recompense. Ned Ward, the scurrilous rascal who wrote *The Wooden World dissected*,[1] says of the sailor, 'He's a rare dog under an honest commander, and will fight everlastingly if he can but have justice at the end of his labours; but to receive all the knocks, and none of the moneys, is the Devil, and gripes him worse than the purser's wine-vinegar'. How

[1] *The Wooden World dissected in the Character of a Ship of War: as also, The Characters of all the Officers, from the Captain to the Common Sailors; by the Author of the London Spy.* The book was written in 1706 and went through many editions during the century.

H

small a proportion of the 'moneys' the seaman received, these examples show:

Captain Fox's convoy action. 1747.	£	s.	d.	*Capture of 'Hermione'.* 1762.	£	s.	d.
Total sum . .	294,486	3	7	Total sum . .	519,165	0	0
Flag[1] . .	36,810	15	8	Flag[1] . .	64,963	3	9
Captain . .	8,615	1	0	Captain . .	65,000	0	0
Lieutenant .	1,049	15	10	Lieutenant . .	13,000	0	0
Warrant officer .	459	5	8	Warrant officer .	4,336	0	0
Seaman . .	24	19	0	Seaman . .	480	0	0

At the capture of Havana in 1769 the Admiral and the General each received £122,000. The seaman's share was £23 14s. 9¾d. By regulation the flag share was one-eighth, and the great difference between this and the other actions quoted is due to a special arrangement having been made as to the division of prize money.

This preposterously unjust division of rewards was another of those abuses condemned in Parliament by Vernon. 'There is one thing indeed which ought to be amended; a very unequal distribution is made of the prize money between the officers and sailors, the sailors' part having no proportion to that of the officers''; and he warned the Government in the plainest terms that unless better treatment, more regular pay, and a fairer distribution of prize money were given, a mutiny might break out when the security of the kingdom was in danger.

One step had been taken in the previous century to mitigate the difficulties of obtaining men quickly on the outbreak of war. That renowned corps, the Royal Marines, was raised in King William's reign for manning the fleet and to form a 'nursery for seamen' as well as for providing small-arms men for battle at sea and men for landing when needed. Though it had been disbanded after the Peace of Utrecht, it was restored in 1740 when the manning difficulty was extreme. The marine was a sea-soldier, a seaman and a soldier in one. He was never supposed to be so finished a performer in 'the minute parts of exercise' of an infantryman as the private in a line regiment; but he must be practised in boarding, the use of the small arms, and picking off the men at the enemies' guns in battle.[2] He must be reasonably

[1] In neither case was the Flag officer present at the action.

[2] John Macintyre, *A Military Treatise on the discipline of the Marine Forces* (1763).

proficient in handling the musket, marching, forming, and charging. To add to this he must be able to go aloft, to reef and furl on the lower yards, and must know the ropes on deck. In peace, he was used partly as a rigger in the dockyards, partly as guard for the dockyards; and each year a certain number would be rated able seamen if found proficient by the dockyard authorities.

Our seaman, having volunteered or been pressed, arrived in due course on board his ship. There he received a ticket for his pay, recording the date he joined, which was signed by the Captain, the Purser, the Master, and the Boatswain. This ticket he must carefully keep for presentation at the end of his voyage, however long that might be, when it would be completed with the discharge. Then he could draw his pay and was 'paid off'. But he must present the ticket in person or he would be mulct one-fifth of the meagre total. As it was quicker and easier to get money on it from the Jew on Portsmouth Hard, he disposed of it only too often at an even greater discount. The pay was small enough. The 'ordinary seaman' got 19s. a month; the able seaman £1 4s. Others who received the same sum as the 'A.B.' were the Midshipman ordinary, the Cook, the Swabber, the Cooper, the Captain's Cook, and the Trumpeter.

If his pay was small, his food offered but small compensation. It was bad, scanty, and monotonous to a degree. The scale laid down in 1745 was as follows:[1]

	Biscuits lb.	Beer galls.	Beef lb.	Pork lb.	Pease pints.	Oatmeal pints.	Butter oz.	Cheese oz.
Sunday	1	1		1	$\frac{1}{2}$			
Monday	1	1				1	2	4
Tuesday	1	1	2					
Wednesday	1	1			$\frac{1}{2}$	1	2	4
Thursday	1	1		1	$\frac{1}{2}$			
Friday	1	1			$\frac{1}{2}$	1	2	4
Saturday	1	1	2					

There are curious 'equivalents'. One gallon of beer was equalled by a pint of wine or a half-pint of brandy, rum, or arrack; a pint of olive oil equalled a pound of butter or two pounds of Suffolk cheese; and one pound of Suffolk cheese was equalled by two-thirds of a pound of the presumably more nutritious cheese named Cheshire.

[1] *Admiralty Regulations*, 1745.

Fresh meat—beef or mutton—was to be supplied, even when in port, on two days of the week only: so that while a fleet lay at St. Helen's or Torbay, assembling, as it might often be forced to do for weeks on end, the men were already living mainly on salt food and undermining their powers of resistance to that dread disease, scurvy. The regulations also provided for an economical use of stores—there should be no waste. If the 'bread'—that is to say, biscuit—was found to be damp, it was 'to be aired on the quarter deck or poop'; but no provisions were to be returned 'on pretence of their being old or unfit for keeping unless there shall be reasonable ground to object against any such provisions'. Thus a ship, when victualling for a foreign voyage, might first be victualled with the oldest provisions in stock, then lie for weeks at Spithead waiting for a fair wind, without which a large convoy could not move down Channel, and then spend many more weeks at sea before she reached, perhaps, Brazil and could get some fresh food and vegetables. What wonder that the ships on foreign stations were short in complement!

The beer was a byword. Hawke, in his strenuous cruising off Brest in 1759, wrote: 'The beer brewed at Plymouth is in reality so little relief to the squadron that I have sent in orders to send no more of it. Our daily employment is condemning of it.' And to the 'naval officer'—'storekeeper' as we should call him to-day—at Plymouth, he wrote: 'The beer brewed at your port is so excessively bad that it employs the whole time of the squadron in surveying it and throwing it overboard. . . a quantity of bread from the *Ramilies* will be returned to you by the *Elizabeth,* though not altogether unfit for use yet so full of weevils and maggots that it would have infected all the bread come on board this day.' One may wonder at what stage of decomposition the bread would have become 'altogether unfit for use'! That was before the battle of Quiberon, one of the boldest and most remarkable actions of a remarkable year—the *annus mirabilis.* England was saved from invasion, but the seaman got no gratitude in the form of betterment in either his pay, his prize money, or his provisions. Conditions may even have been worse, for the contemporary jingle ran:

Ere Hawke did bang
Monsieur Conflans
You sent us beef and beer;

Now Monsieur 's beat
We've nought to eat
Since you have nought to fear.

The losses from scurvy were immense, until the discovery
of the value of lime-juice as an antiscorbutic—a discovery
made before 1770, but not made use of officially until 1795.
It was rare, according to Admiral Geary, for a ship to remain
longer than six weeks without the men 'falling down' from
the disease. A strange cure for scurvy is mentioned by
Admiral Pasley, who, having a tray of earth on board in
which he grew vegetables at sea, put the sick men into the
earth. 'Yesterday the garden did wonders; the men who
were carried and lifted in and out of it incapable of moving
a limb, worked by themselves to-day—wonderful effect. . . .
How fortunate my having a garden!'[1] Provisions, water,
and health are rarely alluded to in the formal histories of
these days; but they played a very great part in the strategy,
they affected the outcome of battles. How great the losses
were is illustrated strikingly in the *Annual Register* for 1763,
which records that in the Seven Years War 1,512 seamen
were killed in battle, while 133,708 died of disease or were
'missing'.

The needs of the sick were provided for by having a 'Convenient Room' prescribed in the regulations for the sick and
hurt, and men appointed by the captain to serve them and
keep the place clean. Fishing tackle was provided expressly
to enable captains to employ men to catch fish for the sick;
the surplus, if any, being divided gratis among the officers
and seamen's messes without favour. But what the condition of the sick and wounded could be in a tropical climate
can be read in Smollett's terrible picture in *Roderick Random*
of the 'tween-decks off Cartagena in 1741.

Hospital ships accompanied some fleets—vessels with
flush gun-decks, without cabins or bulkheads 'except a deal
or canvas one (to roll up) for separating such as have malig-
nant distempers from the rest'.[2] Extra scuttles to improve
the ventilation were cut, and the staff consisted of the
physician of the fleet, an 'able and experienced surgeon'
with four mates and six attendants, a servant of the surgeon,
a baker, and four washermen. Though there were rules

[1] *Private Sea Journals of Admiral Pasley* (1782).
[2] *Admiralty Regulations*, 1745.

governing the qualifications of the physician they were not rigorously observed. The case is recorded of one calling himself 'Dr.' Vincent, who, when in charge of French prisoners, by his practice of bleeding and evacuation 'killed more Frenchmen than all the commanders in the Navy put together'.

The seaman had to run the gauntlet not only of the surgeon. One admiral had his own ideas of medicine in the shape of a belief in the paramount value of James's powders, which he insisted on being used in all cases of fever: though it is but fair to say that when it was represented to him that the result was that the men were dying at the rate of four a day 'he gave up his favourite nostrum'.[1] Even the surgeon was but a warrant officer, with £5 a month for his pay—£1 more than the boatswain and £1 less than the most newly fledged lieutenant in a small ship. He had to provide his own instruments and medicines according to a prescribed scale, and had charge of the necessaries sent on board for the sick, which he was directly enjoined by the regulations 'to keep in custody and not embezzle or mis-apply any part'.

If the poor seaman, after being forced on board if he were not a volunteer, after facing the enemy, stomaching the food, and withstanding the climate, survived also the ministrations of the physician and the surgeon, he might in the end get some reward in the form of a gratuity from the chest at Chatham and possibly a berth in Greenwich Hospital: while if he did not survive he had the satisfaction of knowing that his widow would be entitled to a year's pay, each of his orphans to one-third of a year's pay, and that 'his posthumous children would be deemed orphans'.

THE OFFICERS

Although men from the lower deck could become officers, it was seldom that a bona fide 'seaman', even if he obtained commissioned rank, rose higher than lieutenant.[2] The lower deck was not, nor could it be, a regular road to the quarter-deck and the after cabin. The officer was entered and trained on different lines.

There were many ways of entering the Navy. A boy of

---

[1] W. H. Long, *Naval Yarns, Journal of a Naval Surgeon* (1758–65).

[2] Captain Cook, who entered the Navy as a common seaman, is one of the few remarkable exceptions.

THE LOWER GUN DECK OF H.M.S. VICTORY

thirteen could be entered as a 'servant'. A captain could oblige a friend by this convenient method of taking one of his youngsters on the ship's books. By being thus shown, the boy could reckon the 'time' to qualify for lieutenant, even though he never went on board. If the parent were an officer an additional advantage accrued, for the boy could be entered at the age of eleven. These rules were elastically interpreted. Thus, Admiral Clavell was entered at the age of one; Saumarez was 'borne' for two and a half years without setting foot on board. J. A. Gardner was 'entered' in his father's ship while still at school, aged five, and many never put in an appearance on board for years. A boy could also join as a 'volunteer per order' whose training is outlined in a set of instructions concerning a boy entered from the Naval Academy in 1742:

Whereas the bearer, Mr. William Lloyd, has been educated in the Naval Academy at Portsmouth, and is well qualified to serve his Majesty at sea, you are hereby required and directed to . . . enter him as one of your Complement.

You are to take care that he applies himself to the Duty of a Seaman, and he is to have the Privelege of walking the Quarter Deck. You are to allot him a proper place to lie in without setting up any cabin, and you are to rate him volunteer per order which will entitle him to Able-Seaman's pay.

You are to oblige him to keep a Journal, and to draw the appearances of Head-lands, Coasts, Bays, Sands, Rocks and Suchlike: and you are to take care that the Master, Boatswain and Schoolmaster do instruct him in all parts of learning that may qualify him to do the duty of Able Seaman and Midshipman.

After two years' Service at Sea you are to rate him Midshipman ordinary, or Midshipman if he shall be qualified for it.

When your Ship shall be at Spithead, or in Portsmouth Harbour, you are to direct him to attend the Mathematical Master in order to his further improvement in the Mathematicks, and likewise to attend the lessons given by the other teachers and by the officers of the yard, who are directed to instruct him Gratis.

He is likewise to carry his Journal to the Mathematical Master in order to his examining the same: and representing to us how he has informed himself. And at the end of his Service in the Ship under your Command you are to give him such a Certificate of his Sobriety, Diligence and Skill in the Profession of a Seaman as he shall deserve, as also the length of Time he has served with you either as a Volunteer per order or Midshipman.

A restricted number of midshipmen ordinary was allowed

to each type of ship. Their pay was £1 4s. a month as against the regular midshipman's £2 5s. There was no social difference between the various ranks of young officer. In 1780, in the *Conqueror*, three brothers Nash were serving; one was a midshipman, the two others were captain's servants, and both eventually became captains themselves.

Another mode of entry was through the Naval Academy, a school established at Portsmouth in 1729. The boy could enter at any age between thirteen and sixteen and could remain there either for two years, as the volunteer per order in the instructions already quoted had done, or for three. Thus, between these various ways of becoming an officer, the official age of going to sea could be anything between eleven and nineteen. In practice, however, the greater number went at between twelve and fourteen. One reason for this was to accustom them to the hard life. If they came later, it would deter them from remaining at sea. On this question George III wrote, 'All the sea officers I have ever consulted as to the proper age for sending young officers to sea have concurred in the opinion that fourteen is as late as so hardy a profession can be embraced with the smallest prospect of success'. Notwithstanding this opinion, many officers embraced the 'hardy profession' with success at a later age. Boscawen, noted for his fearlessness in taking responsibility and his independence of view, was over fifteen when he went to sea, and Hood was sixteen; Sir Francis Geary and Benjamin Caldwell were seventeen; Vernon was nearly eighteen when he left Cambridge; and Borlase Warren, after passing through Winchester and Emmanuel College, did not go regularly to sea until he was past eighteen.

Thus varied as the ages were at which boys first embarked, no less varied was their service. Nelson's early service is an example. At the age of twelve he served before the mast in a merchant ship, on a voyage to the West Indies, where, as he wrote, 'if I did not improve my education I returned a practical seaman with a horror of the Royal Navy. . . . It was many weeks before I became reconciled to a man-of-war'. He then had a term in a pilot-cutter, plying in pilotage between the Tower of London and the Forelands, after which a Polar expedition was followed by a voyage to India. This variety of service undoubtedly contributed to that independence of character, that habit of forming his own opinions

productive of the moral courage that is so often lacking in
officers, which made him so great a commander. Howe—an
Etonian—as a youngster went round the world with Anson;
in the course of the voyage he was taken from the orlop deck
into the captain's cabin where he broadened his mind as he
could not have done in the rough surroundings below.
Troubridge, leaving England as a midshipman, went to the
East Indies, and there remained for twelve years, returning
to Spithead at the end of that time as a post-captain commanding the flagship.

This wealth of experience, and the responsibility which
fell upon these boys, not only instilled professional knowledge and developed seamanship; it gave them confidence
and self-reliance. Of some forms of book-learning there may
have been but little, but of education, in a wider sense,
there was much. Instruction, however, was not wholly
neglected. A schoolmaster was appointed to the larger ships
where many midshipmen were borne, who must have ex-
hibited his qualifications of being 'well skilled in the Theory
and Practice of Navigation and qualified to teach Youth
therein' to the Master and Wardens of Trinity House;
though it is to be feared that the Regulations often sat no
less lightly in his case than in that of others. He was sometimes
an indifferent guide in spite of his having also to produce
certificates from 'Persons of known Credit testifying the
Sobriety of his Life and Conversation'; he is described as
being 'frequently a confirmed drunkard and the butt of his
pupils'.[1] He was directed to inform the captain of the
names of such as were 'idle and averse to learning in order
for his taking Course for their Correction'. It would seem
that, as in much later times, the boy's education depended
far more upon the captain under whom he served than upon
any system. A youngster who served under a cultivated
man like Collingwood started with an advantage of every
kind over others who served with men of a more common
mould.

The young officer was not supposed to receive commissioned rank until the age of twenty-one, with six years
service as midshipman or mate. But here again regulations
were interpreted with latitude. Admiral Sir George Elliot
found no difficulty in procuring a certificate that he was

[1] Sir John Laughton in *Papers of Lady du Cane*, Introduction, p. xxxii.

twenty-one when his age was actually no more than sixteen and a half, for the porter at the Navy Board, where examinations were held, supplied these useful documents for the modest sum of 5s. Nelson certified to the necessary age when he was under eighteen, Barrington when he was fifteen. Perhaps the most flagrant case was that of a son of Lord Rodney who became a commissioned officer at fifteen and four months, and a captain five weeks later.[1] But success was too rapid for him and he came early to grief. It is indeed not without interest to note how few of the great sea commanders of this age were the sons of naval officers—Anson, Hawke, Boscawen, Jervis, Rodney, Hardy, Vernon, Saunders were not: while the two most notorious failures, John Byng and Lestock, were.

The certificate once obtained, the examination was not severe, particularly if the examinee had a friend of the family on the board. This ordeal over, the young man might become a lieutenant; he was eligible, but he must await a vacancy. Vacancies were rare in peace, and the 'passed midshipman' might have to wait many a weary year for his advancement. Collingwood, for example, who was a midshipman of the Seven Years War, which ended in 1763, did not get his step until the American War of 1775; nor was his case exceptional.

The young man's pay now rose from 49s. a month to 5s. a day if appointed to a first or second rate, or 4s. in a smaller vessel. The greatest ships had but six lieutenants—a number that compares curiously with the score and more who now are to be found in the corresponding type of ship—the third rate had four, the fourth and fifth rates, three, and the 20-gun sixth rate, one only. Thus, much of the duty performed to-day by commissioned officers was then performed by the seaman class, to the great advantage of promotion. These duties were to keep a watch and command a battery or other duty in action. The junior lieutenant instructed the seamen in the small arms.

This regular method of producing lieutenants was not capable of meeting the needs of expansion in war. The Navy,

---

[1] This record was close-run at a later date by a cousin of Lord Cochrane, who, serving in his father's ship, was made lieutenant at sixteen, commander three months later, and an acting captain at seventeen. He, however, survived this rapid promotion and died at an advanced age as an Admiral.

as we have seen, was reduced to a very small establishment in peace. The twenty 'guard ships' and the frigate squadrons did not carry many midshipmen, and hosts of officers had to seek employment outside the Navy. When, therefore, war broke out and experienced sea officers were needed in great numbers, the 'passed midshipmen' and mates who had been either vegetating on shore during the peace, or serving afloat in the trading ships, were given commissions in hundreds. Each war showed a vast increase, thus:

War of 1739–48.		War of 1756–63.		War of 1775–83.	
No. of Lieutenants.		No. of Lieutenants.		No. of Lieutenants.	
1739	1748	1756	1763	1775	1783
367	640	632	880	836	1349
(a)	(b)	(c)	(d)	(e)	(f)

Thus, from (b) to (c) and (d) to (e) we see that though the number was approximately maintained in peace, the replacements do not actually make up the wastage. As we have seen, the immediate needs were met by wholesale promotions of 'passed midshipmen' and mates and withdrawals from the merchant marine. But these last-named officers were rarely promoted further. It is uncommon to find among the senior officers men whose careers had regularly begun in that service. Assuredly there was no lack of bold and skilful fighting seamen among the masters of the merchants' ships, as the privateer records and the defence of their own vessels plainly show; but good though such men were in the minor ship commands, they were not adapted to the higher stations, and the rule had been established that no one should be promoted who had not served in the Navy, in a subordinate officer's rank, long enough to learn how to command men: a rule whose rigid application undoubtedly deprived the Navy of such fine fighting seamen as 'Commodore Walker' the privateersman, or Paul Jones, Decatur, and Bainbridge in the young American Navy.

No one with experience of command is unaware how difficult it is to discover the exceptional man, bred on the lower deck and limited in outlook, however technically capable, who is fit for command. The skilled seaman, gunner, or other technician—even the technician in courage like

Captain Carkett who bungled Rodney's attack—may make but an indifferent commander of a squadron or a fleet. The bulk of the flag officers were men of education; but others there were who lacked it. Thus, Admiral Thomas Pye in 1773 ends a letter to Lord Sandwich in this manner:

Give me leave my Lord to make one Observation More and I have Don—and that is When You peruse Admiral Pyes Letters you will please not to Scrutinize too Close either to the speling or to the Grammatical Part as I allow my Self to be no proficient in either, I had the Mortification to be neglected in my education, went to Sea at 14 without any, and a Man of War was my University.[1]

There was, however, interchange between the Navy and the mercantile marine which was undoubtedly valuable. The naval officer when out of employment sought it in the trading ship, not only as a youngster but even in higher ranks. Lord Keith, Captain Alms—one of Hughes's captains in the East Indies—and Fanny Burney's naval brother, Captain Burney, are among the many who thus served.

Promotion from lieutenant to captain, or to master and commander, depended on many things. Interest went far— very far; but merit could obtain recognition, though recognition moved more slowly than a friend at court. But if an officer were fortunate enough to come under the notice of his Commander-in-Chief for some good service, he had expectations of advancement. For in war the admiral was on the look out for good men to promote into vacancies, though the First Lord might be pestering him with political and social candidates for promotion. Neither Hyde Parker, Troubridge, Kempenfelt, Pellew, nor Jervis—to mention some of the better known men—had family interest. Pellew was the son of the master of a packet boat; Troubridge's ancestry is uncertain; Hyde Parker had served as a seaman in the merchant service; Kempenfelt was the son of a Swedish artillery officer—the 'Captain Sentry' of the *Spectator*. Some men were naturally more fortunate than others. Nelson was a captain before he was twenty-one; Hawke did not reach that rank till he was twenty-eight.

On board his ship the captain was an autocrat: yet there were many things he might not do. He might not 'be out of his ship from the day of his coming on board to the day of his discharge unless by leave from the Admiralty or his

[1] *Sandwich Papers* (Navy Records Society, vol. lxiv), vol. i, p. 36.

Commander-in-Chief'. A set of fifty-five separate instructions regulated his conduct, regulations which (as regulations when overdone are liable to do) would have occupied every minute of his waking hours if scrupulously observed. His pay varied from £1 a day in a first rate to 6s. in a sixth. He was allowed four 'servants', which gave him an opportunity for providing for his sons, or the sons of his friends; and though the instructions laid down that none would be borne on the books who were not embarked, borne there were many.

Though the pay in the ships of the line was higher than in the smaller classes, captains often—possibly 'generally' would be nearer the mark—preferred a frigate command; for it gave opportunities for making a fortune in prize money. Captain Pasley, when commanding a 50-gun ship—a large frigate, in effect—refused an offer to exchange into a higher-paid 74. 'A 74-gun ship is not the thing in that country.' If, however, he should be offered to exchange into a smart 32-gun frigate, the *Active*, he might accept. 'With my connections I think a Fortune in a couple of years would be a certainty.' Many are the examples of this way of looking at things. No greater favour could indeed be shown to a captain, no better expression of the admiral's favour, than being 'sent on a cruise' where he might pick up some prizes. Nor were admirals averse from sending their ships out 'cruising'; for the flag took, as we have seen, one-eighth of the prize money. The custom was an evil one, though it would have had some advantages if the flag officers' and captains' shares had been reduced and the seamen's increased. The temptation to detach ships for prize hunting would have been less: while recruiting might have gained by the promise of larger rewards to the seaman. The system enriched a small proportion of individuals; but it was demoralising and it led to more than one deflexion of force from its true objectives, and to shady transactions and breaches of friendship in the Service and between the Services. 'No soldier was landed till two o'clock, two full hours after the affair was settled, by which means they are deprived of all shadow of hope. The sole, the only right to Prizes, remains to the Navy alone. . . .' So wrote a captain exultingly of the capture of a Dutch force at Saldanha Bay in 1781.

Eventually, after whatever period circumstances or fortune dictated, our captain became a flag officer. That period varied greatly. Prior to 1747 the Board had selected captains for promotion whatever their place upon the list; but the complaints made by officers who were passed over were so consistent, so powerfully supported, and undoubtedly often so well justified in that day when political favours played so large a part, that promotion by selection was abolished, and officers were promoted in turn into vacancies in the flag list. To avoid employing officers who were not thought fit, the new rank of 'retired Admiral'—colloquially called 'Admiral of the Yellow'—was instituted. Originally available only to officers who had served in the Spanish war (1739–40), it was extended, in 1770, to all captains who had been passed over but had good service behind them. But for all this, there were advantages in promotion by selection. Neither Hawke nor Anson would have commanded in their actions in 1747, nor would Anson have been able to carry out his great reforms, if they had had to wait their turn.

Service in the captain's rank was prolonged. Howe, Bridport, and Hood, captains of 1746 and 1756, served for twenty-four years in that rank. Duncan (1761) for twenty-six, St. Vincent (1760) for twenty-seven, Cornwallis (1768) for twenty-eight, Sir Richard King and Charles Middleton—afterwards Lord Barham and First Lord during the Trafalgar Campaign—for twenty-nine, Sir Hyde Parker (1762) and Sir Peter Parker (1747) for thirty, and Barrington (1747) and Sir Richard Onslow (1762) for thirty-one years. In later years this period decreased, owing to the sweeping promotions made by Lord Howe when that great officer was First Lord. Lord Keith served nineteen years as a captain and Nelson eighteen.

Whatever injustice it may have imposed upon individuals —and injustice it certainly did impose—early advancement and long service in the rank of captain had certain advantages for the country. The system of early promotion placed men in positions of responsibility while still young, unafraid, and without the burden of a reputation to maintain. These men grew up in the habit of trusting to their own judgement and of acting accordingly, without awaiting or asking for orders. Nor did their seniors discourage this healthy spirit.

But the system had also its disadvantages. The very young captain, promoted by interest, had not always learnt to govern himself. He might become, and too frequently was, a tyrant. But this was less characteristic of these forty years than it was at a later time when the greater expansions of the personnel increased the field in jobbery, and parliamentary and social interest were more pronounced.

The flag-officers' list at the beginning of this period—1740—was limited to a total of ten: one Admiral of the Fleet, two Admirals, three Vice- and three Rear-Admirals. This establishment was a relic of the seventeenth century. It represented the needs of tactical command in the great fleets of many vessels of the wars with the Dutch and Louis XIV. The spread of the Empire brought with it new theatres of war in the struggles for America and India. More detached squadrons, and larger, became necessary, and hence more flag officers to command them. Ten flag officers grew to twenty in the war of 1739–48. No reduction was made at the peace in 1748. Not only was it not possible to get rid of the admirals in excess of the earlier establishment, except by death, but the growth of the lieutenants' and captains' lists which the war had caused made it necessary to maintain a larger flag list. At the end of the next war (1765) the flag officers had increased to thirty-seven. The next war added more; in 1783 there were fifty-seven Admirals.

Into this rank our officer who had begun his career at some age between eleven and nineteen at length, if he were fortunate, arrived. He now has a fine state cabin, bare and uncomfortable though it would look to the luxurious modern eye. He has a great stern gallery in which he may walk and survey his fleet's behaviour, if he does not choose to walk the poop. He has respectable emoluments and privileges. As a Vice-Admiral he gets his £2 10s. a day and a retinue of fifteen men; as an Admiral, £3 10s. and the same retinue; as Admiral, £5 and a retinue of fifty. He can advance those whom he thinks fit to advance; and he has that comfortable one-eighth of a share of the money awarded for prizes to any ship serving under his command.

The expansion, in the forty years under review, of the officers in the Navy, brought about by the three great wars of that period, was remarkable. At the beginning there were 315 lieutenants, at the end, 1,349; 36 masters and commanders grew to 184; 171 captains to 412; and 10 flag officers to 57.

The period of Johnson witnessed great happenings in the

Navy. Though the Navy proved unable to save the Old
Empire, as it might have done if it had been more efficiently
provided in peace and directed in war, it saved the nation.
It saved India and other great possessions. It touched great
depths—a Franco-Spanish fleet in overwhelming numbers
even cruised in the English Channel. But it touched also the
highest peaks of glory. It held the sea in dispute for four
years against the three greatest maritime Powers. Though
over 9,000 sail and merchant ships were taken, the flow of
trade never ceased. It won great victories at sea. The Navy
of Johnson's England was rich in great commanders whose
names should be household words—Vernon, Anson, Hawke,
Boscawen, Saunders, Rodney, Howe, Hood; and besides
these many others, less known. John Norris, the wise old
veteran of Queen Anne's wars; the brave, though quarrelsome and erratic, Charles Knowles; Peter Warren, the
amiable and able Irishman, who helped to take Louisbourg,
but lost his chance of remembrance by being struck down by
scurvy in 1747; that stubborn fighter George Pocock, who
never won a victory but by sheer pugnacity and hard hitting
drove his opponent d'Aché from the Indian seas; Steevens,
the dogged seaman who clung to Pondicherry through the
tempestuous weather of the monsoon and compelled its
surrender; Charles Watson, Clive's colleague at the retaking
of Calcutta; Hughes, the solid, stubborn old seaman who
with inferior force foiled the efforts of that greatest of
French commanders, Suffren; and Kempenfelt, better known
to the public because he was overset with twice four hundred
men than for the far more profound reason that he was
a great thinker, a strategist and a tactician, a most able
commander, and a reformer of the first rank. These were
great men indeed, worthy of the age of Johnson.

BIBLIOGRAPHY.—The Admiralty Regulations (1740–66) give information about pay, conditions of service, victualling, duties of officers, entry. Contemporary writings are to be found in the *Recollections of James Anthony Gardner*—an excellent picture of contemporary life and manners (Navy Records Society); *Law and Custom of the Sea* (ibid.), papers concerning Capture, Privateers, Prize customs; SIR GILBERT BLANE's (1749–1834) *Short account of the most effectual means of preserving the Health of Seamen*, telling how scurvy was met. *Lady du Cane's Papers* (Hist. MSS. Comm.) and the *Papers of Captain H. V. Knox* (ibid.) give much information on many aspects of life at sea. FALCONER's *Marine Dictionary* and CHARNOCK's *Marine Architecture*, for matters of general and technical information. SMOLLETT's description of the siege of Cartagena in *Roderick Random* and the *Private Journal of Admiral Sir Thomas Pasley* contribute to a knowledge of everyday life. WARD's *The Wooden World dissected in the Character of a Man of War* is a scurrilous and highly coloured description of officers and men. Difficulties of manning the fleet are dealt with in the *Diary of Sir John Norris* (Brit. Mus. Add. MS. 28132–3), and they are also fully dealt with in HUTCHINSON's *The Press-gang afloat and ashore*. General sketches of the life of the seaman, illustrated with contemporary prints, are to be found *in extenso* in COMMANDER ROBINSON's exhaustive books, *The British Fleet* and *The British Tar in Fact and Fiction*. MASEFIELD's *Sea-life in Nelson's Time*, though it deals with a rather later period, is applicable to an earlier date. ROSCOE's *The English Scene in the Eighteenth Century*, W. H. LONG's *Naval Yarns*, SIR J. K. LAUGHTON's *Sea fights and Adventures*, MARKHAM's *A Forgotten John Russell*, CHILDERS's *A Mariner of England 1780–1817*, furnish many curious details of life at sea. Biographies are numerous. TUCKER's Life of St. Vincent, BARROW's of Howe and Anson, BURROWS's of Hawke, CORNWALLIS-WEST's of Cornwallis are among the most important. The administrative chapters in LAIRD CLOWES's *History of the Royal Navy* give much information on administration and organization. LAIRD CLOWES's *Sailing Ships* (Science Museum) gives in a brief form much information about construction and rigging, and R. G. ALBION's *Forests and Sea Power* (1927) about the problems of supply of masts and spars.

IV

THE ARMY

By THE HON. SIR JOHN FORTESCUE

Our nation may boast, beyond any other people in the world, of a kind of epidemick bravery, diffused equally through all its ranks. We can show a peasantry of heroes, and fill our armies with clowns, whose courage may vie with that of their general.—*On the Bravery of the English Common Soldiers* (added to the *Idler* in the edition of 1767).

JOHNSON was born in the year of Malplaquet and died one year after the signature of the treaty which gave the American Colonists their independence. Such was the period of his life, expressed in terms of British military history. We may put it still more shortly by saying that within his lifetime a British Empire was won and lost. The first British soldier that he ever heard of was Marlborough, the greatest of them all; the last was Cornwallis, who was compelled to surrender at Yorktown.

It may be said that the modern British soldier was the creation of Cromwell. The great Oliver was the man who had taught him discipline and self-respect, had turned him to account for stern government of a distracted nation, and had made him the terror of Europe. Cromwell's army was by no means a wholly contented army, for the officers were not satisfied with the tenure upon which they held their commissions; but he could always obtain as many good recruits as he desired to keep its strength up to fifty thousand men; and the profession of the soldier was held in honour. All this passed away within two years of his death, leaving behind it in the nation a deep hatred of military rule and a permanent distrust and loathing of standing armies.

Nevertheless, a small standing army was established at the Restoration, though it consisted of little more than a bodyguard for the sovereign and garrisons for British possessions oversea. It was not held in high esteem, and its constitution was completely altered. Reverting to the practice of the medieval mercenary companies, officers bought their commissions. Colonels were the proprietors of their regiments, and captains were proprietors of their companies, a system which endured for two centuries until it was finally swept away in 1871. The so-called army was, in fact, not an army at all, but a collection of regiments, in each of which the commanding officer enjoyed considerable independence. The regiment was called by his name; and the number, which signified its precedence, was hardly used in Johnson's lifetime, as it was later, for the purpose of denomination. Nevertheless, even in the time of Charles II, the Army was burdened with the duties which it continued to fulfil, in whole or in part, until the first decades of the nineteenth century. It manned the fleet in time of war and it did the work of the preventive service and of the domestic police at home, as well as of imperial police abroad.

Upon the small foundation left by Charles II his successor, James II, began to build a far more formidable structure with a view to absolute rule. The Royalists or Tories had already been taught to abominate a standing army by Cromwell, and the Whigs learned the same lesson from James. The King, as we all know, was driven from the country before he could go far with his design, and William III, who greatly desired England as a recruiting ground, took his place. Therewith there began the long struggle with France which ended only in the year of Johnson's death.

The Army, when William took it over, was from various causes in a very bad state, nor, being an unsuccessful general, was he the man to make the best of it. But it improved greatly between 1689 and 1697; and to this period belong the best-known English officer and soldier in the world, Captain Tobias Shandy, otherwise Uncle Toby, and Corporal James Butler, otherwise Trim. Laurence Sterne, born four years later than Johnson, was a child of the barrack-yard, and, though *Tristram Shandy* was not published until 1760 and was dedicated to the elder Pitt, it is very evident that the soldiers of William and Marlborough were better known to him than those of Ferdinand of Brunswick, Amherst, and Wolfe.

William died in 1702, bequeathing the task of curbing the exorbitant power of France to Marlborough. Under that greatest of English soldiers the red-coats rose to the highest reputation in Europe. At the Schellenberg (July 2, 1704) their prowess had won the admiration of the entire host of the Allies, and Louis XIV went so far as to instruct his generals to be particularly careful of any part of the line of battle in which they were stationed. Not even under Cromwell had they been more dreaded; but Marlborough was brought to disgrace by the mean intrigues of faction; and after the Peace of Utrecht (1713) the old cry against a standing army became more savage than ever.

From 1714 until 1739 every man's hand was against the Army. Parliament only grudgingly voted the money for a quite insufficient force and declined to provide funds for building barracks. Accordingly, in compliance with the Mutiny Act, which provided, among other things, for the quartering of the Army in Britain, each regiment was split up into six or eight little detachments and scattered among the ale-houses of as many petty towns for maintenance. Then the trouble began. With one voice the petty towns petitioned vigorously for deliverance from the burden. They pestered the Secretary at War with letters of complaint. Their representatives in Parliament 'speeched' that unfortunate individual in the House of Commons. Last and not least, they laid themselves out by every description of malevolence to make the lives of their unwelcome visitors unendurable. Magistrates abused their powers to persecute all soldiers past and present. They would listen to any charge against them, and contrive that even the most innocent should suffer at least some annoyance if not some penalty. Goldsmith, who seems to have had some feeling for old soldiers, describes the old cripple who, when a little charity was granted him,

Shouldered his crutch and showed how fields were won,

and in *The Vicar of Wakefield* he relates how Mr. Burchell paid a guinea to save an old soldier from being whipped through the streets. The two incidents are very full of meaning to those who have studied the military history of that period.

It need not be said that this maltreatment of the soldier provoked retaliation. Officers, it must be confessed, shrank from the dullness of the life in little towns; and, since the politicians had assumed command of the army and would give any officer unlimited leave of absence provided that he could bring political influence to bear, there were many who never went near their regiments. This was a great evil, for the distribution of regiments, already very weak in numbers, into a multitude of detachments encouraged slackness and made the enforcement of discipline very difficult.

It was an effort even for the most conscientious of commanding officers to ride, perhaps, over one hundred miles before he could see all the men for whose conduct he was responsible. Thus it came about that young subalterns, with all the mischief and hardihood of youth, would think out ingenious methods of revenging themselves upon well-to-do citizens who bullied their soldiers. One such citizen prided himself upon the neatness of a patch of grass and a gravelled walk before his house. A cornet of dragoons took occasion to drill his troop thereon, and cut grass and gravel to pieces. Two officers, greatly daring, asked a leading clothier of Trowbridge to dinner, plied him with drink, and, when he was in a condition which made him agreeable to any proposal, pressed a shilling into his hand and enlisted him as a soldier. But the triumph of these two enterprising warriors was short-lived. In every case where the civilian complained of the soldier to the Secretary at War, it was always the soldier who went to the wall, whether rightly or wrongly. The disputes and wrangles between civilians and soldiers nearly drove the Secretary at War to distraction during this period, but the soldier gained little by them.

In spite of the traditional hatred of a standing army in the nation, this intense animosity against the soldier would be difficult to account for, but for one fact—that the army was the only police force that stood between authority and anarchy, and the only preventive service that could enforce the revenue laws. Dragoons were the soldiers chiefly employed to prevent smuggling, and no one can now tell how far that particular duty influenced them for good or evil, for efficiency or corruption. But, as regards the preservation of common order, beyond doubt the soldier stood for a great deal, for the times were inexpressibly lawless. The judicious handling of the Metropolitan Police during a century of life has made the public their friends, ready to appeal to them and second them; and the same spirit extends to the constabulary of the country generally. Things were very different in the middle of the eighteenth century. Few would bestir themselves in the cause of law and order.[1] It

[1] When, in the first week of June 1780, the Gordon rioters carried on their orgy of anarchy and destruction in London, ministers and magistrates were utterly supine, and the situation was only saved by the use of the military at the express injunction of the King.

was impossible to put down even a formidable gang of poachers without the help of the military. And the military itself, being consistently persecuted by the public, was not too trustworthy. Patrols of cavalry failed to make the road safe between London and Kensington. On one occasion Frederick, Prince of Wales, drove down to Whitehall with an escort of dragoons and, when the time came to return, found that every man of them was hopelessly drunk. His Royal Highness raved, his prominent blue eyes starting out of his head with wrath, but not all his imprecations could restore his escort to sobriety. Upon another occasion Kensington Palace itself was burglariously entered, and upon investigation it was found that the guard was acting in league with the burglars. There was nothing surprising in this. The public had chosen to ordain that the calling of the soldier should be held in contempt and disrepute, and the recruits, especially about London, were naturally the scum of the earth. Merciless flogging alone upheld some kind of discipline, but even public executions in Hyde Park could not check desertion. The best of good soldiers, under the infamous law of the land, could not consider himself safe. When called upon to act in aid of the civil power, he was liable to be shot for mutiny if he disobeyed the order to fire, and liable to be tried by a civil court for murder if he obeyed.

But if the condition of the soldier were unhappy at home, much unhappier was it abroad. Colonial garrisons were not many in those days—Gibraltar, Minorca, New York, Nova Scotia, and a few of the Antilles—but they were more than enough to baffle the administrative powers of the War Office. In England the soldiers were quartered in ale-houses. Obviously, therefore, they must be quartered in ale-houses wherever they might be. In Ireland, it is true, it had been found necessary to build them barracks; but the Irish establishment was a thing apart, subject to the Lord-Lieutenant and the Irish Parliament. Food was cheaper there, for Ireland was the victualling yard of the world, and the rates of pay for all ranks were accordingly lower. Ireland could look after herself; but the new Mediterranean garrisons, called into existence by the Peace of Utrecht, were a sad puzzle, for the troublesome places could show no ale-houses. The troops must, therefore, be provided with

roofs over their heads, bedding, fuel, victuals, and all kinds
of troublesome details; and the effort to provide these things
was too great for the War Office. They made contracts for
the supply of food to the troops, but in Minorca they omitted
the item of meat. They considered the old Spanish huts or
baracas sufficient shelter for the garrison at Gibraltar, but,
as they forgot to furnish any supply of fuel, the soldiers were
obliged to burn these huts in order to light their fires. As
to victualling these two fortresses against the event of a
siege, such a thing never occurred to them until it was
actually suggested by the King. In the West Indies the most
important garrison was that of Jamaica, where the quarters
were so unhealthy that the men died like flies. But even
in the nineteenth century the life of a battalion in the West
Indies did not exceed two years. In New York there were a
few weak independent companies permanently attached to
the place, and in one winter an appreciable proportion of
these died from sheer cold. But in all of these quarters there
was at least liquor to be obtained. In Minorca and Gibraltar
wine was cheap. In the West Indies rum, and especially
that poison new rum, was only too abundant. In New
York also there were imported rum and locally made beer.
But in Nova Scotia, a lonely, dreary wilderness, there was
nothing but water to drink, for there were not only no ale-
houses, which the War Office seemed to think must grow up
naturally like trees, but there was no ale. It was actually
necessary for the officers, none too well paid, to brew spruce-
beer for their men at their own cost.

A serious trouble in respect of these foreign garrisons was
the duration of a regiment's stay in them. Poor ignorant
yokels, as most of the recruits were, dreaded the voyage
across the sea. In the first place, the rustic mind has a
strange terror of great waters, and in the second, the poor
lads naturally shrank from the idea of possible transportation for life to a strange land, where they might not find—
and frequently did not find—decent food, bedding, or
shelter. Hence, when a battalion was ordered abroad the
ranks were half emptied by desertion. The War Office had
as yet no idea of an organized system of reliefs. In old days
garrisons had been things apart, inalienably attached to their
fortresses whether at home or abroad, and the War Office
still halted between old methods and new. One battalion

actually remained unrelieved in the West Indies for sixty years. In any case, when a battalion was sent abroad to replace another in a foreign garrison, it generally absorbed into its ranks the men of the old garrison, who had bound themselves to the strange land by ties of wine and women, and were content to stay there until the end of their days.

We know very little of the life of the soldier oversea in time of peace, catching only fleeting glimpses of it from journals begun during a siege and prolonged after the cessation of hostilities. One such journal of the abortive Spanish attack upon Gibraltar in 1727 reveals a few interesting facts. The behaviour of the men during active operations was good, though some five and twenty deserted. The food issued to them was so bad that there were many deaths from dysentery both among officers and men; and the governor himself had to content himself with ships' biscuits in lieu of bread. Still, all hardship was cheerfully borne until hostilities ceased, and then with the return to the dullness of routine the men became troublesome. There was much desertion, much drinking, and endless quarrelling. Two corporals of one regiment fought each other with their fists until both expired. Two sergeants of another regiment fought with swords and killed each other. Two officers, after a dispute over a game of fives, were only prevented from emulating the sergeants by being placed under arrest. Another officer, 'being in discontent' first drank himself drunk and then shot himself. The lash was constantly busy among the men, and the whirligig (a contrivance for making the refractory land-sick) among the women, who seem to have been the very lowest of their kind. But the lash had little terror for many of the soldiers. One of them, who asked leave to marry one of these same disreputable women, was sentenced by his officer to one hundred lashes. He presented himself, with his back all raw, on the following day to repeat his request, which his officer had not then the heart to refuse. Yet another man, a drummer, boasted that he had received twenty-six thousand lashes in fourteen years, and his officers could testify that he had received four thousand more between February 1727 and February 1728. 'And yet,' comments the chronicler, 'the man is hearty and well, and no ways concerned.' The English newspapers of the time show that it was not uncommon for men who were not soldiers to back themselves to take some hundreds of lashes for half a crown.

In spite, however, of these gruesome details it is probable that officers took better care of their men abroad than at home. In the first place, to take the lowest view of the officers, every soldier lost to them through infirmity, death, or desertion had to be replaced mainly at their own expense, so that it was to their interest to stand between them and maltreatment. But beyond doubt there were among the officers gentle and humane men who delighted in their soldiers for their own sake, and would do much for their well-being. If Fielding has painted for us Ensign Northerton, Sterne has given us Uncle Toby and Corporal Trim; and it is remarkable that the most charming portrait in literature of master and man should be the work of a child of the barrack-yard. Roger Sterne, the father of Laurence, was actually an officer of the garrison of Gibraltar in 1727. Nor is it to be supposed that no such officers were to be found at home. The men would never have followed them so readily into action had there not been. But abroad the soldier of that day, helpless outside his native element, was more than ever dependent upon his officer for everything; and there was always the sacred honour of the regiment to form a bond between them. It is a very significant fact that every measure for the welfare of the soldier was initiated by regimental officers long before it was embodied in general regulations, and that a very large proportion of them originated in foreign garrisons.

There is another significant point about the period under review. It is about the year 1740 that the soldier begins to take his place in contemporary art as a feature in the life of the nation. We have reached the time when sovereigns, as a token of their power, delighted to dress their soldiers like dolls and manœuvre them like puppets. Frederick William I of Prussia, that half-insane creature, with his regiment of giants, gave a powerful impulse in this direction which did not escape his brother of Hanover. George II actually caused delineations to be made of a man of every regiment in his army, which still exist, the cavalry in the Royal Library at Windsor, and the infantry (unlawfully spirited away) in the British Museum. There is also at Windsor a series of engravings by Bernard Lens of a grenadier going

through every motion of the hand-grenade exercise, from
the slinging of his musket about him to the replacing of his
musket to the 'shoulder'. In all of these we see the soldier
who fought at Dettingen exactly as he was. The cavalry
have (with one exception) three-cornered hats; they have
long-skirted scarlet coats with divers facings, long heavy
boots above the knee, and ornate housings over the saddle,
while the horses are of the type that is only seen nowadays
in a hearse, black in colour (except those of the Scots Greys)
with tails docked so short as to leave about two inches of
bone with no hair. The foot-soldier likewise wears the
three-cornered hat, a broad-skirted scarlet coat, with wide
facings, a long low flapped waistcoat, scarlet (in some royal
regiments blue) breeches, and long white spatterdash
gaiters, reaching to mid-thigh. He has a very broad buff
leather shoulder belt, an equally broad waist belt, a sword
as well as a bayonet, and a musket at the shoulder; and—
a significant fact—he stands with his legs wide apart. So
Johnson must have seen him when he first came to London,
very smart, very clean, a figure calculated even then to
make an impression upon the female heart.

Better known of course than these delineations (though
they have been frequently reproduced) is Hogarth's painting of the march to Finchley, which so greatly offended
George II. The young grenadier who is the most prominent
figure, if painted from nature, must have been a very favourable type of recruit, and the sergeant who is driving him
away from his girl, a not unusual type of non-commissioned
officer. But quite apart from such great work as Hogarth's
there belong to this time the engravings of guard-mounting
and such-like functions, which prove that these were among
the sights of London. The musicians are few as compared
with those which now attend guard-mounting at St. James's
or Buckingham Palace; but their appearance is rendered
striking by the contrast between extremely tiny drummers
and fifers and gigantic bandsmen with gigantic instruments,
of which the serpent (or something like it) is the most
prominent. Unpopular though he might be, the soldier was
beginning to take his place as part of the pageantry of
London, and as such to be at least tolerated if not admired.

But great changes were at hand for him. In 1739 a quarrel
with Spain raised hopes of great booty to be gathered in the

A TROOPER OF THE KING'S CARABINEERS, 1742

Spanish Indies and the Spanish Main. A raid upon Porto Bello by Admiral Vernon gained that officer such fame that his name has not even yet vanished from the sign-boards of English inns. An expedition was projected to Cartagena; and such power had still the fabled wealth of Spain over ignorant English minds that recruits of a very good class jostled each other in the race to join the colours. There was nothing new in this. When Cromwell sent his expedition to St. Domingo an old officer of the New Model contemptuously described the troops as 'big with expectation of gold told up in bags'. There is no need to re-tell the ghastly story of Cartagena, for it has been told once for all by the young naval surgeon, Tobias Smollett, who saw all of its horrors with his own eyes, and set them down with a vivid and remorseless pen. Of all the young fellows who had donned the red coat to make their fortunes not one in ten returned.

Meanwhile, Europe had embroiled itself in a quarrel over the succession of the Empress Maria Theresa to her father's dominions. France had visions of a partition of the Austrian Empire. Frederick of Prussia without any provocation invaded and appropriated Silesia. George II, as Elector of Hanover, supported the Empress and taking command of his army in person did his best to lead it to disaster at Dettingen. He escaped, thanks chiefly to the valour of his troops. His son, William, Duke of Cumberland, in 1745 replaced him and engaged the Army in the glorious defeat of Fontenoy. Then came the invasion of the Young Pretender, with its astonishing initial successes and its final collapse at Culloden, one or two more unsuccessful actions in the Low Countries, and finally the peace of Aix-la-Chapelle in 1748. The Army, which had been largely augmented for the war, was reduced again with all the old outcry against it in Parliament; and the nation, rather sore and much irritated by the bill that was presented to it for the cost of the war, settled down in some bewilderment to what it conceived to be peace.

But in truth the struggle for the possession of the New World had begun in earnest and, whatever might be the state of affairs in Europe, British, though not yet of the regular army, and French were arrayed against each other both to east and west, both in India and in North America. Ministers and Parliament, however, took as yet little heed of that. The tiny drummers and the huge bandsmen went on guard as usual. There were many more mutilated and crippled men wandering as beggars about the country, not all of them so fortunate as to meet with a Mr. Burchell. In the war department the Duke of Cumberland struggled, with but small measure of success, to make good the many defects which had been revealed by the last war. Thoughtful colonels too began to make changes. It had occurred to Frederick the Great of Prussia that by making men stand with their heels together and shoulder to shoulder, a greater number of muskets could be compressed into a given space, and that as a natural consequence, a greater volume of fire could be delivered from within that space. There must therefore be an end of the old position immortalized by the pencil of Bernard Lens, when the soldier stood with his legs wide apart. It was a small matter, but it transformed the accepted appearance of a battalion on parade, and the transformation has persisted to this day.

For seven years the covert bickering of English and French continued in America and India until at last in America the quarrel came to a head. The French were encroaching on the Ohio—on land, that is to say, which had been bought by a little group of speculators in Virginia. The British Governor was one of these speculators and George Washington was another. In terror for the safety of their investments they invoked the aid of the mother-country to eject the intruders, and two battalions were accordingly sent across the Atlantic to fight in the American backwoods. The fact sounds common-place, but it is difficult to realize nowadays what it must have meant to the soldier. He was packed into a hired transport, probably some old bluff-bowed brig or barque not exceeding two hundred tons in burthen, and packed so tightly that he could hardly move unless half at least of his comrades were on deck. He was hustled and bullied by the captain and the crew for being, quite innocently, in the way in fair weather; and in foul he was battened down below decks, miserably sea-sick and frightened out of his life. His food was chiefly salt pork, very likely mouldy and certainly ill-cooked, eked out with biscuit full of weevils. His allowance of water was strictly limited, and if the voyage were prolonged, very short indeed. Lastly it was extremely doubtful when, if ever, he would arrive at his destination. The

A FOOT SOLDIER OF THE 29TH REGIMENT OF FOOT, 1742

merchant-skippers might be good seamen, but they were
very indifferent navigators, and they were much given to
drink. Details of life in a hired transport at this period are
all too rare, but such few as we can gather concerning it
during the eighteenth century are not pleasant. A sergeant
of Marlborough's army, who journeyed no farther than from
England to Ostend described it as 'a fatigue for the devil—
hell between decks, the pox above board, and the devil at
the helm.' So much for the interior economy of hired
transports: now for their vagaries. General Clinton when
sailing with a force from New York to Charleston, Carolina,
during the American War of Independence, was overtaken
by a heavy gale. Two of his transports were blown clean
across the Atlantic. One of them put in to Falmouth,
Cornwall. The other, being blown through the Straits of
Gibraltar, brought up at Cartagena in a sinking condition.
Her gaping timbers were frapped together with her cables,
and thus she hobbled to Gibraltar where she fell to pieces.
Again in the year 1796 the Captain of a hired transport
bound from the West Indies to England died of *delirium
tremens* a few days after sailing. A major of infantry then
took command, and undertook to bring the ship across the
Atlantic to the Downs. In due time he dropped anchor in
an English estuary, which, however, proved to be that of the
Mersey instead of that of the Thames. His calculations erred
to the extent that he had passed to the north instead of to
the south of Ireland; but things might have been worse, for
at least he did not run his ship ashore on the west coast of
Ireland.

Voyages to more distant lands, such as to India round the
Cape of Good Hope, were a more serious matter, though the
East India Company's ships were famous for excellence.
The passage rarely took less than six months and, if anything
went wrong, might be prolonged for two or three months
more. Robert Clive was nine months at sea when he first
sailed to India as a youth, and had outgrown all of his clothes
before he reached Calcutta. Again, in 1807 a regiment of
light dragoons, which had sailed on the ill-fated expedition
to Buenos Aires, took no fewer than one hundred and eighty
days to return from thence to Deal. By 1807 strict rules as to
ventilation, deodorization and so forth had improved the
conditions on board transports; but the men were so much

cramped and crowded that they could hardly fail to suffer in health. In earlier days the condition of a hired transport was unspeakable.

The two battalions which were sent out to America in 1755 reached their destination without mishap, and duly landed in their panoply of three-cornered hat, wide skirted red coat, spatterdashes, and so forth. It will occur to the reader at once that such a costume was not well adapted to a campaign in the backwoods; but there was no help for that. Nowadays the Army Clothing Department would provide suitable raiment at short notice; but then, and for a century afterwards, it was a colonel's business to clothe his men. Twopence a day was stopped from the pay of every man to meet the expense, and the Colonel, employing a contractor, made, if he could, a profit out of the transaction. It must be premised that a general officer received no additional pay as such and might very well, unless he were the colonel of a regiment or the governor of a fortress, find himself the poorer for his promotion. It was understood that he should make a profit out of his men's clothing, and the temptation to gain money at the soldier's expense had in early days proved too strong for poor human nature. There was one extreme case when a colonel went so far as to clothe his men in the cast clothing of another regiment, and had been cashiered for his pains. Such abuses had been rendered impossible by a regulation laid down by Marlborough (always the soldier's friend) when he was Master-General of the Ordnance in 1707. But it was obviously quite impossible to expect a colonel to re-clothe his regiment specially for some unusual campaign, for he could not, unless he possessed very large private means, afford to do so. Even as things were, peculiar circumstances not unfrequently converted the colonel's profits into very serious loss.

So the two battalions plunged into the bush under General Braddock, clad just as they would have been in London, and it is difficult to conceive of the appearance that they must have presented after they had been at work for a week. However, they were shortly afterwards surprised and cut to pieces, so that it mattered very little what they wore. Two or three years later a young British officer, Lord Howe, who had more sense and enterprise than his contemporaries, raised an irregular corps in America for forest-fighting, cut the hair off his men's heads and the skirts off their coats, and clad them in brown as a practical working colour. But he was early killed in action, though his example was not forgotten later on during the American War of Independence. Meanwhile, the masterly policy which revoked the order prohibiting Highlanders from bearing arms, provided that they would use them in the King's service, had called kilted regiments into being. Their national costumes gave them at any rate freedom of movement for their limbs, and they did very fine service in Canada during the summer. But bare limbs will not withstand a Canadian winter, and the Highlanders might have fared ill had not the good nuns of Quebec, moved rather by considerations of decorum than of the men's welfare, knitted warm garments to cover their nakedness.

Braddock's incursion against the French on the Ohio produced open declaration of war with France in 1756, and the Whig ministers who then governed England sat still and trembled while Minorca was besieged and taken. The elder Pitt presently assumed command in their place, and he began by calling into existence, in 1757, a new class of soldier called the militia man. His design was nothing less than to pass the manhood of England, chosen by ballot, through three years of military training.[1] Singularly little is known to us in detail of this militia, but we learn from the pages of Edward Gibbon's journal that his regiment at least was very efficient, that he was bored to death when once he had learned his duty and that he found the business of the ballot particularly trying. The ballot itself was carried out by the simple process of drawing numbers out of a hat ; but it is easy to understand that the tricks and wiles of rude and illiterate deputy-lieutenants and servile parish-clerks, all intent upon doing some job in favour of some rustic friend or to the prejudice of some rustic enemy, the interminable chatter and the wilful waste of time must have afflicted the nerves of the studious and fastidious Edward. Still he seems to have been a good officer, who did not disdain to think out new methods of intensifying the fire of musketry.

[1] Boswell tells us that Johnson 'was once drawn to serve in the militia, the Trained Bands of the City of London. . . . It may be believed he did not serve in person. . . . He upon that occasion provided himself with a musket, and with a sword and belt'.

Extracts, recently published from an order book of some Yorkshire militia, give us a far better idea as to how the new militia regiments were knocked into shape. At the outset they were casual in the extreme and constantly intoxicated. They would come to roll-call drunk, unpunctual, and irregularly dressed, and would answer their names (or each other's names) and stagger away without waiting to be dismissed. They were only with much difficulty persuaded to be tidy in person and in dress and to take care of their arms; and their sergeants would connive at their shirking of duty by making out false weekly and monthly states. Sentries on duty chattered incessantly, being particularly noisy when the time came for relief, and, if a disorderly militia-man were arrested by the guard, his comrades rose like one man to rescue him. The general in command was actually obliged to remind them that the penalty for insubordination was death. Gradually, however, thanks to the example of two regular regiments which shared quarters in the same town, they were tamed and more or less disciplined. At last the day came when they were trusted with the firing of a few ball-cartridges, whereupon they at once began to squander their ammunition upon private shooting matches (they were always betting and gambling) and upon depredations upon the game of the neighbouring squires. But they seem upon the whole to have been worthy fellows, and would have given a good account of themselves in the event of an invasion.

Meanwhile, they liberated all regular troops for service abroad, and Pitt was insatiable both of recruits and of conquests. His methods of recruiting, imitated a generation later by his son, were thoroughly unsound, but he got men together, good, bad, and indifferent; and the number of regular infantry regiments rose far in excess of one hundred. Never before had there been so many British soldiers; and there was something to show for them. In 1758 the long tide of failure and defeat began to turn with the capture of Louisburg, and in 1759 came the year of victory—the capture of Guadeloupe in the West Indies, the brilliant victory of Minden in Germany, Wolfe's decisive success at Quebec in Canada, and Hawke's brilliant action at Quiberon Bay. In the East the long efforts of Stringer Lawrence and Clive had culminated in the triumphs of Forde and Eyre

THE MARCH TO FINCHLEY

From the engraving by L. Sullivan after the painting by W. Hogarth

Coote, and an Empire had been won in the Orient as well as in the West. Fresh successes followed between 1760 and 1762; and by the treaty of 1763 England was saddled with more territory and more West Indian islands than she realized. Had Pitt been in power there would probably have been a further increase and the catastrophe of 1783 would have been even more humiliating than it was.

There was no idea in those days of making a hero of the soldier, not even for a day. When he had served his purpose he was cast aside and went back to his old status of a plague of the nation. The conquest of the empire imperatively demanded an augmentation of the army for its defence, but Parliament quarrelled even with the quite inadequate force which was proposed for the purpose. Edmund Burke, who had longer sight than most men of his time, complained bitterly of the 'huge increase of the military establishment', which included twenty new regiments. His vision could only conjure up twenty new colonels capable of holding seats in the House of Commons. It never occurred to him that there were a thousand miles of frontier in North America which would require protection against Indians. The wretched men who were scattered among the various fortified posts along that vast line led dreary lives of hardship and isolation with hardly food enough to eat. Moreover, the Indians did actually rise, and swept away not a few of them, causing a most serious situation which, as usual, was saved by the ability and promptitude of an officer and a handful of British soldiers on the spot. The incident cost two or three hundred men their lives and probably not one Englishman in ten thousand had the slightest knowledge of it.

Meanwhile, there was gradually developing the quarrel with the American Colonies over the question of Imperial Defence, which was ultimately to force upon the British soldier much of the most thankless work that he ever did. It is curious that the irritation of the Americans arose principally out of three measures of high imperial policy in which the Imperial Government was undoubtedly in the right. First, there was the question of Colonial contribution to the cost of Imperial Defence. The Colonies admitted the justice of this in principle, but contested it vigorously in practice. Next, there was the Quebec Act, which gave the French in Canada liberty to follow their own religion. This infuriated the bigoted and narrow-minded Puritans of New England. Lastly, another regulation forbade land belonging to Indians in the newly conquered territory to be arbitrarily appropriated by the American Colonists. This alienated many well-to-do gentlemen in the south, George Washington among them, who had for years been dabbling in speculative purchases of land on the Ohio.

To have found a solution of all these difficulties which should more or less satisfy all parties would have passed the wit of man; but most unfortunately the trouble was aggravated by complications at home. Ever since the death of Queen Anne the Whigs had been the dominant party in England, but they themselves were divided by so many quarrelsome factions as greatly to injure the general administration of the government. Realizing this George III had the courage to rid himself of them and appoint ministers of his own choice, as constitutionally he had then a perfect right to do. Thereby he rendered his country a very great service, but he paid the penalty, for the Whigs who had, in all innocence, irritated the Americans to rebellion, now, in considerable numbers, took their side. They did not really want to lose the American Colonies. In fact they were rather dismayed to find themselves ultimately compelled to grant American independence. But they had not realized the possible consequences of their action in Parliament. If ever an important contest were decided by blind chance, it was the War of American Independence.

The man who paid for all this trouble at home was of course the British soldier. He was sent out at first to Boston, the centre of rebellion, to do police-duty, but he was not allowed to act. The soldiers were obliged to submit to every kind of insult, outrage, and persecution, but were not permitted to retaliate. The lives of sentries were made a burden to them. The ruffians of Boston would always attack any individual soldier whom they could overpower, and would maltreat even sick soldiers who could hardly crawl out of hospital. The magistrates behaved as ill as the ruffians. For example a soldier for some petty theft was imprisoned, condemned to pay £70 damages, and in default was sold as a slave for a term of years. It was common for both officers and soldiers to be arrested upon some frivolous charge and to be refused bail; and when, after some period

of confinement, the case came up for trial, no evidence was
offered by the prosecution and the prisoners were instantly
acquitted. All this was greatly the fault of the English
Ministers. It is idle to make a mere menace of force and not
to exert it. But the Imperial Government shrank from strong
measures, because there was always a powerful faction at
home siding with the Americans.

So too, when war, open and unabashed, came at last, it was
not prosecuted vigorously and relentlessly. The commanders,
knowing that they had bitter enemies at home, took the
field with the sword in one hand and the olive-branch in
the other, with the result that when advantages were gained
they were not turned to full account. Thus the soldiers
poured out their blood to no purpose. As a matter of fact
no one wanted to fight, least of all the Americans. Washington's own letters leave no doubt upon that point. On the
other hand the British were in little better case. The men in
the field felt that many of their own countrymen were against
them. Many officers went on half pay rather than serve in
America, some upon political grounds, some because they
thought—and rightly thought—the whole idea of subduing
America by military force sheer madness. Recruits likewise
came in but slowly for service in the Army, since the pay of
the soldier had become utterly insufficient for his needs.
There was nothing very tempting in a campaign against a
civilized enemy in an untamed country—no hope of booty,
no prospect of anything but hardship abroad and perhaps
more bitter hostility than ever at home.

The contest dragged on, thankless and indecisive, until
the disaster at Saratoga put a new and more serious complexion on affairs. It was agreed under the capitulation that
the British prisoners should not be separated from their
officers. Congress without hesitation violated this article,
hoping by maltreatment of the soldiers to drive them to take
service with the American army. Then France openly
joined the American rebels, and therewith patriotic feeling
did begin to awake in England. Troops were drawn from
America for a counter attack upon the French in the West
Indies with brilliant success; but, as usual, the men who had
covered themselves with glory in the operations were mostly
dead of yellow fever within twelve months after their
conclusion. The main scene of action was transferred to the

southern provinces of America, but, in spite of some hard
fighting, neither side made much progress. So little zeal had
the combatants for the struggle that it was said, not without
a strong leaven of truth, that latterly the British and
American Armies were composed of each others' deserters.
At last in its fourth campaign the intervention of the French
fleet was decisive. The disaster of Yorktown determined
Parliament to carry on the war no longer; and the Whigs,
after arranging the terms of peace, proceeded to discharge
soldiers so fast that hardly any army survived at all. Such
men as were left deserted in despair at the impossibility of
keeping body and soul together, and it was in this condition
that the Army opened the wars of the French Revolution and
the French Empire.

In truth the Army, thanks to the incurable vices of British
politics and politicians, gained much less in every way than
it ought from the forty years of almost continuous fighting
from 1740 to 1781. After all even now how few Englishmen
realize that those were years of continuous fighting? How
many actions are known even by name to the ordinary man
who conceives himself to be educated? Perhaps four—
Fontenoy, Quebec, Saratoga, and Yorktown. And how
many men could he name as prominent in the military
history of the period? Probably again four—Clive, whom
he knows from Macaulay's essay, Wolfe, because he fell in
the moment of victory, Burgoyne and Cornwallis, because
they were associated with decisive disasters. Of Minden,
one of the most striking examples of the prowess of the
British soldier, of Warburg, although the elder Mr. Weller's
public house bore the sign of the Marquis of Granby, of
St. Lucia in 1778, the most wonderful instance of success
achieved against vastly superior numbers by perfect concert
between Army and Navy, they have never heard, or at least
could give no coherent account. These were of course,
relatively speaking, small affairs, but ours has always been
a small army and in every war we have been careful to
scatter it over half a dozen fields of operations. In America,
too, the difficulty of feeding troops was so great that it was
a hard task to move even five thousand men over any great
distance. In India the early work of conquest was achieved
principally by mere handfuls of British soldiers, serving under
the command of captains, as spear-heads to small bodies of

sipahis; yet that is no reason why the names of Stringer Lawrence, Knox, Forde, Adams, and Caillaud should be forgotten. However, there the matter is. After all, as regards the Army, we only take our cue from our own politicians.

Nevertheless, the Army did gain some inward profit from all these forgotten campaigns. It was not that the ruling authorities in London turned their lessons to any account. The auxiliary services were as hopelessly inefficient in 1793 as in 1740, and the artillery then sent on active service was horsed according to the obsolete methods of Marlborough's time. In the matter of recruiting again the younger Pitt copied the evil systems of his father with disastrous results. But the British Army, as I have already said, was never an army at all. It was only a collection of regiments, and it was the commanders of those regiments and their officers who laid the lessons of experience to heart. One great tactical change was brought about by the American war. A great deal of the fighting took place in woodland country, where the old rigid formation of infantry in triple rank was useless. Insensibly the triple rank gave place to double, affording a greater front of fire; and the British infantry fire, as was proved at Fontenoy and Minden, was the deadliest in Europe. It is rather curious that at Minden the British found themselves outranged by French Grenadiers armed with rifles, but disposed of them without difficulty by advancing with the bayonet. In America the Colonial marksmen, often armed with rifles, were far more formidable and needed specially trained men to encounter them. One British regiment, the 62nd Foot, became so apt at this work of springing from cover to cover that it gained the nickname of the 'Springers'. Perhaps the most accomplished were bodies of irregulars raised on the spot and commanded by British officers, with a sprinkling of regular non-commissioned officers and privates to stiffen them. But in any case the force of circumstances threw greater opportunity of independent action in the way alike of junior officers and of private soldiers, and thereby strengthened the bond, always stronger in the British than in any other army, between regimental officers and men. In St. Lucia twelve hundred British troops, fresh from active training in America, in a skilfully chosen position held at bay twelve thousand French.

So strenuous was the contest that, when ammunition was needed, a single officer of herculean strength ran back alone and brought up a case under each arm. The cases were opened, and the ammunition was found to be perished and useless. The fight was at its hottest, having just reached its most critical moment, but the British commander could see no alternative but to give the order to cease fire. It was given, and without hesitation every man brought his musket down and calmly awaited the next command. Such perfection of discipline could only be attained by troops who gave not only obedience but confidence and love to their officers; and the officer who records the fact—it was Harris, later Lord Harris, who captured Seringapatam—mentions it with no common pride. A more touching instance of the strong attachment that united men and regimental officers was seen after the capitulation of Saratoga, when the Americans, in violation of their plighted word, separated the soldiers from their officers. The scene at their parting was most distressing. All ranks were in tears, and when the officers were, very reluctantly, removed, the men followed them with shouts of 'God bless your honours', until they were out of hearing. Uncle Toby received the famous wound that disabled him from further service at the siege of Namur in 1695, but the like of Uncle Toby and of his faithful corporal was still to be found abundantly in 1777.

By the time that Johnson died the outward appearance of the soldier was slightly changed. The long white spatter-dashes had given place to shorter black gaiters, and the cut of the coat had been altered so as more nearly to approach to the civilian's fashions. But the man was the same, in the eyes of the nation a curse, in the eyes of his officers one who could be trusted to dare and to endure anything. There were, it is true, occasional outbursts of national pride in his prowess. The vulgar tradition that one Englishman could beat three Frenchmen still persisted, and the soldier was expected to maintain it. Collins wrote, 'How sleep the brave', and Glover sang of a ghastly tragedy in the Navy in the forgotten lines of 'Hoosier's Ghost'. But there were no war-memorials. The very names of the rank and file who had perished on active service were unknown to any but their Colonels until 1793. The soldier might be a hero oversea, but at home he was an outcast. Not until Miss Nightin-

THE ENCAMPMENT OF THE GUARDS IN ST. JAMES'S PARK, 5TH JULY, 1780

gale went out to the hospitals in the Crimea did the nation awake to the fact that this outcast was after all a man, very patient, very gentle, very courteous, and so devoted to her, who cared for them, that they would kiss her shadow on the wall. It was a wholesome lesson for us, even though it had cost us two centuries to learn.

BIBLIOGRAPHY.—For the period under review the best authorities are in manuscript. The most important of these are the Secretary of War's Common Letter Books and the Home Office Military Entry Books, which are to be found in the Public Record Office. Some curious information as to the private soldier may be found in the tiny sheets of the contemporary newspapers. But in the case of all of these much mud must be washed away before any gold is found. BLAND's *Military Discipline* is a sufficient guide to military routine and drill. WOLFE's *Instructions*, a little thin volume, is more human. For the Cartagena Expedition SMOLLETT's narrative in *Roderick Random* remains without a rival; but the official dispatches (unpublished) in the Public Record Office are most valuable. For the war of the Austrian Succession the only matter of real value in English is to be found likewise in the unpublished letters and dispatches in the Public Record Office. The struggle in North America is admirably set forth in the works of FRANCIS PARKMAN, *Half a Century of Conflict* and *Montcalm and Wolfe*. Full use is made here of the contemporary narratives of KNOX and MANTE as well as of American material. For the Seven Years War there are in English the incomplete history by LLOYD, and there are the far more useful compilations in German by TEMPELHOF and WEST-PHALEN, *Feldzüge des Herzogs Ferdinands*. The American War has a dull but trustworthy general historian in STEDMAN, and there are several ancillary narratives too numerous to mention. A newly published and still incomplete life of Washington by Mr. RUPERT HUGHES is a most useful corrective to former American accounts of the War of Independence.

V

EXPLORATION AND DISCOVERY

By JAMES A. WILLIAMSON

What mankind has lost and gained by the genius and designs of [Henry the Navigator], it would be long to compare, and very difficult to estimate. Much knowledge has been acquired, and much cruelty been committed, the belief of religion has been very little propagated, and its laws have been outrageously and enormously violated. . . . But there is reason to hope that out of so much evil good may sometime be produced, and that the light of the gospel will at last illuminate the sands of *Africa*, and the desarts of *America*, though its progress cannot but be slow, when it is so much obstructed by the lives of Christians.—Introduction to *The World Displayed* (1759).

He expressed a particular enthusiasm with respect to visiting the wall of China. I catched it up for the moment, and said I really believed I should go and see the wall of China had I not children, of whom it was my duty to take care. 'Sir, (said he,) by doing so, you would do what would be of importance in raising your children to eminence. There would be a lustre reflected upon them from your spirit and curiosity. They would be at all times regarded as the children of a man who had gone to view the wall of China. I am serious, Sir.—*Life of Johnson* (10 April 1778).

THE third quarter of the eighteenth century witnessed intense energy in European, and particularly in British, exploration. The geographical work begun in the Renaissance was completed by the mapping in broad outline of the coasts and oceans that yet remained unknown; after which the chief interest of exploration shifted to the ice and to the land, to the crossing of the polar regions and to the penetration of the continents. The enterprise which accomplished the advance of the eighteenth century was partly conditioned by the struggle for empire, but its methods and success had their roots in earlier achievements. In effect, the founder of the effort was William Dampier, whose best work was all done before the seventeenth century came to its close.

Dampier was not a great discoverer. His contributions to the world-map are insignificant. His importance lies rather in what he wrote than in what he did in the sphere of leadership. His chosen work was the observation of nature, and his geographical area was the wide world, over which he wandered, collecting notes. As a poor man, he had to work his passage, which he did in various uncongenial capacities. His life was a hard one, but his reward was that he succeeded in the undertaking on which his mind was set.

In 1697, at the age of forty-five, he published a book that lived, *A New Voyage round the World.* The voyage was not an expedition with plan and finish. It was a series of driftings in different ships and employments, to Jamaica to take up plantation work, to Campeachy to cut log-wood, over the Isthmus with buccaneers, back to Virginia to live respectably for a season, then round Cape Horn into the Pacific with other buccaneers, across the Pacific to the Philippines, south to Terra Australis Incognita (to that western part of it which the Dutch called New Holland), thence to the Indian Ocean, with a divergence to Tonquin and Malacca and the islands adjacent, and so to Madras and home by the Cape of Good Hope. The voyage had taken up twelve years of his life, and he reached England with no booty but a painted savage, who was sold to a showman and died of small-pox. Thousands of drifters have done the like, have degenerated and sunk into forgotten graves. Dampier survived by the vigour of his mind, which preserved him unsodden by sloth and despair. He had kept a journal and filled it with the things that inspired him. Somehow he picked up a living whilst seeking a patron and polishing the journal into a book; and six years after his return the *New Voyage* appeared.

The book had an immediate and permanent success. It was what the public wanted. The public was greatly interested in the trading prospects of Spanish-America, the South Sea, and the East Indies. The jealousies aroused by the Darien Scheme were at their height; two rival East India Companies were filling political England with their clamour, which shortly afterwards became a major issue in a general election; and the approaching problem of the Spanish Succession forced the country to consider the future of a decaying empire which possessed all the known Pacific coasts of both the Americas. The *New Voyage* catered for these tastes, for Dampier, although no trader, had an eye for the interests of commerce. Still more had he an eye for the curiosities of humanity and nature, and so also had a large section of the reading public, whom Addison and Steele were in future years to entertain with essays on such topics. The sheer romance of distant travel had also an appeal, not indeed a new one, but one which Defoe was to prove twenty years later to be capable of striking development. The *New Voyage* had something for every man who could read, think, and imagine. It was dedicated appropriately to Charles Montagu, Earl of Halifax, President of the Royal Society and a Lord Commissioner of the Treasury, one of that band of Augustan statesmen which included Robert Harley and the Duke of Shrewsbury, men to whom science and the arts were interests as absorbing as the affairs of the state. Two editions appeared in 1697, a third in 1698, a fourth in 1699; and thenceforward Dampier's works were reprinted separately and in collections on many occasions in the first half of the eighteenth century.[1]

The pioneer work of 1697 was soon supplemented by others. In 1699 Dampier published a miscellany of additional matter under the title of *Voyages and Discoveries*. It broke new ground with the inclusion of 'A Discourse on the Trade Winds', the foundation of scientific observation on that subject. In that year the Admiralty appointed the author to command a voyage of exploration in H.M.S. *Roebuck*. It was planned that he should round Cape Horn and strike across the unknown South Pacific. Had he done so he might have reached New Zealand and Eastern Australia. But Dampier was not cast in the mould of James Cook. He could endure any hardship but cold. The tropics had no terrors for him, but he shirked the frozen sails and icy decks of the Cape Horn passage, of which he already had experience. He went by the Cape of Good Hope and across the Indian Ocean, and so approached Australia on its well-known western side. There he effected some improvements of detail in the chart, and collected material for an account, as lively as the subject permitted, of the fauna and flora of Western Australia, including the Australian aborigines. He passed by the north to New Guinea, and discovered Dampier Passage, the channel between New Guinea and New Britain. He wrote of the latter island as a promising centre for British enterprise, capable of furnishing valuable products, and a potential base for trade in the Western Pacific and for the exploration of the unknown east coast of Australia. But he himself did not explore that coast. His ship was hopelessly rotten, his officers disaffected, his men mutinous. He turned homewards by Batavia and the Cape, but the *Roebuck* could not last out the Atlantic passage. She fell to pieces at Ascension

[1] For these and further bibliographical details see the edition of the *New Voyage* by Sir Albert Gray (Argonaut Press, 1927).

Island, whence her people were taken off by British ships and reached England by way of the West Indies.[1] A court-martial condemned Dampier to loss of pay and rank for harsh treatment of his subordinates. They seem to have deserved it, but as a commander he was discredited. As a writer his fame was heightened by the *Voyage to New Holland*, published in 1703, and subsequently reprinted with his other works.

Dampier had yet privateering ventures to make in the South Sea, but his work of introducing that vast mystery to the eighteenth century was done. Englishmen of the age of Drake had felt the lure of the Pacific, and had even framed plans for a colonial empire in the islands and continent of Terra Australis Incognita. But the project had yielded to another, more immediately practicable. Hakluyt and Ralegh and the propagandists of Atlantic expansion had had their way, and the seventeenth century had witnessed the foundation of the first British Empire in the West Indies and North America. Throughout that century Englishmen were dead to the appeal of the South Sea. With Dampier they grew alive again, and their interest never slackened until its culmination in the achievements of Cook. That interest, as has been said, was scientific as well as mercantile. It was also inspired by national rivalry with France. To forestall the enemy in unknown waters promised glory comparable to that of overthrowing him in Canada and India.

The War of the Spanish Succession, and its pendant, the almost forgotten war with Spain in 1718–19, consolidated the literary interest evoked by Dampier. The Bourbon Philip V ascended the throne of Spain, supported by the French, challenged by the British. Frenchmen assumed freedom of trade with the Pacific dominions of their ally. British privateers, Dampier among them, went out to ravage those dominions in the manner of Drake, although commonly without Drake's success. These operations made the Cape Horn entry to the Pacific familiar, and they sometimes ended with a voyage across that ocean and a return by the Cape of Good Hope ; and, following the precedent of Dampier, the commanders generally published an account of their

[1] An indispensable work of reference for these and all other explorations considered in this chapter is Mr. E. Heawood's *Geographical Discovery in the Seventeenth and Eighteenth Centuries* (Cambridge, 1912).

expeditions if fortune brought them safely home. So were produced the narratives of William Funnell, Woodes Rogers, and George Shelvocke, full of detail about the known tracts of the Pacific, but containing very little of new discovery; for their authors were commerce-raiders, not explorers. Nevertheless they kept the thoughts of statesmen and the public upon the possibilities of the South Sea, and attracted special attention to islands such as the Falklands and Juan Fernandez, whose strategic value had hitherto been unrecognized. In such an atmosphere it was possible to launch the South Sea Company of 1711, with great aspirations, if with little ultimate achievement.

From enthusiasm for narratives of true adventure it was an easy step to a quite novel taste for narratives of fiction. Defoe was the home-staying counterpart of Dampier. Like Dampier, he observed the world, but he did it by reading books and talking to men. He was indeed an experienced traveller in his own 'Island of Great Britain', and so had acquired a canon of practical criticism wherewith to distil reality from the things he learned from others. It was common ground that a soldier who might have served only in Flanders was thereby rendered more competent than a civilian to discuss soldiering anywhere else, or that a sailor who had never been a pirate was better equipped than any landsman to write a history of piracy. Defoe extended the principle to travellers' tales, and opened a new field to men of letters. His Robinson Crusoe coasted Guinea, dwelt in Brazil and the West Indies, and travelled hard through continental Asia. His Captain Singleton crossed unknown Africa, with realistic adventures, satisfying to his contemporaries although rather discounted by the truths revealed in a later age. The effect of such books was to fortify the public backing for actual exploration. For, although the events and the individuals were fictitious, the human types were true to life, and the geographical settings, where real evidence was available, were faithfully depicted. Crusoe's Island, with its climate, its seas, and its savages, was a description of more than one uncolonized spot in the Lesser Antilles (it is hardly necessary to say here that it was not Juan Fernandez); and Will Atkins is a living portrait of the honest, bloodthirsty ruffians who trampled 'natives' into the earth, and seized the rod of empire from the grasp of decadent

Spain. And, having played his ruffianly part in founding a new colony, Atkins remained true to type. He turned to his Bible and became a God-fearing pillar of society when it was time for freebooting pioneers to change into respectable citizens. Thus, with genius partly unconscious, Defoe drew the moral of empire-building.

Jonathan Swift was a man in whom hatred of the unjust was more prominent than human sympathy, and his contribution to the interest in travel was incidental to his onslaught upon shams. The marvellous lands visited by Lemuel Gulliver were avowedly fanciful, but they served to draw attention to the large blanks existing in the world-map of 1726. No one knew what lay between Van Diemen's Land and the northern coasts of New Holland discovered by the Dutch. Swift placed his Lilliput in the gap, and was quite entitled to do so. The North Pacific had likewise an unknown area, and in it Swift located his Brobdingnag of the giants, and his empire of Balnibarbi inhabited by crazy scientists. There was more plausibility in this, since the Dutch had spread the rumour that a civilized country with white inhabitants did actually exist to the east of Japan. The most daring fantasy of all, the land of the Houyhnhnms, seems to have lain south-west of Australia, the region in which geographers since the Renaissance had been depicting a great southern continent, but which no one had yet explored. Every reader of *Gulliver's Travels*, while he enjoyed their satire, must also have been stimulated to muse upon the unknown Pacific; and Swift was quite ready to outline the plan of its exploitation when the discovery should be accomplished:

A Crew of Pyrates are driven by a storm they know not whither, at length a Boy discovers Land from the Top-mast, they go on shore to rob and plunder; they see an harmless People, are entertained with Kindness; they give the Country a new Name, they take formal Possession of it for their King, they set up a rotten Plank or a Stone for a Memorial, they murder two or three dozen of the Natives, bring away a couple more by Force for a Sample, return home, and get their Pardon. Here commences a new Dominion acquired with a Title by *Divine Right*. Ships are sent with the first Opportunity, the Natives driven out or destroyed, their Princes tortured to discover their Gold; a free Licence given to all Acts of Inhumanity and Lust, the Earth reeking with the Blood of its Inhabitants: And this execrable Crew of Butchers, employed in so pious an Expedition, is a *modern Colony* sent to convert and civilize an idolatrous and barbarous People.

Here was a point of view, not indeed characteristic of the eighteenth century, but one which the previous century would not have dreamed of setting forth. It was a seed which multiplied. Yet another hundred years, and the Clapham Sect, the missions to the heathen, and the Aborigines Protection Society, were to enforce the ethics of which Swift had revealed the lack, much as their worthy members would have disliked to print any words of his upon the title-page of their prospectuses.

The great War of the Spanish Succession had left France with her navy discredited, her commerce greatly reduced, and her East India Company in a condition of virtual suspension. As was not unnatural, when recovery commenced after the peace, the French began to take stock of their colonies and distant trades, and to consider the means by which to retrieve their losses. Within five years of the Treaty of Utrecht the Mississippi Company and its cognate schemes produced an enthusiasm parallel to that of the South Sea Bubble in England. Their unsound finance and consequent disaster rendered 1720 a black year in France as in England, but there was nevertheless a substantial achievement. The French colonies in America and the West Indies entered on a new period of prosperity, the African slave trade and the East India Company revived, and Frenchmen began to take an increasing interest in that farthest East which had hitherto been a preserve of the Dutch. These aspirations are reflected in French literature, and that literature was almost as closely studied in England as in France.

In 1722 Jean Baptiste Labat published his *Nouveau Voyage aux Isles de l'Amérique*, a work which took rank as one of the best available descriptions of the West Indies. It was geographical in the wide sense, including treatment of economic, agricultural, and ethnological questions. Labat followed it with his *Nouvelle Relation de l'Afrique Occidentale* (1728), translated into English in 1745, and *Voyage en Guinée, Isles Voisines et à Cayenne* (1730), the trilogy furnishing a comprehensive view of the tropical Atlantic area of mercantile expansion. At the same period another massive work, R. A. C. de Renneville's *Recueil des Voyages . . . de la Com-*

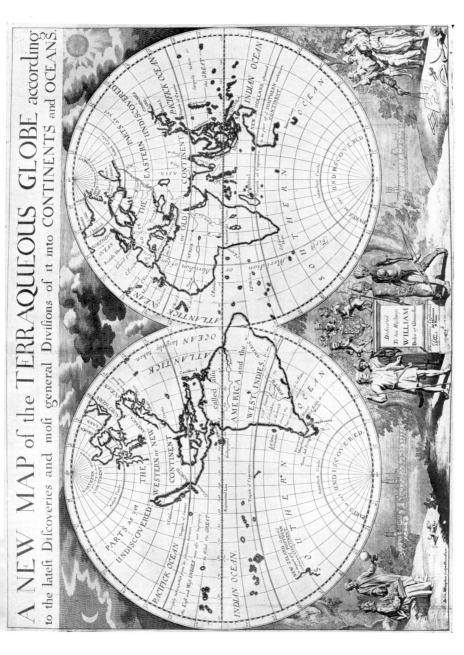

'NEW MAP OF THE TERRAQUEOUS GLOBE', BY EDWARD WELLS, 1722

pagnie des Indes Orientales, first published at Amsterdam in 1702, was reprinted at Rouen (1725). It dealt with the Far East, the voyages in question being those which had established the power of the Dutch East India Company. From the closing years of the seventeenth century the French Jesuits had carried on an active mission in China, and their reports contained much curious and scientific information on an empire about which little had hitherto been known. They were published in many successive volumes under the title of *Lettres édifiantes et curieuses,* and early attracted attention in England. Partial translations appeared in English in 1707, 1714, and 1743. The last mentioned, by John Lockman, was the most complete. Its author claims in his preface to have included all the valuable material, omitting only the miracles and conversions, recounted by the Jesuit fathers: 'it was necessary for me to expunge all Incidents of this kind, (those excepted, here and there, which I presumed might entertain), such appearing quite insipid or ridiculous to most English Readers, and indeed to all Persons of Understanding and Taste.' The fact that the work was undertaken in spite of this strong anti-Jesuit prejudice shows that the subject had a powerful appeal. Meanwhile Pére J. B. Du Halde, out of materials furnished him by the Jesuit missionaries, had produced a comprehensive work on China, which appeared in 1735. Its importance was at once recognized in England, and in the following year an English translation was published as *The General History of China,* in four volumes (London, 1736). Although described as history, it is in the main a geographical work, descriptive of the country and the life of its inhabitants. Another translation followed in 1738.[1]

Meanwhile the period of peace was producing a good deal of actual discovery, although the British took no part in it. The wars had left Great Britain the chief sea-power of the world, and in the materialist Walpole era she was content to consolidate her known advantages whilst leaving to less fortunate rivals the task of examining the unknown. On the cheerless north-east coasts of Asia the Russians under the leadership of the German Vitus Bering launched ships and cleared up the ancient problem of the relation of Asia

[1] There was keen competition between the two translations. The first was several times reprinted.

to North America. Bering established the existence of his strait, crossed it, and reconnoitred the Alaskan shore. Only the bare outline of his achievements became known in England, and much remained to be done in this quarter, a task which was to occupy the last months of the life of Captain Cook. In the Canadian country, west of the St. Lawrence and the Great Lakes, French Jesuits and military officers pushed steadily into the unknown, to follow up the exploits of La Salle and others on the Mississippi in the previous century. The Sieur de la Vérendrye and his sons led this advance from 1731, and ultimately passed through Dakota to the sources of the Missouri. But the fortune of a later war was destined to decide that the French were to be pioneers only, and that the penetration to the Pacific was to be the achievement of a British explorer.

In the Pacific Ocean itself the only notable voyage of discovery in this period was Dutch. In 1721 Jacob Roggeveen sailed with three vessels, two of which rounded Cape Horn whilst the third passed the Straits of Magellan. After re-uniting at Juan Fernandez, they searched for the continental land supposed to exist to the west of that locality. But Roggeveen, although he crossed the Pacific to Batavia, found only small islands. Of these Easter Island was the most remarkable, on account of the mysterious stone figures observed in it, evidently carved by a people who must have differed from the known races of the South Sea. The unknown Terra Australis was expected to stretch farthest towards the tropics in the longitudes of the Pacific, but there were many who believed that its coasts would be found bordering the South Atlantic and Indian Oceans. A vague and ill-authenticated story asserted that in the earliest years of the sixteenth century a French captain named Gonneville had sought to follow the track of the Portuguese round the Cape to India. Storms had driven him out of his course, and he had reached an attractive country somewhere to the southward of the known routes. He had stayed some time and had brought to France a native prince. In 1663 a French priest who claimed descent from this 'Australian' published the tale and advocated the discovery and conversion of the country. There is independent testimony to the voyage of Gonneville, but absolutely no indication of the locality of his find, which may possibly have been Madagascar. The eighteenth century held it to be Terra Australis, in the longitude of South Africa, and in 1738 Lozier Bouvet sailed to rediscover it. In the height of summer, and in latitudes equivalent to those of France, he found icebergs and field-ice, with alternating fogs and gales. He pressed on through this discouraging climate, and was rewarded with the sight of mountainous, snow-covered land in 54° S. Bad weather soon drove him from it, but he was convinced that he had discovered a great continent. He named the part seen Cape Circumcision, but was unable to determine its proper longitude. It is really a small island, whose position has been fixed in modern times, and whose name on present-day maps is Bouvet Island.

With the wars of the mid-eighteenth century began the British effort which, seconded by the French, resulted in the full revelation of the Pacific. War with Spain broke out in 1739, on a question of colonial trade; and in 1740 Commodore George Anson was instructed to lead a squadron of the British Navy to attack the Spanish coasts of the Pacific. Anson's purpose was not discovery, neither did he in fact visit any unknown regions. Nevertheless it is recognized that he was in a certain sense the father of the discoverers of the succeeding generation. One of them, Byron, sailed as a young officer in Anson's squadron. Another of Anson's juniors, Piercy Brett, lived to be one of the Lords of the Admiralty who drew the instructions for Captain Cook in 1768. There was certainly more *liaison* than these facts imply. Anson's expedition was part of a far-reaching policy, the consciousness of which must have persisted in Admiralty circles until the time again became favourable to put it into execution. It is only by inference that we can reconstruct the policy inspiring Anson's voyage, since the instructions issued to him have not come to light. His own account of the expedition, published under the name of his chaplain, Richard Walter, contains only hints, for it was written shortly after his return, while the war was still in progress. Reticence was therefore obligatory. But it seems likely that Anson's mission was to display such force on the coasts of Chile and Peru as to detach those countries from the Spanish empire, not perhaps as British conquests, but as independent states which would open their ports to British trade. When Anson sailed, other British expeditions were operating on the Caribbean coasts of the same colonial possession. Had they succeeded, they would have cut the communications of Peru with Spain, and the project of detaching Peru would have been by no means chimerical. They did not succeed. Anson also failed to bring more than a third of his force to the scene of action; and the Spanish empire emerged intact from the war. The great voyage is thus remembered, not for its strategy, on which its own commander is silent, but as a record of hardship, casualties, and prize-money for the survivors.

Apart from the hidden interest of the voyage, Richard Walter's book is notable for its details of sea life in the eighteenth century, and of the *personnel* of the expedition. The military force allotted to Anson consisted, as has often been recorded, of Chelsea pensioners, most of whom were over sixty years of age. All of them who had limbs and strength to permit of it deserted before the squadron left Portsmouth, and their places were supplied with newly enlisted marines whose only title to be considered soldiers was that they wore uniform. The seamen also were for the most part of very poor quality, and the casualties from disease on the outward passage were enormous. The officers did what they could, and took every opportunity of cleansing the ships 'for correcting the noisome stench on board, and destroying the vermin; for, from the number of our men and the heat of the climate, both these nuisances had increased upon us to a very loathsome degree, and,' adds the narrator reflectively, 'besides being most intolerably offensive, they were, doubtless, in some sort productive of the sickness we had laboured under'. From this and similar passages it is evident that the conditions of sea life in Anson's time were no better than those experienced by Hakluyt's Elizabethans. They also had surmised that uncleanliness produced mortality, and enlightened men among them, such as Sir John Hawkins, had striven to inculcate better habits. But in the early eighteenth century, as in the sixteenth, such efforts were in vain, for the average sailor refused to be kept in health and, says Walter, preserved 'superstitious attachment to such practices as have been long established, and a settled contempt and hatred of all kinds of innovations, especially such as are projected by landmen and persons residing on shore'. All this, it should be remembered, was true of the Walpole period and the War of Jenkins's Ear; but it rapidly ceased to be true in the succeeding generation. A silent revolution was about to be effected in nautical hygiene, and the men who were to accomplish it, Cook and his contemporaries, were already living when Anson's doomed crews set forth upon their voyage. The publication of the narrative of that voyage must have been one of the agents of the change.

Official orders and counter-orders had subjected Anson to six months' delay before setting sail, with the consequence that he had to round Cape Horn at the worst season of the year. The details given by Walter made it appear surprising that he achieved the passage, and it is noteworthy that a Spanish squadron sent out to intercept him was turned back by the weather and took shelter at Buenos Aires after losing a great number of lives. Anson indeed persisted in an almost incredible feat of navigation, but only at the sacrifice of his fighting strength; 'for from hence proceeded the separation of our ships, the destruction of our people, the ruin of our project on Baldivia, and of all our other views on the Spanish places, and the reduction of our squadron . . . to a couple of shattered half-manned cruisers and a sloop'. Whatever the policy embodied in his instructions, he was able to carry out nothing but a superficial raid on the west coast. Thence he crossed the Pacific and captured a Manila galleon of great wealth. He took her to Canton, removed all the valuables, and sold the vessel herself at Macao. His chaplain gives an interesting description of the Chinese, of whom he asserts, from personal experience, 'that in artifice, falsehood, and an attachment to all kinds of lucre, many of the Chinese are difficult to be paralleled by any other people'. Although many English merchantmen frequented Canton, the published information about China available in England was mainly based on the Jesuit narratives, and this from the naval point of view was new discovery. Anson reached England by way of the Cape in 1744.

Thenceforward there was an intermission of Pacific voyages for some twenty years. The Anglo-French rivalry in North America and India became more intense after the peace of 1748, and the disputes in those countries ripened until the outbreak of the Seven Years War in 1756. The struggle decided, for the time, the mastery of the Atlantic and Indian

Ocean, and when it ceased in 1763 the exploration of the Pacific began in earnest.

Meanwhile the literary interest continued unabated. In 1744, just after Anson's return, John Campbell brought out a new edition of Harris's *Voyages*, first published in the reign of Queen Anne. In a sense it was a new work, for Campbell incorporated in the older text a considerable amount of comment and propaganda of his own. He was especially interested in the South Sea, which he believed to contain two southern continents, the Australia or New Holland imperfectly discovered by the Dutch and proved by Tasman's circumnavigation to be insular, and the Terra Australis Incognita between the longitudes of New Holland and South America, of which Tasman's New Zealand was thought to be a projecting portion. Campbell's standpoint was mercantile, and he based a hopeful argument on Dampier's report of New Britain. Of Dampier's work he says: 'It has shown us a new Indies, in which, whenever that Spirit of Industry shall revive, which first extended, and then established our Commerce, we may be able to undertake Settlements as advantageous as any that have hitherto been made by this or any other Nation . . . We cannot entertain the least Doubt of the Possibility of finding, in the Southern Part of the Globe, countries worth our looking after.' Campbell had a strategic plan which is probably the echo of the general thought of the time, and may serve as an indication of one of the purposes underlying Anson's voyage. He advocated the colonization of Juan Fernandez, which a garrison of five hundred men would render impregnable to the Spaniards. From Juan Fernandez a two months' voyage would give access to New Britain and the unknown Eastern Australia:

It is most evident that, if such a Settlement was made at Juan Fernandez, proper Magazines erected, and a constant Correspondence established between that Island and the Terra Australis [here meaning Australia proper], these three Consequences must absolutely follow from thence: I. That a new Trade would be opened, which must carry off a great Quantity of our Goods and Manufactures that cannot, at present, be brought to any Market, or at least, not to so good a Market, as if there were a greater Demand for them. II. It would render this Navigation, which is, at present, so strange and consequently so terrible to us, easy and familiar, which might be attended with Advantages that cannot be foreseen, especially since there is, as I before observed, in all Probability another Southern Continent, which is still to be discovered. III. It would greatly increase our Shipping and our Seamen, which are the true and natural Strength of this Country.

Finally, Campbell proposed that the South Sea Company, which had never yet sent a ship into the South Sea, should be the agent of this enterprise, to which the Royal African Company could contribute by creating a base in Madagascar for approach from the opposite direction. The East India and Hudson's Bay Companies were already exploiting large maritime monopolies, and the combined effect would be a very pretty stranglehold upon the extra-European commerce of the globe. It was in such an atmosphere that William Pitt developed the fierce imperialism that was to make him the terror of the Bourbon powers.

Imaginations, both in Great Britain and France, were fascinated by the unknown, and upon it they grafted the social speculations characteristic of the age which culminated in the French Revolution. Swift had dealt in social speculation of the satirical kind, exploiting the exotic in order to castigate the world in which he lived. The mid-century speculators aimed at uplift rather than denunciation. The 'perfectibility of the species' was their theme, illuminated by the conception of 'the noble savage', who lived a higher life in his state of nature than was possible to the over-civilized European. The American colonists, hewing their way into primeval forests, were thought in France to be nearer than any other white men to this desirable state; and from this belief proceeded much of the public enthusiasm for the American Revolution. Paris ran mad after Benjamin Franklin, and no doubt the shrewd old man partly divined the reason—that to his admirers he was in some sort a 'noble savage' in the flesh.

In this connexion some references to Johnson are of interest, not as indicating that he went deeply into the subject, but rather as showing that it had its place in the thoughts and work of a man of letters. In the earlier part of his career indeed he did some geographical pot-boiling, which included a translation of Lobo's *Voyage to Abyssinia* (1735), a life of Sir Francis Drake (1740), an essay on China (1742), and a translation of a French account of the Amazons (1741), the last three all anonymous and appearing in the *Gentleman's Magazine*. They have an obvious topical relation to the war with Spain and the expedition of Anson. The Seven Years War evoked similar work from Johnson in the shape of reviews of books on maritime and colonial subjects (1756); an introduction to *The World Displayed*, a collection of voyages and travels published in 1759–61; and a preface to *Rolt's Dictionary of Trade and Commerce* (1756). Boswell remarks that 'the enquiry into the state of foreign countries was an object that at all times interested Johnson'. He would have been exceptional if it had not, in view of the large place such studies occupied in the literature of his period. Other geographical prefaces followed, together with a pamphlet in 1771 on Falkland's Islands, a burning question which was threatening to produce a new war with the Bourbon powers. To such conceptions as 'the noble savage' and 'the state of nature' Johnson's attitude was John Bullish and contrary to that of the French *philosophes*: 'What a wretch he must be', he remarked, 'who is content with such conversation as can be had among savages'; and in his Hebridean tour he had some amusing passages with Lord Monboddo, a primitive evolutionist who surmised that men had once had tails and walked on all fours, and that apes could be taught to speak English. In these and other conversations Johnson was a stout supporter of civilization.[1]

In constructive speculation the most notable work before the Seven Years War emanated from France; and since it was subsequently reproduced in English it is part of the literature of Johnson's England. Charles de Brosses, President of the Parliament of Dijon, studied for several years the history of Pacific exploration, and in 1756 he published his *Histoire des Navigations aux Terres Australes*. The book was more than a record of past efforts; it was an exhortation to the author's countrymen to undertake a great work for science and civilization. The argument, based on discoveries already achieved, and on current physical theories, was that there must be a great southern continent covering the whole antarctic cap of the globe and projecting north-

[1] For the above references to Johnson the writer is indebted to Professor E. G. R. Taylor, who very kindly lent him the notes of a lecture she had delivered on 'Dr. Johnson and Geography'.

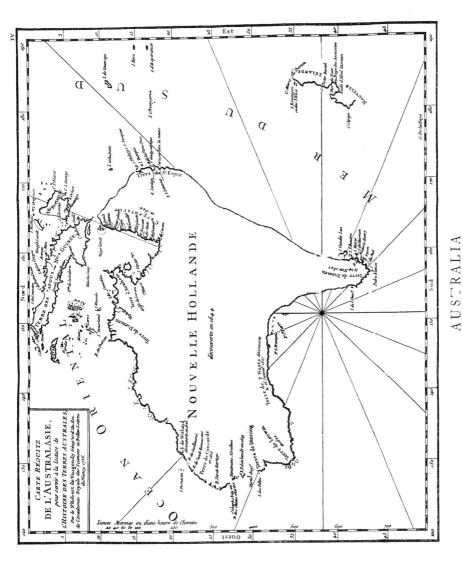

AUS⌐RALIA

From C. de Brosses, Histoire des navigations aux Terres Australes, 1756

wards into temperate latitudes. Australia indeed had been proved by Tasman to be an island, but the continental coast must lie not far to the south of it; and elsewhere that coast had been sighted, in New Zealand, in Bouvet's Cape Circumcision, in various reported discoveries of land which we now know to have been only icebergs or cloud-banks. These, in de Brosses' reasoning, were all made to do duty as projections of Terra Australis Incognita. So far, de Brosses was not original, for the great continent had been part of the geographical system since classical times. His argument from physics was twofold: water was lighter than land, and if there were nothing but water in the unknown south, the earth's axis of rotation could not lie in the direction in which it was observed to lie; moreover sea-water (it was believed) did not freeze except in thin icefields, and the mountainous bergs reported in the southern ocean must have been extruded from the mouths of mighty rivers, which necessitated the existence of a no less mighty continent. The glacial origin of icebergs did not occur to de Brosses. He was not content with Antarctica as known to the twentieth century. He insisted on the rivers, rivers of running water in the summer season although frozen in the winter; and he posited for his southern continent a climate no worse than that of Canada, while parts of it would be in far milder latitudes.

From such a base the *philosophe* imagination could leap to great heights. This land must contain peoples, animals, and products all unknown, cut off from all influence of the existing world, and by consequence utterly different and of immense interest to science. Europe could confer benefits on these peoples, at least the benefit of Christianity, and they in their turn might have much to teach their discoverers. Savages, it was true, were not all noble—some fairly ignoble specimens had been observed in Australia—but in favourable circumstances they might rise untutored to idyllic gentleness. There was ample room for Houyhnhnms as well as Yahoos. Civilizations might conceivably be found, and, if found, the enlightened eighteenth century would not destroy them as the sixteenth had destroyed the Incas and the Aztecs. Moreover, such enterprise would well repay its cost. Commerce would accrue to the exploiting nation, and the opportunity for planting colonies, which would strengthen the position of that nation among the dominant peoples of the world. De Brosses foresaw a great future for *colonies de peuplement*, and he imagined French dominions in the south comparable to those since developed by the British. Social reform also entered into his plans. He was eloquent upon the reclamation of criminals by transporting them to new surroundings where they might retrieve their past, uncontaminated by the evil associations of their old homes. It is to be noted, however, that he did not advocate colonies solely composed of convicts and their guards. He argued rather that colonies of normal good citizens would be able to absorb and purify a large proportion of undesirables whom the mother country found herself unable to reform. All this was very much in the doctrinaire style of the writer's country and period. There was evidence, in America and the West Indies, in whose light these questions might be practically examined. De Brosses did not pay attention to it. He theorized in the abstract. But he was a genuine humanitarian, and not the least impressive of his passages is a contrast between the glorious, beneficent enterprise of the South and the waste and misery produced by European warfare. How could any enlightened people hesitate to choose between them? France, to his sorrow, did not hesitate. As his book was passing through the press the opening moves of the Seven Years War were taking place.

In effect, the work of de Brosses was the most weighty combination of history and propaganda as yet devoted to the enterprise of the South Sea. It did not fall to the ground, although it was applied to uses which its patriotic author would have regretted. There can be little doubt that it was read by cultured men in England while the war was in progress. 'We conquered France, but felt our captive's charms' was a line written of an earlier struggle, but it was valid until the Revolution of 1789. Hostilities did not impair the British respect for French thought in the arts and sciences. Three years after the Treaty of Paris, de Brosses appeared in a British guise, as John Callender's *Terra Australis Cognita*, published at Edinburgh in 1766. Although Callender includes some matter of his own, his book is in the main a translation of de Brosses, whom he reproduces, *mutatis mutandis*, as propaganda for British expansion, with a somewhat grudging acknowledgement to the original author. From this date the South Seas made a large appeal to ardent minds on both sides of the Channel.

Another British enthusiast, Alexander Dalrymple, was prepared to act not only as a propagandist but as a leader in action. He had been many years in Asiatic waters as a servant of the East India Company, and he had independently studied the voyages of the past and the evidences of a great southern continent. In particular, he had found that New Guinea and Australia were not a single land-mass as they were commonly drawn upon the maps, for he had seen a Spanish document recording the voyage of Torres in 1606 through the Straits that now bear his name. This discovery had never been made public by the Spaniards. It has been generally asserted, on the authority of Matthew Flinders, who knew Dalrymple, that the latter learned of it from a memorial acquired at Manila by the British expedition which captured that place in 1762. Recent investigation has shown that Dalrymple had his knowledge earlier, and that he saw the first evidence of it at Madras before the Seven Years War.[1] That evidence probably came from Manila, but there seems to be no reason for rejecting Flinders's statement that a document was also captured there in 1762, for Dalrymple was at pains to collect everything he could on the subject. However that may be, Torres Strait was a comparatively minor part of his investigations. He was fired with the conception of the Southern Continent in its most magnificent form, and he cast himself for the part of its discoverer and conqueror. In the sixties he was back in England seeking to be placed in command of an expedition for the purpose. He pressed his claims on the Admiralty and the Royal Society, and was recognized as a man of knowledge. By 1767 he had written a book on the subject of his ambition.

Meanwhile the French and British Admiralties had in-augurated the new period of discovery. In 1763, the year of the peace, Louis Antoine de Bougainville sailed from St. Malo with an expedition for the colonization of the Falkland Islands, whose strategic importance on the thres-hold of the Pacific was by this time well understood. Bougainville reached the islands and founded a small colony at Baie Saint Louis (Berkeley Sound) in February 1764.

---

[1] He says, 'before the siege of Madras', referring to Lally's siege of 1759. See Royal Australian Historical Society, *Journal*, vol. xiii (1927), pp. 55–6.

He returned to France, and again visited the colony with supplies in the following year. This was the beginning of his career as a navigator. Before the Seven Years War he had been in the diplomatic service, and during the struggle he had fought as a soldier at Quebec. His record typifies the change in his country's interests and prospects. France had lost an empire in North America, and was bent upon the examination of the South Pacific as a new area of expansion.

The British authorities were probably aware of the French interest, but did not know of Bougainville's actual intentions, since his destination had been kept secret. In 1764 the Admiralty selected Commodore John Byron, one of Anson's former officers, to command an expedition to the South Seas. He was instructed to search the unknown areas for islands and continental coasts, and, as a preliminary, to obtain full information of the Falklands, described as already 'His Majesty's islands'. Accordingly, Byron came to the Falklands in January 1765, and took formal possession after discovering and naming the fine harbour of Port Egmont. He did this without knowing that the French were in actual occupation at St. Louis. He then steered for the Pacific. More than twenty years earlier he had entered it with Anson by way of Cape Horn, with damages and casualties sufficiently terrifying. On this occasion he chose to proceed by the Straits of Magellan. He had a very rough passage, protracted to seven weeks, but nevertheless recommended the Straits as less perilous than the Horn. 'One great advantage of this passage', he remarked, 'is the facility with which fish is almost everywhere to be procured, with wild celery, scurvy grass, berries, and many other vegetables in great abundance; for to this I impute the healthiness of my ship's company, not a single man being affected with the scurvy in the slightest degree, nor upon the sick list for any other disorder.'

In the Straits Byron saw a French ship, but had no communication with her. He learned afterwards that she was commanded by Bougainville, on his second visit to his colony. The Falklands were destitute of wood, and Bougainville was collecting a supply in the eastern reaches of the Straits. The subsequent history of this colony may be briefly noted. In 1766–7, in consequence of Byron's report, the British Admiralty sent Captain McBride in the frigate *Jason* to investigate the islands more fully. McBride established a little settlement at Port Egmont, and surveyed the coasts, but he had been there nearly a year before he happened upon the French colony at St. Louis. Its existence was a complete surprise, and he at once protested that it had no right to be there. However, it was in time of peace, and he had no authority to commence hostilities; and either party therefore continued to maintain its occupation. Meanwhile, the Spanish Government had heard of the French colony but not of the British. It contended that the islands belonged to Spain. The French Government accepted this view, and in 1766 Bougainville sailed once more, to hand over the possession to Spanish officers from Buenos Aires. It was only then that the British intrusion became known to the representatives of the Bourbon powers. Although the British were known to be in the islands, the Spaniards did not encounter them until 1769. There was an interchange of notes between the rival commanders, each claiming to be the legal occupier, and then, in 1770, a Spanish force was sent, which captured the British settlement and deported its people. A first-class international crisis ensued, and nearly resulted in war. But at the last moment France decided not to support Spain, and the latter, unable to fight alone, gave way. The British possession at Port Egmont was formally restored, and the incident terminated.[1] Neither British nor Spaniards maintained permanent occupation, and true colonization did not begin until the nineteenth century.

The attention drawn to the Falkland Islands was in reality the most important result of Byron's voyage, for his crossing of the Pacific yielded no discoveries of moment. After leaving the Straits of Magellan he went northwards to latitude $27\frac{1}{2}°$ S. and then turned to the westward. A large land was supposed to exist in this region at no great distance from South America, but Byron found no trace of it. Unfavourable weather caused him to edge northwards into the tropics. He sighted one or two minor islands of the Low Archipelago, crossed the equator, and visited the Ladrones, after which he passed through the Dutch East Indies and circumnavigated the globe. His Pacific route was unenterprising, for it was one that had been frequently traversed since the pioneer voyage of Magellan. The unknown area

[1] For this subject see *The Falkland Islands*, by V. F. Boyson (Oxford, 1924).

lay in the south, but Byron's crews had become sickly, and he did not feel justified in attempting it.

The next expedition made a really important discovery. Three months after Byron's return in 1766, the Admiralty equipped his ship the *Dolphin* to go again to the Pacific under Captain Samuel Wallis. A smaller vessel, the sloop *Swallow*, was sent in company under the command of Captain Philip Carteret. They passed together through the Straits of Magellan but were separated by stress of weather soon afterwards. The story thenceforward becomes that of two independent expeditions. Wallis, hampered like Byron by sickness, followed approximately the same general route, except that in mid-Pacific he kept a little more to the southward than his predecessor. By this means he sighted several units of the Low Archipelago, and in June 1767 discovered a large island whose interior slopes rose to considerable heights. The natives were numerous and in the main friendly, although given to stealing and to childish outbursts of temper. They called their country Otaheite, a name now rendered as Tahiti. Wallis christened it King George the Third's Island. He described the country as one of the most delightful in the world, blessed with pure air, covered with wood and herbage, pestered with no venomous animals, its inhabitants happy in constant health. He had no high opinion of their morals or civilization or of any solid commercial advantage to be expected from the discovery. But it was a valuable place of refreshment for scurvy-stricken crews, and he stayed for over a month trafficking for hogs and fruit. Wallis was a prosaic realist, lacking the romantic French eye for the wonders of the unknown world. That eye, as will be shown, was shortly to view Tahiti, with expansive consequences to the theory of the noble savage so dear to the *philosophes* of Paris.[1] To Wallis the romance of Tahiti was of the sordid kind. The women were alluring, and the sailors found that, while they valued a shilling as little as a halfpenny, they had a businesslike appreciation of iron and copper nails. The nails in the ship's stores were reserved for the purchase of foodstuffs. The men therefore drew the

---

[1] 'A gentleman'—very likely Boswell refers to himself—once expressed to Johnson a wish to go and live for three years in Tahiti or New Zealand. Johnson did not encourage him. Boswell was given to praising savage life, and he mentions Tahiti on several occasions.

nails from all accessible parts of the ship's structure. Wallis, not a man of quick perception, was at first puzzled to account for this. When the truth dawned upon him he determined to make an example of an offender:

I called all the people together upon the deck, and after taking some pains to explain his crime, with all its aggravations, I ordered that he should be whipped with nettles while he ran the gauntlet thrice round the deck. My rhetoric, however, had very little effect, for most of the crew being equally criminal with himself, he was handled so tenderly, that others were rather encouraged to repeat the offence by the hope of impunity, than deterred by the fear of punishment. To preserve the ship, therefore, from being pulled to pieces . . . I ordered that no man except the wooders and waterers, with their guard, should be permitted to go on shore.

Wallis's methods of discipline seem rather mild for the eighteenth century, but he was in weak health, as were his two lieutenants, and in these long voyages a captain was very much at the mercy of his crew.

After leaving Tahiti, Wallis followed Byron's example in steering for Tinian, in the Ladrones, and thence by Batavia and the Cape for England, where he arrived in May 1768.

Carteret in the *Swallow* crossed the Pacific somewhat to the south of the Tropic of Capricorn, and by so doing passed southward of Tahiti. Bad weather, sickness, and the wretched condition of his little ship then compelled him to work northwards, although less markedly so than Wallis had done. He rediscovered Santa Cruz and certain of the Solomon Islands, visited by the Spaniards two centuries earlier, but never again seen by Europeans until the *Swallow* drew near. The position of the Solomons had been so badly recorded that Carteret did not realize their identity. In fact, one of his remarks about the Solomon Islands reported by the early Spaniards implies that he doubted if they had any real existence. The experience of their native people must surely be unique. In 1567 white men in great ships visited their coasts, spent months there in trafficking, fighting, and exploring, and sailed away, purposing shortly to return and conquer. They never returned, and for two hundred years not a white sail broke the sea-line nor a gun disturbed the silence of the shore. Then in 1767 came Carteret, the precursor of many others of his kind. Did any legend of the earlier visitation survive through half a dozen generations of the islanders? It is a question to which the answer is unknown.

Carteret was conscious that great exploring remained to be done to the west and south-west of his new islands. But the debility both of his crew and of his ship precluded the attempt, and Eastern Australia had to wait four years longer for the advent of its discoverer, 'for if we had got into any gulph or deep bay, our crew was so sickly, and our ship so bad, that it would have been impossible for us to have got out again'. It was indeed lucky that discretion prevailed, since the reception awaiting the pioneer was worse than any gulf or bay. It was the Great Barrier Reef, from whose perils it is morally certain that not a man of the *Swallow*'s crew would have escaped. As it was, Carteret had still a useful discovery to make. He bore north-westwards in search of refreshment at Dampier's highly recommended New Britain, and he found a passage—St. George's Channel—splitting it into two islands, of which he fitly named the lesser New Ireland. Thence he sailed for the Philippines and home by the usual route of the Dutch Indies and the Cape. Although he had covered virtually the same distance as Wallis, the *Swallow* was so slow that the voyage took ten months longer to complete.

We left Bougainville engaged in handing over the Falkland Islands to Spain. That business occasioned a delay which prevented him from passing through the Straits of Magellan until January 1768. His orders were to cross the Pacific in or near tropical latitudes and to search for the lands which were now exciting an international attention among geographers and governments. He had two ships, the frigate *Boudeuse* and the store-ship *Étoile*. He knew nothing of the discoveries of Wallis and Carteret, who had preceded him by some months. Like the Englishmen, he looked first for the continent supposed to lie in the latitudes of Chile and not far from its coast. Like them also, he sailed over the position it should have occupied, and satisfied himself that the theoretical geographers were wrong. His comment has its value to-day, when unproved and mutually destructive theories about the earth and the universe are as freely published as they were in the eighteenth century: 'Geography is a science of facts; in studying it, authors must by no means give way to any system formed in their studies, unless they

would run the risk of being subject to very grave errors.'
It was a point of view implicit in all the navigators' writings,
and a corrective to the airy castle-building indulged in by
the philosophers. The required facts were hard to come by,
and the temptation to theorize in advance of them was great.

In April 1768 Bougainville came to Tahiti. He learned
from the natives that he was not its first discoverer, but he
took formal possession for the crown of France. He was
greatly pleased with the people and the climate, of which
he gave an account essentially similar to that of Wallis,
although more enthusiastically worded. To the French the
easy morals and incurable thievishness of the islanders
seemed less reprehensible. What appealed was their gaiety
and freedom from care: 'the inhabitants are happy, and
arrive at old age without feeling any of its inconveniencies.'
Elaborations of that theme furnished rich meat to the school
of Rousseau and the return to Nature.

Bougainville passed on from Tahiti to the discovery of the
Samoa group and of the New Hebrides. He called the former
the Navigators' Islands, and the latter the Grandes Cyclades
—their present name is that bestowed by Cook a few years
later. Thence he pushed westwards to probe the mystery
of Eastern Australia. He drew near to the tangles of shoals
and reefs, but dared not penetrate them, since the prevailing
wind would have made it almost impossible to extricate
himself. He indeed thought it probable that a channel
existed by which to pass through to the westward, but it was
only a chance; he had not seen the evidence of Torres Strait
which Dalrymple had obtained. He therefore turned away
to the north-east, and even so had a hard task to clear the
eastern end of New Guinea. His subsequent track followed
rather closely that of Carteret. He visited certain of the
Solomon Islands and, like Carteret, failed to recognize them;
and in his chart he made a parallel remark to that of Carteret,
that the existence of the Solomon Islands was doubtful. He
went on to New Britain and entered a haven in search of
refreshment, and there one of his men picked up a fragment
of a leaden plate upon which were decipherable the broken
words '. . . HOR'D HERE . . . ICK MAJESTY'. The plate
had been set up by Carteret, and torn down by the natives
after his departure. Carteret's journal does not give the
text of the inscription, but says: 'we nailed upon a high tree

a piece of board, faced with lead, on which was engraved
the English union, with the name of the ship and her commander, the name of the cove, and the time of her coming
in and sailing out of it.' It was a strange coincidence that
Frenchmen should reach the very spot ten months later, and
find his fragment buried in the sand. Bougainville continued
his voyage by northern New Guinea to the Dutch islands and
thence to France by the Cape of Good Hope. In mid-
Atlantic he overtook Carteret and exchanged compliments.
The Englishman told how the little *Swallow* had crossed the
Pacific, but Bougainville did not produce the leaden plate
or avow in his turn how the *Boudeuse* had followed her
precursor round the world. In fact Bougainville's lieutenant
assured Carteret that the *Boudeuse* was an East Indiaman
returning from a trading voyage to Sumatra, although one
of the French crew blabbed that they had come through the
South Sea by the Straits of Magellan. And so they parted,
Bougainville pluming himself on having deceived his rival,
Carteret confirmed in the traditional faith that 'mounseers'
were too polite to be honest.

The four commanders considered above, Byron, Wallis,
Carteret, and Bougainville, had all sailed with the quest of
the southern continent as one of their primary objects. They
had all failed to close with the problem, and for the same
reason, namely, that when they approached the scene of
action their crews had become too sickly and their ships too
feeble in hull or gear to permit of a struggle with the tempestuous weather of the south temperate zone. All had therefore
edged northwards into the tropics for supplies and repairs,
and had left the great task unattempted. The same circumstances had likewise compelled them to leave the eastern
coast of Australia unexplored. It is not to their discredit
that, substantially, they failed. All of them were sound,
competent, and courageous leaders of the type ordinarily
bred in the fighting services of England and France. But
the South Sea demanded something more. It demanded an
extraordinary man, extraordinary in resolution, in scientific
knowledge, and in qualities of seamanship and command.
At length it found him in James Cook; and after Cook had
led two expeditions all the major problems of the South Sea
were solved. In seven years he did the work which it would
probably have needed another thirty years of the Byrons and

the Wallises to accomplish. In his third and final expedition he began to deal with the problems of the North Pacific and the Arctic, and we may be assured that, but for his untimely death in his fiftieth year, knowledge of those regions would have been advanced more rapidly than was actually the case. It is not possible in this chapter to give a systematic account of Cook's voyages. For that the reader must turn to the biographies of Cook, of which the best is that by Mr. Arthur Kitson, published in 1907.[1] Here it will be feasible only to consider the general plans and the outstanding events, and to show their relation to the life and thought of contemporary England.

Cook's first expedition had a twofold origin: the Royal Society wished to make accurate observations of the transit of Venus predicted for June 3, 1769; and the Admiralty desired a more intensive exploration of the South Pacific than had hitherto been accomplished. A transit of Venus had been observed first by an Englishman, Jeremiah Horrocks, in 1639. The phenomenon had occurred again in 1761, but the preparations to record it had been inadequate, and no increase of astronomical knowledge had resulted. After 1769 no recurrence could be foreseen for a century to come, and the Royal Society was insistent that for the credit of England the opportunity should not be missed. Its committee reported that suitable stations would be in Hudson's Bay, at the North Cape of Norway, and in mid-Pacific between the equator and 30° S. Since the northern observations were very likely to be spoiled by cloudy weather, the Society placed most reliance upon the Pacific, and urged the King to provide a naval expedition for the purpose. This was in 1767, and Alexander Dalrymple took part in pressing the project, for he realized that it could be combined with his own ambition to discover the Southern Continent. The Society recommended his appointment as a scientific observer, but he would be satisfied with nothing less than the command of the expedition. The Admiralty, whilst agreeing, on the King's gracious instructions, to forward the project, declined to entrust it to any but a naval officer, and so Dalrymple, in a very bad humour, refused to go at all. There

[1] Sir Walter Besant's short *Life*, in *English Men of Action*, can hardly be described as one of the successes of that series, for its author did not perform the research necessary to a mastery of his subject.

can be no doubt that, in spite of his knowledge and enthusiasm, he was unsuitable for command, for he was eccentric
and intolerant and incapable of working harmoniously with
others. The Admiralty looked among its own servants for a
commander, and in a fortunate hour selected James Cook.

Cook had had nothing to do with the origination of the
project and, so far as is known, had evinced no special
interest in the South Sea. His early life had been spent in
the merchant service, in which he had risen to be mate of an
east-coast collier. At the opening of the Seven Years War
he volunteered for the Navy and was almost immediately
promoted to warrant rank. He served as master of a battle-
ship in the Louisbourg and Quebec campaigns of 1758–9,
and after the peace he continued on the North American
station, making surveys of the coasts of Labrador and
Newfoundland. His excellent work and sterling character
commended him to his superiors, but he was still a warrant
officer when he was chosen for the South Sea command.
For that purpose he was commissioned as lieutenant in
May 1768. Character was the touchstone in the decision.
There were officers available who had sailed round the world
with Byron and Wallis. Cook had never even been in the
tropics, and when in his great voyage south he crossed the
line for the first time, he was duly ducked by Father Neptune
like any first-voyager.

The expedition contained another man of outstanding
merit in the person of Joseph Banks, 'a gentleman of large
fortune', who, at the age of twenty-six, was already a Fellow
of the Royal Society. He was primarily a botanist, but was
able to hold his own in any scientific company and to take
part on equal terms with Cook in the astronomical observations. It says much for the good sense of both men that they
worked in harmony, with a mutual respect that survived a
three years' voyage. For the position was by no means easy
—a commander risen from the ranks, with nothing but his
pay of five shillings a day, dependent for his future upon
the favour of the great, and yet wholly responsible for the
conduct of a hazardous expedition and the discipline of
all its members; and a young man of rank, ready to
spend £10,000 on doing his world-tour in style, full of
enthusiasm and initiative, and unbroken to the order of sea
life. The odds were that they would fall out, and that the

expedition would suffer. They held together, and there is no hint in the writings of either of them that the strain was at any time considerable. But when circumstances prevented Banks from accompanying a second expedition Cook expressed no heart-felt sorrow.

The Admiralty's secret instructions were made public only in 1928,[1] but they accord with what had been inferred by Kitson from a variety of indications. Cook was to sail first by way of Cape Horn to Tahiti, and there to set up the apparatus and observe the transit. Thence he was to go southward as far as 40° S., to look for the coasts of the Southern Continent. If he found them, he was to report on their geography, products, and inhabitants; to cultivate friendship; and to annex places convenient for trade. If there should be no continent south of Tahiti, he was to sail westward between the latitudes of 40° and 35° until he reached New Zealand, which country he was to explore as fully as his resources permitted. This was as much as the authorities expected from one expedition, and there is no instruction to explore the eastern coast of Australia.

A single ship was employed, the *Endeavour*, of 368 tons, described as a cat-built bark. She was not a naval vessel, but an east-coast collier, purchased at Whitby, undoubtedly on the advice of Cook, who had served in such craft in his early years. For exploration he wanted a ship which should be weatherly and easily handled, able to ride comfortably in exposed anchorages, and of moderate draught to take the ground for repairs without elaborate dockyard facilities; and he judged that a Whitby ship would meet these requirements better than a fighting frigate. It is noteworthy that he did not favour the copper sheathing then being introduced, and that the *Endeavour* was sheathed in the old manner with planking over a layer of felt and hair. Copper, although a complete preventive of worm, was in the experimental stage, and difficult to renew if damaged. With the old sheathing the worm bored through the outer planking and was killed by the hair within.

After fitting out in the Thames, the *Endeavour* sailed from Plymouth on August 26, 1768, with ninety-four men on

[1] See Navy Records Society, *The Naval Miscellany*, vol. iii, pp. 343-50 (1928); and *Geographical Journal*, February 1929, pp. 105-6.

board. They rounded Cape Horn and steered north-west for Tahiti. The track lay well to the southward of those followed by previous voyagers, and passed over an area in which Dalrymple had been confident that land would be discovered. But there was no land, and on the whole passage to the Tahiti group nothing was sighted but a circular coral reef enclosing a lagoon. The date of arrival at Tahiti, April 12, 1769, allowed nearly two months for the astronomical preparations, and on June 3 the transit was successfully observed amid perfect weather conditions. Cook's men, like those of Wallis, stole nails for their personal traffic with the natives; but Cook, on detecting an offender, gave him two dozen lashes with the cat, which probably made more impression on his tough hide than Wallis's farcical flogging with nettles. But even Cook's severity was very moderate by the standards of the age.

After leaving Tahiti, Cook spent a month in discovering the neighbouring islands. He named the whole archipelago the Society Islands, and in August, when the Antarctic winter was drawing to its close, he bore away for the south. He crossed the fortieth parallel, according to instructions, but found no sign of land, and then turned in a general westerly direction for New Zealand. That country had only once been reported by a European discoverer. Tasman had found it in 1642. He had seen only a portion of its western coast; and he had misunderstood its nature. His belief was that New Zealand was a projecting peninsula of the great continent, and would be found to extend illimitably to the southward. Cook now approached the unknown eastern side, which he discovered on October 7 in latitude 38° 40′ S. He circumnavigated both the North and the South Islands and traversed the strait between them. The resulting chart was substantially accurate, except that Stewart Island in the far south was represented as continuous with the South Island. As the *Endeavour* coasted that shore her officers were in a state of eager anticipation, for a great problem was to be decided. Would the land broaden into a continent, or would it terminate in a southern ocean? Banks, with unabated zest, hoped for a continent, but he hints that most of the others welcomed an end to the toilsome probing of dangerous coasts amid dirty weather. The points of view of the passenger and the sailor were inevitably different. At length the

shoreline turned, the course led westward and then northward, and New Zealand took the shape we know. The great
continent had once more shrunk into the waste of southern
waters. Cook, unlike his companions, expressed neither
hopes nor fears. He was there to settle a problem and he
cared not at all what the solution might be. He seems to have
been absolutely untouched by the romantic glamour of
Terra Australis, and would have been just as well satisfied to
prove that it did not exist as that it did. As for an end to
exertion, that had no place in his calculations. With his six
months' circumnavigation of New Zealand he had fulfilled
his instructions, and could sail home certain of high commendation. But he found himself with stores in hand which
made it unnecessary to seek refreshment for another six
months to come. He embarked without hesitation on a
further plan of discovery.

There were two possible courses, to recross the ocean to
Cape Horn in a high southern latitude, searching for the
continental coast, or to continue westward and visit the
eastern side of Australia, never yet described by a European.
He chose the latter, for it would lead him towards the Dutch
Indies and a refit, whilst for the tempestuous south the ship's
gear was already becoming inadequate. In April 1770,
therefore, the *Endeavour* drew near to the Australian coast.
Tasman had visited Van Diemen's Land before passing on to
New Zealand, but he had not determined whether it was
continuous with Australia. Cook also left this question open,
for he sighted Australia at a point north of the dividing
strait. He coasted steadily northwards with the object of
charting the general outline of the country and the dangers to
navigation, although time did not permit of the investigation
of every detail. Thus he made a thorough survey of Botany
Bay, but did not enter Port Jackson, the more desirable
harbour a few miles to the northward, on which Sydney was
afterwards to arise.[1] As he pushed on he found himself
enclosed between the land and the Barrier Reef. The *Endeavour* struck one of the innumerable heads of coral in this
channel and had to be beached for repairs. It was a narrow
escape, and Cook passed through an opening and continued

[1] For the voyage in general the authority of Kitson is here followed, but
the Australian exploration is more fully described and criticized in G. A.
Wood's *Discovery of Australia* (1922).

the voyage outside the Barrier. Here again all were within an ace of destruction, for a failure of the wind left the ship at the mercy of the ocean swell, which threatened to hurl her upon the reef. The timely discovery of a gap enabled the boats to tow her through to safety. These were the risks, the mere surmise of which had hitherto deterred navigators from closing with this coast. Cook persisted to the end, and crowned the achievement by passing through Torres Strait, and so by the south of New Guinea to Batavia. Dalrymple had imparted to Banks his evidence for the existence of Torres Strait. But Dalrymple was not a man of sound judgement, as Cook may well have perceived, and moreover he had been unable to furnish any chart of the maze of islands, shoals, and shallows through which the channel had to be sought. Cook had to make all this discovery for himself. He was very modest about it, and, after all, he had no need to be emphatic, for it was but one among many perilous passages of his great voyage.

Cook left the coast of Eastern Australia, which he named New South Wales, in August 1770. He made a prolonged stay at Batavia and reached England by the Cape of Good Hope in July 1771. His seamanship, scientific knowledge, and inflexibility of purpose had been among the more obvious causes of his success. But a comparison of his voyage with others reveals a no less important merit, the honest equipment of the expedition, and the careful attention to hygiene and to the discipline essential to its maintenance. Carteret and Bougainville had approached Australia with stores depleted and crews weakened by sickness. Cook approached it with stores in hand and every man fit. The few deaths in his ship had been from accident, but there had been no disease. Later on, it is true, he lost a number of men, but that was from tropical fevers contracted at Batavia. His attention to detail and insistence on discipline had brought his crew across the Pacific without an outbreak of scurvy. Quarters were frequently scrubbed and fumigated, and no man dared to come dirty into his captain's presence. The sailors were by no means grateful, and more than once in his journals there are entries recording their opposition to measures for their own welfare. On one occasion they refused to take an antiscorbutic which was served out. Cook then ordered that it should be reserved for the cabin, whereupon all hands

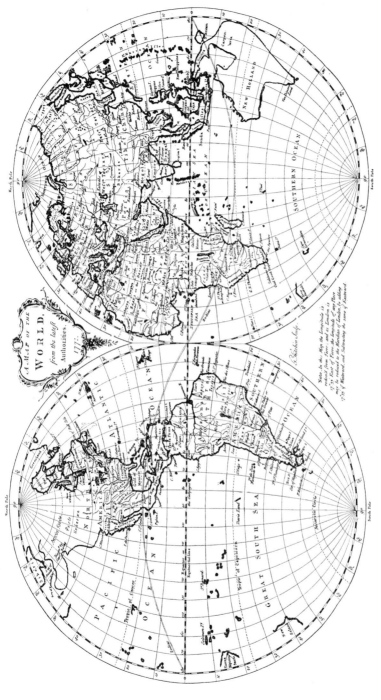

A MAP OF THE WORLD

From Kitchin's Atlas, 1771

became eager for a share of it. In connexion with hygiene, it may be mentioned that the majority of eighteenth-century seamen, Cook included, were unable to swim. Presumably there was very little bathing from the ship, even in tropical waters, and the sailor of those days did not make a habit of falling overboard. That accident, to judge from recorded instances, happened only once in a man's career.

The Admiralty decided to publish immediately an account of the voyage. Cook's journals were written in a plain and lucid style which in our day would be preferred. The taste of the eighteenth century was for embellishment, and all the documents were therefore entrusted to Dr. John Hawkesworth to be worked into proper literary form. The result was unfortunate, for Hawkesworth garbled Cook's facts with foolish comments and deductions in such a manner that the truth was indistinguishable from the editorial imaginings. Cook was displeased, and Boswell, who met him some years later, told Johnson that Cook had referred to many exaggerated passages in Hawkesworth's book. Fortunately, copies of Cook's own account have survived and are now available in published form.[1] The result of the voyage had been to push the Southern Continent farther southwards than the believers had allowed, but not to destroy the possibility of its existence. This, moreover, applied only to the longitudes of the Pacific; elsewhere the question remained in its previous state, and in the southern Indian Ocean strong hopes rested on Bouvet's Cape Circumcision, sighted half a century previously. The Admiralty now determined to clear up the doubt. Cook was appointed to sail with two ships in 1772. His instructions[2] were to rediscover Cape Circumcision and trace the coastline to which it was attached. If he could not find it, he was to sail south until he reached some solid obstacle, and then to circumnavigate the globe in touch with that obstacle, and in as high a latitude as might be necessary. Cook followed his instructions. His second voyage was thus primarily an Antarctic, and only incidentally a Pacific, expedition. It was the first of its kind sent forth from Europe. The knowledge already gained can have left little hope of the discovery of some southern Utopia from whose exploitation profit would accrue, and we must credit

[1] Edited by Admiral Sir W. J. L. Wharton, 1893.
[2] *Naval Miscellany*, vol. iii, pp. 351–6.

the British Government with promoting the expedition in the cause of scientific learning.

Banks purposed to accompany Cook once more, but withdrew on finding that adequate accommodation was not to be provided for himself and the large scientific staff he desired to take with him. Cook was not altogether sorry. There was tough work in prospect, and a crowd of landsmen might be inconvenient. The civilian members were therefore reduced to a modest half-dozen, headed by John Reinhold Forster, a German naturalist, who took his son with him as his assistant. Forster, although a man of undoubted learning, was socially a caricature. He was the comic German who has become a stock figure of humorous literature. He was imbued with the immensity of his own importance, convinced that he had nothing to learn, even of the handling of ships, self-assertive, and heavily censorious of the shortcomings of the English, for whom he had a perfect contempt. He describes on more than one occasion the negligence and unseamanlike conduct of Cook and his officers. Even before sailing he began to afford sport. Disliking his cabin, he required the master to exchange with him, and being refused, he threatened to report his adversary to the King and have him expelled from the Navy. The sailors took up the jest, and for some days were heard threatening one another that they would be 'reported to King George and turned out of the sarvice'. Altogether, Forster must have been an asset in promoting cheerfulness amid the hardships of the Antarctic.

On July 13, 1772, the two ships sailed from Plymouth. They were both north-country colliers, built at Whitby, and were named the *Resolution* (462 tons, commanded by Cook) and the *Adventure* (336 tons, commanded by Tobias Furneaux). They did not find Cape Circumcision, whose locality had not been correctly recorded. Cook crossed the Antarctic circle and reached $67\frac{1}{4}°$ S. without seeing land. His plan was to examine as much of the southern ocean as possible during the short summer, and then to turn north and winter among the Pacific islands. In this manner he completed the circuit of the Antarctic in the summers of 1772–3, 1773–4, and 1774–5. During the second season he passed the latitude of 70° S. and discovered the permanent ice-barrier. In the third he visited South Georgia and Sandwich Land in the extreme South Atlantic. But they were only islands, desolate and valueless. There was definitely no Southern Continent except the rocks which might lie for ever buried beneath the polar ice-cap. As might be expected, Cook was not idle while wintering in warmer climates. He struck hither and thither in the south Pacific, visiting New Zealand on three occasions, and discovering new islands or rediscovering those reported by seventeenth-century navigators and almost forgotten. For the greater part of the voyage the *Resolution* was alone, her consort having parted company in bad weather. Throughout the voyage there was abundance of hardship in the south, of doubtful encounters with the natives in the islands, and of peril everywhere from ice or unknown reefs. Cook was ever watchful and prepared for surprises, but he did not refrain from taking risks. To do so was part of his duty, without which he would have accomplished nothing. Forster hated the whole business, and espccially the southward probings amid the icebergs. He was moderately happy only when anchored in some snug island roadstead and censuring mankind at his ease. For the rest his judgement of Cook's proceedings was that 'rashness and reliance on good fortune became the principal roads to famc, by being crowned with great and undeserved success'. The *Resolution* reached England in July 1775, after what a London newspaper described as 'an agreeable voyage round the world'. Her commander was honoured with an interview with the King, a commission as post-captain, and an appointment at Greenwich Hospital worth £200 a year. On this occasion the official account of the voyage was written by Cook himself, with advice from a clergyman appointed as editor.

Cook had disposed of the Southern Continent, a speculation as old as the science of geography itself. In the north there was another unsolved problem, not quite so ancient, but dating from the discovery of America at the close of the fifteenth century. It was that of the North-West Passage, the supposed sea-channel joining the Atlantic and the Pacific round the northern extremity of America. A multitude of expeditions, for the most part English, had sought this passage from the Atlantic side. They had proved it practicable as far as Hudson's Bay, but the connecting link from that water to the Pacific had yet to be revealed. The work of Bering in the early eighteenth century formed a contribution by proving that a strait divided north-eastern Asia from

north-western America. Whether it was possible to pass that
strait and then sail eastward to Hudson's Bay was yet un-
determined. There was also another possibility, that of a
passage opening through the coasts which are now British
Columbia and Southern Alaska. These coasts were known
to be deeply indented, but they had never been properly
surveyed, and it seemed likely that one of the sounds might
prove to be the opening of a continuous waterway. Such
were the possibilities that provided the motive of Cook's
third voyage.

The Admiralty was determined to have this work done and
knew that Cook was the man to do it, yet it did not care to
order him out from the easy place he had so justly earned
at Greenwich. But he was not the man to hold a soft job
when there was a hard one to be done. As soon as the difficulty
was apparent he volunteered. It was not in truth his choice
but his destiny; being what he was, he could not do otherwise. He was now the representative not only of England
but of civilization, and civilization acknowledged it. During
this last expedition war broke out with France, and the
French minister of marine issued orders to his admirals 'that
Captain Cook shall be treated as a commander of a neutral
and allied power, and that all captains of armed vessels who
may meet that famous navigator shall make him acquainted
with the King's order on this behalf'. It was the War of
American Independence. Benjamin Franklin was in Paris
issuing American commissions to French privateers, and
they contained a similar injunction. So also did the Spanish
fleet's instructions when Spain joined in the conflict in 1779.[1]
The twentieth century has some things to learn from the
eighteenth.

With the *Resolution* and the *Discovery* (yet another
Whitby ship bought for the purpose) Cook left Plymouth in
July 1776. He rounded the Cape of Good Hope and sailed
eastward to New Zealand, and thence by various island
groups to the equator. At the close of 1777 he entered the
north Pacific and for the first time traversed its waters. In
20° N., midway between Asia and America, he came upon a
group of islands, of which the largest bore the native name
of Owhyhee, now spelt as Hawaii. He called the archipelago
the Sandwich Islands in honour of Lord Sandwich, the First

[1] Kitson's *Cook*, p. 356.

A DANCE in OTAHEITE

From Cook's Third Voyage, 1784

Lord of the Admiralty. As it was still early for Arctic work he passed six weeks in examining his discovery, and then in the spring of 1778 sailed northwards. He touched the Californian coast and made a rapid survey, not for the purpose of accurate charting, but solely to detect signs of a channel through the continent. There was none, and he went on through Bering Strait. To the eastward, in the direction of the Atlantic, ice blocked progress. He tried westward, along the Arctic shore of Asia, for a North-East Passage was also a possibility. But the season ended before he had achieved any success. He returned to winter in the Sandwich Islands, with the intention of trying again in the following summer. For Cook, alas, there were to be no more summers. The people of the islands were friendly but thievish, and, like all those of the Pacific, of uncertain temper. A boat was stolen at Owhyhee. Cook went on shore to recover it, and tried to arrest a chief as a hostage. The tribe resisted with threatening gestures. It was an ugly situation, but one such as he had often dealt with before. He made a dignified retreat to the beach. The boats were lying off, and before they could pull in the crowd made a rush. Cook and his landing party fired in self-defence, and in a general scuffle men were killed on both sides, but the natives abstained from attacking him personally. He then turned to stop the firing and call the boats in. It was a fatal action, for as soon as his gaze was off them the savages struck, and he perished under clubs and spears within a few yards of safety. It was the fourteenth of February, 1779.

Cook's death coincides with the end of a period, for his work had completed the outlining of the world map begun by the explorers of the Renaissance. Thenceforward there were many details to be filled in, but in the habitable regions of the world there were no more long coastlines to be viewed for the first time from the decks of a white man's ship. In his chosen sphere Cook fulfilled the purpose of his age. In his personality he was an example of its highest quality. Although his temper was sometimes hasty, his intellect manifested that calm balance and unerring sense of proportion which his century so greatly valued, and to them were added an unconsciousness of self and an objective absorption in duty which are rare among great men of action in any phase of the world's affairs.

BIBLIOGRAPHY.—The eighteenth century witnessed the revival of the publication of general collections of voyages and travels. Richard Hakluyt, in the reign of Queen Elizabeth, had been the greatest, although not the first, English editor of this kind of material. Samuel Purchas followed, under James I, and published his largest collection in the year of that monarch's death. Thereafter the practice waned, whilst public interest was turning from discovery to colonization and trade in well-known regions. With the War of the Spanish Succession and the renewal of interest in the unknown, collections again came into fashion. In 1704 JOHN CHURCHILL, the publisher, brought out the first four volumes of *A Collection of Voyages and Travels*; volumes v and vi, which completed the work, were delayed, somewhat curiously, until 1732. Following hard upon Churchill, JOHN HARRIS edited in 1705, *Navigantium atque Itinerantium Bibliotheca, or A Compleat Collection of Voyages and Travels*, containing over 400 items in two large volumes. During the Jenkins's Ear and Austrian Succession Wars, JOHN CAMPBELL revised and enlarged Harris's collection, which he brought out in four volumes in 1744–8. To the same period belongs T. ASTLEY's *A New General Collection of Voyages and Travels* (4 vols., 1745). In the following year the Abbé Prévost began in France the issue of his *Histoire Générale des Voyages* (20 vols., 1746–89), of which the first seven volumes represent a translation of Astley's work. The Seven Years War produced another large English collection, *The World Displayed, or A Curious Collection of Voyages and Travels*, 20 vols., with a preface by Samuel Johnson (1759-61). This work had a large popularity and reached its fourth edition in 1774–8. It had a less bulky competitor in *The Modern Traveller: being a Collection of Useful and Entertaining Travels* (4 vols., 1776). The special interest of the South Sea produced the collections of De Brosses and Callender, already mentioned, together with ALEXANDER DALRYMPLE's *An Historical Collection of the Several Voyages and Discoveries in the South Pacific Ocean* (2 vols., 1770–1). This was written, but not published, before Cook's departure on his first expedition. It was translated into French in 1774. The dates of the above publications suggest that the wars of Queen Anne and of the mid-eighteenth century, and the triumph of discovery after 1763, were the stimulating influences. And indeed, the contents and editing of most of the collections indicate that the interest was not purely historical, as with present-day readers of Hakluyt and Purchas, but that it was largely topical and inspired by the ambitions and rivalries of the moment. Eighteenth-century Englishmen studied exploration partly for its scientific appeal but chiefly in order to learn how to out-distance the French.

VI

TRAVEL AND COMMUNICATIONS

By H. L. BEALES

Curiosity is, in great and generous minds, the first passion and the last; and perhaps always predominates in proportion to the strength of the contemplative faculties.—*The Rambler* (24 Aug. 1751).

You and I, Sir, have, I think, seen together the extremes of what can be seen in Britain:—the wild rough island of Mull, and Blenheim Park.

There is nothing which has yet been contrived by man, by which so much happiness is produced as by a good tavern or inn.—*Life of Johnson* (21 March 1776).

'HAVING passed my time almost wholly in cities,' wrote Dr. Johnson in the closing paragraph of *A Journey to the Western Islands of Scotland*, 'I may have been surprised by modes of life and appearances of nature, that are familiar to men of wider survey and more varied conversation.' Had Dr. Johnson's knowledge of his own limitations been a commoner endowment among the travellers of the eighteenth century, posterity would have known his England better than it does. There is no dearth of travel records, but all too often they are little more than travellers' tales, tales that must be sifted with caution if their essential truth is to be discerned And the sifting is not always easy. The traveller is himself no more than human: he has his own peculiar limitations of personality and experience. He bears with him, too, the characteristics of his age, whether it be romantic fervour, or the sentimentalist's regard for the better things of days gone by, or a predisposition to Gothic gloom, or impatience at the slow supersession of the old by the new. He would serve the historian best who could combine Defoe's avidity for concrete fact, Johnson's sturdy scepticism of second-hand information and his sane belief in the material progress of his day, and Arthur Young's sharp eye for needless inefficiency. He who could see in early turnpikes and tentative river improvements the future triumphs of Telford and Brindley, would give a true account of the communications of the day, and the more so in that he would remember the packhorse train and the travelling pedlar as well as the touring grandee and the flying coach.

Though the first beginnings of river improvement, the first

canals, and the first mysterious outlines of colliery tramways
had already taken shape when road improvement had become a constant concern of all progressive areas, these were
still the projector's or the speculator's field. It was the road,
its amenities and its dangers, that mattered most to legis-
lator at Westminster and business man in the already growing industrial areas. For the greater part of the century to
travel by road was to travel slowly and often hazardously.
Yet the complaints of time lost and bones all but broken do
but mask a continuous improvement. The truth is that
times were changing, and standards tending ever upward.
The roads of yesterday were always behind the needs of
to-day, and to-day's best could scarcely satisfy to-morrow.
The story of the English road in this period is the story of
a restless search for the first principles of constructional
technique, and that story must be surveyed against a poor
inheritance both of engineering and of local government.
The picturesque adventures, whether of coaches lost in
swollen streams or of highwaymen preying incessantly upon
helpless journeyers, must be seen in perspective.

So rapidly was trade increasing, so regularly was the
occasion for travel expanding, that the enlargement of the
requisite facilities was a permanent pre-occupation. As
time went on, too, the demand for quicker as well as more
commodious travel became more urgent. Boswell and Johnson on their autumn holiday tour to the Western Islands
might be content 'with the gentle pace of a Scotch driver,
who having no rivals in expedition neither gives himself
nor his horses unnecessary trouble'. But not so the business
man, impatient of the cost and the delay of slow going. His
necessities gave news-value to unusual occurrences, such as
that noted in 1770 in a Bristol paper: 'The London Mail did
not arrive so soon by several hours as usual on Monday,
owing to the mailman getting a little intoxicated on his way
between Newbury and Marlborough and falling from his
horse into a hedge, where he was found asleep, by means of
his dog.'[1] A far truer general idea is to be gathered from
the optimism of a writer in the *Gentleman's Magazine* in 1754
than from the narration of exceptional events: 'Were the
same persons,' he declares, 'who made the full tour of
England thirty years ago, to make a fresh one now, and a

[1] Quoted by R. C. Tombs, *Bristol Royal Mail* (n.d.), p. 17.

third some years hence, they would find themselves in a land of enchantment. England is no more like to what England was, than it resembles Borneo or Madagascar.'[1]

A careful examination of the famous expletives of Arthur Young shows clearly that this expectation was justified.

The definite evidence from the examination of the Tours [says Professor Gay] confirms the impression gathered from other contemporary sources that a progressive betterment of the roads had been proceeding for several decades before Young wrote. It did not extend equally to all parts of England; it was impeded by imperfect technical knowledge and administrative parochialism; the country or cross-road lagged behind turnpikes. But improvement in transportation, following the demand of increasing traffic, was continuous.[2]

It is noticeable that Young was far more careful in his road observations in his Northern Tour than in his Southern, and the reason is obvious. The advance of industrialism was throwing into relief the needs as well as the accomplishments of the north. Sensitive to these needs, Young wrote as a propagandist. His execrations of the bad are more entertaining to read than his praise of the good. Thus, when we read of certain southern roads that 'they continue mere rocky lanes, full of hugeous stones as big as one's horse', we must remember that the very phrase shows purposive exaggeration. And it is worth noting that the paragraph in which this picturesque sentence occurs contains also a recommendation of the last sixteen miles to Cowbridge as 'exceeding good; the stones bound firmly together, no loose ones, nor any rutts'. In any case, Young was individual in his point of view. As traveller he loathed bad turnpikes: as farmer he deprecated the rural exodus.

To find fault with good roads, or any such public convenience, in this age [he wrote,[3]] would have the appearance of paradox and absurdity; but it is nevertheless a fact, that giving the power of expeditious travelling, depopulates the Kingdom. Young men and women in the country villages, fix their eyes on *London*, as the last stage of their hope; they enter into service in the country for little else but to raise money enough to go to *London*, which was no such easy matter, when a stage-coach was four or five days creeping an hundred miles; the fare and the expenses

[1] *Gentleman's Mag.* (1754) vol. xxiv, pp. 347–9.

[2] *Quarterly Journal of Economics*, vol. xli, May 1927: E. F. Gay, 'Arthur Young on English Roads', pp. 545–51.

[3] A. Young, *The Farmer's Letters to the People of England* (1767), p. 340.

ran high. *But now!* a country fellow, one hundred miles from *London*, jumps on to a coach-box in the morning, and for eight or ten shillings gets to town by night; which makes a material difference.

But Young is a witness in so many causes. As sociologist he disapproved the swelling-out of London at the expense of the countryside: as economist, he could not but record with appreciation the transforming effect of a turnpike in a backward area.

There is such an instance of the benefit of a turnpike there (at Horsham), [he writes in 1789] as is very rarely to be met with: the present road to London was made in 1756; before that time it was so execrably bad, that whoever went on wheels, were forced to go round by Canterbury, which is one of the most extraordinary instances that the history of non-communication in this country can afford.[1]

There was opposition to the making of this road, but when it was finished, rents rose at once from 7*s.* to 11*s.* an acre, and an era of prosperity began. And this was to be attributed, as Young was careful to point out,

not to the power of carrying heavy loads to London, but to the general impetus given to circulation; new people—new ideas—new exertions —fresh activity to every branch of industry ... and all the animation, vigour, life and energy of luxury, consumption, and industry, which flow with a full tide through this Kingdom, wherever there is a free communication between the capital and the provinces.

No better summary could be found of the road experience of this improving age.

The heralds of a better England had already sounded their challenge long before Young. A sign of the times had been the appearance of Defoe's *Tour Through the Whole Island of Great Britain* (1724–6). Defoe's book had a definitely utilitarian purpose—to make the whole country familiar to those who lived in it. It was based on the knowledge acquired in 'seventeen very long circuits or journeys and three general tours'. But its author pointed out that no perfect description could be given because 'new foundations are always laying, new buildings always raising, highways repairing ... new projects enterpriz'd, new designs laid'. It was the more necessary on that account, and it became the parent of a prolific stream of books with the object of guiding travellers to the places of importance.

---

[1] *Annals of Agriculture* (1789), vol. xvi, p. 292.

BLOSSOM's INN,
LAWRENCE-LANE, CHEAPSIDE.

Chester Original Flying Waggon,
IN FIVE DAYS,
TO THE
BLOSSOM'S INN, CHESTER.

SETS out every Saturday, in the Afternoon, at Six o'Clock, and Arrives at CHESTER early every Friday Morning, and forwards GOODS for the following Places, and all Parts of *North Wales*:

Parkgate,	Denbigh,	Holywell,	Conway,
Frodsham,	Ruthen,	Bala,	Corwen,
Neston,	St. 'Asaph,	Carnarvon,	Bangor,
Mold,	Abergaley,	Northop,	Beaumaris,
Leefwood,	Llanruft,	Llangernew,	Holyhead.

Whitchurch and *Wrexham* Old Conftant Flying Waggons,

Set out every Saturday, in the Afternoon, and convey GOODS to the following Towns, and all Places adjacent:

Four Croffes,	Newport,	Prees,	Handly,
Street Road,	Turnhill,	Sandford,	Bangor,
Ivetfea Bank,	Market Drayton,	Malpas,	Overton, &c.
Pavelane,	Hinftock,	Barnhill,	

Performed by JAMES SCOTT and Co.

The BRIGHTON Elegant POST COACHES, DILIGENCES, and LONG COACHES, fet out from Hence, as ufual, every Morning at Half paft Seven o'Clock, to SCOTT's *New Inn and Hotel*, BRIGHTON.

From the road literature of the middle and later decades of the century, a lifelike picture of the roads of Johnson's England can be made. There were the 'tolerable good ways' of the great northern post road from London to York, and of the other northern road by way of Northampton, Leicester, and Nottingham. Defoe had to warn travellers against the deep clay area of the Midlands which was

so surprisingly soft, that it is perfectly frightful to travellers, and it has been the wonder of foreigners, how, considering the great numbers of carriages which are continually passing with heavy loads, those ways have been made practicable; indeed the great number of horses every year kill'd by the excess of labour in those heavy ways, has been such a charge to the country, that new building of causeways, as the Romans did of old, seems to me to be a much easier expence.

But he could praise the turnpike system, which was found admirable in Essex and Suffolk, between London and Ipswich and Harwich, and in parts of Hertfordshire, Cambridge, and Bedford, as well as farther afield. If the metropolitan area was particularly mentioned as that where improvement was most conspicious, Defoe was careful to note that much remained to be done. Yet, "'tis more than probable, that our posterity may see the roads all over England restor'd in their time, to such a perfection, that travelling and carriage of goods will be much more easy both to man and horse, than ever it was since the Romans lost this island'.[1] And he was entitled to claim that a good beginning had been made. If only those editors to whom the revision of Defoe's *Tour* was entrusted from time to time had brought to their work the same powers of observation and the same care to provide trustworthy information, the successive editions would have presented a useful bird's-eye view of the means of travel and communication over half a century of change. They were hack-workers, however, and did little more than make the sprightly original into a commonplace guide-book. The cross-post through all the west of England, for example, was described in 1778 in the same terms as in 1725, and even Defoe's September snow on the hills beyond Rochdale was still visible fifty years later! Evidence from other sources must be found to complete the story which

[1] Defoe, *Tour through England and Wales* (Everyman edition), vol. ii, pp. 115–32, Appendix on roads.

Defoe had begun; yet it is worth noting that in 1778 the 'Gentlemen of Eminence in the Literary World' who refurbished Defoe's text and its continuation 'by the late Mr. Richardson, Author of *Clarissa*', were able to write freely of the northern counties. Westmorland and Cumberland, they declared, 'were formerly considered as little better than barren and inhospitable deserts, and, being so remote from the Metropolis, were seldom visited as the objects of pleasure, till the amazing improvements lately made (and still making) in all the roads through the Kingdom, gave a spur to travellers of independent fortunes, who have now made us almost as well acquainted with the northern as we before were with the southern parts of our island.' The time was already in sight when, as Wilberforce remembered in his later years 'the tour to the Lakes had become so fashionable that the banks of the Thames were scarcely more public than those of Windermere'.

The middle years of the century provide a turning-point in the history of internal communications. Not only did the 'Forty-Five' emphasize the necessity of road improvement and lead to the opening-up of considerable parts of Scotland by road construction, but the turnpike system began to be very widely extended and to be pruned of its major weaknesses.[1] The earliest turnpike Acts, those of 1663 for Hertford, Cambridge, and Huntingdon and of 1695 for the London-Colchester road, provided useful preliminary experience, which was embodied in the numerous Acts that were secured in the first two decades of the eighteenth century. These Acts made provision for the repair and maintenance of short sections of road. Duties under them were entrusted to boards of trustees, named in the Acts, not to the justices of the peace as formerly. Conceived as supplementary to the older system of road improvement and maintenance through the statutory *corvée*, the turnpike system came in time to supersede it, or to absorb it, save for local roads of no 'through' importance. The turnpike trustees were given a free hand for the twenty-one years which was their usual span of life before reconsideration of their Trust. They were

---

[1] The new road authorities, the Turnpike Trustees, were authorized to erect 'toll-houses', 'toll-bars', 'turnpikes', 'crates', or 'gates' at any points which seemed suitable to them on the roads over which they had control, and to exact tolls at the points in payment for passage. The term 'turnpike' was used both for the toll-gate and, by a natural extension, for the road itself.

responsible to no central authority either regarding their expenditure, or the extent of their borrowing, or the efficiency of their work. On the other hand, their work was conditioned from time to time by overriding general regulations imposed by Parliament, and their behaviour was criticized in the most violent way by the furious attacks of riotous mobs. Parliament was still concerned, as it had been since the extension of wheeled traffic in the seventeenth century, to discover means by which vehicles could be prevented from damaging the highways. It regulated the size of wheels and of vehicles and the number of horses: it authorized the use of weighing-engines at toll-gates, and even made them compulsory within a thirty-mile radius of London. It also ejected inn-keepers from the holding of offices of trust —doubtless not without reason— and insisted on a substantial property-qualification for trustees.

That the watchful attention of Parliament was necessary is proved by the grumbling of travellers and by the complaints from the trusts of the evasion of their tolls. The latter was positively encouraged by the tenderness of Parliament to the interests of the gentry. The extra tolls fixed in 1741 upon vehicles whose weight was over three tons, did not apply to gentlemen's carriages, farmers' vehicles, or wagons in the King's service. Perhaps, too, the desire to exempt from payment those best able to pay had something to do with popular hostility to the extortions of the toll-gate officer. An Act of 1728 imposed stringent penalties for attack on the toll-gates—three months' imprisonment and a whipping for the first offence, and seven years' transportation for the second. A little later the death penalty was introduced. Even so, the attacks continued. It was reported in 1749 in Bristol that 'about 400 Somersetshire people cut down a 3rd time the turnpike gates on the Ashton road . . . then afterwards destroy'd the Dundry turnpike, and thence went to Bedminster, headed by two chiefs on horseback . . . the rest were on foot, armed with rusty swords, pitch-forks, axes, guns, pistols, clubs . . .'.[1] The year 1749 was a bad year in Bristol. On another occasion, turnpike riots lasted for several days, and almost all the turnpikes and turnpike-houses were demolished. It required six troops of dragoon guards to quell the rioters, who are described in the *Gentleman's*

[1] *Gentleman's Mag.* (1749), vol. xix, p. 376.

Magazine as 'a body of Gloucestershire people, some naked with only trousers, some in their shirts, some naked with their faces blacked'.[1] They were equipped with gunpowder for the purpose of blowing up the posts, and they forced a passage for the cattle and colts they were taking to the fair even against the commissioners themselves, who 'took it by turns about a dozen in a body to stand at the gates', suitably supported, 'to awe the people'.

Even those in the highest places occasionally forgot their rectitude.

Returning by way of frolic, very late at night, on horseback, to Wimbledon, from Addiscombe . . . Lord Thurlow, then Chancellor, Pitt and Dundas, found the Turnpike Gate situate between Tooting and Streatham, thrown open. Being elevated above their usual prudence, and having no Servant near them, they passed through the gate at a brisk pace, without stopping to pay the Toll; regardless of the remonstrances or threats of the Turnpike man, who running after them, and believing them to belong to some Highwaymen, who had recently committed depredations on that road, discharged the contents of his Blunderbuss at their backs. Happily he did no injury.[2]

Individual delinquencies of this order mattered little, but it is impossible to believe that turnpike riots and the persistent fraudulent evasions of tolls had no justification outside the law. It is likely that the more serious riots were protests against high costs of living in hard times, summary judgements of the price-raising effect of the tolls levied at the toll-bars. They may well have expressed also popular disapproval of inefficiency and corruption. Evidence of mismanagement can be discovered from parliamentary inquiries made from time to time. A mid-century examination of the application over a decade of time of highway funds collected by virtue of any Act of Parliament provided a number of striking instances. Not for the first time the Kensington turnpike came in for criticism. A striking case, too, was that of the turnpike between Cranford Bridge and Maidenhead Bridge. This road was shown ordinarily to be administered by small farmers: at a particular meeting, attended for once by the wealthier commissioners, it was

---

[1] *Gentleman's Mag.* (1749), vol. xix, p. 376.
[2] Sir N. Wraxall, Bt., *Historical Memoirs of My Own Time* (1815), vol. ii, p. 473.

ordered that the practice of exempting commissioners from payment of tolls should be discontinued, whereupon the receipts increased by some £3 or £4 per week, and the 'three or four draught teams, which used to go to London with heavy loads of meal and other goods, several times in a week', and were kept by some of the farmer-commissioners, no longer escaped their due share of upkeep costs.[1] Rules had to be prescribed to prevent the recurrence of these acts of corruption and habits of inefficiency in the future, but a long period elapsed before the important discovery was made in the technique of government that voluntary service had very considerable limitations and was apt to be more expensive than professional paid service. When, in 1711, the trustee system superseded the old system of administration by justices of the peace, the substitution of professionals for amateurs had not been accomplished. Inefficiencies still crept in. It is reasonable to regard popular hostility to the exaction of tolls as having some justification, therefore, however inadmissible it may have been as a mode of criticism.

The public history of road legislation throws a far clearer light upon the history of road transport than does the more popular method of stringing together travellers' expletives. The dry-light of statistics shows that in the first half of the century upwards of four hundred road Acts were passed by Parliament; between 1751 and 1790 there were four times as many.

Against this background we can safely place the recorded experience of individual road-users.

In my journey to London [declares one in 1747], I travelled from Harborough to Northampton, and well was it that I was in a light Berlin, and six good horses, or I might have been overlaid in that turnpike road. But for fear of life and limb, I walk'd several miles on foot, met twenty waggons tearing their goods to pieces, and the drivers cursing and swearing for being robbed on the highway by a turnpike, screened under an act of parliament.

Upon this experience the *Gentleman's Magazine* makes editorial comment:

These complaints we have found experimentally true, in a journey to Derby, and rather than travel the said bad and dangerous road

[1] *House of Commons Journals*, 25 Geo. II, 1752, vol. xxvi, p. 491.

twice, chose to go several miles about into another turnpike road.[1]

This ride from Leicester to Northampton [wrote Parson Moritz in 1782] I shall remember as long as I live. . . . My companions on the top of the coach, were a farmer, a young man very decently dressed, and a black-a-moor. The getting up alone was at the risk of one's life; and when I was up, I was obliged to sit just at the corner of the coach, with nothing to hold by, but a sort of little handle, fastened on the side. I sat nearest the wheel; and the moment that we set off, I fancied that I saw certain death await me. All I could do, was to take still faster hold of the handle, and to be more and more careful to preserve my balance. The machine now rolled along with prodigious rapidity, over the stones through the town, and every moment we seemed to fly into the air; so that it was almost a miracle, that we still stuck to the coach, and did not fall. We seemed to be thus on the wing, and to fly, as often as we passed through a village, or went down a hill. At last the being continually in fear of my life, became insupportable, and as we were going up a hill, and consequently proceeding rather slower than usual, I crept from the top of the coach, and got snug into the basket. 'O, sir, sir you will be shaken to death!' said the black; but I flattered myself, he exaggerated the unpleasantness of my post. As long as we went up hill, it was easy and pleasant . . . but how was the case altered when we came to go down hill; then all the trunks and parcels began, as it were, to dance around me . . . and I every moment received from them such violent blows, that I thought my last hour was come. . . . I was obliged to suffer this torture nearly an hour, till we came to another hill again, when quite shaken to pieces and sadly bruised, I again crept to the top of the coach and took possession of my former seat.[2]

No wonder Moritz looked like 'a crazy creature' when he reached London, after what he described as 'hardly a journey but rather a perpetual motion, or removal, from one place to another, in a close box', the last stage from Northampton having been accomplished as an inside passenger. A generation of crowded road history separated these two experiences: between 1747 and 1789 big changes had been effected.

Those who journeyed to the south-western counties complained in the middle of the century that after the first fifty miles from London, no turnpike was discoverable for 220

[1] *Gentleman's Mag.* (1747) vol. xvii, pp. 232–3. Quoted by W. T. Jackman, *Development of Transportation in Modern England* (1916), vol. i, p. 85.

[2] *Travels of Carl Philipp Moritz in England* (reprinted 1924, Oxford Miscellany ed.), pp. 211–14.

THE HYDE PARK CORNER TURNPIKE

with a view of st. george's hospital, 1798

miles. In the far north there was a lack of guide posts in Northumberland—as Hutchinson put it in 1776—to 'mitigate the grievances of travelling', but in this county and in Durham from 1742 onwards the roads were reasonably good, apart from heavy gradients.[1] In Yorkshire and Lancashire, where growing industries were constantly creating new needs, improvements were made but never rapidly enough. It was in this area that John Metcalfe set so startling an example of road engineering.[2] Though blind, Metcalfe succeeded in securing a succession of contracts for road construction. He rode fearlessly over the wildest country and was valued as a reliable guide. He showed business aptitude as well as technical resourcefulness as a pioneer in road construction, and was responsible for surveying and building some 500 miles of excellent roadways. The difficulty was to keep pace with traffic expansion, and success could not be expected till road engineering was improved. That was Metcalfe's achievement. The short lengths of road for which he contracted were usually difficult, and his work in the Leeds, Wakefield, Skipton, Knaresborough, Harrogate, Burnley districts was astonishing, in itself, and not only as the achievement of a blind man. In these areas, as in the Midlands, the road alone could not be made to suffice: rivers and canals had to relieve the roads and cheapen transport before their expansive energies could be fully liberated.

The metropolitan area presented unusual difficulties, and it took a long time to hammer out a technique adequate to it. A summary of the situation at the end of the century is worth quoting. 'To the improvement of the roads (compared with the state they were in forty or fifty years ago) may be attributed the present safe, cheap and expeditious conveyance in mail-coaches, in which Britain is unequalled. In the variety of construction of public carriages for the conveyance of passengers London excels all other places.' So wrote the reporter to the Board of Agriculture regarding

[1] Hutchinson, *View of Northumberland* (1776), vol. i, p. 131; *Victoria County History, Durham*, vol. ii, p. 244.
[2] See *The Life of John Metcalfe; formerly called Blind Jack of Knaresborough; with many entertaining anecdotes of His Exploits in Hunting, Card playing &c., some Particulars relating to the Expedition against the Rebels in 1745 . . . and a succinct Account of his various Contracts for Making Roads, erecting Bridges and other Undertakings* (a new edition, improved, 1812).

Middlesex in 1798, and no one could dissent from his statements. But he goes on in a surprising strain.

Most of the *parish highways* in this county, are superior to any other of equal extent I have ever seen. They are hard and clean in every sort of weather; so much so, that gentlemen may ride along them, even directly after rain, and scarcely receive a splash. The *turnpike roads*, on the contrary, are, generally, very bad; although at the toll-gates of this county, there is collected a very large sum of money, probably not less than £130,000 a year; which is uselessly expended in sinking wells, erecting pumps, building carts, and hiring horses and men to keep the dust down, by watering, instead of more wisely scraping it off. . . .

The turnpike from Hadley through South Mimms is 'unsufferably bad'; the Edgware road is of the same description; the road from Tyburn through Uxbridge, 'supposed to have more broad-wheeled waggons pass over it than any other in the county', is almost impassable for horsemen and light carriages; the road from Hyde Park corner through Brentford and Hounslow, 'notwithstanding His Majesty travels this road several times every week', is equally deep in filth; Highgate and Hampstead hills are 'a tax, of one horse in every team, on the farmers of Finchley and Hendon'.

If this was the part of the country where most could be expected, the remote south-west was the part where least could be looked for, since its main industries were losing their oldtime resilience. Yet the zeal for improvement extended even to the remote west country. Devonshire highways, at one time more like 'watery ditches than public roads', were said, in 1784, to be 'equal to those of any other county; our narrow Lanes sufficiently widen'd, the watery Places drain'd, the deep and hollow Parts raised, and the Ascents of the Hills facilitated'.[1] In the first half of the eighteenth century none of the roads of Devon, Dorset, or Cornwall were turnpiked; there were a hundred turnpike Acts between 1751 and 1790. The Exeter Trust, established in 1753, and the pioneer of progress, was made responsible for 150 miles of road radiating from the city; a few years later it was found possible to speed up the London-Exeter coach, the four days previously required being halved. But this advance must be attributed to improvements in coach-making as well as to road-betterment. The two-day coaches of 1764 were

[1] See references in G. Sheldon, *From Trackway to Turnpike* (1928), p. 122.

'machines', not stage-wagons, with the driver mounted on the box, not walking or pony-riding by the side of the vehicle.

The whole position can best be appreciated retrospectively. When the stage-coach ushered in a new era, great progress was made, but it was still inadequate.

With regard to the roads of England and Wales [reported Telford as late as 1819] they are in general very defective, both as to their direction and inclinations; they are frequently carried over hills, which might be avoided by passing along the adjacent valleys; the shape or cross sections and drainage of the roads are quite as defective as the general directions and inclinations; there has been no attention paid to constructing good and solid foundations; the materials, whether consisting of gravel or stones, have seldom been sufficiently selected and arranged; and they lie so promisciously upon the roads as to render it inconvenient to travel upon them, and to promote their speedy destruction. The shape of the road or cross-section of the surface is frequently hollow in the middle; the sides encumbered with great banks of road dirt, which have accumulated in some places to the height of six, seven, and eight feet; these prevent the water from falling into the side drains, and also throw a considerable shade upon the road, and are great and unpardonable nuisances.[1]

The pages of Defoe's *Tour* nearly a century earlier had made lively reference to the droves of turkeys, the Highland and Welsh cattle, the flocks of sheep, the geese, the fast fish carriages, and other new users of the roads. The volume of traffic constantly increased, and more and more the traffic was borne on wheels. Legislation of the most perplexing variety was tried in the attempt to fit the vehicle to the road, but it was never even moderately successful. The coach-builders were constantly making new types of vehicle. Caravans or stage-wagons drawn by four or five horses carried a score or so of passengers, unable to pay for better and faster accommodation. Except on the Liverpool-London road they seldom changed horses, but used the same team throughout.[2] The ordinary stage-coach, with four horses, carried only half a dozen passengers, who travelled inside, till road-improvement made outside-accommodation feasible. Even then, they seem to have shared the roof with the luggage, and accidents were common.[3] These coaches

[1] Evidence before the Committee of House of Commons, quoted by Sir H. Parnell, *A Treatise on Roads* (1838), p. 234.

[2] H. E. Malet, *Annals of the Road, to which an added Essay on the Road by Nimrod* [i.e. C. J. Apperley] (1876), p. 11.

[3] W. C. A. Blew, *Brighton and its Coaches* (1894), p. 24.

before about 1750 were springless, and some of them carried baggage (and occasionally passengers) in baskets slung on the back. The flying-machines were steel-sprung from 1754 onwards; the earlier Brighton flying-machine (1745) was 'fashioned something like the Brighton bathing-machines.' No one was carried on the roof; but subsequently there was added a big basket contrivance, called a 'conveniency', behind, for the accommodation of half-price passengers.[1] The Brighton diligence ran daily, carrying three passengers at 3*d*. a mile each, and in 1787 three light post-coaches, two heavy coaches, and three wagons ran on the London-Brighton road. This was not satisfactory to all travellers. An advertisement of 1791 in the *Sussex Advertiser* shows this.

There are [it reads] two modes of conveyance, either by common stages or by a post-chaise. By the common stage, you are classed with company of every description, and who may very frequently turn out very disagreeable. You are also paid no attention to at the inns where you stop, although you pay exorbitant for refreshment, and are frequently insulted by the indecent behaviour of the coachman, and besides your fare, you have a considerable sum to pay for luggage. On the contrary, if two or three passengers choose to travel together, they may, by travelling in a post-chaise, not only avoid all these inconveniences—but suit their own convenience in point of time, and be at less expence—besides meeting with genteeler treatment at the inns on the road.[2]

Sir Walter Gilbey quotes a contemporary description of the mid-century stage-coach—

covered with dull black leather, studded by way of ornament with broad-headed nails, with oval windows in the quarters, the frames painted red. . . . The roof rose in a high curve with an iron rail around it. The coachman and guard sat in front upon a high narrow boot. . . . Behind was an immense basket supported by iron bars. . . . The machine groaned and creaked as it went along.[3]

Compared with this type of vehicle, the many varieties of private carriage were light and elegant. It is impossible to describe them all. Writing from Paris in 1770, Jeremy Bentham tells how he 'set out from London this day sennight with Mr. Clark in his Titiwhiskey' and reached Paris, after travelling 'on Horses, Asses, in Boats, Chamber Pots (Pots de Chambre, a kind of two-wheeled, two-horsed

[1] W. A. C. Blew, *Brighton and its Coaches*, p. 33.
[2] Quoted Blew, ibid., p. 45.
[3] Sir W. Gilbey, Bt., *Early Carriages and Roads* (1903), p. 82.

A GENTLEMAN DRIVING A PHAETON

From the picture in the National Gallery by George Stubbs

voiture, clumsy to the most exquisite perfection) and a floating kind of Black Hole'.[1] Parson Cole, Horace Walpole's friend, journeying to Paris five years earlier, found French hackney coaches dirtier and more shabby than English, but 'easier than ours, being hung lower and upon Leather in a different Manner'.[2] French postilions are 'cleaner and cleverer Fellows', but 'our Equipages exceed those of France for Lightness, Ease and Convenience'.[3]

The Turnpike Act of 1803 admitted the levying of tolls on coaches, calashes, chariots, landaws, berlins, chaises, chaises marines, cars, chairs, caravans, hearses, and litters. The remoter parts of the county were unaware of the variety of vehicles that frequented the busier roads, and a strange list of survivals could have been compiled even in the progressive days of Queen Victoria. As with road-engineering, so with vehicle-building, a good deal of progress has to be reported. These improvements were gathered up in the solid and spectacular achievement of Palmer's mail-coaches, which were as much better than the old stage-coaches in speed, safety, and comfort as were the main roads on which they were driven than the roads of George II's day. Palmer's work marks the end of one era and the beginning of another in travel as well as postal facilities. John Palmer had shown an enterprising spirit when he secured the first royal patent for a provincial theatre. He had found by experience that fast travelling was possible with good horses: he often performed the journey between Bath and London in a day. Realizing that the post was the slowest and least safe mode of conveyance in England, he set to work to devise a plan of improvement. When in 1784 he promised a sixteen-hour service between Bristol and London at 28s. a passenger, he challenged the established services. It is true that his mail-coaches afforded accommodation for only four inside passengers as against six inside and a variable number outside on the usual vehicles. But the advantages of speed and safety—armed guards and coachmen had to give security to the proprietors for their good conduct—were irresistible. Through services and cross-services were multiplied, and the great days of the coaching era had arrived. De Quincey's

[1] Quoted by C. W. Everett, *The Education of Jeremy Bentham* (1931), p. 52.
[2] The Rev. W. Cole, *A Journal of My Journey to Paris in 1765* (1931), p. 47.
[3] Ibid., p. 326.

picture immediately comes to mind. 'Seated on the old mail-coach, we needed no evidence out of ourselves to indicate the velocity. . . . The vital experience of the glad animal sensibilities made doubts impossible. . . . we heard our speed, we saw it, we felt it as a thrilling: and this speed was not the product of blind insensate agencies, that had no sympathy to give, but was incarnated in the fiery eyeballs of the noblest among brutes, in his dilated nostril, spasmodic muscles, and thunder-beating hoofs.'

When allowances have been made for road-straightening, and all the other improvement of the century, and when individual idiosyncrasies of all sorts have been eliminated, there seems to be no doubt that fifty to sixty miles was a good average day's journey in the middle years of the century, and perhaps twice that mileage in the later. The chief gain was not in the speed on the road but in the elimination of stops and in the better service of horses. Little satisfaction can be got, however, from the attempt to discover average times and speeds. What impressed people was the phenomenal achievements of the fastest vehicles. The Newcastle-London coach left Newcastle at 10 p.m. and reached London at the close of the third day, in 1785; it required 6 days in 1754. The fastest time between Birmingham and London in 1752 was 2 summer days: it was only 19 hours in 1785. It took $4\frac{1}{2}$ days to travel from Manchester to London in 1754, 28 hours in 1788. These times are instructive not only as showing the changed travelling habits, but as indicating the narrowness of the advantages offered by railways in their first phase. It is not surprising, in view of the high speeds of the early nineteenth-century coaches, that the great possibilities of the railway remained concealed, and that railway building seemed at first to be little better than an act of misplaced faith. The ten to twelve miles per hour of the coaches of the 'twenties represents at least a doubling of rates in the course of the century. It is not to be wondered at, then, that the railway pioneers were bred upon the coalfields where the special track and the special locomotive were first brought together. If the earliest railways are discoverable long before Palmer's coaches, and the first Trevithick locomotive in 1804, the slow elaboration of these beginnings must not be regarded as the mark of an unprogressive age. The reverse, rather, is the truth. The improve-

ment of the road and the coach, and the introduction of
the canal made railways unnecessary until further economic
expansion rendered these older agencies inadequate.

It is difficult to estimate the cost of road-travel. Stage-
coach fares varied. Partly they were fixed by reference to
the cost of the alternative means of riding post or by wagon;
custom was the main factor, however. Rates were constant
in the early decades of the eighteenth century, but like
other costs, they began to rise in the 'sixties. Thomas
Somerville's experience in 1779 must have been typical.

I returned to Scotland . . . in the beginning of June. It is a circumstance not unworthy of notice, because it shows the increased
expense of travelling, that we paid no more than 7d. per mile for
posting from London to York. Finding the horses not so good, we
paid 9d. per mile (which was the ordinary charge), for the remaining
part of the journey. The duty on posting (2d. per mile) did not commence till July 1, 1779.[1]

Somerville's last journey from Scotland by stage-coach in
1800 cost him twice as much as the £7 he paid for his first
in 1769.[2] A common summer-rate was 2½d. per mile, the
winter rate being ½d. more. The fare from London to Edinburgh was about £4. 10s.[3]

What regular coach-services could the traveller command?
Set out in a list, they appear considerable, but regarded in
reference to the population, they are scanty. In the summer
of 1740 the service from London to Bath comprised three
coaches three times a week—three on Mondays and Fridays,
two on Wednesdays, and one on Thursdays. In winter, two
coaches were available on Mondays and Thursdays only.
The direct Bristol service, in summer, included three 'flys'
on Mondays, Wednesdays, and Fridays, and for the rest of
the year there were coaches on Mondays and Thursdays.
These set out from the 'Three Cups' in Bread Street, 'the
Bell Savage' in Ludgate Hill, and the 'One Bell' in the Strand.
Exeter had one coach twice weekly, from the 'Saracen's
Head' in Friday Street, while Plymouth had no regular ser-
vice of coaches and had to depend on a weekly car. The
Universities had considerably better provision made for
them. The summer service to Oxford, from the 'Bolt and
Ton' in Fleet Street, the 'Bull and the Black Swan' in

[1] *My Own Life and Times* (1861), p. 190.   [2] Ibid., p. 140.
[3] Jackman, *Development of Transportation*, vol. i, p. 138.

Holborn, and the 'Oxford Arms' in Warwick Crescent was made up of four coaches three times a week, one service or more being available on all days but Sundays. In the winter there were only three coaches twice weekly and an additional coach on Thursdays. Cambridge had one coach on Tuesdays, Wednesdays, Thursdays, and Fridays. There were regular services to Channel ports—to Dover, two coaches three days a week in summer, and half that service in winter; to Southampton four coaches a week in the summer, three in winter; to Harwich, five coaches weekly. Coaches to York, Newcastle, and Edinburgh left the 'Black Swan', Holborn, on three days in the week in summer, and on two in winter.

Towards the end of Johnson's life, on the eve of the Palmer régime, the traveller had a considerable service at his disposal. Beau Nash had made Bath so attractive that it was served by five coaches every day, four coaches running daily with the exception of Saturdays, and four which ran three times a week. There was an improvement in the choice of starting-times too. Instead of a 4 a.m. start the traveller could, if he preferred, choose to set out from the terminal inn at 5 a.m., 8 a.m., 2 p.m., 4 p.m., or 9 p.m. The Bristol service consisted of three coaches every day, two coaches daily except on Saturdays, and two others which ran on Mondays, Wednesdays, and Fridays. Exeter was served by one daily coach, one daily except Saturdays, two on three days in the week, and a daily diligence. Plymouth had two daily coaches, two on three days a week, and two daily diligences. Oxford had five daily coaches, and an additional coach and diligence three times a week. Cambridge still required a less elaborate service—one daily coach, two coaches three times a week, and a daily diligence. A considerable growth in the channel-port services had taken place by 1783. Dover had five coaches and four diligences daily; Southampton two coaches and two diligences daily as well as a second diligence three times a week; Harwich was now content with one coach three times weekly, which was less than formerly. The northern services had become profuse by 1783. A daily coach and a daily diligence to York were supplemented by further services of two coaches three times and one diligence twice a week. Newcastle was served by three daily coaches and a daily diligence, and a further coach on three days a week. The Edinburgh service comprised four daily coaches, one daily diligence, and one coach daily except Saturdays.

To some extent the cost of travelling was conditioned by the frequency of toll-gates. There were six on the London-Dover road, and six on the Brighton road via Reigate. But there were only six between London and York, four on the Chippenham route to Bristol, and two on the Henley route to Oxford. A study of the road-books shows the number decreasing as the century advanced, these figures being taken from Cary's well-known *New Itinerary* (1798).

Innkeepers usually organized coach services, confining their business to their own locality or to one system of roads. Originally they were interlopers, who encroached upon the functions of the postmaster. But postmasters were often innkeepers, as innkeepers were often farmers. It was only with the growth of more elaborate services that functions were more strictly differentiated.

The dangers of the road have figured so often in the pages of Horace Walpole and others that a romantic glamour has attached itself to the exploits of the highwayman. Probably his activities, like crimes of violence against property in our own day, were less frequent in good times than in bad, when food was scarce and employment irregular. It may be said confidently that the prevalence of highway robbery has been exaggerated, and that the perpetrators were common pests. Richard Turpin, alias John Palmer, hanged at York, on April 7, 1739, 'gave £3 10s. to 5 men who were to follow the Cart as Mourners, with Hatbands and Gloves to them and several others', as the *Gentleman's Magazine* reports;[1] but there seems to be no other evidence that either he or his partner, Tom King, ever deserved their immortality. Turpin was not even the hero of the perennially famous ride to York: he was merely sentenced to death for stealing a black mare. 'Blueskin' Blake and Jack Sheppard were no better, though a crowd of thousands watched the last moments of Sheppard, expecting, it may be, that prince of escapers to achieve his masterpiece. Jerry Abershaw, terror of the Kingston-Wimbledon area, covered his head when the

---

[1] *Gentleman's Mag.* (1739), vol. ix, p. 213. Turpin faced his death so bravely that the mob snatched his body from the surgeon's dissecting-knife and procured it a Christian burial. Executions were in the nature of public spectacles, almost sporting events, and the crowd appreciated a good performer.

judge put on the black cap to sentence him, and went gaily
to the gallows with a flower between his lips. But, in truth,
these hardened reprobates were no heroes, however interesting as social phenomena. *The Beggar's Opera* has imposed
a legend upon us.

From the memoirs, correspondence, journals, and newspapers of the time there may be culled many stories, often
picturesque in their details and romantic in retrospect, of
the exploits of the aforementioned scoundrels and others
less notorious. A highwayman might be most gentlemanly
in appearance; might combine great daring and success in
his operations with an objection to wanton cruelty and the
appearance of meanness:[1] but as a rule the 'gentleman of
the road' had no compunction, and robbed the poor post-
man and the toll-house keeper as readily as the quality.[2]
He was not invariably successful, for the intended victims
were sometimes sufficiently courageous and sufficiently well
armed to defend themselves;[3] but at all times he was an
intolerable nuisance and a source of apprehension to the
peaceable traveller who saw nothing at all romantic in having
his journey interrupted and his pocket picked.

There was a persistent belief that highwaymen were all
too commonly in league with innkeepers. This belief doubtless had occasional justification. The perpetrator of a daring
mail-robbery near Selby at the end of the century was not
discovered, but demolition operations in 1876 at an inn in
Churchill, near that town, led to the finding of human
remains and the missing mail-bag. In this case the con-
federates seem to have fallen out. It is unnecessary to
attach an unduly black character to innkeepers, even though
many of them did succeed, to the benefit of their houses, in
impeding road-improvement through their position of advantage as road-trustees, a fault in road management which
was remedied by the Act of 1753. But highwaymen, without
any doubt, clustered most thickly near London. Opportunity was greatest in the metropolitan area. Not only was
traffic, by day and night, more frequent than elsewhere in
the country, but there were better chances of disposing of

[1] Cf. *Gentleman's Mag.* (1757), vol. xxvii, p. 382; *Annual Register* (1761),
pp. 51–4.
[2] Ibid. (1753), vol. xxiii, p. 293; (1750), vol. xv, p. 569.
[3] e.g. ibid., p. 378; (1769), vol. xxxix, p. 210.

O RARE TURPIN.

AS I was riding over Hunslow Moor,
There I saw a lawyer riding before,
And I asked him if he was not afraid.
To meet bold Turpin that mischievous blade.
CHORUS.—I asked him if he was not afraid,
To meet bold Turpin that mischievous blade.
Says Turpin to the lawyer and for to be cute,
My money I have hid all in my boot,,
Says the lawyer to Turpin they mine can't find,
For I have hid mine in the cape of my coat behind.
I rode till I came to a powder mill,
Where Turpin bid the lawyer for to stand still
For the cape of your coat it must come off,
For my horse is in want of a new saddle cloth.
Now Turpin robbed the lawyer of all his store,
When that's gone he knows where to get more,
And the very next town that you go in,
Tell them you was robb'd by the bold Turpin.
Now Turpin is caught, and tried and cast,
And for a game cock must die at last,
One hundred pounds when he did die,
He left Jack Ketch for a legacy.

A Broadside in the collection of Sir Charles Firth

stolen goods and better places of concealment. The Clare Market area was notorious, with its slums and its taverns, as a highwaymen's head-quarters, and on the outskirts of London, as Tucker complained, there were so many heaths and commons which could 'answer no other end but to be a Rendezvous for Highwaymen and a commodious scene for them to exercise their Profession'.[1] They could acquire, too, a most varied apprenticeship. There were the pockets of theatre-goers to be picked round Drury Lane, and there were the spoils of the river to be collected in days when the lack of adequate warehouse and dock accommodation opened up a wide and lucrative field for adventurous plunderers. Colquhoun's *Treatise on the Commerce and Police of the River Thames*, though published in 1800, was no less true of earlier decades in its descriptions of the varieties and prevalence of crime.

The traveller's comfort in the inns was of quite outstanding importance in the days of road travel. 'Let the Traveller observe', Dean Tucker counselled, 'the condition of the public Inns on the great Roads: for they are a kind of Pulse, by which you may discover the Riches or Poverty of a Country.' That doubtless was true, but creature comforts counted for more than economic measurement, and to be sure of them necessitated knowledge of the country's habits as well as a good purse. The Abbé Le Blanc found, at Northampton, that each political party had its favoured hostelry, and 'if a member of Parliament is in opposition to the Court, he is under a necessity of going to an inn of his party, or he is a lost man'.[2] The historian Somerville, frequenting simpler hostelries it may be presumed, carried his own knife and fork with him when travelling, to make good the deficiency of equipment he experienced from time to time.[3] Travellers passed on their experience usefully to friends planning journeys. The Dean of Exeter, writing to a friend in 1767, 'cannot commend the inns at Plymouth, they are like those in other seaports, neither very neat nor quiet'.[4] Arthur Young in his Southern Tour made a list of

---

[1] Josiah Tucker, *The Elements of Commerce* (1755), in *Selected Works of Tucker* (ed. R. L. Schuyler, New York, 1932), pp. 102–3.

[2] Quoted by E. Smith, *Foreign Visitors in England* (1889), from M. l'Abbé Le Blanc, *Letters on the English and French Nations* (1747).

[3] T. Somerville, *My Own Life and Times, 1741–1814* (Edinburgh, 1861), p. 356.   [4] G. Sheldon, *From Trackway to Turnpike* (1928), p. 105.

the inns at which he had rested, and condemned six out of thirty-seven as very bad and very dear, the 'Bush' at Wanstead being 'dirty and impertinent', and the 'George' at Winchester 'dirty and dear but civil'.[1] Saint Fond found the inns generally good save for one in Manchester and one in Edinburgh, where the charges were 'extravagantly high'.[2] Manchester had a bad name for its inns. Others grumbled at them, notably the Irish gentleman who complained in 1785 that they were 'the most inconvenient, incommodious, and in all respects the worst that can be well imagined'.[3] The younger George Colman, the dramatist, and his companion left their beds 'to rest themselves' at one place, and Grosley, at Dover, grumbled at being roused at three o'clock in the morning from the bed he had occupied since six the previous evening, when his room was wanted for new-comers.

The increase of travel in the course of the eighteenth century had its effect upon the inns of the period. If English coaching inns did not reach the height of their excellence until the end of George III's reign, they yet made steady progress. Rebuilding and new building went on constantly.

People at this period, 1770, were rebelling against antique discomfort. The rooms of the average inn were at this time panelled in deal, but the furniture in the best rooms was of mahogany. Hence it was that the curtains—rep and chinz—together with extra candles and the needle-work bell-pulls, came to be charged on the bills. It was at this time that travellers insisted on the use of the warming-pan before venturing between sheets.[4]

Inns were constructed on a conventional pattern—courtyard with arched entry, reception hall, main staircase, coffee-room and dining-parlour. Some had a special dining-room for coach-passengers only. There were often smaller apartments, too, known by the names Sun, Moon, Star, Crescent, or Paragon.[5] The great terminal inns were considerable establishments. The 'George and Blue Boar', Holborn, for example, whence ran the first direct Glasgow coach, had

[1] A. Young, *A Six Weeks Tour through the Southern Counties of England and Wales* (1768), pp. 282–4.

[2] F. St. Fond, 'Travels through England and Scotland to the Hebrides', in Mavor's *British Tourists*, vol. v, p. 100.

[3] An English Gentleman (Thomas Newte), *A Tour in England and Scotland in 1785*, p. 42.

[4] A. Groom, *Old London Coaching Inns and their Successors* (1928), p. 25.

[5] Ibid., p. 112.

40 bedrooms, stabling for 52 horses, 7 coachhouses, and a dry drive 70 yards long.[1]

Landlords were often substantial folk, stage-coach proprietors and postmasters. They held a key position at election times, being courted by the squirearchy.[2] 'They charged according to what they considered their guests would grumble at—and pay', it has been said,[3] but there is plenty of contrary evidence.

At the 'Lion', Liverpool, an Irish gentleman and three fellow passengers paid only 6d. each for 'a very good supper, consisting of veal cutlets, pigeons, asparagus, lamb and salad, apple-pie and tarts'.[4] The 'Lion', he said, was accounted 'one of the best ordinaries in England, as you've the nicest and most uncommon dishes at only 8d. per piece' at the one o'clock meal. At Leicester, however, things were less satisfactory. 'After we had very often called for eggs, the waiter at length brought two and protested there was no more in town to be bought.'[5] It has to be remembered that coaches had the habit, for obvious reasons, of starting very early. Four a.m. and even two a.m. were common times of leaving terminals for long-distance journeys. This must have been a standing handicap to innkeepers. They might well be impatient with the casual traveller, who turned up at irregular hours.

Innkeepers were as various as inns. Pastor Moritz, travelling on foot, often had occasion to grumble at his hosts. He was particularly unlucky at Windsor. At the first attempt to find lodging he was offered a room which 'much resembled a prison for malefactors'.[6] Refusing that, he was invited to go on to Slough and was compelled to find solace in reflecting upon 'this impudent ill-usage from people, who ought to reflect, that they are but the servants of the public; and little likely to recommend themselves to the high, by being insolent to the low'. Yet Moritz did find a kindly mannered

---

[1] A. E. Richardson and H. D. Eberlein, *The English Inn, Past and Present* (1925), p. 22.

[2] C. G. Harper, *The Old Inns of Old England* (2 vols., 1906), vol. i, p. 51. Johnson's friend, the Rev. Dr. Taylor of Ashbourne, numbered among his other friends two retired inn-keepers. The daughter of one of them, Brian Hodgson, married Beilby Porteus, Bishop of Chester in Johnson's lifetime, and afterwards of London.

[3] A. Groom, *Old London Coaching Inns and their Successors*, p. 51.

[4] An Irish Gentleman, *Journey through England* (1752), p. 12.

[5] Ibid., p. 63.   [6] *Travels of C. P. Moritz in England*, p. 115.

host elsewhere in Windsor, though the host's civility did not extend to a similar behaviour either in the chamber-maid or the waiter. The former sneeringly invited him to seek accommodation elsewhere, but the host's intervention procured him another room which he shared uneasily with a drunken fellow: the waiter served him with an ill-grace and demanded a tip on his departure. 'I gave him three halfpence', said Moritz, 'on which he saluted me with the heartiest God d——n you, Sir! I had ever heard. At the door stood the cross maid, who also accosted me with "pray remember the chamber-maid!" Yes, yes, said I, I shall long remember your most ill-mannered behaviour, and shameful incivility; and so I gave her nothing.'[1] Moritz would doubtless have fared better, foot-passenger though he was, had he passed a night under John Freeth's roof in Birmingham. Freeth's hobby-horse and practice for thirty years, he tells us in his *Political Songster*,[2] was to write songs upon the occurrence of remarkable events and to sing them while their subjects were upon every man's mind. This practice was profitable, crowding his house with customers, travellers in the mercantile line from every county. Had Moritz been present in 1769, he might have heard Freeth celebrate in an Ode on Inland Navigation the bringing of the first boat load of coals to town.

> And sure that plan must be of noble use,
> Which tends in price provisions to reduce.
> Blest Navigation!. source of golden days
> Which Commerce finds, and brightens all its ways.

Among the great achievements of Hanoverian England was the improvement of inland water communications. First came schemes for rendering rivers navigable; then followed the construction of canals. The impulse in both cases came quite inevitably from the expanding industrial areas. The profits of the colonial trade in sugar, cotton, tobacco, and slaves not only galvanized Liverpool and such lesser ports as Whitehaven into a more active life than they had ever experienced, but provided the sinews of economic growth in the manufacturing areas they served. The need of better facilities for the transportation of goods, and the consciousness

[1] Ibid., p. 124.
[2] John Freeth, *The Political Songster, or a Touch on the Times, on various Subjects and adapted to common Tunes* (Birmingham, 6th ed., 1790).

of that need, led to the furthering of river improvement
and thence to the construction of canals. The means to
their carrying out in Lancashire, Yorkshire, and elsewhere
were found in the resources of merchants and country
gentlemen. An investing public came into being who, in
their enterprise and their credulous optimism, were the true
parents of the railway maniacs of George Hudson's day.
In the early days of the Restoration Andrew Yarranton had
shown how Dutch experience in river engineering could be
applied in this country. Before the eighteenth century
opened, some progress had been achieved in Lancashire,
where the Mersey was made navigable as far as Warrington.
In the first decade of the century Liverpool embarked upon
plans for the construction of a dock, and a River Weaver
Navigation Bill was promoted. In the speculative mania of
1719–20 these and quite a crop of river schemes attracted
attention.[1] The Weaver navigation was opposed by the
road interests, but a scheme by which Wigan coal could be
taken by water to the estuary of the Ribble slipped through
Parliament, only to be left undeveloped upon the bursting
of the South Sea Bubble. Revived a few years later, this
River Douglas Navigation was ultimately carried through,
and with the Weaver and the Irwell and Mersey schemes
made a considerable contribution to Lancashire progress.

These early river improvements were typical of the dawn
of industrialism. They were opposed by particular interests,
such as the owners of river fisheries, and by justices of the
peace, who averred that only private profit, not public gain,
would be served by these projects. They were linked up
with road improvements, either originating in criticism of
the facilities for land communication or through requirements which were imposed on them to contribute out of
their earnings for the repair of highways. They made the
way both for further road developments and for further
river improvements, and they gave birth, in time, to canals.

The canal era proper may be dated conveniently from
1754. Two projects were brought forward in that year—one
for a 'cut' between Salford and Wigan by way of Leigh,
the other to connect the coalpits of St. Helens with Warrington and Liverpool. There followed soon after a Mersey-Trent

[1] A. P. Wadsworth and J. de L. Mann, *The Cotton Trade and Industrial
Lancashire* (1931), pp. 212 ff.

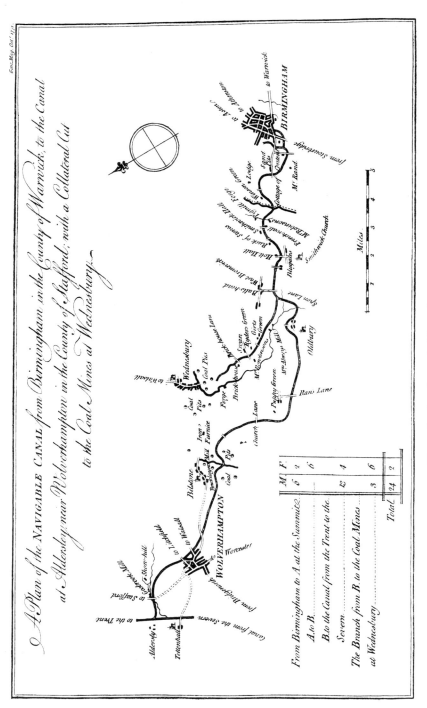

From the Gentleman's Magazine, *1771*

plan, and a plan for the extension of the Calder Navigation from Wakefield to Halifax. The possibilities of canals were in many people's minds. Some of these schemes had appeared earlier. They and others had already a backing in thoughtful opinion. Dean Tucker, in his *Instructions for Travellers*, opined that there were not many rivers naturally navigable in this country, and that 'the high Tolls or Duties laid upon' those that had been rendered navigable were 'a great check to Navigation'. But further improvements might be made 'at the public Expense, under the Direction of the Board of Trade', and England 'might be intersected at least in 8 or 10 places, so as to open a Communication with almost every Town of Note throughout the Kingdom'. He instanced as the more obvious communications which might be made links between 'the *Avon* of Bristol, the *Kennet* and the *Thames*—the *Avon* of Bristol and the *Avon* of Salisbury—the *Avon* of Bristol and the *Thames* by way of Letchlade and Cricklade—also between the *Severn*, the *Stroud* and (by the Help of a short Land Carriage) to Cirencester, and so on to the *Thames* at Cricklade—the *Severn*, the *Steur*, the *Penk*, the *Trent*, and the *Humber*—the *Severn*, the *Avon* (of Stratford) with a small Land Carriage to Banbury on the *Charwell*, and so to the *Isis* at Oxford.'[1] If the list was a little parochial, the reverend economist was at any rate thinking in terms of the future. So was the Duke of Bridgewater, who took up a plan his father had toyed with twenty years before, got his Worsley collieries linked up with Manchester in 1761, and then found the half-illiterate Brindley's magnificent imagination irresistible. Bridgewater realized that high transport costs narrowed the market for his coal. He saw the social as well as the economic relief that a reduction of these costs would bring. Brindley, a millwright by trade, was able to persuade the Duke that the canal idea was quite practicable. Both had unlimited courage and determination. The untaught civil engineer carried through a series of brilliant engineering exploits, and his employer a series of brilliant financial exploits, so important that they deserved even Smiles's Victorian eulogies.[2] But these things should be described in terms wider than those of individual heroism. The promoters and

[1] *Instructions for Travellers* (1757) in *Selected Works*, pp. 232–3.
[2] In *Lives of the Engineers*, vol. i.

organizers of the canal system were the business men of the day; the non-business community, whether the greater or lesser landowners, came but slowly to follow the pioneers' lead; the speculators did not achieve a canal mania till 1793. The gap between initial survey and accomplishment was usually a long one, though a million pounds had been expended on Lancashire and Cheshire schemes by 1780. The Birmingham innkeeper sang that

> *Navigation Bills* create,
> Strange confusion, strange debate;
> Public good, the stale pretence,
> Mockery is to common sense;
> With the OLD and with the NEW,
> Lucre is the only view.[1]

It was the canal that mattered, of course, not the financial opportunism or the obstructiveness of promoters or opponents. The enrichment of the life of the community was of first-class importance, however much the proprietors of a superseded river navigation might complain. Pennant, in his *Journey from Chester to London* (1782), singled out a fundamental gain.

Notwithstanding the clamors which have been raised against this undertaking [he wrote of the Grand Trunk Canal, by which Trent and Mersey were linked together] in the places through which it was intended to pass, we have the pleasure now to see content reign universally on its banks, and plenty attend its progress. . . . The cottage, instead of being half-covered with miserable thatch, is now covered with a substantial covering of tiles or slates, brought from the distant hills of Wales or Cumberland. The fields, which before were barren, are now drained, and, by the assistance of manure, conveyed on the canal toll-free, are cloathed with a beautiful verdure. Places which rarely knew the use of coal, are plentifully supplied with that essential article upon reasonable terms; and, what is of still greater public utility, the monopolizers of corn are prevented from exercising their infamous trade; for, the communication being opened between Liverpool, Bristol, and Hull, and the line of canal being through countries abundant in grain, it affords a conveyance of corn unknown to past ages. At present, nothing but a general dearth can create a scarcity in any part adjacent to this extensive work.[2]

The conquest of local famine marks a stage in the history of

---

[1] J. Freeth, *The Political Songster*, pp. 61–2.
[2] T. Pennant, *A Journey from Chester to London* (1782), p. 75.

THE BRIDGEWATER CANAL AT BARTON BRIDGE, 1794

any civilization. The gains resulting from reduced transport costs are equally noteworthy, and with them must be reckoned the gains that issued from increased transport facilities. Fortunately the canal companies were not allowed to be public carriers on their navigation systems till 1845, and those who organized the quick or fly trade and the slow or heavy trade could specialize on the development of adequate services. The early attempts to develop passenger services—the Duke of Bridgewater made useful profits from his packet-boats for passengers—did not amount to much, though canal transport for poor law children, for whom speed of transit was of no urgency, and cheapness was paramount, survived to Victorian days. The secrecy of the canal transport agencies about their operations and the personal character of their relationship to their clients makes any exact estimate of their influence upon the cost of commodities impossible. That they successfully challenged highway services is unmistakeable and that they reduced the charges for goods of all sorts very considerably is equally certain. Professor Jackman's very careful estimate is that 'the cost of canal carriage normally did not exceed one-half, and in most cases was from one-fourth to one-third, of the cost of land carriage'.[1] The speed, however, even of the fly-boats was under four miles an hour, and of the heavy barges about half that. Resourceful experiments were made by Jonathan Hulls in 1736; the Duke of Bridgewater tried steamboats for towing barges a generation later; hundreds of spectators watched Symington's steam-boats move at five miles an hour in 1788, and seven miles an hour in 1789. But the elaboration of these precocious efforts belongs to a later period. It was the horse- or man-hauled barge that won success in Johnson's England. Its achievements and its possibilities, demonstrated beyond cavil by the Bridgewater-Brindley combination, led to the rapid linking up in the second half of the century of all the main centres of expanding economic activity and of some areas whose promise remains unfulfilled. 'How is the whole face of this country changed in about twenty years!' said that indefatigable traveller, John Wesley, of the Potteries, 'and the country is not more improved than the people.'[2]

1 W. T. Jackman, op. cit., vol. i, p. 449.
2 John Wesley, *Journal* (ed. Curnock), vol. vi, pp. 309–10.

The establishment of Palmer's mail-coaches is an epoch in the history of postal services as well as in the history of travelling. Between 1720, when Ralph Allen was raised from the postmastership of Bath to a position of national importance in the postal service, and the advent of Palmer, the most that can be said was that the English system was improving and better than that of most countries. That was the opinion of Macky, who in the early years of Allen's work, described the English Post Office as the best in Europe. 'Here everything is so regularly disposed, that Villages at the greatest distances from the great Roads are truly served.'[1] It was Miege's view forty years later: 'There is no considerable market-town in England but has an easy and certain conveyance for all letters. The charge thereof is easy, and the expedition very great and convenient'.[2] But these were generous views. Corruption prevailed to a truly oriental extent, and safety was by no means assured. The privilege of 'franking' had been made to cover the postal costs of a host of people who could afford to pay them, and a good deal of fraud as well. Parliament tried to check the abuse of franking in 1764 but failed. No right to compensation was admitted for the losses sustained in the post. For a variety of reasons, then, the habit of using non-governmental postal facilities was firmly established. The Post Office was unpopular, and not undeservedly. Delays, inconvenience, cost, irregularity, and uncertainty were all too common. An increase of charges was momentarily threatened when turnpike trustees carried out their statutory obligation to erect milestones on the roads they maintained. Statute miles were much shorter than post office miles; Edinburgh was measured thus as 339 miles from London; formerly it had been counted as 262 miles distant. Costs were adjusted for the traveller, which is largely the explanation of the increased charges of which travellers complained, but the old mileage was retained for the post. This forbearance to exact the pound of legal flesh was valuable. So was Allen's reorganization of the cross posts, and the Postmaster General's improvement of the express posts. The old habit of travelling post on horseback gave place to travelling by post-coach, to the detriment of the innkeepers (save when they were postmasters), who had

---

[1] J. Macky, *Journey through England* (1722), vol. i, p. 233.
[2] G. Miege, *Present State of Gt. Britain* (revised by S. Bolton, 1757), p. 150.

supplied a service of horses. After Allen's death in 1764 a further enlargement of mail services was carried out, but progress was insufficient for growing needs. A legal case cleared obstacles out of the way in 1774. It was decided that within the limits of a postal area the delivery of mail should be free. The slow response to the demand for improvement, even after this case had turned against the Post Office, showed the need of new ideas. These came from the outside, again from Bath, where John Palmer was a theatre-proprietor. He had kept his eyes open, and observed what the weaknesses were which crippled the postal system. His idea was to combine passenger travel and mail delivery, and make the former pay for the latter. The post-coach should be speedy—not slower than the stage-coach as it was—and safe. Fortunately England had Pitt in office. He insisted on Palmer's system being given a trial, and it was an immediate success. On 2nd August, 1784, the first mail coach ran from Bristol to London. Palmer's promises were kept. The journey ordinarily took seventeen hours, and soon the mail-coach was familiar on all the main roads of England. The work done under Palmer as Comptroller-General was epoch-making. It included the ending of mail-robberies, and the provision of a mail service that was abreast of the times. That service contributed in no mean way to economic progress.

To the inland postal improvements was added reform of the Continental mails.[1] By Dover and Harwich there were two posts a week, but they were in doubtful hands. The packets had a bad record for smuggling at Harwich, and Falmouth was no better. There were only thirty-six packets altogether, twenty-one being at Falmouth, but though only small vessels, their cost exceeded a million pounds a year.[2] The grossest corruption existed, but it was ended in 1787.

Travellers coming into England or leaving it usually have more to say about the weather they experienced than about the quality of their accommodation on board. It was common to travel in ships engaged in trade. Regular packets, running two and later three times a week, had been established by the middle of the century, but these services were

---

[1] Details are given in H. Joyce, *History of the Post Office* (1893), pp. 236–48.
[2] The Falmouth packets are described by a seaman named Samuel Kelly. See his Autobiography, edited by Crosbie Garstin (1925).

supplemented as traffic demanded. The usual route to France was between Dover and Calais, but there were crossings from other ports as well, and these included Brighton and Rye, from which there were sailings to Dieppe and Boulogne respectively. The passage was sometimes long, and often it was delayed till a full complement of passengers had been made up. There was discomfort at landing when the tide was low or weather conditions were bad. Whatever the conditions, nothing checked the rage for Continental travel. In the earlier part of the century the polite world toured to Italy; in the later France was more popular. The comprehensive tour included both.

The English, said the Abbé Le Blanc in 1745, 'look on their isle as a prison; and the first use they make of their love of liberty is to get out of it'. Horace Walpole suggested that 'gaming has transported half' of those English people who were swarming in France, Nice, and Switzerland. Whatever the impulse that urged people to foreign travel, its strength grew greater as the century advanced. The Grand Tour became, in fact, a habit of the wealthy. 'Where one Englishman travelled in the reigns of the first two Georges', it was said, 'ten now go on a grand tour. Indeed, to such a pitch is the spirit of travelling come in the kingdom, that there is scarce a citizen of large fortune but takes a flying view of France, Italy and Germany in a summer's excursion.'[1] As a form of education the Continental tour was scarcely comparable with the period of residence at a foreign university which was then a common custom. It had a different object and was designed to be educational in a broader sense. Its value was conceived to be social and political rather than academic. Professors from the Universities or clerics of the established Church could be hired as travelling tutors. The language of France or Italy could be studied. The tourists, armed with letters of introduction, could meet interesting people. And they could all enjoy themselves. The history of so admirably conceived an institution remains to be written. There is an abundance of evidence of interesting contacts established on foreign soil; cross-currents in literature, political thought, and behaviour, thus initiated, can be charted. To what extent the Grand Tour really was a liberal education it would be diffi-

[1] *Letters concerning the Present State of England* (1772), p. 240.

cult to say. It doubtless yielded varying results. To some it was adventure and no more; to others it brought the broadening of horizons; to others still, a wild-oats interlude before the serious business of life and career-making began. There is no need to take too seriously Dean Tucker's explanation of the Grand Tour as a social institution, that it was a device of parents to get rid of their sons during a troublesome period of their careers. In his *Instructions for Travellers* (1757), which was *A Plan for improving in the Moral and Political Theory of Trade and Taxes by means of Travelling*, the Dean tempers his acidity by a recognition of other reasons for foreign travel.

Persons who propose to themselves a Scheme for Travelling, generally do it with a View to obtain one or more of the following Ends, viz. *First*, to make curious Collections, as Natural Philosophers, Virtuosos, or Antiquarians. *Secondly*, to improve in Painting, Statuary, Architecture and Music, *Thirdly*, To obtain the reputation of being Men of Vertu, and of an elegant Taste. *Fourthly*, To acquire foreign Airs, and adorn their dear Persons with fine Cloaths and new Fashions, and their Conversation with new Phrases. Or *Fifthly*, To rub off local Prejudices (which is indeed the most commendable Motive, though not the most prevailing) and to acquire that impartial view of Men and Things, which no one single Country can afford. . . . As to that Species of Beings found only here in England (a Country of universal Freedom and Opulence) who go abroad with no other view but because they are tired of staying at Home, and can afford to make themselves as ridiculous every where as they please: It would be a Loss of Time to take any other Notice of them, than just to observe, that they are sure of returning Home as Wise as they went out, but much more Impertinent, less Wealthy, and less Innocent.[1]

Tucker's view instantly recalls that of his fellow economist Adam Smith, twenty years later.

In England [wrote Smith] it becomes every day more and more the custom to send young people to travel in foreign countries immediately upon their leaving school, and without sending them to any university. . . . In the course of his travels a young man generally acquires some knowledge of one or two foreign languages; a knowledge, however, which is seldom sufficient to enable him either to speak or write them with propriety. In other respects he commonly returns home more conceited, more unprincipled, more dissipated, and more incapable of any serious application, either to study or to

---

[1] *Instructions for Travellers* in *Selected Works*, pp. 223–4.

business, than he could well have become in so short a time had he lived at home.[1]

As travelling Tutor to the Duke of Buccleuch, Adam Smith had had a studious and well-behaved pupil; he had been well paid and had acquired a life pension of £300 a year. His indictment of the system must presumably have been due to the character of the grand-tourists whom he observed on his travels.

Jonas Hanway, Merchant, who wrote an interesting journal of his travels into Russia and Persia, closed his book with a series of moral and political reflexions inspired by his experience. It was his view that the passage of a merchant from one country to another should not be regarded in the same light as the travels of a man of letters in search of arts or learning.

But if in the course of their observations they have supported one common spirit of national affection; in proportion to their advantages of education and national abilities, the effect will be in a great degree similar. Their own country must necessarily become the dearer to them, according as they discover the superiority it enjoys in laws and government above other nations. Being thus excited by a generous emulation instead of bringing home the vices of other countries, they will strive to plant the virtues which are more peculiar to foreign climes, and not the proper growth of their own soil.[2]

A travelling age could not but discover how English England was. That discovery was quite inevitably a powerful influence. It explains much of what happened in the transition from Johnson's England to the England of Queen Victoria.

BIBLIOGRAPHY.—A. *Contemporary sources:*

(a) Foreign Travellers in England: DON MANOEL GONZALES, *The Voyage of . . . late Merchant of the City of Lisbon, to Gt. Britain 1731* (1808); C. DE SAUSSURE, *A Foreign View of England in the the Reigns of George I & II* (1902); W. WENDEBORN, *View of England towards the Close of the 18th century* (1791); *Travels of Carl Philipp Moritz in England in 1782* (ed. Matheson, 1924); B. FAUJAS ST. FOND, *Travels through England and Scotland in 1784* (ed. Geikie, 1908); M. GROSLEY, *A Tour to London, 1765* (1773); P. KALM, *Visit to England* (1748); M. L'ABBÉ LE BLANC, *Letters on the English and French Nations* (1747); DU BOCCAGE, *Letters Concerning England, Holland and Italy, 1750,* (1770).

(b) British Travellers in England: D. DEFOE, *Tour through the Whole Island of Gt. Britain* (1st ed. 1724–7, and of subsequent editions those of 1748 and 1778); J. WESLEY'S *Journal*; G. MIEGE, *Present State of Great Britain and Ireland* (1757); THOMAS SOMERVILLE, *My Own Life and Times, 1741–1814*

---

[1] *Wealth of Nations* (ed. Cannan), vol. ii, p. 261.
[2] Hanway, *Travels*, vol. ii, pp. 349–50.

(1861); R. Pococke, *Travels through England in 1750 and 1751* (2 vols., 1888–9);
R. Patching, *Four Topographical Letters written in July 1755*; A. Young,
A Six Weeks Tour through the Southern Counties (1768); *A Six Months Tour
through the North of England* (1771); *The Farmer's Tour through the East of
England* (1771); *The Farmer's Letters to the People of England* (1767);
The Travels of the Imagination (1773); J. Pennant, *Journey from Chester to
London* (1782); *Tour from London to Isle of Wight, 1787* (1801); S. Shaw,
Tour to West of England in 1788 (in Pinkerton's *Voyages*, vol. ii).

(c) Road construction and management: J. Shapleigh, *Highways* (1749);
R. Brown, *Description of the Present Great Roads and Principal Cross Roads*
(1765); J. Hawkins, *Observations on the State of the Highways* (1763); H. Homer,
Inquiry into the Means of Preserving and Improving the Public Roads (1767);
B. Bayley, *Observations on the General Highway and Turnpike Acts* (1773);
D. Brown, *A Treatise upon Wheel Carriages* (1763); John Metcalf, *His Life*
(1795). J. Cary, *New Itinerary; or Delineation of the Great Roads throughout
England and Wales* (7th ed., 1817).

(d) River and Canal Improvements: R. Whitworth, *The Advantages
of Inland Navigation* (1766); Anon., *The History of Inland Navigation* (1766);
J. Phillips, *A Treatise on Inland Navigation* (1785); E. Leach, *A Treatise of
Universal Inland Navigation* (1790); J. Cary, *Inland Navigation* (1793);
P. Colquhoun, *A Treatise on the Commerce and Police of the River Thames*
(1800).

(e) Periodicals: *The Annual Register; The Gentleman's Magazine; The London
Magazine; The Grand Magazine of Universal Intelligence.*

B. *Secondary Works:* W. T. Jackman, *The Development of Transportation
in Modern England* (2 vols., 1916). Contains a very full bibliography of printed
and manuscript material; the most careful survey of the history of inland
transportation yet made. S. & B. Webb, *English Local Government: The Story
of the King's Highway* (1920). Primarily a study in road administration;
invaluable for its copious references to contemporary sources. C. H. Hartmann,
The Story of the Roads (1927). Popular short history. S. Smiles, *Lives of the
Engineers* (3 vols., 1861; many reprints). E. A. Pratt, *History of Inland
Transport* (1912). H. Joyce, *History of the Post Office down to 1836* (1893).
A. D. Smith. *Development of Rates of Postage* (1917). J. C. Hemmeon, *The
History of the British Post Office* (1912). C. Maxwell, *The English Traveller in
France, 1689–1815* (1932). Mainly extracts from contemporary travellers.
Useful bibliography. G. Sheldon, *From Trackway to Turnpike* (1928).
Traces the history of Devonshire roads. R. C. Tombs, *Bristol Royal Mail* (1899),
The King's Post (1905). W. Gilbey, *Early Carriages and Roads* (1903).
S. Harris, *Old Coaching Days* (1882). *The Coaching Age* (1885). A. Groom,
Old London Coaching Inns and their Successors (1928). C. G. Harper, *The Old
Inns of Old England* (2 vols., 1906). A. E. Richardson & H. D. Eberlein,
The English Inn, Past & Present (1925).

VII

LONDON AND THE LIFE OF THE TOWN

By M. DOROTHY GEORGE

Why, Sir, Fleet-street has a very animated appearance; but I think the full tide of human existence is at Charing-cross.—*Life of Johnson* (2 April 1775).

When a man is tired of London, he is tired of life.—*Life of Johnson* (20 Sept. 1777).

> What's not destroy'd by Time's destroying hand?
> Where's Troy, and where's the may-pole in the Strand?
> Pease, cabbages, and turnips once grew, where,
> Now stands New Bond-street, and a newer square;
> Such piles of buildings now rise up and down,
> London itself seems going out of town.
> Our fathers cross'd from Fulham in a wherry,
> Their sons enjoy a bridge at Putney-ferry.
>
> J. BRAMSTON, *The Art of Politicks*, 1729.

IT would be hard to exaggerate the importance of London in Johnson's England: in life and letters, in politics, in commerce, the capital played a more important part in the country then than now. 'On peut dire que toute l'Angleterre est condensée dans sa capitale', wrote a foreign visitor in 1741.[1] And Johnson's own deep affection for London and his close association with almost every side of London life give it a very special interest. London was the only great urban community in the kingdom, the only place where town life was cut off from country life—where the country visitor was like a being from another world. Its glamour was correspondingly great; it was a miracle of wealth and splendour, its crimes and its luxury, its pleasures and its opportunities were legendary:

> Such London is, by taste and wealth proclaim'd
> The fairest capital of all the world,
> By riot and incontinence the worst.
>
> Cowper, *The Task*, Book i, ll. 697–9.

'He that is tired of London is tired of life, for there is in London all that life can afford', said Johnson after thirty years of life there. 'London, good God,' wrote Chatterton after a few days in town, 'how superior is London to that despicable place Bristol!'

[1] *Lettres du Baron de Bielfeld* (2 vols., 1763), vol. i, p. 264.

A View of LONDON BRIDGE before the late Alteration as in the Year 1757.

Engraved from the Original Painting.

London was growing with a rapidity which seemed dangerous and portentous: its growth and its many places of amusement were thought to be the chief signs of a tide of luxury
which threatened to submerge the nation. It was a common
topic that the capital was 'a head too big for the body', and
when Cobbett called it a wen he was repeating a commonplace
of two centuries.[1]

To the intelligent foreigners who visited England in such
numbers, London was the epitome of a country strangely
different from the rest of Europe. To quote Archenholtz, a
Prussian, 'England is so different from all the other states of
Europe in the forms of its government, in its laws, its customs, and in the sentiments and manners of its inhabitants,
that it almost seems to belong to another globe. . . .'

During Johnson's literary life there, London was constantly changing, and the accumulated changes of nearly
half a century were revolutionary. A process of civilization
was going on, both in the aspect of the town and in the
manners of its inhabitants; it grew more rapidly in bricks
and mortar than in population; the streets which had been
notorious, even by the standards of the day, for dirt and
unevenness, became the admiration of Europe. When Johnson came to London in 1737, it was the London which
Hogarth has drawn—the London of *Gin Lane* and the *Four
Stages of Cruelty*. There was only one bridge over the river
and the houses were still standing on it. In spite of the ever
increasing number of coaches and carts the Thames was
still a main thoroughfare. The streets were filthy and ill-
paved, the kennel (channel) in the middle was the natural
receptacle for dead cats, as in Hogarth's *Morning*. From the
houses in Cheapside and Fleet Street and elsewhere huge
signs swung on ornamental iron brackets, often decorated
with dangling casks or bunches of grapes, or other emblems
of the wares for sale. They were often beautiful, but
they obstructed light and air, and in a wind they creaked

---

[1] 'London . . . has been complained of for ages past as a kind of monster,
with a head enormously large, and out of all proportion to its body. . . . And
yet . . . when this complaint was first made (about 200 years ago) the buildings
. . . hardly advanced beyond the City bounds. . . . If therefore the increase of
buildings . . . was looked upon to be no better than a wen or excrescence upon
the body politic, what must we think of those numberless streets and squares
which have been added since?' J. Tucker, *Four Letters to the Earl of Shelburne*
(1773), pp. 174, 182.

atrociously. Temple Bar was still regarded as the appropriate place for the heads of traitors. In August 1746 Horace Walpole 'passed under the new heads at Temple Bar where people make trade of letting spy-glasses at a half-penny a look'. These were the heads which Goldsmith pointed out to Johnson, repeating to him the words which Johnson had just quoted in the Poets' Corner in the Abbey: *Forsitan et nostrum nomen miscebitur* ISTIS. There were other executions for treason in Johnson's lifetime, but the Jacobites of 1746 were the last whose heads adorned Temple Bar.

In many things, the signs, the posts in the streets, the greasy uneven cobbles, the London of 1737 was still the London of Gay and Swift. But it was not quite the London of the Mohocks and Jonathan Wild; the process of civilization was going on and a significant change was noted by Johnson: 'In the last age, when my mother lived in London, there were two sets of people, those who gave the wall and those who took it: the peaceable and the quarrelsome. *Now* it is fixed that every man keeps to the right: or, if one is taking the wall, another yields it; and it is never a dispute.' Gay (in 1716) had advised the walker not to attempt to regain the wall if he had once relinquished it:

> Yet rather bear the show'r, and toils of mud
> Than in the doubtful quarrel risque thy blood. *(Trivia.)*

It is true that Johnson wrote in *London*,

> Prepare for death if here at night you roam,
> And sign your will before you sup from home,

and it is true that watchmen and harmless citizens were sometimes the victims of drunken broils, and footpads were far from uncommon, but on the whole the streets were growing safer, and as compared with foreign cities they seemed safe. Gay himself had written,

> Happy Augusta, law-defended town!

A new London was growing up in the west in complete contrast with the older parts of the town, but in 1737 the western part of Piccadilly was still bordered by inns and the yards of statuarys and stone-masons. May Fair still meant a disorderly fair carried on in May on ground behind Piccadilly, to the annoyance of the 'Great', whose houses were fast encroaching on the fields. Georgian London, though so much

more compact than modern London, was to a far greater
extent a collection of different districts and different worlds.
The cleavage between the City and St. James's—'the polite
end of the town'—was profound, fostered by social, political,
and commercial jealousies. The City's narrow tortuous streets
(some main thoroughfares excepted) were very different from
the streets and squares of the new London which was growing
up on both sides of the Tyburn Road. The City was associated with wealth, vulgarity, and factiousness in politics—
a tradition dating at least from the Restoration. Addison's
survey holds good for Johnson's London:

When I consider this great city in its several quarters and divisions,
I look upon it as an aggregate of various nations, distinguished from
each other by their respective customs, manners, and interests. The
courts of two countries do not so much differ from one another, as
the court and city, in their peculiar ways of life and conversation. In
short, the inhabitants of St. James's, notwithstanding they live under
the same laws, and speak the same language, are a distinct people
from those of Cheapside, who are likewise removed from those of
the Temple on the one side, and those of Smithfield on the other, by
several climates and degrees in their ways of thinking and conversing
together.

The cleavage was accentuated by the drift of fashion
westwards.

Within the memory of many now living [wrote Fielding in 1752]
the circle of the People of Fascination included the whole parish of
Covent Garden and a great part of St. Giles in the Fields: but here
the enemy broke in and the circle was presently contracted to
Leicester Fields and Golden Square. Hence the People of Fashion
again retreated before the foe to Hanover Square: whence they were
once more driven to Grosvenor Square and even beyond it, and that
with so much precipitation, that had they not been stopped by the
walls of Hyde Park, it is more than probable they would by this
time have arrived at Kensington.

The topography of this must not be taken too literally
though it is substantially sound. And Fielding rightly called
people of fashion, 'People of Fascination': the stigma of
living among 'cits' appears in the shame with which Evelina
admits to Lord Orville that she is staying 'in Holborn'.

The City, a world apart, within its Bars and its gates, was
a barrier between residential London on the west and industrial London on the east. London was spreading east as

well as west. On the west, town-planning was actually in process on the building estates of the great ground landlords, where the names of streets and squares record the names, marriages, and properties of the governing families who were so powerful in the eighteenth century.[1] These plans were based on squares as centres for streets intersecting at right angles. When Johnson came to London, Cavendish and Hanover Squares were not twenty years old; Grosvenor Square, its garden designed by Kent, was the latest and the most admired of the squares; Berkeley Square was not yet finished, though it had been designed many years before. The new parish of St. George's, Hanover Square, the church consecrated in 1724, had been carved out of St. Martin's-in-the-Fields as a result of the rapid building on the Grosvenor estate.

On the east, the development was almost entirely without plan. Along the river there was an urban belt of varying width stretching to Limehouse. Wapping was a world apart, largely given up to sailors and the harpies who preyed upon them. Johnson, speaking to Boswell and Windham of 'the wonderful extent and variety of London', 'observed that men of curious enquiry might see in it such modes of life as few could even imagine'. 'He in particular', writes Boswell, 'recommended us to *explore Wapping* which we resolved to do.' When at last they did explore it, in 1792, Boswell records, 'Whether from that uniformity which has in modern times, in a great degree, spread through every part of the Metropolis, or from our want of sufficient exertion, we were disappointed'.

The beauty of the river, crowded with shipping, was some compensation to the riverside parishes for the squalor of their lanes and alleys. Wapping was distinguished by the gallows at Execution Dock, still the place for the execution of pirates at low tide. Its open spaces were chiefly rope-walks.

[1] A good example of this nomenclature is the Harley building estate: Cavendish Square, Henrietta and Holles Streets are named after the wife of Edward Harley who succeeded his better-known father as Earl of Oxford in 1724 and died in 1741. She was Henrietta Cavendish Holles, daughter of the Duke of Newcastle. Margaret Street was probably named after this lady's mother. Oxford and Mortimer Streets record the family titles; Harley Street the family name; Welbeck and Wimpole Streets the family estates. Vere Street appears intended to imply a connexion with the de Veres, Earls of Oxford, which did not in fact exist. See G. E. C., *Complete Peerage*, vol. vi (1893), p. 177 n.

Shoreditch and Whitechapel were urban and squalid. The journeymen weavers had spread eastwards from Spitalfields to Mile End and Bethnal Green, still technically hamlets, with a population of the poorest sort. There was a straggling ribbon development along the highways: the great Essex Road leading from Aldgate through Whitechapel; the Ratcliffe Highway with an evil reputation. This district was partly rural, partly industrial: among fields and market gardens were tenter grounds and small, closely-packed industrial settlements. All these eastern parishes were 'burdened with a numerous poor', as the ratepayers constantly complain.

To the north of the City the watchmakers were taking possession of Clerkenwell. The chief industries of Islington were 'cow-keeping' for the London milk-supply, and the numerous tea gardens and places of entertainment which were so crowded on Sundays and holidays. Hackney was still almost rural. It had been deserted by the quality, but was noted for its boarding schools and the number of 'country boxes' belonging to well-to-do citizens.

While on the east and north-east London merged squalidly into the fields, in the more fashionable quarters the town was defined, and the prospect of the 'northern heights' was carefully cherished. Great Ormond Street, like Great Russell Street, was part of the frontier of London. Queen Anne's Square had been left open to the north for the sake of the view. Bedford House filled the north side of Bloomsbury Square and like Montagu House in Great Russell Street faced London on one side, the country on the other. Tottenham Court Road, its south end abutting on the squalid district of St. Giles, still (in 1737) ran chiefly through fields and was bordered with cow houses and farms. Tottenham Court, a hamlet at its northern end, the scene of Hogarth's *March to Finchley*, was famed for its inns and tea gardens. St. Pancras was a small village in the fields. Although building had begun in the south-east of the parish of Marylebone round Cavendish Square, the old village of Marylebone was still partly rural and famed for the goodness of its air. Cavendish Square looked northwards over open fields. Lord Oxford had built Oxford Market and a chapel (in Vere Street) to encourage building on his estate, but 'the new buildings' did not extend beyond Vere Street on the west. Wigmore Row (now Street) was built only on one side, and the old White Hart inn in the new (and partly built) Welbeck Street was the place for examining pistols before crossing the fields to Lissen Green (now Lisson Grove), which was part of the country village of Paddington.

South of the Tyburn Road, building was proceeding actively, but it seemed as if the wall of Hyde Park was a permanent boundary to London. Lanesborough House, a recent outpost of London at Hyde Park Corner, had become St. George's Hospital, opened in 1734. Buckingham House stood at the west end of St. James's Park; behind it were marshy fields. Surrounding the Abbey was old Westminster, which had changed comparatively little since the Civil War. The new church of St. John's was the centre of a new and poor district bounded to the west by the curve of Horseferry Road. The common of Tothill Fields was an open space of squalid character into which Rochester Row projected, a line of almshouses and charity schools. On the river at Mill Bank, the site now occupied by Mowlem's yards, was Grosvenor House, long regarded as the last house in London. Beyond it the Five Fields stretched to Chelsea. The parishes on the south of the river had their own character and their own trades. The northern part of the Borough was old and closely built; its great inns had long been the head-quarters of much of the traffic with the southern counties. Such was the extent of the capital when Johnson and Garrick arrived there from Lichfield.

To do justice to the changes in London between 1737 and 1784 would need a volume. Among the chief landmarks are the arching over of the Fleet river ('a stinking and offensive ditch') for some distance north of the Thames, and the building of Fleet Market, opened in 1737 on the ground thus gained. The Stocks Market was then closed and the site was used for the Mansion House. This did much to alter the appearance of the City. The building of Westminster Bridge was begun in 1738; at midnight on November 17, 1750, it was opened for traffic. It was immensely admired and was generally regarded as the finest bridge in Europe. A view was thrown open of the curve of the river to Somerset House and St. Paul's (the view of Wordsworth's sonnet), and it became at once one of the favourite 'walks'. 'The surprising echo in the arches, brings much company with French horns to entertain themselves under it in summer; and with the upper part, for an agreeable airing, none of the public walks or gardens can stand in competition', said the *Gentleman's Magazine*.[1] It roused the jealous emulation of the City: in 1757 London Bridge was widened and the houses were cleared away, and after many delays Blackfriars Bridge was opened to wheeled traffic in 1769.[2]

Between 1760 and 1767 the City gates were taken down. In Westminster two older and more interesting gates were sacrificed to improvements. Parliament Street (like Bridge Street) was cut through some squalid places, but it involved the destruction in 1759 of the beautiful gate next the Banqueting House known as Holbein's Gate.

Another significant change in Westminster was the extension of building on the west of the Green Park, obscuring the view of the open country which had been its great beauty. George III wanted to buy the ground for the gardens of Buckingham House, but Grenville refused him the necessary £20,000 from the Treasury; the fields were sold to builders, and houses were built on the site of what is now Grosvenor Gardens.[3]

During the whole time building was in progress on both sides of the Tyburn Road (or Oxford Street); about 1764 Portman Square was begun and was the centre of a district then spoken of as 'the new buildings in Marylebone'. A little later systematic building began both west and east of Tottenham Court Road. 'Rows of houses shoot out every way like a polypus,' Walpole wrote to Mann in 1776; 'and, so great is the rage of building every where, that, if I stay here a fortnight, without going to town, I look about to see if no new house is built since I went last. America and France must tell us how long this exuberance of opulence is to last.' There was in fact some check to speculative building during the American War, and a fresh wave of activity directly after it.

But in the meantime the town had been transformed by

---

[1] 1750, vol. xx, p. 586.

[2] The Act was obtained in 1756; the first pile was driven in 1760. Johnson in the interests of his friend Gwynne advocated the semi-circular arch in three letters to the *Gazetteer*, in place of the elliptical arch of Mylne which was adopted. Wheatley and Cunningham, *London Past and Present* (1910). See also *The Architect* (1877), pp. 13 ff.

[3] H. Walpole, *Memoirs of the Reign of George III* (1845 ed.), vol. ii, p. 160; vol. iii, p. 4.

the removal of the signs and by the paving of the streets on
a new system. This was done by a series of Acts obtained by
different parishes and districts, but only after many previous
attempts had been defeated. Johnson himself describes the
state of the streets before the new Acts, in a speech which he
puts into the mouth of Lord Tyrconnel during a debate in
1741 on one of these abortive Paving Bills:

The filth, Sir, of some parts of the town, and the inequality and
ruggedness of others, cannot but in the eyes of foreigners disgrace our
nation, and incline them to imagine us a people, not only without
government, but without delicacy, a herd of Barbarians, or a colony
of Hottentots. The most disgusting part of the character given by
travellers, of the most savage nations, is their neglect of cleanliness,
of which, perhaps, no part of the world affords more proofs, than the
streets of the British capital: a city famous for wealth, commerce, and
plenty, and for every other kind of civility and politeness, but which
abounds with such heaps of filth, as a savage would look on with
amazement.

If that be allowed which is generally believed, that putrefaction
and stench are causes of pestilential distempers; the removal of this
grievance may be pressed from motives of far greater weight than
those of delicacy and pleasure. . . .

That the present neglect of cleansing and paving the streets, is such
as ought not to be borne, that the passenger is every where either
surprised and endangered by neglected chasms, or offended and
obstructed by mountains of filth, is well known to every one that
has passed a single day in this great city; and that this grievance is
without remedy, is a sufficient proof, that no magistrate has at
present power to remove it. . . .

When at last, twenty-one years after these words were
written 'in a garret in Exeter Street', the old, hopeless system,
by which every man was responsible for removing the dirt
and mending the pavement in front of his own door, was
given up, things rapidly altered. The first of the Westminster
Acts was in 1762; the City followed in 1766. Raised foot-
pavements replaced the protective posts, and flat stones the
'uneasy pebbles' of the roadway. The signs were removed or
placed flat against the houses. Boydell's print shop is no
longer 'The Unicorn, the corner of Queen Street in Cheapside', but '90 Cheapside'. Clearly something was lost when
the signs went, but they were unregretted. To quote the
biographer of Jonas Hanway, a pioneer of civic improvement:

How comfortless must be the sensations of an elderly female, stopped in the street on a windy day, under a large old sign loaded with lead and iron in full swing over her head, and perhaps a torrent of rain and dirty water falling near from a projecting spout, ornamented with the mouth and teeth of a dragon. These dangers and distresses are now [1787] at an end; and we may think of them as the sailor does of a storm that has subsided, but the advantages derived from the present uniformity and cleanliness can be known only in their full extent by comparing them with the former inconveniencies.[1]

Hence the neglect of an important phase of London history by modern writers. The removal of the filthy broken pavements was an important part of the transformation which caused a marvellous improvement in the health of London. It also reversed the relative positions of London and Paris. Dr. Douglas, visiting Paris in 1749, found it much superior in point of 'pavements and cleanliness', although in breadth, length, and straightness of streets 'the greater part of London is far superior'.[2] By the seventies London visitors are shocked at the dirt of Paris. 'Mrs. Gregory and I', writes Mrs. Montagu, in 1776, 'are not yet cured of our astonishment at the dirtiness, the stinks, and the narrowness of the streets. . . .'[3]

The endless comparisons between London and Paris give the best view of the town as it appeared to contemporaries. No agreement was reached as to relative size and population: 'A quoi bon cette rivalité d'étendue et de population?' asks the Abbé Coyer. 'Plus les deux Capitales entasseront d'Hommes, plus il y aura d'infection dans l'atmosphère, plus de maladies épidémiques, plus de luxe, plus de cupidité, plus de cherté dans les vivres, plus de crimes; plus, en un mot, elles corrompront les deux Empires.' This was the luxury theory, expressed by Fielding, Goldsmith, Smollett, Cowper, and Dr. Priestley among a host of others, and consistently opposed by Johnson. Smollett, in the guise of Matthew Bramble, called the capital 'an overgrown monster, which, like a dropsical head, will in time leave the body and extremities without nourishment and support'. Though Johnson 'owned that London was too large', he added, 'it is nonsense to say the head is too big for the body'.

---

[1] Pugh, *Life of Jonas Hanway* (1787). Hanway had actively promoted the paving and improvement Acts.
[2] See the whole passage in C. Maxwell, *The English Traveller in France* (1932), pp. 68–72.
[3] *Mrs. Montagu, 'Queen of the Blues'* (ed. R. Blunt, 2 vols., 1923), vol. i, p. 327.

Foreigners in general were astonished at the way in which people of rank were content to live in houses in no way differing from those of rich merchants. The few private palaces were admired: Bedford House, Montagu House (which became the British Museum, opened to the public in 1759), Northumberland House, Burlington House, Chesterfield House, and a few others; but the general absence of the *porte cochère* and the *hôtel* surrounded by a wall never failed to surprise. The consequent uniformity and simplicity of the houses was often admired. Foreigners and natives alike agreed in despising St. James's Palace. Even Walpole called it 'the little tottering ruined palace in St. James's Street'. All were impressed by the magnificence of Greenwich and Chelsea Hospitals: 'Les Rois de la Grande Bretagne', wrote von Bielfeld, 'sont logés au Palais de St. James comme des invalides, et les invalides de l'Armée et de la Marine comme des Rois à Chelsea et à Greenwich.'[1] The safety of pedestrians in London (and their danger in Paris) was matter of universal comment. All these things, like the licence of the populace and the press, seemed to the foreign observer an outcome of English liberty: 'One sees that their laws are not made and executed entirely by those who always ride in chariots', recorded Madame Roland in 1784.

As for the traffic of the streets and the river no one disputed that this was incomparably greater in London than in Paris. All visitors to London, native and foreign, were impressed by the thronging crowds and ceaseless traffic. 'Most of the streets in Paris are as little frequented on week days as those of London on Sundays', wrote Dr. Douglas in 1749.[2] And in the eighties Wendeborn notes that 'more people are seen in London at midnight than in many considerable towns of Europe at noon-day'. The contrast of the two rivers was even more striking. The Seine had its quays, while the Thames could only be approached at certain stairs and landing-places, but the traffic was a delight to the eye.

---

[1] This appears to derive from,

> To lofty Chelsea, or to Greenwich dome,
> Soldiers and sailors all are welcom'd home.
> Her poor to palaces Britannia brings,
> St. James's hospital may serve for kings.
>
> BRAMSTON, *The Man of Taste* (1733).

[2] See the whole passage quoted in C. Maxwell, *The English Traveller in France* (1932), pp. 68–72.

COACHES IN A LONDON STREET

From a print of 1750

Between Poplar and London Bridge the ships filled the river with a forest of masts and sails. 'Above Bridge' were the barges and the tilt boats and the wherries of the watermen. 'The whole surface of the Thames', wrote Lydia Melford, 'is covered with small vessels, barges, boats, and wherries, passing to and fro, and below the three bridges, such a prodigious forest of masts, for miles together, that you would think all the ships of the universe were here assembled.'

The river and the streets, the shops, the coffee-houses and taverns, the parks and the places of amusement were the chief sights of London. Its more conventional sights, the Tower, with its lions and its armoury, the Abbey, the British Museum, Bedlam (where visitors could take tea with the inmates), Mrs. Salmon's Waxworks, were full of varied interest, but here they take a second place since they were more removed from the daily life of the town. Beginning with the streets, Johnson's dictum must not be forgotten: 'Sir, if you wish to have a just notion of the magnitude of this city, you must not be satisfied with seeing its great streets and squares, but must survey the innumerable little lanes and courts. It is not in the showy evolution of buildings, but in the multiplicity of human habitations crowded together, that the wonderful immensity of London consists.' It was a characteristic of the older parts of London, and especially of that part of it which is most essentially Johnson's, lying between Charing Cross and St. Paul's, that there were great thoroughfares of roaring traffic, bordered by courts and lanes to which the foot-passenger could escape from turmoil. Some indeed were sordid, others were quiet oases, like the long narrow court shaded with trees, in or near the Temple, which Johnson called his walk. This sudden transition from crowds and noise is best described by Wordsworth. The London of his first visit (in 1791), which he describes in *The Prelude*, is in essentials the London of Johnson:

> Meanwhile the roar continues, till at length,
> Escaped as from an enemy, we turn
> Abruptly into some sequester'd nook,
> Still as a shelter'd place when winds blow loud!

The noise of the streets was indeed deafening. Hogarth's *Enraged Musician* (1741) shows only some of the daily noises of the town, the chief perhaps being the thunder of iron-shod wheels and the clatter of hooves. Gay apostrophizes Venice,

> O happy streets, to rumbling wheels unknown,
> No carts, no coaches, shake the floating town. (*Trivia.*)

It was far otherwise in London. Many of the stage-coaches and wagons, whose head-quarters were in the great inns of the City and the Strand, left and arrived at night. And though the night was far from silent, and was broken periodically by the watchman's cry, morning was heralded with noise.

The street cries, always varied and shrill, altered as the decades passed, but there were some which linked the London of Shakespeare with that of Johnson. One of the oldest and most melancholy of London cries survived. 'Sir,' wrote Johnson in *The Idler*, 'as I was passing lately under one of the gates of this city, I was struck with horror by a rueful cry, which summoned me *to remember the poor debtors*.'[1]

The ballad-singer was for generations a familiar London figure:

> Let not the ballad singer's shrilling strain
> Amid the swarm thy list'ning ear detain:
> Guard well thy pocket: for these *syrens* stand
> To aid the labours of the diving hand:
> Confed'rate in the cheat, they draw the throng,
> And cambrick handkerchiefs reward the song.

Gay's warning was often repeated by Sir John Fielding in his far from unsuccessful attempt to teach the art of living in London by advertisements in the newspapers. The newspaper boys, crying their wares with the help of a horn, multiplied as the newspapers multiplied. Wandering musicians were numerous, street cries were shrill. Wordsworth writes of

> Private courts
> Gloomy as coffins, and unsightly lanes
> Thrilled by some female vendor's scream, belike
> The very shrillest of all London cries.

Another ancient and melancholy cry was that of the beggars who in Gay's time lay in 'the publick square'

> Where all beside the rail, rang'd beggars lie,
> And from each other catch the doleful cry.

[1] No. 22, Sept. 16, 1758. The gate was Ludgate, one of the City prisons.

'A constant reader' wrote in 1766 to a newspaper complaining of 'two great nuisances', one, 'the many ballad singers in St. Paul's Church Yard singing obscene songs on evenings (sometimes till eleven o'clock at night), whilst opposite to them are half a dozen wretches lying on the ground and crying out in a most lamentable tone of voice *God Almighty be your Guide, &c.* which makes a medley capable of chilling the blood of any thinking person'.[1]

The hand-bell was used to aid the voice: the scavenger with his cart rang a bell to announce his approach. The collectors for the 'penny post' also rang a bell. This evoked a complaint from the long-suffering Londoner, who wrote to a newspaper appealing for the abolition of a dangerous noise, which might be done, he says, by opening a few more receiving offices and keeping them open till ten o'clock at night. He signs himself 'Good Order and therefore Anti-Bell'.[2] It is characteristic of the period that movements for reform in things small and great are apt to begin with a letter to the press.

The streets of London were a perpetual pageant—not only in retrospect, now that they have receded into a costume play, and not only to strangers, but to Londoners. The spirit of the innumerable prints depicting the life of the town and the perennial interest in the Cries of London are evidence enough—apart from the verse and prose of a long tradition which includes Taylor the Water Poet, Gay, Wordsworth, and Lamb, as well as a host of forgotten names. It is clear that Hogarth saw the beauty and romance as well as the comedies and tragedies of the streets; his followers depict the humours of the town with less of cautionary intent: the lamplighter on his ladder dropping oil on the passers-by, the milliner tripping along with her bandbox and alluring glance, the barber hurrying with his wig boxes, a comb stuck in his hair, the ballad-singer, always slatternly and impudent, with a sheaf of some *New Song* for sale (in the *Enraged Musician* it is *The Ladies Fall*). There are apple women, Billingsgate wenches, gilt coaches, sedan chairs, link boys. Almost inevitably, at least one little chimney-sweep, with his short brush and bag of soot, is a grinning spectator of the scene. Though their lot was so hard, these children were the licensed *gamins* of the streets: while other apprentices were

---

[1] *Gazetteer*, Aug. 14, 1766.   [2] *Public Advertiser*, Oct. 23, 1783.

kept indoors their duty was to 'cry the streets' in the early morning and by mid-day their work was over and they were free. The humiliation of the fine lady and the beau—more especially of the French fop—is a perennially popular theme: he is lean and beggarly, but is decked out in ruffles, bag-wig and *chapeau-bras*. Indeed, it was a common jest that the Frenchman 'for the sake of wearing ruffles' was content 'to go without a shirt'.[1]

The pervading spirit of this popular art is that in the London streets the populace is supreme. Fielding's irony was rooted in fact when he called 'the mob' 'that very large and powerful body which forms the fourth estate in this community'.[2] It was indeed the mob which decided whether the punishment of the pillory was to be a shameful torture or a triumph, and which took upon itself to punish pick-pockets by chasing, thrashing, and ducking or 'pumping'. During Johnson's lifetime the treatment of foreigners markedly improved, but the sight of a French *petit-maître* was highly provocative. A Frenchman warns his countrymen to be careful of their dress: 'the populace of England must be considered as sovereign as regards the costumes of its country.'[3]

Although mobs were frequent and alarming, and the under-world of London was always a threat to its security, yet on the whole the good order which accompanied much turbu-lence and an almost complete absence of police are remark-able. The roughness of the populace was tempered with humour and good nature. This was apparent in the crowded streets. Grosley, visiting London in 1765, was impressed by 'the great care they take to prevent the frays almost un-avoidable, amidst the eternal passing and repassing of carriages in the most frequented streets, some of which are exceedingly narrow. If, notwithstanding the great care of the coachmen and carmen to avoid them, there arises some confusion and perplexity, their readiness to turn aside, to retire, to open, and to lend each other a hand . . . prevents this confusion from degenerating into one of those bloody frays which so often happen at Paris'.

Besides the daily pageantry of the streets, the more formal

---

[1] *Connoisseur*, July 18, 1754.
[2] *Covent Garden Journal*, June 13, 1752.
[3] Decremps, *Le Parisien à Londres* (Amsterdam, 1789), p. 91.

Cittings del.

Blake sculp.

MAY-DAY IN LONDON.

From the Wit's Magazine 1784

pageantry of the procession still played a great part in London life. The procession on Lord Mayor's Day, by water as well as through the streets, was an immense attraction for which stands were erected and windows let at a high price. The civic barges were followed by a crowd of decorated boats. Once in six weeks there was the dreadful procession to Tyburn: with its halt before St. Sepulchre's church, the cart or carts followed by hearses and mourning coaches for those who could afford that luxury, it had a macabre impressiveness. A 'hanging day' was a popular holiday in London, and not with the rabble only. The scene at Tyburn resembled a fair. Politics were to an extraordinary extent a part of the life of the town and conspicuously a part of its pageantry. Many times did the gilt coaches of the city notables go in procession to St. James's, carrying sometimes remonstrances, sometimes loyal addresses, but always escorted by a crowd.

> The rabble all alive,
> From tippling benches, cellars, stalls, and styes,
> Swarm in the streets. The statesman of the day,
> A pompous and slow-moving pageant, comes.
>
> (Cowper, *The Task*, Book VI, ll. 694-7.)

Occasionally the statesman was pelted with mud or even dragged from his coach.

The shops and shop-windows of London were admittedly supreme. Paris had some famous shops much patronized by English *milords* for *articles de luxe*, but she had nothing to compare with the number and magnificence of those in London. 'Let us take a walk from Charing Cross to White-chapel,' said Johnson to Goldsmith, 'through I suppose the greatest series of shops in the world.' 'The magnificence of the shops is the most striking thing in London,' said Archenholtz; 'they sometimes extend without interruption for an English mile. The shop front has large glass windows and a glass door. In these the merchant displays all that is finest and most modern, and as fashion compels him to make considerable changes, the variety and the symmetrical arrangement provide for the passers-by the most brilliant *coup d'œil*.' The display in the windows of the silversmiths, he says, with 'prodigious heaps of gold and silver', gives some notion of the wealth of the island. 'The largest shops of this kind in Paris, in the Rue St. Honoré, are mean compared to those in London . . .' Cole, writing (in 1765) for his own eye alone, is unrestrained: 'The shops at Paris are the poorest gloomy dungeons you can possibly conceive, however rich their contents may be: as the Brilliancy & Shew of ours in London make one of its cheif beauties and Ornaments, so the dead gloom of the City of Paris is nothing beholden to its Tradesmen in shewing their Goods to the best Advantage....'[1]

The shops played a large part in the life of the town. Shopping was more of a social activity then than now, and great demands were made on the complaisance of the London shopkeeper. He was expected to humour all the caprices of those who came with no other object but to while away an idle hour. Here are the qualifications for 'a gold and silver laceman' set down in all seriousness. 'He ought to speak fluently, though not elegantly, to entertain the ladies: and to be the master of a handsome bow and cringe: should be able to hand a lady to and from her coach politely, without being seiz'd with a palpitation of the heart at the touch of a delicate hand, the sight of a well-turned and much expos'd limb, or a handsome face....'[2] Foreign visitors were impressed with the urbanity of the London shopkeeper. Forster speaks of his *complaisance parfaite*: 'If a two-shilling purchase is made he will offer to send it to the other extremity of the town, and if the customer spends several pounds he is sure to be invited to his table or at least regaled with a glass of wine, a cup of chocolate or some other refreshment. The richest merchant never shows ill-humour, even if asked to unfold more than a hundred pieces of stuff.'[3]

A bookseller's shop in particular was far more than a place for the selling of books. Who can forget that it was in the parlour of Tom Davies in Russell Street, Covent Garden, that Boswell was drinking tea, when Johnson unexpectedly came into the shop and the momentous meeting was effected?

The print shops were veritable picture galleries, attracting crowds of window-gazers. They displayed both serious portraits and caricatures of those in the public eye. Johnson of course was both 'scraped in mezzotinto' and caricatured. This was one of the ways in which London characters (who

---

[1] *Paris Journal* (ed. F. G. Stokes, 1931), p. 50.
[2] R. Campbell, *The London Tradesman* (1747), p. 147.
[3] *Voyage philosophique et pittoresque en Angleterre . . . en 1790*. See also Goldsmith in *The Citizen of the World* (first printed, *Public Ledger*, Sept. 22, 1760).

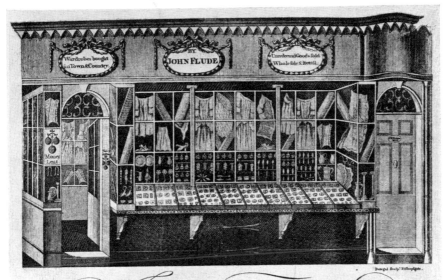

John Flude

PAWNBROKER *and* **SILVERSMITH**

N.º 2 Grace Church Street

London.

Lends Money on Plate, Watches, Jewells & Wearing Apparel, Houshold Goods, & Stock in Trade.

NB

Goods Sent from any Part of y Country directed as above, shall be duly attended too & the Utmost Value lent thereon.

were of all ranks) became familiar, being eagerly watched in the parks and elsewhere. The freedom with which outrageous political satires and caricatures of the Great were displayed astonished foreign visitors.

But it was in the coffee-houses that the national passion for politics found its chief expression. The coffee-house and the tavern played a very important part in London life. Indeed, Colman and Thornton begin their 'view of the town' with a survey of the principal coffee-houses.[1] Different professions and classes and groups had their favourite coffee-houses. To these men went at all times of the day (often beginning with breakfast in dressing-gown and slippers) to read the newspapers, and there the writers for the newspapers went to learn the news and the 'latest lie of the town'.[2] The staple of the coffee-man was as much news as coffee; the character of the news differed: merchants frequented the coffee-houses that clustered thickly round the Royal Exchange, notably Garraway's, Jonathan's, Tom's, and Lloyd's. The booksellers met at the Chapter off Paternoster Row, the doctors at Batson's. Temple Bar and Covent Garden were the centres for authors and wits; men of fashion were to be found there, but their chief resort was to the coffee-houses and chocolate-houses of St. James's Street and Pall Mall.

The coffee-house was a godsend especially to the young men who came to town, as Johnson did, to earn a living from the booksellers. It mitigated the squalor of Grub Street, offered a chance of introduction to the wits, and provided the necessary good address: as Johnson was told before he came to London, 'a man might live in a garret for eighteen pence a week; few people would enquire where he lodged, and if they did, it was easy to say, "Sir, I am to be found at such a place." By spending threepence in a coffee-house he might be for some hours every day in very good company'.

As the coffee-houses were embryo clubs, so when the formal club developed out of them it was a sign that their decline was beginning. When Johnson came to London the club in this modern sense had recently come into being at White's Chocolate-house in St. James's Street. This had been a resort of men of fashion for high play since the end of the

---

[1] *Connoisseur*, No. 1, Jan. 31, 1754.
[2] Cf. Tom Restless (who was Johnson's friend Tom Tyers) in *The Idler*, No. 48, March 17, 1759.

seventeenth century. Shortly before 1736 its *habitués* formed a club (one black ball to exclude) with rules to keep outsiders from their 'Subscription Rooms'. The rest of the house remained open to the public, but before long the whole building was absorbed by the club, and eventually the members became owners of the premises.[1] Other coffee- and chocolate-houses went through a similar evolution: Tom's in Russell Street, Covent Garden; the Cocoa Tree, first in Pall Mall and then in St. James's Street; Boodles and Almack's (soon known as Brooks's), both in St. James's Street.

It was White's that fascinated and horrified the public for its deserved reputation for extreme fashion and high play. 'The citizens put on their double chanelled pumps', wrote Walpole in 1755, 'and trudge to St. James's Street in expectation of seeing judgments executed on White's, angels with flaming swords and devils flying away with dice boxes; like the prints in Sadeler's Hermits.' A coat of arms for 'the Club at White's' was designed at Strawberry Hill to illustrate with dice boxes and other emblems the gaming which went on there. This reputation was afterwards rivalled by Brooks's, started in 1764 by Macall (or 'Almack') for purposes of high play, which attracted to itself the greatest gamblers (and notably Charles Fox) from White's on the opposite side of the street, and became associated with Fox and his party.

City coffee-houses had a corresponding development but their outcome was an embryo Stock Exchange and (ultimately) the modern Lloyd's. By Addison's day, Lloyd's coffee-house was one of the chief commercial sale rooms in the City, especially for those interested in shipping and foreign trade. Its early possession of accurate shipping news led to the publication of *Lloyd's List*. The desire to exclude outsiders and those who dealt in gambling insurances induced some of the *habitués*, in 1771, to open a New Lloyd's coffee-house (first in Pope's Head Alley and in 1774 in the Royal Exchange) with an outer room for the public and an inner 'Subscribers' Room'.

These coffee-house clubs had their own activities: as that of Lloyd's was (*inter alia*) the sale and insurance of ships, and that of Jonathan's and Garraway's was stock jobbing, so that of the fashionable clubs of St. James's was betting

[1] W. B. Boulton, *A History of White's* (2 vols., 1892).

The Coffee-house Politicians.

From an engraving in Every Man's Magazine, *1772*

and high play with the occasional organization of a ball or masquerade.

Covent Garden was the centre for wits, authors, actors, and to some extent of artists. The Bedford coffee-house 'under the Piazza' (not to be confused with the Bedford Head tavern close by) was their head-quarters. It was the resort of Fielding, Hogarth, Murphy, Foote, and Colman, as Button's or Will's had been that of Dryden, Addison, and Steele. Indeed in 1751 Dr. Hill (Fielding's enemy) placed here for the use of his short-lived paper *The Inspector* the Lion's head letter-box which Steele had used at Button's for contributions to *The Guardian*,[1] and thus 'once more placed the dominion of wit in Covent Garden'.[2] 'This coffee-house', say Colman and Thornton, 'is every night crowded with men of parts. Almost every one you meet is a polite scholar and a wit, jokes and *bons mots* are echoed from box to box; every branch of literature is critically examined, and the merit of every production of the theatres, weighed and determined.' It was not exclusive: 'A student never launches from Oxford or Cambridge, a lawyer's clerk never claps on a sword or a haberdasher's apprentice a cue wig, but he makes his appearance here.' It was a peculiarity of the Bedford that politics were 'seldom brought upon the carpet'.[2] The other coffee-house of similar standing and character was George's in the Strand near Temple Bar. Lloyd writes of the lawyer-wit,

> Supreme at George's, he harangues the throng,
> Censor of style, from tragedy to song.

Old Slaughter's in St. Martin's Lane was the resort of artists and of foreigners, especially Frenchmen, and Johnson is believed to have frequented it when he first came to town in order to learn to speak French, but, says Hawkins, 'he never could attain to it'. This is the scene of his famous remark, made 'when a number of foreigners were talking loud about little things', 'does not this confirm old Meynell's observation—*For any thing I see, foreigners are fools*'.[3]

When Murphy came to London in 1751 he made his way

[1] From Button's it had gone to the Shakespeare's Head tavern next door to the Bedford. See J. Timbs, *Clubs and Club Life in London* (1872), pp. 323 et seq.

[2] *Memoirs of the Bedford Head Coffee-House* (2nd ed., 1763).

[3] Sir I. Hawkins, *Life of Johnson* (2nd ed., 1787). Loud talk was a breach of English coffee-house etiquette: see quotation from Archenholtz.

at once to George's and the Bedford and so made the acquaintance of 'the town'. He wrote in 1805: 'London at that time had many advantages which have long since been lost. There were a number of coffee-houses where the town wits met every evening; particularly the Bedford . . . and George's. . . . Young as I was I made my way to those places.'[1]

Though the literary coffee-houses are naturally prominent in the writings of 'authors by profession', most coffee-houses were places for talking politics and reading the newspapers. Foreigners invariably comment on the passion of the Englishman for politics and news. Archenholtz contrasts a London coffee-house with a French café: in the former no billiard tables or gaming tables are seen, no noise is heard, every one speaks low so as not to disturb the others. The chief object is to read the newspapers, an occupation which is a positive necessity for the English. The most frequented coffee-houses have ten or twelve copies of the same paper and also the best periodicals. One house files the newspapers of the year, which are carefully preserved.[2] The *habitué* can behave as if in his own house, make appointments, and have his letters addressed there.[3]

It is with the tavern more than with the coffee-house that Johnson is associated. 'The tavern chair' was to him 'the throne of human felicity'. It was at the Turk's Head tavern in Gerrard Street (not to be confused with the Turk's Head Coffee-house in the Strand which Johnson also frequented) that The Club first met. Here the members supped weekly at seven and 'generally continued their conversation to a pretty late hour'. Such clubs were common to the evening life of all classes. This, the most famous of them all, differed from others only in the character of its members.[4] It, like some other clubs of the period, went through a similar evolution

---

[1] J. Foot, *Life of Murphy* (1811), p. 11. In 1767 Hume complained 'men of letters have here no place of rendezvous; and are indeed, sunk and forgotten in the general torrent of the world'. J. H. Burton, *Life of Hume* (2 vols., 1846), vol. ii, p. 385.

[2] Probably Peele's in Fleet Street at the east corner of Fetter Lane. Its files of the *Gazette* dated from 1759 and of other papers from 1773, &c. Timbs, op. cit., p. 361.

[3] Archenholtz, *Tableau de l'Angleterre* (2 vols., 1788), vol. ii, p. 104. (A slightly abridged translation.)

[4] See Goldsmith, 'A Description of various Clubs', *Busy Body*, Oct. 13, 1759. (Essay iv in the edition of 1766.) M. D. George, *London Life*, pp. 273 et seq.

to that which turned the *habitués* of a coffee-house into a club in the modern sense: when it grew larger, lost its intimate character, and became a dining society[1] it also migrated to the more fashionable end of the town, and Johnson lost some of his interest in it and was one of the more frequent absentees. 'He loudly proclaimed his carelessness *who* might be admitted, when it was become a mere dinner club.'[2] At the end of his life he attempted to renew the traditions of the earlier and more homely type of club by trying to revive the club which had met at Horseman's chop-house in Ivy Lane.

Above all taverns it is with the Mitre in Fleet Street, with its 'orthodox high church sound', that Johnson is chiefly associated. It was at the Mitre that Johnson agreed with Murphy to accept the pension which delivered him from poverty. Boswell successfully begged to be allowed to pass an evening with him here, and here fifteen years later Johnson agreed to his proposal 'to dine by ourselves at the Mitre, to keep up the old custom, the custom of the manor, "custom of the Mitre".' Close to the Mitre was a yet more famous tavern, the Devil (or the Old Devil) at Temple Bar, so-called from its sign of St. Dunstan pulling the Devil's nose with a pair of tongs. Its literary associations range from Ben Jonson to Samuel Johnson. For its great room known as the Apollo (used in the eighteenth century for concerts and lectures) Ben Jonson had drawn up the famous *Leges conviviales*. Here, on Johnson's proposal, the Ivy Lane Club celebrated 'the birth of Mrs. Lennox's first literary child', as he called her book, by a whole night spent in festivity. Johnson crowned the lady with a wreath of laurel, and the night passed 'in pleasant conversation, and harmless mirth, intermingled at different periods with the refreshments of coffee and tea. About five, Johnson's face shone with meridian splendour, though his drink had been only lemonade. . . .'[3]

The tavern, like the coffee-house, had an important, but a declining, part in the life of the town.[4] The larger taverns

---

[1] It must be remembered that four was then a late and fashionable hour for dinner. See S. Walpole, 'The Dining Societies of London' in *Essays* (1908).

[2] *Johnsonian Misc.* (ed. G. B. Hill, 2 vols., Oxford, 1897), vol. i, pp. 229–30.

[3] Hawkins, *Life of Johnson*, p. 286.

[4] 'It is worthy of remark . . . how little these houses of entertainment are now frequented and what a diminution in their number has been experienced in London and Westminster in a period of about forty years backward.' Ibid., pp. 87–8.

had great rooms which were used for formal dinners,
political meetings, concerts, and the meetings of clubs and
societies. The Crown and Anchor in the Strand (where Johnson and Boswell sometimes dined) and the St. Albans Tavern
were the scenes of some great political meetings before
and after 1784. The London Tavern in Bishopsgate Street
(opened in 1766) was a byword for civic luxury with its
great tanks in which turtles swam till they were wanted. At
the other end of the scale were alehouses or 'taverns of the
second rank', as they are styled by a foreign visitor, who
informs us that they had always two rooms and sometimes
three; the first, being for the populace, had neither cleanliness nor decorum; the second was the parlour to which only
decently dressed and mannered people were admitted; here,
in a thick cloud of smoke, since pipes were given gratis, the
clients played draughts and read the newspapers. The third
room was reserved for the meetings of clubs.[1]

Foreign visitors saw in the London parks as in the coffee-
houses something of the 'peculiar genius' of the English
people: their passion for 'the promenade', the mixture of
classes which was so strangely tolerated. Walking to see and
to be seen was a favourite amusement, and the Mall in St.
James's Park was pre-eminently the 'public walk' of the
century—both of 'the World' in the limited sense of 'the
Great' and of their acquaintance,[2] and of the people who
went to stare as well as to amuse themselves in ways not
always decorous. Besides the formal promenade of the Mall,
shaded by its double avenue of limes and elms, were other
walks, and also the Canal, the Decoy, and Rosamond's Pond.

'La promenade fait maintenant mes delices', wrote Baron
von Bielfeld in 1741, describing how he made the tour of St.
James's Park every morning, and found combined there 'le
spectacle de la campagne, de la guerre, de la ville, et de la
cour'. 'La campagne' was represented by 'un troupeau de

---

[1] Decremps, *Le Parisien à Londres.* Cf. M. D. George, *London Life,*
p. 273. The great coaching inns which were the head-quarters of the country
stages and wagons, such as The Swan with Two Necks in Lad Lane, The Golden
Cross in the Strand, the White Hart in the Borough, were in a different
category and are associated rather with travel than with the daily life of the
town. The same applies to the coaching inns used by gentlemen who drove to
town, such as the Hercules Pillars in Piccadilly where Squire Western put up.
All along the roads leading into London there were a number of inns, many of
them humble places frequented by drovers and carters.

[2] Cf. Fielding, 'A Modern Glossary', in *Covent Garden Journal,* Jan. 14, 1752.

'THE CANAL, CHINESE BUILDING, ROTUNDO, ETC., IN RANELAGH
GARDENS, WITH THE MASQUERADE'

COVENT GARDEN, 1741

vaches' 'sur un beau tapis vert', the nymph by the milk-maid who milked the cows for those who came there for their morning draught of 'what the English call "cillibub"': they brought a glass one-third filled with Spanish wine which the nymph filled with exquisitely flavoured milk straight from the cow. There were, he says, some twenty walks, some straight, some serpentine, and all kept with the utmost neatness. He admires the ducks and the water-birds, visits Duck Island (in the Decoy), picks flowers there and admires the building 'rustic but pretty' which had been associated with the famous St. Evremond. Then he sees the footguards being drilled, not without oaths. From the camp he approaches the Court, represented by the Mall, where he admires the ladies, en négligé, but admirably neat and well shod. Here he meets ministers, courtiers, petits-maîtres, and co-quettes, and remains till it is time to go to Court or to dine. Here in fact every one of note in eighteenth-century London must have walked. Here Richardson and 'Mrs. Belfour' (Lady Bradshaigh) made their assignations. It was in the Mall (in 1764) that little Mozart was walking with his family when, as his father delightedly records, 'the King and Queen came driving by, and, although we were all differently dressed, they knew and saluted us; the king in particular threw open the carriage window, put out his head laughing, and greeted us with head and hands—particularly our Master Wolfgang. . . .'[1] Here Fanny Burney saw the Duchess of Devonshire when she first astonished the town with her youth and beauty walking in a déshabillé which she stigmatizes as slatternly, followed by a servant 'in superb livery'.

The fine folk were often incommoded, sometimes seriously, by those who went to jostle and stare; the most familiar incident is that of the Gunnings. The Park was also one of the places for scenes of low life. From about 1763 there is a succession of newspaper protests against the indecorum of the Park and of suggestions for reform. The milkmaids are spoken of as 'the insolent milk-women', and the stands for cows near Spring Gardens turn the place into a dung-yard. Disorderly people 'infest' it, and the seats are decayed. Among the proposals for reform are an entrance fee of a penny after 6 p.m., the money to be used to erect lamps; many

[1] E. Holmes, Life of Mozart (Everyman ed.), p. 25.

prostitutes and robbers would thus, it was said, be kept out. Rosamond's Pond, 'where so many have been drowned', should be filled up, and also 'the canals or rather ditches about that island, which are so noxious to the health of the neighbouring inhabitations, especially in Downing Street and Duke Street, from the aquatic and stinking exhalations of those waters . . . which disagreeably and even dangerously affect all persons who walk or inhabit thereabouts'. In 1766 the magistrates took steps 'to prevent the indecent practices in St. James's Park by a set of disorderly persons, playing and betting at unlawful games, bathings, running of races naked, &c., particularly on the Sabbath Day'.[1] Disorders in the Park were always being 'suppressed' and always renewing themselves. This is not surprising since the Park was not lighted, was a favourite place for 'the rabble', was the nightly resort of soldiers off duty, and was not watched or guarded except for an occasional raid from Bow Street. Though the gates were locked at ten at night, 6,500 persons (according to Archenholtz) had keys for which they paid a guinea, while a much greater number were known to have false keys.

Rosamond's Pond and the Decoy and its ditches with their stinking exhalations were removed in 1770 or 1771 when the Park was 'new modelled' under the direction of Capability Brown. In the Academy exhibition in May 1771 there was a picture by Charles Catton of the filling up of Rosamond's Pond.[2] It was less easy to curb the disorders of the Park: 'the nuisance of beggars, gamblers, and other disorderly persons', the gamblers being those who 'set up teetotum tables, dice tables and other arts of gambling, such as throwing at oranges or pitching for halfpence on the top of a small stick'.[3] In 1773 the Bow Street Justices announced their intention of issuing warrants to take up the disorderly till 'St. James's Park and its environs be brought into that state of decorum that his Majesty's subjects may enjoy the privilege of walking and passing through that delightful spot without nuisance or interruption'.[4]

Another picture of 'the disorders' of the Park illustrates also the way in which they were sometimes suppressed—

[1] *Gazetteer*, June 21, 1766.
[2] R.A. Catalogues in British Museum, Print Department.
[3] *Public Advertiser*, Jan. 6, 1768; Aug. 27, 1770.   [4] Ibid., Feb. 15, 1773.

SKAITING SCENE *in* HYDE PARK.

From the Wit's Magazine, 1785

probably the threat was sufficient: 'Complaints having been made . . . of the notorious prophanation of the Lord's Day, the last time the Canals there were froze over, by hundreds of skaiters and spectators shouting and whooping in time of divine service, and in view and hearing of the royal family; we have the satisfaction to be informed, that for preventing this impious outrage tomorrow, if the Civil Power be too weak, a strong Press-gang will attend to make a draught of such of the skaiters &c. as may be thought proper for serving their country against the French, upon the frozen lakes of Canada.'[1]

The populace regarded the Park as theirs, although it was Crown property, hence the story told by Walpole: 'Queen Caroline spoke of shutting up St. James's Park, and converting it into a noble garden for the palace of that name. She asked my father what it might probably cost; who replied, "*only three crowns*". '[2] The untrammelled access of the vulgar to a royal park was one of the things which confirmed foreigners in their belief that in London the populace was supreme.

Between 1730 and 1733 Queen Caroline did succeed in altering and extending Kensington Gardens in accordance with the fashionable landscape gardening introduced by Bridgeman and Kent. She extended it to the north as far as 'the road to Acton', and on the east at the expense of Hyde Park. The formal gardens to the north and south of the palace disappeared, the broad walk was laid out, 'the basin' (now known as the Round Pond) was formed, and a string of ponds and the waters of the West Bourne were transformed into the Serpentine. With the earth excavated from it 'the Mount' (levelled to the ground in the nineteenth century) was formed in the south-east corner of the Gardens. On its apex was a revolving shelter, shaped like a temple, which protected a seat from the prevailing wind. Inevitably this was used for a political parable directed against Sir Robert Walpole. The seat is the king's chair; this is turned due south by 'a certain corpulent man who seemed to be his chief minister', so as to direct his master's attention to his own villa on the Thames in Chelsea, although the king himself desired to look 'to the left, which opened to him the

[1] Ibid., Jan. 12, 1760.
[2] Horace Walpole, *Walpoliana* (2 vols., 1799), vol. i, pp. 8–9.

prospect of a large and populous city, the great centre and foundation of all his power'. The new modelled gardens are described as 'Paradise itself': 'The whole extent of it was laid out in the most regular manner, and yet so artfully design'd with vistas, terras walks, and canals, with little ascents, declivities and vallies, with open areas and gloomy recesses, that it put me in mind of that beautiful description in *Windsor Forest*,

> Where order in variety we see,
> And where, though all things differ, all agree.'[1]

Kensington Gardens, thus transformed, became a fashionable resort at the expense both of the Ring in Hyde Park and (on Sundays at least) of St. James's Park. It was more orderly since 'the rabble' were excluded. 'For the better regulating the company, servants are placed at the different entrances to prevent persons meanly clad from going into the garden.'[2]

The vistas (a chief feature of the new gardening, depending mainly on the ha-ha or sunk fence) opened views from Kensington Gardens into Hyde Park. This had then something of the appearance of Richmond Park to-day; it was rural without laid-out 'walks', though the Ring for riding and driving dated from the time of Charles I. Deer were kept in an enclosure in the north-west corner and the king occasionally hunted there, at least till 1768.[3] It had its Cake House or Cheese Cake House. This park was a noted duelling resort, the scene of some famous encounters during our period, as for instance (in fact) the duel between Fox and Adam in 1779, and (in fiction) that between Booth and Colonel Bath, on that spot 'which may properly be called the field of blood, being that place a little to the left of the Ring, which heroes have chosen for the scene of their exit from this world'.[4]

The curious mixture of fashion, squalor, and the macabre which characterized Johnson's London, and had long characterized it, was conspicuous in the two parks. In Hyde Park a spot near the site of the Marble Arch is marked in Rocque's maps as 'Stone where soldiers are shot'. St. James's Park was the scene of the dreadful floggings then inflicted on soldiers.

---

[1] *The Craftsman*, No. 305, May 6, 1732.   [2] *A Sunday Ramble*, n.d., c. 1774.
[3] J. Ashton, *Hyde Park* (1896).   [4] *Amelia* (1751), Book V, chap. v.

A General Prospect of Vaux Hall Gardens. Vue Generalle des Jardins de Vaux Hall.
Shewing at one view the disposition of the whole Gardens.

Printed for John Bowles at the Black Horse in Cornhill.

VAUXHALL GARDENS, 1751

The parks, a morning resort, were part of the fashionable life of the town, as were the auctions conducted by a succession of eminent auctioneers: among many others, Cock (the Mr. Auctioneer Hen of Fielding's *Historical Register*), Langford (the Puff of Foote's *Minor*), and Christie, the first of a dynasty. Their rooms were 'fashionable lounges' and meeting places. So were certain shops, for instance Deard's,[1] Betty's, the famous fruit-shop in St. James's Street, Wedgwood's, and, for a time at least, the Foundling Hospital for its music and its pictures. For 'sporting gentlemen' there was Tattersall's at Hyde Park Corner (opened in 1766) with its Subscription Rooms for members of the Jockey Club. A rehearsal at the Opera House in the Haymarket was a meeting-place for 'the World' in its limited sense.[2] Thus the *haut ton* killed time before dinner. Lord Townshend writes of 'Squire Hanger', a macaroni (or beau):

> At Tattershall's, Wedgwood's, and eke the Rehearsal,
> Then straightway at Betty's he's sure to converse all:
> At Arthur's you meet him, and then all in a sweat
> At Kensington Garden's he's posted vidette.

It was one of the commonest topics of the day that the places of amusement in London were excessive, a chief manifestation of unbounded luxury. The passion of the English for amusements was noted by a long succession of foreign visitors, who were particularly impressed by the crowds which thronged all places of entertainment. These, like the streets, were thronged as in no other European city. As for the theatres: 'What is called in other countries *un spectacle rempli*', writes Archenholtz, 'is in England *une salle vide*. The expression *a full house* is used only when the spectators are heaped up one against the other and some hundreds have not found places, which happens at almost every performance of good plays.' 'The houses indeed are filled, let the play be never so bad,' writes a correspondent of *The London Museum*, 'but thousands for want of room are sent away.'[3] Wendeborn records that at both theatres before the doors were open 'there is generally for an hour and longer such a mobbing that many a one stays away

[1] Cf. 'Deard's bill for baubles shall to thousands mount'. Bramston, *The Man of Taste*.
[2] Cf. F. Burney, *Cecilia*, 1782, Book I, chap. viii.
[3] Op. cit. (1770), p. 45. Cf. *infra*, vol. ii, chap. xx.

because he does not like to be jostled about for such a length of time'.[1]

Of the ring of pleasure gardens which surrounded London Vauxhall and Ranelagh are in a class apart. Naturally, they are styled 'the two grand seminaries of luxury'.[2] Vauxhall was the more popular and the more amusing, Ranelagh more select and more decorous; but it was a chief attraction of both that the notabilities of the day were to be seen at close quarters—ribbons and stars, as well as wits and beauties and the characters of the town. Humbler folk, like Beau Tibbs, could half pretend and half believe that they belonged to this *beau monde*. At both there were concerts, and gardens lit by lamps fixed to the trees. Vauxhall had much larger gardens, in which nightingales sang, with the dangers and attractions of the 'dark walks' of Evelina's adventure. The supper party too was the special charm of Vauxhall, since at Ranelagh, except on gala nights, only tea and bread and butter were served. 'After the music is ended for the night, 'tis vastly agreeable to wander round the ranges of pavilions, and gaze at the numberless parties (some of whom are frequently attended by French horns) supping in their several bowers. . . . Many have wondered how it could be possible for three or four hundred persons to be regularly entertain'd at different tables at one and the same time.'[3] Of all the Vauxhall supper parties of fact and fiction, two stand out pre-eminently. There is the one described by Walpole when Lady Caroline Petersham, 'looking gloriously jolly and handsome', minced seven chickens in a china dish; a party which took up 'the whole attention of the Gardens, so much so, that from eleven till half an hour after one we had the whole concourse round our booth. . . .' The other is that of Beau Tibbs and his wife, the Man in Black, and the Chinese Philosopher, when they missed seeing the waterworks (or the cascade), and failed to get a genteel box, since the keepers of the boxes 'chose to reserve genteel boxes for what they

[1] Wendeborn, *View of England* (2 vols., 1791), vol. ii, p. 244. A mezzotint of the pit door at Drury Lane shows a struggling crowd; the ground is strewn with hats, ribbons, and buckles lost in the fray, and a fainting lady is being revived with smelling-salts. A play-bill on the wall shows that it is Oct. 21, 1784, and that Mrs. Siddons was to play Euphrasia in Murphy's *Grecian Daughter*, while Kemble in *Hamlet* is billed for the following night.

[2] 1761 edition of Defoe's *Tour*.

[3] *A Sketch of the Spring Gardens at Vauxhall*, n.d., c. 1750.

judged more genteel company'.[1] In spite of the constant
'affrays' at Vauxhall, and the misadventures of Amelia and
Evelina, and the dangers of 'the dark walks', it was evidently
as Boswell says, a place of 'elegant and innocent entertainment' and one 'peculiarly adapted to the taste of the English nation, there being a mixture of curious shew—gay
exhibition—musick, vocal and instrumental, not too refined
for the general ear; for all which only a shilling is paid: and
though last not least—good eating and drinking for those
who choose to purchase that regale'. Minute chickens and
ham of a paper-like thinness were the traditional fare at
Vauxhall.[2]

At Ranelagh the adventures and affrays, common enough
at Vauxhall, were almost unknown. The gardens were much
smaller, the chief attraction was the great Rotunda with its
orchestra and its walls lined with tiers of boxes, each holding
seven or eight people. The lights and the crowd in a smaller
space than in Vauxhall were very impressive. Johnson
thought the *coup d'œil* of the Rotunda 'the finest thing he
had ever seen'. 'When I first entered it,' he told Boswell,
'it gave an expansion and gay sensation to my mind, such
as I had never experienced elsewhere.' The company took
tea in boxes, listened to the music, and walked round and
round the Rotunda, sometimes in an atmosphere of solemn
hush.

Vauxhall and Ranelagh opened in the spring and closed at
the end of August, while the quality deserted town at the
beginning of June, so that their season was short. In 1772
the Pantheon was opened to be a winter Ranelagh and to
be a place for assemblies, concerts, and masquerades, which
should compete with those of Mrs. Cornelys in Soho Square.
Its magnificence was universally admired, though it was of
course stigmatized as a manifestation of luxury. 'In point
of ennui and magnificence', wrote Gibbon, 'the Pantheon is
the wonder of the eighteenth century and of the British
Empire.'[3]

The ring of pleasure gardens encircling the town is one of
the most characteristic features of Johnson's London. They
were then in their hey-day—a competitive development

[1] Goldsmith, *The Citizen of the World*.
[2] *Connoisseur* (Colman and Thornton), No. 68, May 10, 1755.
[3] *Misc. Works* (5 vols., 1814), vol. ii, p. 74.

from the Spring Gardens, Wells, and Bowling Greens of the immediate past. It was the beginning of a long decay when, in 1778, Marylebone Gardens were sacrificed to the builders. Distinctions can be drawn, though the categories merge, between music gardens, wells or spas, and tea-gardens. A more essential distinction is that between places of entertainment for the evening, frequented by the gentry, and usually closed on Sunday, and places whose chief custom was on Sunday, when music and entertainments were forbidden. Marylebone Gardens was primarily an evening music garden, but it was also a tea-garden noted for its plum cake. Angelo calls this a place for the gentry rather than the *haut ton*, and it never succeeded in rivalling Vauxhall. Fireworks were its speciality, especially those of Torré (the subject of a Latin poem by Johnson, and better known for his attempt to provoke a riot on a damp night when the advertised display was not given). Almost all were resorts for Sunday afternoons and many were places of evening entertainment on other days. They clustered most thickly just north of the City, in St. Pancras, Islington, and Kentish Town. Here were the most noted places of their kind: Bagnigge Wells, Sadler's Wells, and White Conduit House, Islington Spa (earlier called the New Tunbridge Wells). This last had a brief period of fashion after Princess Amelia visited it to drink the waters. The crowds at these places astonished foreign visitors—it was an aspect of the life of 'the middle and lower ranks' which was then unique.

Within the environs of the capital [wrote Archenholtz] there is a prodigious number of tea-gardens. The happy arrangement, the order, the cleanliness, the promptitude of the service, the company—always numerous and agreeable—make these gardens as pleasant as they are interesting. At Bagnigge Wells, in fine weather, it is surprising to find from ten to twelve hundred people taking tea. In one called Shakespeare's Garden[1] the eye is delighted by a number of pictures representing the principal characters in his works distributed in all the alcoves of the garden. These places are frequented only by the middle and common class; people of distinction come rarely, ladies of quality never.

[1] This is Dobney's Bowling Green, on Islington Hill (now submerged in Pentonville Road), which at the time of Garrick's famous Jubilee at Stratford (1769) changed its name to the Shakespeare Tavern and Jubilee Gardens. It was chiefly noted for the equestrian feats of Price and others. *A Sunday Ramble* (n.d., c. 1774), and Wroth, *London Pleasure Gardens* (1896), pp. 141–4.

An Inside View of the Rotunda in Ranelagh Gardens

Vue de l'Interieur de la Rotonde dans le Jardins de Ranelagh.

Bagnigge Wells and White Conduit House were the two classic tea-gardens:

> Ah, I loves life and all the joy it yields,
> Says Madam Fussock, warm from Spittle Fields.
> *Bon Ton*'s the space 'twixt Saturday and Monday,
> And riding in a one horse chair o' Sunday:
> 'Tis drinking tea on summer's afternoons
> At Bagnigge Wells with china and gilt spoons![1]

The humours of a London Sunday were a favourite subject both for prose and verse. A Grub Street poet describes White Conduit House:

> Human beings here
> In couples multitudinous assemble,
> Forming the drollest group that ever trod
> Fair Islingtonian plains. Male after male,
> Dog after dog succeeding, husbands, wives,
> Fathers and mothers, brothers, sisters, friends,
> And pretty little boys and girls. Around,
> Across, along the garden's shrubby maze
> They walk, they sit, they stand. What crowds press on,
> Eager to mount the stairs, eager to catch
> First vacant bench, or chair in long room plac'd.[2]

The features of a London pleasure garden were walks, lawns, clipped hedges, shrubberies, as much ornamental water as could be managed, with a grotto, fountains and statues, vistas and views. In fact, though few gardens of course could combine all these attractions, they were cockneyfied and eclectic adaptations of the gardening fashions of the century. There were arbours and boxes for tea-drinking, often, as at Vauxhall and Ranelagh, decorated with paintings. The larger places had a long room with an organ for concerts and balls, also used on Sundays for tea-drinking. There was usually a house or rooms for drinking and smoking, often forbidden in the more genteel walks; sometimes there was a bun house or a cake house. Among the common amusements were skittles, Dutch pins, and bat, trap and ball. At White Conduit House there was a field where cricket was played, the landlord supplying bats and balls. Copenhagen House was famous for its fives. There was often fishing and

---

[1] Garrick's prologue to Colman's *Bon Ton*, 1775.
[2] W. Woty, *London Chronicle*, 1760, vol. vii, p. 531.

occasionally a swimming bath as at the Dog and Duck and the Peerless Pool (the last, however, belonged to a different type of pleasure garden). In most of these places, and indeed at nearly every tavern and alehouse near London, there was a Sunday Ordinary where citizens went to dine at prices varying between ninepence and eight shillings.[1] The almost savage gormandizing which went on at such places was a stock subject of satire, written and pictorial. 'As Mr. Quin has observed, it is not safe to eat at them without a basket-hilted knife and fork.'[2]

There was an important group of pleasure gardens on the south side of the river. Of these the Dog and Duck (a spa whose contaminated waters Johnson recommended for Mr. Thrale) had by the end of Johnson's life become one of the few pleasure gardens which were definitely disreputable. It was here that, as a boy, Francis Place saw people waiting to see the highwaymen mount their horses and 'the flashy women come out to take leave of the thieves at dusk and wish them success'.[3] There were other places with a similar character which had a brief career towards the end of the century, but on the whole the London pleasure gardens were places for family parties like those of Johnson's *Zachary Treacle*, whose wife dragged him on Sundays 'to Georgia, or Hornsey Wood, or the White Conduit House', and where he grudged the cost of 'tea, and hot rolls and sillabubs, and cakes for the boy', not to speak of the occasional expense of a hackney coach or one horse chair.[4]

But almost every inn and alehouse within reach of town transformed itself weekly into a Sunday resort, and there

[1] The ninepenny or shilling ordinary was a common subject of ridicule; Archenholtz notes that at some as much as 8s. was charged.

[2] *St. James's Chronicle*, May 2, 1761.

[3] M. D. George, *London Life*, p. 305.

[4] *Idler*, No. 15, July 22, 1758. Needless to say, they did not escape the attentions of those who thought places of amusement excessive and pernicious. 'It is said that the number of houses of entertainment in the Environs of London to which the lower ranks of people resort on Sundays and holidays will be taken under consideration in the ensuing Sessions of Parliament; as it is well known that of the many thousands that resort to such places, very few can support the expense, which brings many of the men to the gallows and the women upon the town. If the morals of the public requires that the number of theatres should be confined and licensed, by the Police, the same reason holds for confining the number of tea-drinking places, public wells &c. &c. which strips the apprentices and chambermaids of their pocket money and drives those who have none to bad practices for their supply.' *Public Advertiser*, Sept. 29, 1775. (I suspect this of emanating from Bow Street.)

THE DOG AND DUCK

From a print in the Guildhall Library, 1789

were cheese-cake houses and bun houses, the most notable being that at Chelsea, patronized by royalty. Places in Stepney Fields and Mile End were the resort of sailors and their women. 'It is incredible how many thousand buns are devoured in that one day at Chelsea and Paddington, and how much beer is swallowed at Islington and Mile End', say Colman and Thornton.[1] Many taverns provided rough sports such as duck-hunting, dog-fighting, and badger-baiting. The sign of the Dog and Duck (a spaniel with a duck in its mouth) indicates a pond for duck-hunting—in the forties there was one in Carrington Street, Mayfair. Access to most of such sports round London was by means of a public house, but the Long Fields immediately behind Montagu House seem to have been free and were noted for gatherings which the magistrates were always trying to suppress, in war time by means of a press-gang, at other times by a raid of constables. The magistrates in 1764 had 'under consideration' 'ridding the fields and places adjacent to this metropolis of those swarms of loose, idle and disorderly people who daily assemble therein, particularly in the Long Fields . . . to play at cricket, tossing up &c, which usually terminates in broils and is the cause of various kinds of mischief . . . for it is well known that the major part . . . are gamblers and thieves. . . .'[2] A raid on a Sunday in June was headed by the high constable of Holborn 'when he found upwards of two hundred and fifty dog-fighters, bullies, chimney sweepers and sharpers all assembled and at work. As soon as he and his officers entered the ring (which was in the time of divine service) they set their mastiff dogs at them, who had more humanity than their brutal masters. . . .' The principals were brought before Johnson's friend, Justice Welch, at his office in Lichfield Street.[3] (This office—an embryo police court—Johnson attended for a whole winter only to find 'an almost uniform tenor of misfortune and profligacy'.)

London had the great beauty of a town with views of open country. From its neighbouring heights the prospect of the city was immensely and justly admired, especially when, as from Greenwich Hill, the river with its shipping could be seen. This, however, did not mean that the fields surrounding

[1] *Connoisseur*, No. 26, July 25, 1754.
[2] *Public Advertiser*, Aug. 3, 1764.   [3] *Daily Gazetteer*, June 10, 1766.

the town were all pleasant places. They had the disadvantages of the immediate neighbourhood of a great city before the age of sanitation, and when transport was so relatively primitive that cattle had to be driven there on foot, and bricks made near the spot where they were to be used. These fields were also the natural lurking-places of footpads and vagrants and were notoriously unsafe. The author of a *Life of Pope* (1744) makes an illuminating remark. Pope's schoolmaster, he says, removed to a house near Hyde Park Corner (on the site of Down Street), which had previously belonged to a market gardener, 'and consequently having a large open space adjoining thereto was not pleasant'. The approach to London from the north in 1772 is thus described by Gilpin, that specialist in picturesque tours. After Highgate Hill, he writes, 'the country is gone. London comes on apace; and all those disgusting ideas with which its great avenues abound—brick-kilns, heaps of collected soil,[1] and stinks of every denomination—clouds of dust rising and vanishing from agitated wheels, pursuing each other in agitated motion—or taking temporary possession of the road, by becoming the atmosphere of some cumbersome, slow-moving wagon—villages without rural ideas, trees and hedgerows without a tinge of green. . . .'[2]

This gloomy picture is far from universally true. West London protected by parks was far more favourably situated, but it too was not without its blemishes. The prospect from the Green Park, in 1749,[3] then uncurtailed by the extensions to the gardens of Buckingham House, was a rural landscape in which the chief incidents were the newly built Chesterfield House, St. George's Hospital, the Rotunda of Ranelagh, and Chelsea Hospital, Chelsea Church nestling in trees, the 'Surrey hills' now lost in the streets of Battersea and Clapham. But there was also 'the Pot House', a conical building emitting clouds of smoke close to St. George's, and shown in Rocque's map as a brick-kiln. These places were a real nuisance and West London did not escape. 'Fine streets and squares, most of them regularly laid down and well paved,' wrote Wendeborn in the eighties, 'present palaces to the

---

[1] That is, night-soil.
[2] *Observations relative chiefly to picturesque Beauty made in the year 1772* (2 vols., 1786), vol. ii, pp. 267–8.
[3] Print in the Crace Collection, British Museum.

BAGNIGGE WELLS

From a drawing by F. Sanders, 1772

eye . . . where a little while ago nothing was to be seen but uncultivated grounds, brick-kilns and even dung hills.' But when all is said, this easy access to the fields was an enormous boon to the Londoner and was taken advantage of to the full. On Sunday mornings these fields were invaded by 'dirty blackguards and poor parentless children who have not any friends to take care of them, going about the fields and ditches where wild-honey-suckles, nettles and thistles grow, with bottles and catching of bees, wasps, lady birds, blue bottles and other winged insects'.[1]

The darker side of London life has hardly been touched on here: the homeless deserted children and young vagrants who grew up to form gangs of thieves are described by Defoe in *Colonel Jacque*. They were one of the saddest sights of London and at night were to be seen sleeping on bulks and under stalls. Johnson told Miss Reynolds that 'as he returned to his lodgings about one or two o'clock in the morning, he often saw poor children asleep on thresholds and stalls, and that he used to put pennies into their hands to buy them a breakfast'.[2]

That London, with its underworld, its dangerous rookeries, and twopenny lodging-houses, its turbulent population and its turmoil of traffic, was yet on the whole an orderly place is a strange phenomenon. It is true that riots were frequent and that in 1780 the forces of disorder got the upper hand, but only after months of incendiary propaganda, and after days of virtual encouragement to burn and plunder. On the whole, the Gordon Riots, examined in detail, confirm the impression that the population, beneath its turbulence, was fundamentally law-abiding. As compared with Paris, and as judged by modern notions, London was without a police; yet it was admittedly a safer place than Paris both as regards crimes of violence and the dangers of the unregulated street traffic. Much was due to the efforts of Bow Street and a few public-spirited magistrates. The testimony of an American in 1779 is valuable, since he was by no means uncritical: 'The number of places of dissipation and pleasure are inconceivable,' he writes; 'Sundays are days of riot, excursion and dissipation.' But he also notes, 'How willingly people submit to practices or usages calculated for the common benefit, is evident in large cities. The urbanity in the City of London is

---

[1] *Low Life* (3rd ed., 1764).   [2] *Johnsonian Misc.*, vol. ii, p. 251.

extremely remarkable. No coercive laws would obtain so implicit an obedience as is here *voluntarily* given to customs calculated for convenience.'[1]

BIBLIOGRAPHY.—*Contemporary Authorities*: Maps are numerous; the best is that of ROCQUE (1746) reproduced by the London Topographical Society, 1913. Among a number of topographers and topographical historians the most useful are: editions of STOWE's *Survey* by Strype (1720), by 'R. Seymour' (1733–4); the histories of W. MAITLAND (editions of 1739, 1756, and 1772) and J. NOORTHOUCK (1773); T. PENNANT's *Of London* (1790 and later editions). J. P. MALCOLM's *Londinium Redivivum* (4 vols., 1802–7) excellently combines history and description; his *Anecdotes of the Manners and Customs of London during the Eighteenth Century* (1808) is a useful compilation from contemporary sources. *The Microcosm of London* (3 vols., 1808–9), aquatints by PUGIN and ROWLANDSON, text by W. H. PYNE and W. COMBE, and W. HONE's *Every Day Book* (1826–7) are also useful.

Letters and memoirs, plays, novels, and essays are a mine of information; especially useful are FOOTE's plays, FIELDING's *Amelia* (1751), SMOLLETT's *Humphry Clinker* (1771), F. BURNEY's *Evelina* (1778, ed. Sir F. D. Mackinnon, 1930); for the underworld, DEFOE's *Colonel Jacque* and *Moll Flanders* (both 1722). Among periodical essays *The World* (1753–4) and *The Connoisseur* (1754–6) are particularly valuable for their view of 'the town'; JOHNSON's *Rambler* (1750–2) and *Idler* (1758–60) contain much information on London life, as do GOLDSMITH's essays, especially *The Citizen of the World*. Besides the classic letters and lives of the period, H. ANGELO's *Reminiscences* (2 vols., 1828–30; illustrated, 1904) and J. T. SMITH's *Book for a Rainy Day* (ed. W. Whitten, 1905) and *Nollekens and his Times* (ed. Whitten, 2 vols., 1929) are useful. The impressions of foreign visitors are numerous and valuable, e.g. LE BLANC, *Lettres d'un François* (2 vols. 1745); BARON VON BIELFELD, *Lettres* (2 vols., 1763, visit 1741); J. P. GROSLEY, *Londres* (3 vols., 1770, visit 1765); C. MORITZ, *Travels through various parts of England in 1782* (ed. P. E. Matheson, 1924); ARCHENHOLTZ, *Tableau de l'Angleterre* (2 vols., 1788); Wendeborn, *A View of England . . .* (2 vols., 1791).

Secondary Works: H. B. WHEATLEY and P. CUNNINGHAM, *London Past and Present* (3 vols., 1910), an indispensable reference book; H. B. CHANCELLOR's *The Eighteenth Century in London* (1920) is well illustrated, as are a number of other pleasant topographical books by the same writer. M. D. GEORGE's *London Life in the Eighteenth Century* (1925) is chiefly concerned with the life of the humbler classes. Parish histories are numerous and useful, e.g. J. NELSON's *Islington* (1811), T. FAULKNER's *Chelsea* (1810) and *Kensington* (1820), PINK's *Clerkenwell* (1865), J. MACMASTER's *St. Martin's in the Fields* (1916). Among the enormous number of books on special aspects of London life the following are especially useful: A. DOBSON's *Eighteenth-Century Vignettes* (three series) and other collected essays published in the *World's Classics*; W. W. and E. A. WROTH, *London Pleasure Gardens of the Eighteenth Century* (1896); W. B. BOULTON, *The Amusements of London* (2 vols., 1901), and the same writer's anonymously published *History of White's* (2 vols., 1892); J. TIMBS, *Clubs and Club Life in London* (1872); SIR A. GEIKIE, *Annals of the Royal Society Club* (1917); H. HUMPHERUS, *History of the Company of Waterman* (n.d.), vol. ii; A. I. DASENT's *St. James's Square* (1895) and *Piccadilly in three Centuries* (1920); W. RENDLE and P. NORMAN, *The Inns of Old Southwark* (1888). J. IRVING's *John Gay's London* (1928) is a convenient guide to the light verse on London before and after GAY's *Trivia*.

[1] H. C. Van Schaack, *Life of Peter Van Schaak* (New York, 1842), pp. 162, 238.

A BAGNIGGE WELLS SCENE, or NO RESISTING TEMPTATION.

VIII

TOWN-LIFE IN THE PROVINCES

By G. D. H. COLE

Here sit poor I, with nothing but my own solitary individuality; doing little, and suffering no more than I have often suffered; hearing nothing that I can repeat; seeing nothing that I can relate; talking, when I do talk, to those whom you cannot regard, and at this moment hearing the curfew which you cannot hear.—*To Mrs. Thrale from Lichfield* (July 26, 1775).

A small country town is not the place in which one would choose to quarrel with a wife; every human being in such places is a spy.—*To Dr. Taylor* (Sept. 3, 1763).

WHY do men live in towns? One reason is 'Because they like it'; and there are towns which appear to exist only for this reason. But the great majority of men cannot simply follow their inclinations in deciding where to dwell. They have to earn their livings, and to take up their habitation where their business lies. Most towns, in modern times at any rate, exist because they serve an economic end; and accordingly their character reflects the forms and needs of the dominant economic system.

In eighteenth-century England there were pleasure-towns, such as Tunbridge Wells and Cheltenham and, above all, Bath. There were seaside holiday resorts, such as Scarborough and, later in the century, Margate, Brighthelmstone, and Weymouth; for this was the age in which the fashionable world discovered sea-bathing in addition to popularizing the inland spas. There were cities and towns, such as Exeter and King's Lynn and Stamford, that, apart from their trade, were noted for the number of gentlemen who had good houses in and around them. There were decayed boroughs, such as Winchelsea and Great Bedwin, that seemed to have no reason for existing at all. There were, finally, cathedral towns, such as Wells and Johnson's own Lichfield, that owed most of their importance to the Church, and clustered, almost in medieval fashion, about the Close; and there were, hardly less ecclesiastical in tone, the ancient university towns of Oxford and Cambridge.

But most English towns in the age of Dr. Johnson owed the greatest part of their wealth and activity to some form of trade. There were, first of all, market towns, any number of them, scattered over the entire face of the country, and serving the surrounding villages as centres of exchange. Thither the rural producer brought many of his wares to sell, either directly to the consumer, or to a middleman who would carry them away to some greater market. And thither the country dweller, too, came to buy, either from stalls or booths in the market-place, or from regular shops. For in eighteenth-century England every town, even the smallest, already had some shops; and their number and importance increased steadily and rapidly as the century advanced. Markets and fairs were indeed far more important then than now; and most towns had a regular market once or twice a week. The poorer people dealt not at the shops, but in the market; but in or near most market towns there were enough of the richer sort to keep at least some shops alive.

The shops flourished especially in those market towns which served a countryside well filled with seats and villas of the gentry. Stamford, for example, where Robert Owen served his apprenticeship as a linen-draper, was a famous shopping-centre throughout the century. Guildford, where the old clothing trade had almost completely disappeared, was another; and, indeed, towns of this sort, which lived largely by supplying the gentry, were scattered thick and fast over most of southern England. No one who glances through one of the old *Road Books* of Cary or Paterson will take long to discover that 'gentlemen's seats' were regarded as the most important feature of the eighteenth-century landscape, or that every road in the south was studded with them. The number of these country houses increased very greatly as the century advanced; for it was a great time for building. But they were plentiful throughout Dr. Johnson's age; and the latter half of the century was especially fertile not only in mansions for noblemen and successful merchants, but also in eligible villa residences for the lesser gentry.

Many market towns in the south were places of little trade apart from this lucrative business of supplying the gentlefolk with provisions and draperies, and catering for their more occasional needs of travel and amusement. If the town stood on a main road, it would have at least one tolerable inn, over and above the alehouses and lesser 'publics' which drove a thriving trade on market days. At this inn there

R. de Greene Delin.

S. Wood Sculp.

An East View of the Cathedral Church & Close of LICHFIELD.
Taken from STOW-pool near S.t CHAD'S Church 1745.

would probably be a local Assembly Room, which could be used for balls, dinners, and other entertainments, and would sometimes house a troop of players—for there were regular theatres only in the larger towns. If the place was a borough or the county town, and accustomed to contested elections, it would almost certainly have two rival inns, used as head-quarters by the contending parties. But some boroughs, where the representation was virtually owned by a single landlord, or put up to the highest bidder by a close corpora-tion, were not used to election contests, and recked little of political affairs. One inn, in addition to the many public houses, might serve their needs.

Other market towns in the south were much more than mere shopping centres for the surrounding gentry, and for the country folk on market days. For they were also the focus of a vigorous industrial life. The west of England, especially, was full of little towns which lived chiefly by their activities in the woollen trade. These were industrial towns long before the coming of the Industrial Revolution, which indeed to a great extent stole their industry away. The growing competition of the Yorkshire manufacturers, who were undercutting its old-established products by new methods of production and with cheaper and less durable goods, though much complained of, had not yet prevented the growth of the industry in east or west; for the total demand was expanding rapidly with the increase of foreign markets. The western counties lived by sheep and by the woollen manufacture; and on this trade and industry the life of their towns was chiefly based.

These west-country towns were not merely centres for buying and selling, but active hives of manufacturing industry. The rich merchant clothiers, whose chief business was trade, were mainly concentrated in the larger towns, such as Exeter and Taunton. But in each smaller town—Bradford-on-Avon, Devizes, Witney, Malmesbury, Honiton, Axminster, and a host of others—there were gathered the actual producers of woollen stuffs. For whereas spinning of wool was at this time carried on by unskilled labour, chiefly that of women and children, scattered among innumerable villages all over the country as well as in the towns, weaving was for the most part a skilled urban occupation. The weavers had little or no connexion with the land, though

they might help at harvest time; and they were mainly
gathered together in towns and large villages that were far
more urban than rural. Wool-combing, too, was a highly
skilled and highly paid urban occupation, even more concentrated in the larger centres than weaving. Wool-combers,
and to some extent workers in the finishing trades, might
labour under the roof of a substantial employer; but the vast
majority of the weavers were home-workers, plying their
craft in their own cottages or in workrooms attached thereto.
The west-country weaving town was a place not of factories
but of substantial cottages each containing a loom, or perhaps two or three.

Very similar conditions existed in the eastern counties,
save that there Norwich was the metropolis of the woollen
trade to a far greater extent than any single town or city in
the west. Indeed, any one who wishes to recapture the
spirit of the old English woollen industry will find in Sudbury, Lavenham, Long Melford, Stoke-by-Neyland, and
other old clothing towns and villages of the eastern counties,
an outward shape less changed by time than anywhere in
the west.

The western counties and East Anglia, with Yorkshire, of
which more anon, were the greatest centres of the woollen
manufacture. But many other counties had their clothing
towns and villages not greatly unlike those of Suffolk or
Devonshire. Kendal, Rochdale, Burnley, Bacup, Knutsford,
Darlington, Godalming, Leominster—the list could be almost
indefinitely prolonged, even without going to Scotland or
Wales for additional examples. The woollen manufacture
was in the eighteenth century England's most widely
diffused, as well as her greatest, industry; and it stamped its
peculiar imprint on half the towns in the country. Moreover,
the less important, but still considerable, manufactures of
linen and silk, the knitting trade in the east Midlands, and
cotton itself before the introduction of the new machines,
created towns and villages of very similar appearance and
social structure.

In Yorkshire, however, the woollen manufacture was
carried on under somewhat different conditions, and with
different effects on the structure of town life. For the
representative figure of the Yorkshire woollen trade in the
eighteenth century was neither the rich merchant clothier

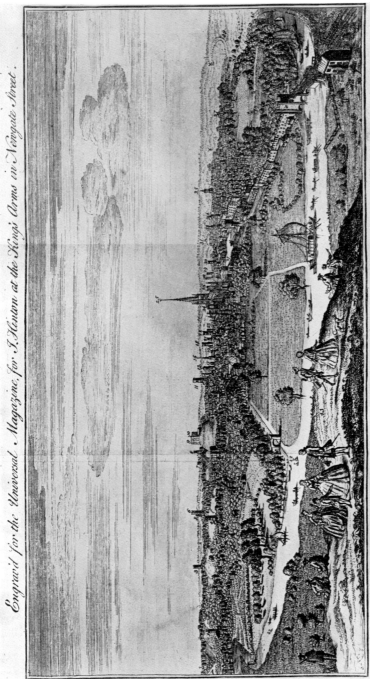

Engrav'd for the Universal Magazine, for J.Hinton at the King's Arms in Newgate Street.

The South-East Prospect of the CITY of NORWICH.

From the Universal Magazine, *1753*

nor the urban home-worker, but rather the small master-craftsman working with his own hands and employing one or two journeymen under his own roof. There were, of course, rich merchants in Leeds and Halifax and Bradford; but they were not for the most part nearly so rich or so gentlemanly as the merchant clothiers of Exeter or Taunton. There were home-workers too; and spinning was, until about the end of the century, an unskilled occupation carried on by women and children in town and country alike. But weaving, the main skilled occupation, was a good deal less urbanized than in the south; and Defoe's famous description of the country round Halifax continued to hold good in the latter part of the century. The Yorkshire manufactures grew up scattered, wherever a river or streamlet afforded a supply of good water for washing and bleaching and, later, for the application of water-power. Its typical unit was a substantial workshop attached to a farm-house; and the typical employer remained at least one part a farmer till quite late in the century.

In these circumstances, there grew up in Yorkshire no such plenty of small clothing towns and large villages as in the west. The Yorkshire clothing towns—Leeds, Halifax, Bradford, and the rest—were centres rather of trade than of actual production. Their chief importance lay in their famous cloth markets, to which the small masters from all the country round brought in their wares. Only with the introduction of steam-power and the factory system did Leeds and Halifax and Bradford become primarily manufacturing, rather than trading, towns.

This, of course, does not mean that no manufacturing was carried on within their limits. Wool-combing and carding, and the pressing and finishing of the woven stuffs, were urban occupations in the north as well as in the south; and there were weavers and spinners in Leeds and Halifax as well as in the surrounding country. But the towns themselves got their social atmosphere and their importance from trade rather than manufacture; and their leading citizens were merchants rather than employers.

Our journey to the north has carried us from the small market towns with which we began to larger urban centres; for Leeds and Bradford and Halifax were all considerable places in the eighteenth century. Richard Price gives the population of Leeds as 17,000 in 1775, and Halifax, with its surrounding countryside, had long been noted as the 'most populous parish in England'. But, even so, Leeds was only a third as populous as Norwich, and about half the size of Birmingham or Liverpool. Chester was nearly as big as Leeds as late as 1750.

Of course it is necessary to speak with great caution of town populations in the eighteenth century, when there was no such thing as an official census, and different authorities often gave wildly different estimates. Sometimes these differences arise because the varying estimates are not for the same areas, some being confined to the borough limits and some including the surrounding suburbs. For example, very different figures are given for Manchester, according as the quotation is for the town itself, or for the wider parish, or for the whole area of the Manor of Manchester.

It is, however, possible, from the estimates quoted by Arthur Young, Macpherson, and other economic writers and travellers, and by Richard Price in his famous *Essay on the Population of England*, and sometimes from local censuses of varying accuracy, to get some idea of the size of the principal towns in the third quarter of the eighteenth century. London was, of course, immensely the largest—even bigger in relation to the total population of eighteenth-century England than modern London is in relation to the England of to-day. For London was the great centre of trade as well as of fashion, arts, and government; and, at any rate in the south, the London market dominated the trade of the smaller towns to a very great extent. In the south, London's only serious rival was Bristol, which alone drove a thriving independent import and export trade, and provided an alternative point of focus for the industries of South Wales and the western counties, including the Severn country and even, to a great extent, Birmingham and the West Midlands with their rapidly growing manufactures of iron and brass.

Bristol was, indeed, easily the second town in England, with a population of about 100,000, and a flourishing glass and china manufacture in addition to the trade of its port. Manchester, growing at a very rapid rate, had only 30,000 inhabitants in 1769, according to Arthur Young, and even with Salford and the suburbs no more than 50,000. Young put the population of Liverpool at 40,000 in 1769; but Price made it only 34,500 in 1773, and the latter estimate is probably nearer the truth unless the surrounding villages are included with it. Birmingham in 1770 had about 30,000 people according to several authorities, Hull from 20,000 (Young) to 24,000 (Macpherson), and Sheffield from 20,000 (Macpherson) to 30,000 (Young). These, with Norwich, variously estimated at from 40,000 (Young) to 60,000 (Macpherson), were the largest towns, followed by Nottingham and Leeds, each with about 17,000. Chester had about 15,000, Shrewsbury about 13,000, and Worcester from 11,000 to 12,000, according to varying estimates by Price and Young, while Bolton had only 5,000, and Northampton no more. Newbury, in Berkshire, with 4,000 people, was as big as Bradford; and the great majority even of the more flourishing lesser towns had only from two to four thousand inhabitants. Chippenham, for example, had 2,400 (Price), and High Wycombe 2,500 (also Price).[1]

Ordinary market towns and even flourishing industrial centres were, then, even in the latter part of the eighteenth century, no larger than populous villages of to-day; and even the great trading centres, except Bristol, were no larger than very minor modern provincial towns. We must bear this smallness of the typical eighteenth-century town constantly in mind, if we mean to get a true picture of its character and way of life. For a town even of forty or fifty thousand people cannot be far removed from the country; and a town of five thousand will, unless it be quite exceptional in its way of life, still retain many of the characteristics of a village.

It is necessary to keep this consideration in mind above all in passing judgement on the sanitation and methods of government of the towns of the eighteenth century. For it is very easy to condemn them, on both grounds, by the application of wholly inappropriate standards. We read of the lack of a proper water-supply, of paved streets, of an adequate police force, and of one after another of the essentials of modern town life, in, say, Leeds or Birmingham; and we are apt to think what these great cities would be like now if they had to do without these vital services. But, in fact, neither Leeds nor Birmingham in the eighteenth century was in the least like the Leeds or the Birmingham of to-day; and we

[1] In 1781 Lichfield had less than 4,000 inhabitants (Harwood) and in 1789 Oxford rather more than 8,000 (Parker).

cannot afford to be so proud of the water-supply or the urban amenities of many of our large modern villages as to cast stones very readily at the great majority of eighteenth-century towns for doing without them. Doubtless, the towns of the eighteenth century would have been healthier, and perhaps happier, if they had been better 'policed', in the eighteenth-century sense of that term. But they were by no means so ill off for want of this as the modern reader is apt to imagine, or as the scandalized Utilitarians who drew up the *Report on Municipal Corporations* in 1835 were disposed to suggest. The sanitary problem became desperately urgent only when the trading and hand-working towns of the eighteenth century turned into industrial towns under the factory system and steam-power, and found their populations vastly increased in a few years by the concentration of workers which the factory system involved.

It is, however, true enough that urban government throughout the eighteenth century was in a bad way. Many of the newer towns, like Manchester and Birmingham, were not incorporated, and had no fully developed municipal institutions of their own. But this did not always mean that they were any worse off than a borough in possession of a fully fledged Municipal Corporation, with a charter from the Crown, and valued privileges which rendered it immune from the jurisdiction of the county. For the typical Municipal Corporation of the eighteenth century hardly regarded itself as a local government authority in the modern sense, or accepted any responsibility for the adequate development of sanitary services and amenities on behalf of the whole body of inhabitants. There was an immense variety of municipal constitutions; and the municipal corporations ranged from bodies regularly elected, at least in theory, by nearly all the householders to narrow oligarchies of the wealthier tradesmen and merchants, with perhaps a few independent 'gentlemen', renewing themselves by co-option without any shadow of a representative method of choice. These self-elected oligarchies were indeed the predominant type; and bodies elected by the householders were relatively few. But there is positively, through all the century, no sign of serious objection on a national scale to the principle of self-election, or of a sense that things ought to be otherwise arranged, though it is significant that the more progressive towns, when they needed new services, seldom thought of entrusting them to the existing Municipal Corporations. There were plenty of movements in the latter part of the century, like that of the Yorkshire freeholders and the agitations led by Cartwright and Horne Tooke, for a reform of parliamentary representation. But neither the earlier reformers nor the democrats at the end of the century had ever turned their attention seriously towards municipal reform.

The eighteenth-century Municipal Corporation was, indeed, and considered itself as being, far less an organ of local government in the modern sense than an institution for the management of a corporate property. Membership of this privileged body had come to be regarded almost as a property right, and the property of the Corporation almost as belonging to its members as individuals rather than to the town. Civic feasts, such as we associate with the London Livery Companies of to-day, seemed a more appropriate use for the civic funds than the provision of an adequate water-supply or the paving or lighting of the streets; and the right to send Members to Parliament came to be regarded rather as a property right of the members of the Corporation than as a right of representation in the counsels of the country. The right of electing Members to serve in Parliament was often vested in the Corporation, and seats were often put up for sale, without shame or sense of shame, to the highest bidder. Indeed, the buying of seats was often justified as a desirable means of securing the return to Parliament of men of property who lacked territorial influence; and often the best and most independent Members sat for the rottenest boroughs. Sometimes, of course, when a large part of the borough was owned by a single great landowner, the Corporation simply carried out his will in the election of Members to Parliament; but, where property was more distributed and the Corporation was free to act as it chose, it was usually far less inclined to aim at getting its own point of view represented in the House of Commons than to return some man of wealth who was prepared to pay for the privilege. The truth is that most of the eighteenth-century boroughs had no particular desire to be represented in Parliament. They wanted, not to be better governed, but to be left alone.

Nor did things usually work out any better when the

parliamentary franchise was vested, not in the Corporation, but in a wider body of freemen, or in all the householders paying scot and lot. For this, as a rule, only diffused corruption over a wider field, causing a plentiful outpouring, at election time, of free dinners, free beer, and very often free money as well. These wider bodies of electors were no more disposed than the oligarchical Corporations to take their privilege of representation seriously. Even such famous open constituencies as Westminster, Preston, and Coventry, where real elections were fought in the early nineteenth century on real issues of political principle— though not without a good deal of corruption even then— only gained their reputation after the revolutions in America and France had sent men back to political first principles, and effectively roused the democratic spirit from its long sleep. Whatever virtues the eighteenth century had, it was assuredly not democratic. It did not want to be democratic; and accordingly, even when democratic instruments were placed in its hands, it did not commonly care or trouble to use them.

Parliament, however, was far away; and it may seem surprising that the provincial notables, even if they could not be bothered with governing the country, did not make more effort to provide for the good government of their own towns. But, in fact, in many of the older towns the members of the Municipal Corporation were hardly conscious that a problem of local administration existed at all. As Mr. and Mrs. Webb have pointed out in their monumental study of English Local Government, the very phrase 'Local Government' was not coined until after the middle of the nineteenth century. This, of course, is not to say that the notion had not existed for many centuries. But it had been associated, in the minds of the Municipal Corporations of Tudor and Stuart times, primarily with the regulation of local trades and industries, that is, with forms of administration which changing economic conditions had rendered obsolete. What remained of the old functions was judicial rather than administrative; and the Borough Justices, inferior in social status to the country gentlemen who manned the county bench, were in most towns a good deal more active in local affairs than the Municipal Corporations. Here and there, as at Liverpool, an energetic and on the whole enlightened

Corporation was to be found. But Liverpool was exceptional; for its rapidly growing prosperity depended obviously on the efficiency of its docks and its trading organization, and the merchants who controlled its administration had a strong interest in the proper conduct of municipal affairs. Manchester might have been just as efficient if it had possessed the appropriate local institutions. But Manchester was not a Corporation at all; it was still under the old manorial jurisdiction.

Most of the English towns in the mid-eighteenth century were still unconscious of problems calling for strong municipal government. Such a matter as the cleaning of the streets was still imposed as an obligation on each individual householder, whose duty it was to keep the space in front of his own dwelling clear, as far as the middle of the road. Street cleaning was thus a citizen's obligation, to be enforced by the justices, rather than a public obligation. The supply of water was indeed coming in the early part of the century to be felt as a pressing need in some of the larger towns; and this service was sometimes taken in hand by the Corporation. But eighteenth-century travellers always commented with surprised fervour when they found a town, such as Exeter, publicly supplied with water in leaden pipes; wells and pumps still supplied the needs of townsmen in most places, as they do to this day the needs of the majority of villages.

What is remarkable is that when, as the century advanced, increasing population and improving sanitary knowledge began to force the problems of municipal organization into public notice, the commonest way of getting new services developed was not by means of the Municipal Corporations, but by the establishment, side by side with them, of new and independent authorities. Under various names, one town after another set up in the course of the eighteenth century a body of Improvement Commissioners, created by a special Act of Parliament, and given power to lay a limited rate upon the whole of the householders. These bodies of Commissioners were doing, in the latter part of the century, far more to introduce new municipal services than all the Municipal Corporations taken together. They chiefly set about lighting, cleaning, and paving the streets, providing a rudimentary police-force of night-watchmen, regulating traffic, and in many ways both removing 'nuisances' and improving local amenities. This is not surprising in towns such as Manchester, which lacked corporate rights and organization: what is at first sight astonishing is that bodies of this sort were set up almost as much in towns which already had Municipal Corporations, and that in most cases the entrusting of the new duties to the existing authorities seems not to have been even considered. There could be no clearer sign of the extent to which incorporation had come to be regarded as conferring not duties but privileges on the members of the corporate body. This attitude fitted in well enough with the common opinion of eighteenth-century England about the scope of government and the rights of property. *Laissez-faire*, save in matters of foreign trade, was not a nineteenth-century invention, or a product of the machine age. It flourished even more, inside the country, after the 'Glorious Revolution' of 1689 had established the country gentleman's right to be let alone by Parliament, and the spread of the 'domestic system' through the market towns and country districts had destroyed the old regulative functions of Gilds and Municipal Corporations.

Another important reason for the lethargy of the Municipal Corporations was the prevalence of religious Dissent among the merchants and tradesmen of the developing towns. For though the Test and Corporation Acts were not enforced, and Acts of Indemnity were regularly passed on behalf of those Dissenters of an accommodating spirit who took office in spite of them, the Municipal Corporations retained throughout the century a strong flavour of religious orthodoxy, enough to exclude the more vigorous and conscientious members of the dissenting connexions. It was partly under the influence of the latter, and in order to secure their collaboration, that the new purely secular and undenominational bodies of Improvement Commissioners were brought into being; and it was through these new bodies that the Dissenters came to be a power in the municipal world.

Apart from such clearly public functions as the lighting, paving, cleaning, and watching of the streets, there were plenty of other municipal duties awaiting the energies of the local reformers as the century advanced. Outside London, the movement to establish hospitals for the use of the poor seems to have begun with the opening of a public hospital

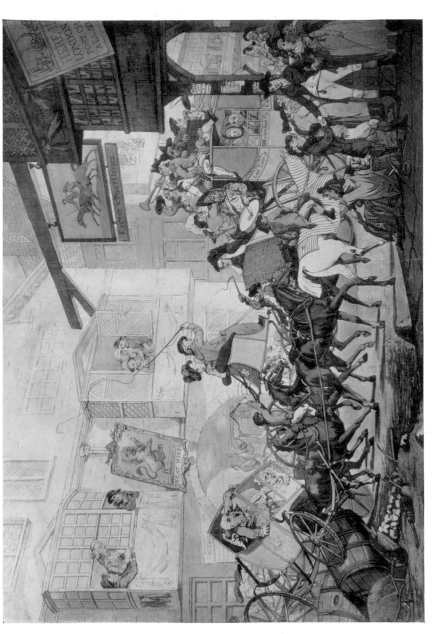

SCENE IN A COUNTRY TOWN AT THE TIME OF A RACE MEETING

From an engraving after the painting by W. Mason

at Winchester in 1736. This was intended to serve the needs of the entire county; and the funds for it were raised by public subscription among the wealthier inhabitants—a method followed for most subsequent institutions of a similar kind. Bristol, York, and Exeter all established hospitals within the next few years. Liverpool's Infirmary was founded in 1749 and Manchester's in 1752. Manchester added a Lunatic Asylum in 1765, and Public Baths in 1751. Newcastle-on-Tyne began a Lying-in Charity in 1765, and Norwich a hospital in 1771. Finally, in 1784, came Dr. Thomas Percival's famous Report on the Health of Manchester to the County Justices, followed by the setting-up of the Manchester Board of Health.

Thus, even before the middle of the century, attention was already turning towards medical and sanitary reform, and thereafter this movement rapidly gained force in several of the larger towns. In this field of action, Manchester, under the vigorous leadership of Dr. Percival, was well to the front; and indirectly John Howard's national crusade for prison reform, which began in 1773, exerted a powerful influence on the movement. Howard's *State of the Prisons* appeared in 1777; and he included hospitals and similar institutions within the scope of his enlightening surveys. But reform was slow. William Tuke's Retreat at York—the first humane Lunatic Asylum—was not founded until 1791; and the creation of separate fever hospitals was only beginning at the end of the century. The Manchester Fever Hospital, created under Percival's influence, dates only from 1796.

The spirit of philanthropy was not confined to hospital subscriptions. The latter half of the century was also marked by the growth of other charitable bodies, from Friendly Societies, under the patronage of the rich, to such institutions as the Norwich Society of Universal Good Will, first founded as the Scots Society in 1776, for the relief of poor strangers in the town. The movement to set up Charity Schools connected with the Church of England had by 1750 exhausted its impetus and ceased to expand; but sporadic Sunday Schools, such as Hannah Ball's at High Wycombe (1768), were founded even before Robert Raikes began work at Bristol in 1780. Hannah More was at that time still pursuing her literary career in London, on intimate terms with Dr. Johnson and his circle. Her philanthropic ventures at Cowslip Green, near Bristol, began only after 1785.

This growth of philanthropic activities is closely bound up with the rise of Wesleyanism and the Evangelical movement. Of these, Wesleyanism counted for much the more in the provincial towns. Wesley's famous *Journal* is full of accounts of his visits and preachings not only in Bath and Bristol, but also in the growing towns of the north, in all of which from the middle of the century he began to have a considerable following. Wesleyanism was, indeed, concerned with men's souls far more than with their bodies; and Wesley himself as well as his leading followers abhorred all forms of Radicalism. This came to matter greatly at a later stage, when the age of political excitements had set in with the Revolutions in America and France. But in the middle part of the century there was little political unrest to impel the religious reformers to turn their backs on the demand for social reform; and in the provincial towns the Wesleyan revival was undoubtedly a factor making for the development of the social conscience.

The lead, however, was taken at this stage not by the Wesleyans, but by older types of Dissenters, and especially by Unitarians and Independents, and in some places, such as York, by the Quakers. The Unitarians, headed by Richard Price and Joseph Priestley, were made up of far more intellectual elements than any other group of Dissenters; and their Academies, such as the New College at Warrington, where Priestley taught, followed by Dalton the chemist after its removal to Manchester, were notable centres of social as well as religious enlightenment. Certain of the most successful merchants of Liverpool and other fast growing centres of industry and commerce got their education at the Dissenting Academies, which spread a knowledge of popular science as well as of religious and political speculation.

Closely connected with the growth of education and enlightenment among the younger generation of merchants is the creation of Literary and Philosophical Societies in the leading mercantile towns. Robert Owen has left, in his *Autobiography*, a graphic record of the impression made on him in his youth by the discussions at the Manchester Society, which was led by Dr. Percival and Dr. Barnes, and included Dalton, as well as Owen, among its members.

Coleridge came to address it while Owen was there; and in other towns besides Manchester societies of this type became centres of reforming zeal as well as of literary and philosophic illumination. They gathered together valuable libraries for their members' use; and their debates and discussions were taken very seriously indeed.

In some cases, the formation of a subscription library came first. Liverpool, well to the front as usual, began one in 1757, and added a weekly 'Academy' in 1774, the year in which the Chamber of Commerce was founded. Manchester, on the other hand, began with informal weekly discussions in an hotel; and out of them the 'Lit. and Phil.' developed in 1781. No lasting subscription library came into existence till 1792, though there had been earlier attempts. Leeds, under Priestley's influence, formed a Subscription Library in 1768; and a Debating Society followed in 1793, but died out in a few years. The Leeds Philosophical and Literary Society dates only from 1818.[1]

By these and other means, standards of taste and knowledge rose very rapidly in the larger manufacturing towns during the latter half of the eighteenth century. A further contribution to the development of more polished manners and a less rude way of living, and perhaps, though not so certainly, to higher cultural standards as well, came from the growing number of boys from the families of the squire-archy who were being apprenticed to trade, especially in the merchant houses of Liverpool. There were many tales narrated about the discontent of these new recruits at the rough ways of speech and living current even among the richer members of the merchant class, at the very early and long hours of work, and at the Puritan ideas so widely spread in the industrial districts. The gentry who took to trade brought with them some shadow of the habits and customs of the fashionable world—a cultivation of dancing, concerts and assemblies, and a taste for music and the fine arts. The Liverpool Musical Society grew out of the great Musical Festival held there in 1784; and exhibitions of pictures began about the same time to be shown in some of the leading provincial towns.

[1] The circulating libraries established by booksellers in the larger provincial towns also helped to spread knowledge and to encourage the liking for books. For the circulating libraries and the booksellers, see *infra*, vol. ii, ch. xxv.

The theatre and the newspaper also spread through the leading provincial centres in the course of the eighteenth century, and especially after 1750. In the earlier part of the century, strolling players used mainly tents or booths, and the superior travelling companies and the 'stock' or repertory companies which existed already here and there used any available hall, and did not provide regular daily performances. But in the latter part of the century there was a rapid building of provincial theatres, such as the Nottingham Theatre of 1760 and the Manchester Theatre Royal of 1775. Often the theatres in several towns were under the same management; and companies changed places one with another. Bath, indeed, had its first theatre as early as 1705, with a stock company, and the plays selected by the leaders of fashion who were there to take the waters. But the venture came to an end about 1738, and for a time plays were given at an inn or in a cellar under the Rooms. Not until 1750 did the elder John Palmer, of whom more anon, open his theatre in Orchard Street (now the Masonic Rooms). His son, who succeeded to the control, developed a group of theatres in Bristol and other neighbouring towns, with circulating companies in which many of the leading actors and actresses of the day made their names. Mrs. Siddons, who had begun her career at Birmingham, was a member of the Bath company from 1788 to 1792, when she went to Drury Lane. Elliston, Macready, and Kean, as well as Henderson, the leading Bath star, also first made their reputations at the Bath theatres under Palmer's management.

Booksellers' shops and printing houses, often associated with a local newspaper, already existed by the middle of the century in most provincial towns of any size. Dr. Johnson's father was a bookseller in Lichfield; for his parchment-making, at which he lost money, was only an auxiliary venture. New and second-hand bookselling were not then divided; and the trade was a much less stable one than it is to-day. It was also more laborious; for the provincial bookseller used often to go from town to town, opening a stall on market-days, in addition to his permanent shop in some one centre. Johnson's father, for example, went regularly to Birmingham with his wares on market-days; and William Hutton, the historian of Birmingham, travelled a regular round of towns for some time, carrying his books long distances upon his back. We also find him walking in 1749 from Nottingham to London and back, in order to buy better tools for his trade as a bookbinder. There is no eighteenth-century autobiography so rich as Hutton's in materials for the study of the provincial life of tradesman and artisan in the Midland counties.

Apart from theatres and concert-rooms and the assembly rooms of the fashionable resorts and the county towns, the centre of the recreative life of the provinces was very often the racecourse. At Manchester, regular race-meetings at Kersal Moor began about 1729, and gave rise to a great deal of controversy. A pamphlet, attributed to John Byrom, was written denouncing them; and in 1745 they were suppressed for a time. But they were renewed in 1760, and a grand stand built by subscription in 1777, followed by a ladies' stand, equipped for refreshments, in 1780. Nottingham racecourse, which belonged to the Corporation, was leased to the noblemen and gentlemen of the county in 1777, under a trust deed, and did not revert to the Corporation until 1845. Doncaster, already celebrated for its races, was also a famous hunting centre; and Defoe tells how, about 1725, it was full of great inns, and the Mayor, who kept one of them, had a pack of hounds, and was deemed fit company for the gentry. Another sport was also gaining in popularity. In 1771 Nottingham and Sheffield met in their first cricket match. Less innocuous was the prevalence of cock-fighting and bull-baiting as sports of rich and poor alike.

This consideration of amusements and recreations leads us naturally back to the world of fashion; for in the eighteenth century almost all sports and recreative arts depended on the noblemen and gentlemen for their patronage. And, in the world of fashion, all roads seem to lead to Bath, which began its career of triumph right at the beginning of the century and kept its ascendancy undimmed to the very end.

Bath, the city of Beau Nash, of John Wood, John Palmer, and Ralph Allen, of Dr. Oliver and Sally Lunn, and, incongruously, of Lady Huntingdon as well, had its first Pump Room in 1704—three years before its first theatre, and its first Assembly Room (Harrison's) in 1708. Nash, Allen, Oliver, the elder Wood, and the elder Palmer were all dead and gone before Dr. Johnson visited Bath with the Thrales

in 1776; but the younger Wood with his new buildings and
the younger and more celebrated Palmer with his mail-
coaches, were in the height of their glory. Most of Bath's
notable buildings had already been erected, and the new
Assembly Rooms, built by the younger Wood, had recently
been opened (1771). Henderson was already playing Shakespeare at the theatre, and Thomas Sheridan and Linley were
there, teaching elocution and music. Ralph Allen's house
at Prior Park was no longer a great resort of literary folk
as in Pope's day, and Bath society was broken up far more
into sets and coteries than earlier in the century. But, save
in one important respect, Bath was still much as Nash had
striven to make it in the early years, a place of resort for
the upper and middle classes alike, where the observed
routine of bathing and drinking the waters was in fact subor-
dinated to the hardly less regular discipline of social events.
The company still gathered largely for breakfast in the
Assembly Rooms, with a dip in the Baths still earlier for
those who fancied it. After breakfast they resorted to the
Pump Room to drink the waters, and then, if so disposed,
to morning service in the Abbey. Walking, riding, or driving
filled in the time until dinner, varied by a visit to the booksellers to read the papers; and after dinner there were more
parades in the Pump Room or the Orange Groves, followed
by five o'clock tea, often taken at the Rooms, and a ball or
a visit to the theatre in the evening.

By the time Dr. Johnson paid his visit, Bath was in the
third and most enduring phase of its popularity. It began its
career, like Harrogate and other places of resort to the
waters, as a centre of attraction for invalids. It passed,
under Nash's influence, rapidly into a haunt of fashion; but
in this second phase one of its chief attractions was the
opportunity which it afforded for open and organized gambling. Till 1745 Nash made most of his money out of the
commission of $2\frac{1}{2}$ per cent. which he received from the bank
on its takings at each EO table—for EO was the favourite
form of gambling. But in 1745 public gambling was suppressed by law, to Nash's heavy loss; and thereafter, while
it went on to some extent in taverns and private houses, it
ceased to count as an important attraction of Bath life.
Gamblers resorted abroad, or to the new racecourses; and
Bath society was none the less fashionable or enticing to the

COMFORTS OF BATH

From the drawing by T. Rowlandson

mind of the public for its disappearance. Thereafter Bath, haunt of wickedness as it appeared to John Wesley and the circle of Lady Huntingdon—who lived there none the less—followed in the main a very innocuous round of pleasures. Its favourite plays were classical tragedies, by Otway or the Elizabethans, and its favourite dance was the stately minuet. It was, indeed, the great match-making centre of England, and a great place for innocent flirtations. But as a den of vice, save the minor vices of idleness and frivolity, it left much to the Wesleyan imagination.

Bath's appeal was in no wise weakened by the rapid growth of other centres of fashionable resort, such as Cheltenham and Tunbridge Wells and Harrogate, or by the growing popularity of seaside watering-places as the century advanced. Of other inland spas, Knaresborough, near the Harrogate waters, was the oldest, and Harrogate grew up as a separate place of resort by the middle of the century. Tunbridge Wells also developed about the same time as a new town grouped round the waters; and Cheltenham was just becoming popular when Richard Pococke visited it in 1750. But its lodgings were then, in his view, no more than tolerable. Cheltenham and Tunbridge Wells modelled themselves on Bath, and reproduced faithfully its routines and observances, whereas Harrogate, frequented chiefly by Northerners, was a good deal less ceremonious.

But the chief resort in the north, and the pioneer of all seaside watering-places, was Scarborough, already famous for its waters in the seventeenth century. From Dr. Wittie's encomium on the virtues of Scarborough Spa in 1667 to Dr. Peter Shaw's *Inquiry into the Contents, Virtues and Uses of Scarborough Spaw Water* in 1734 much was written about the special health-giving properties of the place; and Sir John Floyer's *History of Cold Bathing* (1734) and Shaw's *Inquiry* gave it a new accession of popularity. Sea-bathing was by this time coming much into fashion as a cure; and, in imitation of the inland spas, drinking the sea-water was also widely recommended. These new fashions led to a great growth of watering-places in the south. Brighton, or Brighthelmstone, was only a poor fishing village in Defoe's day; but by 1750 Pococke records it as 'greatly improved of late by the concourse of people who come to it to bathe and drink the sea-water', and as possessing a good coffee-house, a large room for company, and carriages for the convenience of bathing. Pococke has much the same to say of Margate, where he notices especially 'the conveniency of covered carriages, at the end of which there is a covering that lets down with hoops, so that people can go down a ladder into the water and not be seen, and those who please may jump in and swim'. Deal and Eastbourne and Portsmouth were among other resorts that became popular in the first half of the eighteenth century, followed a little later by Weymouth and many other places. Much of the fashionable

For Bathing in the Sea at MARGATE,
BEALE (the Inventor of the Bathing Machine) and SAYER in Co.
At the ORIGINAL ROOM, accommodated for BATHING,
Provides Lodgings, Stables, &c.

world went on to a seaside resort after passing the earlier part of the summer at Bath or some other inland spa.

But no more space can be devoted to the haunts and habits of the noblemen and gentlemen, or of those prosperous merchants and tradesmen who came more and more either to imitate their manners, or to work out a round of pleasure for themselves as standards of living advanced and the earlier forms of Puritanism relaxed their hold. For in the eighteenth century, as at other times, towns were mainly workaday places, and the great majority of their inhabitants belonged to the working classes. It is time, then, to glance at the position of the urban workers, their wages and conditions of work, and the environment in which they spent their leisure.

It must be observed in the first place that it is of even less

SCARBOROUGH IN 1735

From an engraving after the painting by J. Setterington

use to generalize about working-class conditions before the Industrial Revolution than in the nineteenth century or to-day. For prior to the coming of the factory system the distinction between the working classes and the social groups nearest to them was even less clear-cut than it is in the modern world. A prosperous skilled artisan earning a weekly wage might be quite as well off, and as respectable in his social status, as a small master or shopkeeper; and in the days of the·'domestic system', the lines between small masters, sub-contractors, and working journeymen were not at all easy to draw. In the building trades especially, the same man often worked sometimes as a small contractor and sometimes as a journeyman drawing a wage; while the 'domestic' worker might be either an independent producer working with his own tools and upon his own materials or a dependent using tools and materials which were the property of some one who was virtually his employer, and paying rent for the use of the instruments of production—'loom-rent' for example. There was, in addition, a far wider gulf between skilled artisans and mere labourers than there is to-day, both in wages and in degree of education and social standing. The cultural gulf between labourer and artisan was usually much wider than the gulf between artisan and small employer or tradesman.

For information about wages outside London, the most valuable sources are Arthur Young's *Tours*; for he recorded, wherever he could, the prevailing wages for urban as well as rural workers. His figures have, however, to be taken as very rough estimates, mostly derived from employers' information; and statements about the earnings of piece-workers under the domestic system are especially liable to error. It is, nevertheless, possible to obtain from his writings, with such confirmation as can be secured from other sources, a fairly clear picture of prevailing wage-standards in many of the principal towns.

Thus, in Manchester it appears that, about 1770, the wages of highly skilled male workers in the textile trades did not often rise above 7s. 6d. a week, though a few exceptionally skilled hands might sometimes get up to 12s. A large number of skilled men got no more than 5s. or 6s., and some as little as 4s. a week. Skilled women workers appear to have made less, but not a great deal less, than the majority of

men; and in a number of cases Young records that they were
paid at the same rates. Children earned from 1s. 6d. a week
upwards, according to age and trade. Eden, writing almost
thirty years later, in the midst of the great rise in prices
during the French War, put the wages of skilled men as
high as 18s. a week, and women's from 6s. to 12s., with
unskilled labour at 2s. or 2s. 6d. a day.

This sharp advance in men's wages was due in part to the
rise in prices, but also to the rapid growth of the cotton
trade. Lancashire was a low-wage area until the Industrial
Revolution. The old-established woollen industry in Yorkshire paid the male workers rather better. Thus, in Leeds,
Arthur Young gave the earnings of men weavers as from
5s. to 12s. a week, with an average of 7s., and of broadcloth
weavers at 10s. 6d., and wool-combers 6s. to 12s. But, while
highly skilled women weavers made in some cases as much
as men, their average earnings were only from 3s. 6d. to
4s., and at spinning—an unskilled occupation—women got
only from 2s. 6d. to 3s. Moreover, all these rates were for
full-time work; and Young comments that they were often
seriously reduced by intermittent employment.

Earnings tended to be lower in the north of England than
in the south, at least for the most highly skilled grades of
workers. Thus, dyers in Norwich are said to have earned
15s. a week, and cloth pressers 13s., while wool-combers in the
Western Counties averaged 13s. Weavers in Witney got
from 10s. to 12s. a week all the year round—an exceptionally
prosperous group; for weavers even in London earned on the
average no more than from 12s. to 15s. a week. Young gives
the average earnings of men employed in industry in the
western counties as 11s. a week, in the eastern counties as
6s. 6d., and in the south as 9s. 4d.

There were, thus, wide differences in wages both from trade
to trade and from place to place. Artisans in the older crafts
in the larger towns—shoemakers, tailors, cabinet-makers,
and so on—and the minority of highly specialized craftsmen, such as wool-combers and dyers, in the larger industries
did best, while the condition of the main body of wage-
earners varied very greatly from one town to another. But
it has to be remembered that costs of living were a good
deal lower in the north and east than in the south, and in the
market towns than in the larger cities.

It is exceedingly difficult to say how far the industrial workers in the eighteenth century were organized in Trade Unions for collective bargaining about wages and conditions of labour. No modern Trade Union dates from this period; and those which did exist have left no records of their own behind them. But there is plenty of evidence of the widespread existence of certain forms of combination. The journeymen in the larger towns certainly had their regular Trade Clubs, which were often Friendly Societies as well as Trade Unions, and negotiated freely with the small masters, usually without any interference from the law. There was, indeed, on the Statute Book a general embargo on working-class combinations enacted under Edward VI; and many specific statutes were passed in the eighteenth century prohibiting combinations in particular trades. But the small Trade Clubs of the urban artisans were seldom molested, the severities of the law being directed rather against the larger Unions which arose from time to time among the weavers of a whole county, or some similar widespread group. The wool-combers seem to have maintained a nation-wide organization without being suppressed; and persecution of Trade Unionism was intermittent and casual until the fears of Jacobinism came to render all working-class bodies suspect of treasonable designs.[1]

These eighteenth-century combinations often sought to influence wage-rates not so much by collective bargaining as by appeals to the law. Again and again the weavers and other groups are found petitioning Parliament or the Justices for the fixing of a legal rate of wages. This method was hardly used by the smaller urban groups; but they were fully prepared to invoke the law when a master endeavoured to employ unapprenticed labour, and so to break down the monopoly of the trained craftsmen. These appeals to the law took place under the Elizabethan Statute of Artificers, which was still in force, though the justices had long ceased to fix regular rates of wages for the various urban trades, and even the fixing of agricultural rates had largely lapsed or become formal and meaningless. The restrictions on

[1] See Hedges and Winterbotham, *Legal History of Trade Unionism*; J. L. and B. Hammond, *The Skilled Labourer* (2nd ed. 1926); S. and B. Webb, *The History of Trade Unionism* (1920); and an article, 'The Combination Laws Reconsidered', by Mrs. George, in *Economic Journal* (1927).

apprenticeship continued to be enforced to a substantial extent in the older crafts and towns; but over the greater part of the textile trades these too had lapsed. They were never enforced in the case of the new Lancashire cotton industry, or in the woollen industry except in Norwich and a very few other places.

The real strength of working-class bargaining power in the eighteenth century lay among the minority of highly skilled craftsmen in the small-scale industries of the towns; for the expansion of wealth gave these skilled groups a valuable monopoly of labour, and the small scale on which their trades were carried on put them nearly on a bargaining equality with their employers. Their small Trade Clubs were powerful monopolies, within their narrow range. But they showed little disposition either to combine on a national scale, or to establish federal relations between club and club, even in the same town. The urban artisans formed less a class than a number of groups of persons lifted well above the common run of labour in both status and earning power, and divided by no more than a narrow line from the typical urban employer. The employer, indeed, was much further removed from the merchant than from his own journeymen until the new class of factory employers began to develop with the advent of power-driven machinery.

It follows from what has been said that it is impossible to generalize about the habits and social conditions of the eighteenth-century workers, any more than about their wages and industrial status. The colliers of the midland and northern counties, the metal-workers of the Black Country, the iron-workers and certain other groups not primarily urban, were doubtless rough and uncivilized enough. But most of the urban workers who responded to the preaching of Wesley and his followers, or were soon to be roused by the appeal of Radical doctrines, had at least some education and some pretension to a civilized way of living.

It has to be remembered that, in many of the urban crafts, apprenticeship was still fully in force, and the apprentice still often went to dwell in his master's house, under conditions which made his master responsible for his training in manners as well as at his trade. William Hutton learnt his trade in his uncle's house at Nottingham, and Robert Owen was apprenticed first to a draper at Stamford. Such men, whatever their origin, usually emerged from their period of servitude with manners like their masters'; and while these might be rough and brutal enough at times, there were many Dissenting or Wesleyan households in which high moral standards were enforced, while in places like Liverpool and Bristol and Norwich the main body of the skilled craftsmen had a long tradition of self-respect and importance in the town's affairs. The common labourers were much below the artisans in these respects; but even for them Wesley and Whitefield did much as the century advanced. Nor must we regard deliberate efforts at working-class education as beginning with Robert Raikes or the Sunday School movement. They were in fact going on all the time, in chapels, Trade Clubs, and other societies, as well as in the course of apprenticeship and in the daily contacts of ordinary life.

There was, however, a town mob in most of the larger cities, and it made its presence felt long before the Gordon Riots in London or the burning of Joseph Priestley's house and laboratory in Birmingham at the time of the French Revolution. Arkwright had his first factory burnt down; and there were frame-breaking troubles in Nottingham and other East Midland towns half a century before the Luddites. But the commonest cause of mob action in the middle of the eighteenth century was the high price of provisions; and again and again, in town after town, we hear of more or less serious bread-riots in times of scarcity and unemployment. These movements had, however, little or no political complexion. What Radicalism there was existed among the most highly skilled of the artisans and among the tradesmen who formed the backbone of the Revolution Societies for celebrating the triumphs of 1688, and not among the mob. For some time after the French Revolution, the mobs were loyalist, and not Jacobin, and far more liable to demonstrate against Popery or Jacobinism than against an iniquitous Government.

But that there existed the material for intense mass excitement the preaching of Wesley and Whitefield and their followers abundantly demonstrated. There are many passages, even in Wesley's *Journal*, which cannot but fill the modern reader with sheer astonishment. We read of sinners who, listening to Wesley's preaching, were overcome with terrible physical pains, and rolled in torment on the ground,

while the enthusiasts of the new gospel knelt round and
prayed for their spiritual deliverance. We read of vast
masses moved out of themselves by the call to repentance
far beyond anything that has marked the revivalism of more
recent times, though not perhaps beyond the achievements
of latter-day American evangelists. We get an impression
throughout Wesley's *Journal* that he is appealing to persons
incapable of an intellectual response, whose souls must be
saved by other and more ferocious means, and we are confirmed in this impression by the attitude of many of Wesley's
own contemporaries towards his preaching. It was not only
among the votaries of the Established Church that the
Wesleyan enthusiasts were derided as throw-backs to an
earlier and less civilized age, but almost equally among the
more intellectual members of the earlier Dissenting con-
gregations. It is customary nowadays to regard Wesleyanism
as a great humanizing and civilizing influence; and so in
many ways it was. But it has its other aspect as well; for,
setting out to catch mens' souls by all means, it used
methods of approach which played upon the fears of the
uneducated and the illiterate without qualm or remorse. And
it was able to do this with the less compunction because
from the outset it would have no truck with political democracy in any form.

But Wesleyanism after the days of the early preachings
was speedily toned down as the Methodists gathered regular
bodies of adherents in the various towns and built themselves
chapels. They developed into orderly Dissenting congrega-
tions which had much in common with the Nonconformist
groups already in existence. Throughout the middle of the
eighteenth century the Methodists were busy creating for
themselves regular places of worship in one after another
of the towns where Wesley had gathered his first disciples
by preaching in the streets or on the open moor. The
Methodists did not cease to remind their hearers of hell fire
even in these changed surroundings; but when once they
had settled down they began to educate men for this world
as well as to save their souls, and perhaps the most important
part of the education which they provided was the training
in self-government which arose out of the working and
organization of the local chapel and its contact with the
wider Wesleyan connexion.

Go to-day to some small town—Sudbury, in Suffolk, Chipping Norton, in Oxfordshire, or even Appleby in Westmorland—which has preserved much of its outer appearance as it was in the eighteenth century, and you have the means, with a little imagination, of visualizing the outer appearance of the typical town, or even city, of two hundred years ago. But in order to make the picture correct, you have to people these towns very differently, and to think of many of them far more as independent manufacturing centres than as markets and shopping-places. Some, indeed, such as Stamford, owed their importance to their use as markets and meeting-places for the surrounding countryside; but, taking the country as a whole, far more had some special manufacture of their own—some branch of one of the textile trades, or pin-making as at Gloucester, or pottery as at Burslem, or tanning (not yet brewing) at Burton-on-Trent. Industry was far more scattered then than now; but, contrary to a common opinion, it was even then mainly urban, if market towns as well as boroughs are included in the conception of a town. Urban areas were very numerous, and for the most part very small; and they were also, as we have seen, exceedingly diverse in their character and ways of life. And above them all stood London, the only town worthy to be thought of as a considerable town at all by our modern standards. But London deserves—and gets—in this volume a chapter to itself.

BIBLIOGRAPHY.—Among contemporary authorities some of the most valuable are the tours of various travellers, English and foreign, from DANIEL DEFOE's *Tour through the Whole Island of Great Britain* (1724–7) to WILLIAM COBBETT's *Rural Rides* (1821–32, new ed. 1927). Defoe's work went through many editions after its first issue, and was corrected for later developments by subsequent editors, including Samuel Richardson. The dates of the various editions are 1738, 1742, 1748, 1753, 1764, 1769, 1778. For the middle of the century the most valuable source is DR. RICHARD POCOCKE's *Travels through England in 1750 and 1751*, printed by the Camden Society in 1888–9. C. P. MORITZ's *Travels in England in 1782* (ed. P. E. Matheson, 1924) is another well-known source; and there is a little urban amid much rural information in PEHR KALM's *Visit to England in 1748* (first published in Swedish in 1753, and in English in 1892). There is a great deal of information, especially about wages and working conditions, in ARTHUR YOUNG's various tours—*Six Weeks Tour through the Southern Counties of England and Wales, Six Months Tour through the North of England*, and *Farmer's Tour through the East of England* (1768–1771). See also THOMAS PENNANT's *Journey from Chester to London* (1782) and various other descriptive tours; JOHN AIKIN's *Description of the Country from Thirty to Forty Miles round Manchester* (1795); and JOHN CAMPBELL's *Political Survey of Britain* (1774). See also some material in

EDWARD and JOHN CHAMBERLAYNE's various editions of *The Present State of England*, especially that of 1770, and in the numerous road books from JOHN OGILBY to PATERSON and MOGG.

With these may also be grouped JOHN WESLEY's famous *Journal*, which contains many sidelights on urban manners.

Of other contemporary sources the most important for working-class conditions is Sir F. M. EDEN's *The State of the Poor* (1797).

For the political condition of eighteenth-century towns see T. H. B. OLD-FIELD's *Representative History of Great Britain* (1816). There are also many eighteenth-century or early nineteenth-century town histories—far too numerous to chronicle; and the reports of the Royal Commission on Municipal Corporations (1835) are full of valuable sidelights on eighteenth-century conditions.

Useful contemporary autobiographies include JOSEPH PRIESTLEY's, WILLIAM HUTTON's, for Birmingham and the Midlands; ROBERT OWEN's, for Newport, Montgomery, and for Stamford and Manchester. See also, for Bath, OLIVER GOLDSMITH's *Life of 'Beau' Nash*. This list might be greatly prolonged. There is also much material in modern biographies, such as E. METEYARD's *Life of Josiah Wedgwood*, SAMUEL SMILES's *Lives of the Engineers, Lives of Boulton and Watt, Industrial Biography*, &c.

Among modern books for the political condition of the towns see E. and A. PORRITT, *The Unreformed House of Commons*, and for local government Mr. and Mrs. SIDNEY WEBB's *English Local Government* (especially the account of *ad hoc* bodies set up during the eighteenth century in the volume entitled *Statutory Authorities for Special Purposes*, which also contains a summary of the authors' conclusions concerning the general structure and working of local government from the seventeenth to the early nineteenth centuries). See also Mr. and Mrs. WEBB's *History of the English Poor Law*, and Miss D. MARSHALL's *The English Poor in the Eighteenth Century* (1926). For hospitals and other philanthropic agencies the most useful book is B. KIRKMAN GRAY's *History of English Philanthropy* (1905). See also JOHN HOWARD's *State of the Prisons* (1777), and his life.

Of modern accounts of English economic conditions in the eighteenth century the most useful is that of P. MANTOUX, *The Industrial Revolution in the Eighteenth Century*. ARNOLD TOYNBEE's *Industrial Revolution*, though old, is still useful, and there is much material in E. LIPSON's *English Economic History*, vols. ii and iii, *The Age of Mercantilism*. Reference may also be made to various works by EDWARD and THOMAS BAINES, including *Yorkshire, Past and Present; Lancashire, Past and Present*, and *A History of the Cotton Manufacture*, and to the writings of SAMUEL SMILES mentioned above.

For population problems see G. T. GRIFFITHS, *The Population Problem in the Age of Malthus* (1926), and for sanitary conditions M. C. BUER's *Health, Wealth, and Population, 1760–1815* (1926). Reference may also be made to Sir JOHN SIMON's *English Sanitary Institutions* (1890).

Much material can naturally be derived from contemporary novelists—for example SMOLLETT, especially *Humphry Clinker*, FIELDING, and FANNY BURNEY. Modern town histories and the *Victoria County History* are also invaluable storehouses of information.

IX

INDUSTRY AND TRADE

By H. HEATON

There was never from the earliest ages a time in which trade so much engaged the attention of mankind, or commercial gain was sought with such general emulation. The merchant is now invited to every port, manufactures are established in all cities, and princes who just can view the sea from some single corner of their dominions are enlarging harbours, erecting mercantile companies, and preparing to traffick in the remotest countries.—*Preface to* ROLT's *New Dictionary of Trade and Commerce* (1756).

Do not be frighted; trade could not be managed by those who manage it, if it had much difficulty. Their great books are soon understood, and their language,

> If speech it may be call'd, that speech is none
> Distinguishable in number, mood, or tense,

is understood with no very laborious application.—*To Mrs. Thrale* (Nov. 16, 1779).

There are few ways in which a man can be more innocently employed than in getting money.—*Life of Johnson* (March 27, 1775).

IF Johnson's interests had resembled those of Defoe or Young, his writings could have been a mine of material for the economic historian, since he had abundant contact with economic problems and ample opportunity for observing industrial and commercial conditions. Book-selling, brewing, and bankruptcy loomed large over his life; his father's impecuniousness cut short his university career, Porter's bankruptcy left the future Mrs. Johnson only her dowry, while the rewards of authorship could not keep even a famous lexicographer free from arrest for debt on one occasion. Johnson knew men who were playing leading parts in the industrial life of Birmingham. Among his friends was John Taylor, 'who, by his ingenuity in mechanical inventions and his success in trade,' became High Sheriff of Warwickshire and left £200,000, made chiefly out of gilt buttons and snuff boxes. He was intimately acquainted with Lewis Paul, inventor of the spinning frame, and tried at least twice to straighten out the financial tangles caused when Paul borrowed money to develop that machine. He knew something about the working of Thrale's big brewery, and was able to compare its output with that of M. Sansterre, the leading brewer in Paris. He knew Adam Smith, and, though at their

3832

G g

first meeting the two men 'did not take to each other', Johnson in later years snubbed those who condemned *The Wealth of Nations* as arm-chair philosophy by suggesting that 'nothing requires more to be illustrated by philosophy than trade does'. In the Society for the Encouragement of Arts, Manufactures, and Commerce, Johnson met those who were interested in innovation and improvement. In 1758 he wrote a preface for Payne's *New Tables of Interest*, having in the previous year done a similar service for Rolt's *New Dictionary of Trade and Commerce*—but without reading the book. He reviewed works on experiments in bleaching, and on ventilation in ships. He travelled over most parts of England during decades when great economic developments were on foot; he even allowed himself to be taken to see the pottery works at Derby. But he was not impressed by what he saw; he let Boswell go alone to see the famous silk mill in that town, and when the two visited Birmingham he preferred to 'sit placidly at tea with his first love' while Boswell was taken off to marvel at 'the vastness and the contrivance of some of the machinery' in Boulton's great factory at Soho. He cared little for such things; he rejoiced that Lichfield had so few industries while Birmingham had so many. 'Sir, we are a city of philosophers; we work with our heads, and make the boobies of Birmingham work for us with their hands.' He was willing to express opinions on almost every economic topic, from the level of wages and the value of money to Walpole's commercial policy and the effect of a money economy on Scottish feudal relations; but he wrote and said little that will aid the writer of this chapter.

Fortunately there are many other sources on which we can draw. Defoe at the beginning of the period and Young at the end were tourists with an eye for economic facts. The fashion for dictionaries and encyclopaedias overflowed into the 'useful arts'. The rising tide of interest in technological advance and experiment influenced even the *Gentleman's Magazine*[1] and the *Annual Register*. The pamphleteers were busier than ever, the Parliamentary Journals and the blue books became thicker. The metropolitan press was supplemented by provincial papers, in which advertisements occupied more space than did the clippings from London news-sheets. Finally some business firms tucked their records

---

[1] Its sub-title for 1732–5 was the *Trader's Monthly Intelligencer*.

away in places from which the student has later been able to dig them. There is no lack of material.

That very plenty makes the picture all the more difficult to paint. Is it to be a twilight scene or a dawn? Is it to show the dusk of what had survived from the Middle Ages and of the elaborately regulated Mercantilist society of Tudor and Stuart days, or to depict the dawn of Victorian capitalism and *laissez-faire*? If we were brought up in the belief that the last ten or fifteen years of Johnson's life witnessed the sudden melodramatic break-up of an old order by the sledge-hammer blows of machinery, steam, and *The Wealth of Nations*—an 'industrial revolution' such as Toynbee described—we shall want two pictures, of peaceful eve and stormy morning. But if we accept the view of a later generation that 'on the vast stage of economic history no sudden shift of scene takes place'[1] and that there is 'no hiatus in economic development, but always a constant tide of progress and change, in which the old is blended almost imperceptibly with the new',[2] our task is easier, for the developments which marked certain parts of English economic life after 1760 will 'but carry further, though on a far greater scale and with far greater rapidity, changes which had been proceeding long before'.[3] The features which we associate with the nineteenth century were not absent from the seventeenth, and much of the social and economic system of the days of Anne retained vitality into those of Victoria. Our picture, then, is a study in growth and motion, and of the changes in structure and method which growth and new knowledge made possible and necessary.

The first important growth was that of the population. It becomes very marked after about 1730; at the beginning of the century some writers felt that England was under-populated, but at the end of it the lamentations of Malthus were in a different key. The best available estimates suggest an increase, in England and Wales, of about 1,250,000 (23 per cent.) between 1700 and 1760, and of over 2,000,000 (32 per cent.) during the next forty years.[4] This unprecedented increase was due, not to any marked growth in the

[1] H. Sée, *Modern Capitalism*, p. 137.
[2] E. Lipson, *Economic History of England* (3 vols., 1920–31), vol. iii, p. 53.
[3] W. J. Ashley, *Economic Organization of England* (1914), p. 141.
[4] See M. C. Buer, *Health, Wealth, and Population in the Early Days of the Industrial Revolution* (1926), chap. iii.

birth-rate, but to a big drop in the death-rate, especially among the young, which in turn was due to two main causes —a better food supply and improved medical services. Up to 1765 England produced a surplus of grain; there were few bad seasons, and bread was cheap. The days of the cheap loaf came to an end in the 'sixties, but, meanwhile, the increasing production of grasses and root crops was making possible a better winter-feeding of live stock, and fresh meat was taking the place of salted, while more milk was available. Spirit-drinking declined rapidly after 1750.[1] Medical knowledge and practice were improving; the provision of hospitals and dispensaries became more widespread in the capital and the provinces; the rudiments of public health began to be understood, and perhaps the patent medicines which were advertised in the newspapers did some good. Progress in the attack on mortality figures was slow. 'You must remember', said Johnson when consoling Boswell for the loss of a child, 'that to keep three out of four is more than your share. Mrs. Thrale has but four out of eleven.' Still, progress was sure, and it gave each child born a little better chance of reaching maturity. The supply of producers and consumers was growing as it had never done before, though there were some who lamented that it was still only one-third or one-fourth that of France.

The output of commodities was also growing, partly in the old industries which had been England's staples for centuries, but especially in industries which were comparatively new to Europe or new to England. Of the old industries, the manufacture of woollen cloth was by far the most important. Its leaders described it as 'the staple manufacture of the country', and when they spoke Parliament listened with respectful attention. For its benefit farmers were forbidden to export wool to feed foreign looms, and the 'owler' who wafted bales abroad to 'the perfidious foe' was threatened with punishments which made the laws, like those of Draco, seem to be 'written in blood'. To nourish the clothier's market prohibitive duties were imposed on foreign cloth, the import and production of cottons was repressed, and the manufacture of cloth in the colonies was frowned on; to keep the Portuguese and Brazilian markets for British weavers, Englishmen were expected to drink port and brave the

[1] Cf. *infra*, pp. 312–14.

ravages of gout in the interests of a trade so favourable to England; and in the name of industrial morality Parliament passed eleven laws during Johnson's lifetime to regulate the making and makers of Yorkshire cloths alone.

The worker in wool had his worries. In his attempt to check the growing popularity of cotton fabrics he was waging a losing battle, and in his export trade he faced disturbances caused by war and tariffs. The West of England, supreme in the production of high-grade cloths, supplied the aristocrat, the officer, and the upper middle class from Russia to Brazil, and the Alleghanies; the West Riding clothed the masses, the private, and the fur-trader over the same area. Hence the frequent European wars closed markets, while the American Revolution wrought havoc, for one-third to two-fifths of the woollen exports crossed the North Atlantic. Tariffs hurt sometimes. The desire for industrial self-sufficiency permeated continental Europe, and military necessity suggested the wisdom of making cloth and munitions at home. Hence at frequent intervals there were cries that Austria, Hanover, Prussia, or Russia had made its tariff prohibitive; and in the 'eighties the Brazilian market seemed doomed to disappear when Portugal, disregarding the Methuen Treaty of 1703, began to raise its import and harbour dues and foster a native cloth manufacture.

Yet despite all dangers, the spoilt child of English commercial policy did prosper. The export figures probably tell the rough truth when they record an expansion in wool textile exports from £3,000,000 in 1720 to £4,000,000 in 1750, and £5,000,000 in 1790. For the West Riding industry trustworthy information is available, since a record was kept from the reign of George II to that of George IV of the number of cloths milled at the fulling mills of the area. These figures show that the West Riding was producing six broad cloths in 1786 for every one made sixty years before. During the same period the manufacture of worsted fabrics had advanced rapidly; East Anglia's old supremacy as worsted centre was successfully challenged by Wakefield, Halifax, and Bradford; the prophecy made in 1737 by a Halifax worsted pioneer that the manufacture of Bocking Bays and Exeter Serges 'will come in spite of fate into these northern Countrys' was proving true; and in 1784 the men who were to make Yorkshire superfines and blankets rival those of

Stroud and Witney were serving their apprenticeship. Kay's flying shuttle was taken up by Yorkshire weavers a generation before any one in Norwich understood how to use it, and the inventions of Hargreaves and Arkwright were quickly adapted and adopted east of the Pennines in the 'seventies to accelerate the spinning of wool. Lord Sheffield might lament in 1785 that the West of England industry was decaying before the competition of Yorkshire and cottons; others might regret that 'folly and fashion have got the better of reason and sound policy in dress', and agree with the pamphleteer who said that if the cotton machines 'be suffered to destroy our woollen and stuff manufactures they will prove the most fatal discoveries ever made in Old England'.[1] But Yorkshiremen did not complain; they were watching developments across the Pennines, and while they were willing to take all the benefits that protection and a non-exportable wool supply might give them, they looked more to the profit which machinery, power, and improved methods would bring. They were willing to learn from Norwich, from the West, even from Lancashire.

What could Lancashire teach them? It could present a remarkable picture of an industry built up on raw materials imported from afar, developed in face of fierce hostility at home and keen competition abroad, imitating, initiating, inventing, and winning its way because it supplied what was desired by a public that eventually stretched all the way from China westward to Panama. Lancashire's textile pilgrimage went from woollens and linens to worsteds, small wares such as ribbon and tape, to fustians made of cotton and linen yarn, and finally to pure cottons. Manchester and Liverpool merchants brought linen yarn from Ireland and cotton from the Levant; the ships of the East India Company brought from the Orient striped, checked, and richly-patterned fabrics which created a keen demand among consumers, violent opposition among silk and woollen producers, and desire to imitate in London and Lancashire. The opposition scored legislative triumphs in 1701 and 1721, for the first act forbade the importation of any Indian pieces except plain calico, while the second forbade the use of home-made

---

[1] 'The Contrast, or a Comparison between our Woollen, Linen, and Silk Manufactures' (1782), quoted in J. Bischoff, *History of the Woollen and Worsted Manufactures* (1842), vol. i, p. 234.

THE WOOLLEN MANUFACTURE

(A) Sheep Shearing. (B) Washing. (C) Beating. (D) Combing
of Wool

From the Universal Magazine, *1749*

or home-printed fabrics containing any cotton. But plain calico could come in to be printed and exported; Indian prints could enter provided they were re-exported; and, most important of all, fustians—half cotton, half linen— were exempted from the ban of 1721. They could be made in Lancashire for sale either at home or abroad, and they were well protected in the home market by the prohibitions set out above.

The home market was almost as large as Lancashire cared to make it, and was limited chiefly by the cost of the raw material, which doubled between the first third of the eighteenth century and the 'seventies. Striped, checked, and plain fabrics served the clothing needs of the poor, 'furniture checks' competed with woollen hangings for beds and windows, while cotton velvet and velveteen offered a superior dress material. The foreign market meant chiefly the West Indian plantations and the slave trade, and in this field Liverpool eventually surpassed London and Bristol. The trade was triangular. Liverpool shipped a cargo of Lancashire cottons to West Africa, exchanged it for slaves, took the slaves to the West Indies, and there turned them into a cargo of cotton, sugar, and tobacco for England. There was also direct trade, for the plantation owners wanted cotton goods for slave clothing. The profits made in this way made Liverpool rich, and the wealth flowed into the hinterland to finance textile production, improve transport facilities, and made modern Lancashire.

The expansion of cotton manufacture can be measured roughly. In the first ten years of the eighteenth century the annual average consumption of raw cotton was about 1,000,000 lb. In the 'forties it was just over 2,000,000 lb., and in the 'seventies over 5,000,000 lb. By that time machine-spinning had come, and consumption jumped from 5,000,000 lb. in 1780 to 22,000,000 lb. in 1787; the next decade saw the invention of Whitney's gin, which revolutionized the task of cleaning the raw material and opened the way to the vast expansion of production in the United States cotton belt. The export trade grew even more rapidly, from £14,000 in 1739 to £109,000 in 1759, and to £303,000 in 1779. The African trade absorbed about one-third of the exports till nearly 1770, while the American and West Indian colonies and plantations bought about half of them. But the

Lancashire checks met keen rivalry from Indian cloths in the African market, and after 1770 India ran Lancashire for a time almost out of that market. But compensation was found in continental Europe, where Manchester cottons found a ready sale during the peace which began in 1763.

When Johnson died, the cotton industry was already becoming the classic illustration of a new industrial order. The failures of Paul's spinning machine in the 'forties and 'fifties were forgotten in the triumphs of the next three decades; Hargreaves, Arkwright, Crompton, and scores of men whose names are scarcely known solved the problem of producing yarn abundant in quantity and good in quality, while the repeal of the ban on the use of cotton fabrics in 1774 formally opened the road to free enterprise. By 1784 spinning factories were sprinkled over Nottinghamshire, Lancashire, and the Glasgow-Paisley areas; in them machines were being turned by hand, animal, and water power, and steam was being tried. Arkwright, a self-made rich man, was being held up to ambitious young men as an example of the way opportunity should be welcomed when it knocked at the door; Manchester had had its first really nasty experience of fever, and the cotton country had heard what other areas were destined to hear at times in the next forty years—the yell of rioters, the smashing of glass, and the breaking of machines.

Cotton had to fight vested interests: pottery had to fight technical problems and difficulties of transport, and when enthusiasts coupled Wedgwood's name with that of Watt and Arkwright they revealed the popular estimate of the service that Wedgwood had rendered British industry. In the words of his memorial tablet, he converted 'a rude and inconsiderable manufacture into an elegant art and an important branch of national commerce'. In one respect he faced the same task as did the men of Lancashire, i.e. the production of a commodity the taste for which had been created by imports from the Orient. Western Europe knew how to make vessels of clay; but, with some exceptions, the product was crude, fit for use but not for ornament, little more than badly glazed yellowish earthenware. At table, therefore, the rich had used glass, silver, plate, or pewter; the poor used leather 'bottles', wood platters, or crude earthenware. The arrival of porcelain in the holds of East

Indiamen stirred some potters to search for the secrets of Chinese success. How was that fine texture obtained, that remarkable whiteness, that translucence, that beautiful colour and pattern? Florence, Delft, Meissen, Dresden, and Sèvres did much to raise the standard of European production during the seventeenth and eighteenth centuries. Delft ware, copied assiduously in London, Bristol, and Liverpool, was scarcely distinguishable from Nankin China—until the piece was handled. Chelsea, Derby, and Worcester took China and Dresden as models, while the stoneware made near Liverpool was said in 1747 to 'come nearest to the Porcelain or China Ware of anything we have; if properly made it has the transparency of that Manufacture, and no doubt would receive the same Colour if judiciously applied'.[1] But, continued Campbell, the potters in and about London 'never will encourage an improvement in the Stone Ware, for fear of interfering with their own Branch, and I am of Opinion that those of Liverpool are not able to be at the expense of proper Experiments'. At best the potters were producing wares which were too costly for any but the upper middle class, and when Boswell admired the 'ingenuity and delicate art' of the Derby workers Johnson 'justly observed' that the product 'was too dear: for that he could have vessels of silver of the same size as cheap as what were here made of porcelain'.

Wedgwood's ambition was to cater for all classes, to build up a Useful Branch as well as an Ornamental Branch, and to reach a big market both at home and abroad. Son of a potter, he resented the haphazard way in which the Staffordshire industry was conducted, the careless selection of materials, the lack of system in mixing glazes, and the happy-go-lucky methods of firing the kilns. Quality was uneven, results were uncertain, taste was lacking, and prices were low. The 'Five towns' in 1738 had a population of barely 4,000; houses were miserable huts; land was poorly cultivated; and roads which were almost impassable 'cut off our part of the country from the rest of the world, besides rendering it not very comfortable to ourselves '(Wedgwood). Fortune favoured Wedgwood, for in 1755 a rich deposit of kaolin—the hard white clay used by the Chinese—was found in Cornwall. But Cornwall and Staffordshire were two

---

[1] R. Campbell, *The London Tradesman* (1747), p. 185.

H h

hundred miles apart as the crow flies; the Severn was forty miles away from Burslem, the Weaver twenty, and the Trent thirty. Wedgwood therefore fought for turnpikes and canals in the West Midlands, and thus reduced the cost of transport and the percentage of breakages.

The rest was a study of methods of production and organization. In the factory at Burslem (1759) and, later, at Etruria (1769) Wedgwood experimented ceaselessly with clays, glazes, colours, and kiln temperatures; he built new ovens and then tore them down; he engaged artists to make moulds and designs; he developed greater division of labour, and tried to turn 'dilatory and drunken idle worthless workmen' into skilled operatives. He stumped round the works on his wooden leg, smashed any piece that failed to please him, and chalked on the bench, 'This won't do for Josiah Wedgwood'. He studied foreign models, ancient and modern, and tried to pick up trade secrets; he watched costs, ploughed back his profits into the business, pondered over marketing methods, sent out illustrated price lists, and opened a fashionable show-room in London. Beyond England and the colonies he saw a vast foreign market waiting to be won if only tariff barriers could be reduced; so he joined hands with hardware and cotton to support the Anglo-French commercial treaty of 1786 and to urge the Government to make similar treaties with the rest of Europe, thus opening up 'new channels of consumption'. The treaties were not made, but markets were found nevertheless by Wedgwood and his fellow-potters. By the early decades of the nineteenth century a traveller could report that 'from Paris to Petersburg, from Amsterdam to the farthest point of Sweden, and from Dunkirk to the extremity of the south of France one is served at every inn upon English ware. Portugal, Spain, and Italy are supplied with it, and vessels are loaded with it for both the Indies and the continent of America'. Eating and drinking became more hygienic and delicate, pewter passed into the antique shop, and 'washing up' became a heavier domestic drudgery.

From Staffordshire to Birmingham was an easy journey, especially after 1777, when canals linked up the Mersey, the Cheshire salt works, the Potteries, the Black Country, Birmingham, Burton, and the Trent. Let us take it, for, despite Johnson, the boobies of Birmingham lived in one of the most interesting industrial spots in all England. Since at least Tudor times Birmingham's fame as the home of small metal wares had grown steadily greater. Leland and Camden found it full of smiths, cutlers, lorimers, and nailers. By 1700 the variety of its products had been enlarged; swords, cane-heads, snuff-boxes, guns, locks, keys, and hinges were now made there, and legend says that when William III lamented that no guns were made in England, Sir Richard Newdegate informed him that 'the men of Birmingham can do whatever skill and metal can do'. A picture of the town published in 1730 described it as 'a market town which, by the art and industry of its inhabitants, has for some years past been rendered famous all over the world for the rare choice and invention of all sorts of wares and curiosities in iron, steel, brass, &c., admired as well for their cheapness as their peculiar beauty of workmanship'.[1]

Three causes contributed to this reputation. Supplies of coal and iron were drawn from the coal- and iron-fields to the west, copper and tin were brought from Cornwall, but zinc and much of the steel came from the Continent. In the second place Birmingham, like Manchester, was free from any state or municipal restraints on economic freedom. No gild or company ordinances forbade this or that action, no code of laws such as controlled the woollen worker was ever passed for hardware; apprenticeship was virtually optional, religious dissent was too strong to be penalized, and new-comers, whether alien or native, could settle without much fear of molestation. Birmingham was 'a city of free trade'.

In the third place, its inhabitants had developed and passed down from generation to generation an ingenuity and capacity for highly skilled work. They had reached a high degree of division of labour, the co-ordination of which was the work of factors; and of them, as of their counterparts in Wolverhampton and Sheffield, Tucker said in 1757 that 'almost every Master-Manufacturer hath a new Invention of his own, and is daily improving on those of others'.[2] Birmingham men had to be on the alert for changes in fashion and demand. While buckles were used for fastening shoes, Birmingham made them; but when in the 'eighties 'the effeminate shoe string' became popular, and 'fashion, void

---

[1] 'Prospect of Birmingham in 1730', in Birmingham Public Library.
[2] Josiah Tucker, *Instructions for Travellers* (1757), p. 21.

of feeling and deaf to argument', deserted the buckle, the makers, after a futile appeal to the Prince of Wales, turned to other things. Fortunes were made in brassware after 1740; Taylor, Johnson's friend, reaped a rich harvest by improving the methods of gilding, plating, and lacquering, and the town, following his lead, gilded common metal buttons which found a ready sale since they looked like brass or even like gold. Whatever mankind wanted in metal, whether swords, guns, pistols, or stirrups for its wars, or wine-strainers, punch-ladles, bread-baskets, or skewers for its peace, the toyshop of Europe could supply; and if it be true that of the 12,000 houses standing in the town in 1790, 8,000 had been built since 1760, then mankind was an eager customer.

To this busy hive Matthew Boulton brought James Watt in 1774. Boulton, who belonged to a Lichfield family, had built up perhaps the largest hardware concern in the country, and in 1762 had spent £20,000 in building and equipping a new factory at Soho. In it he had skilled workmen—six hundred of them; and for it he needed more power than could be generated by the local brook. He had met Watt once or twice and realized that the Scot's improvements on existing steam engines might be made the basis of a profitable manufacture of engines. And he had on his books as a bankrupt debtor the name of Roebuck, who had founded the famous Carron ironworks in 1760, and who had done his best to give substance to Watt's ideas in face of crude tools and unskilled mechanics. Boulton therefore took Watt off Roebuck's hands, and opened a new chapter in the history of power.

Ever since the Middle Ages at any rate there had been slow but sure advance in the use of various sources of power. The treadmill and the treadle had their place, and many an apprentice obtained part of his training by turning a wheel. Animals worked gins and windlasses; Paul used two donkeys, Cartwright harnessed a cow, and the first two power-looms set up in Scotland were driven by a Newfoundland dog. Wind was used, and the Dutch had done wonders with it. But it was too fitful for regular service in England, and water was therefore the main source of power where large quantities were needed. Gearing equipment had improved to such an extent that most ingenious combinations of cogwheels were possible. Fulling stocks, millstones, saws, and ore-crushers were driven by water, and around mines and metal furnaces waterwheels raised and lowered loads in the shaft, worked the pumps, and provided draught for the furnace. The pumps which elevated town water supplies from river to reservoir or water-tower were driven in the same way; on the Severn a wheel, 100 feet in diameter, ground flints for the pottery industry. But the highest level of ingenuity was reached in Lombe's silk mill at Derby, where one wheel, revolving three times a minute, turned—so said the factory guide—26,586 wheels and caused 97,746 mechanical movements, any one of which could be stopped independently of the others. The textile machines which came after 1769 relied on human, animal, and water power, but increasingly on the last. The mills to house them were built in the valleys of the Peak and Pennine countries; old corn-mills were converted into spinning works, and in Yorkshire it was common to find a single wheel supplying power for grinding corn, fulling cloth, and scribbling wool. Where the fall or supply of water was insufficient, steam engines were often used to pump water which had already been over the wheel back to a height from which it could do its work again.

The steam engine was born as an aid to pumping, and was made possible by the scientific work of men like Torricelli, Pascal, Hooke, and others on the vacuum and atmospheric pressure. They discovered that when steam was condensed in a closed vessel a vacuum was created; they also realized that air had weight. If, therefore, a piston was at the top of a steam-filled cylinder, and the steam was condensed, the air would weigh the piston down; and a pump attached to the piston could thus be made to work. This was good news to the men of Cornwall and other mining areas. Deposits near the surface were nearly exhausted, yet any attack on the lower levels was a tragic losing fight against flood. Savery and Newcomen therefore saw the engine as 'the miner's friend', and by 1720 Newcomen had so far solved the problems of construction and operation that several engines were at work. Smeaton made further improvements in details of construction, and by 1769 was able to draw up a list of a hundred engines on the northern coal-fields alone. Some of them were big and powerful; one had a cylinder 6 feet wide, a piston stroke of over 10 feet, a rating of 76 h.p., and a theoretical ability to lift 307 cwt. of water at one stroke. Such engines moved slowly—ten to fifteen strokes a minute; they exerted themselves only on the downward stroke of the piston, and could not be used to provide continuous power and turn machinery; and they wasted much heat. But they met the needs of those few industries which required power in large quantities during the first three-quarters of the century, and the waste of heat was unimportant at a pit-head where coal was abundant and cheap. Hence even as late as the 1830's many of them were still at work.

Watt's engine was at first little more than an improved Newcomen machine, and its only virtue, that of saving heat and fuel, scarcely interested many potential users. Only in the 'eighties did his use of steam to push the piston both ways and his plans for rotary motion result in the production of an engine capable of turning the wheels of industry. When Boswell visited Soho in 1776 Boulton announced, 'I sell here, Sir, what all the world desires to have—POWER.' But 'all the world' was at that date limited to mines and metal plants, and was slow to become conscious of any unfulfilled desire. Between 1775 and 1785 only sixty-six Watt engines were built; all were small in power, and only two were used to turn textile machinery. Not till the 'nineties, or even later, was the steam engine able seriously to challenge the supremacy of water-power in the manufacturing industries.

Two other industries must be noted in our survey of economic growth. Iron and coal both had long histories reaching back to at least the Middle Ages, but while coal-mining could, in 1700, look forward to continued steady growth, the outlook for iron was dark. The problem of the iron industry was that of securing a fuel supply, which as yet meant charcoal. The exhaustion of local timber supplies had put out the furnaces in one district after another, and the need for conserving timber in the interests of shipbuilding and the navy provoked controversy concerning the relative national value of ships and iron. Until another fuel was found iron production could make no progress; in 1739 only about sixty furnaces were at work in the whole country, producing about 17,000 tons per annum, or about one ton daily per furnace. Those who made iron or steel wares had to lean more and more heavily on Sweden, Russia, and

'AN IRON WORK FOR CASTING OF CANNON; AND A BORING MILL. TAKEN FROM THE MADELEY SIDE OF THE RIVER SEVERN, SHROPSHIRE.' 1788

Spain for their raw material, and on the hope that the American colonies would come to their aid. Yet coal was a satisfactory fuel in most other industries. It served the domestic hearth wherever it was available. Brewers, distillers, producers of tiles, salt, sugar, soap, glass, and even of metal goods used it. But despite many attempts to use it for iron smelting, and the isolated successful effort of Dudley in 1619, coal offered no salvation to iron until the eighteenth century.

Even then relief came slowly. Abraham Darby, maker of cast-iron and copper kettles and pans at Coalbrookdale, was using coke by 1709, the year of Johnson's birth. His son, Abraham the Second, used a Newcomen engine which pumped water up to a pond; the water then ran over a waterwheel which provided a stronger furnace draught and thus improved the combustion of the coke. But the new fuel was only slowly adopted elsewhere; even in 1762 the Society for the Encouragement of Arts, Manufactures, and Commerce was offering prizes to those who could make iron with coke which would be as good as that made with charcoal fuel. Cleaner coke and a more powerful draught were needed; but the problem had been partly solved by Darby and the iron famine was ended. The output of pig-iron rose from 17,000 tons in 1740 to 68,000 tons in 1788, doubled between that year and 1796, and doubled again by 1806.

To produce cast-iron in quantities was good; but more was needed, especially cheaper and better methods of turning cast-iron into malleable iron, which would bend rather than break; and beyond that lay the need for more steel. Cort and Onions in the early 'eighties found a new way to make malleable iron; in 1740 Huntsman had shown the Sheffield cutlers how to get steel by intensely heating iron and a pinch of carbon in small clay crucibles; but mass production of steel had to wait for Bessemer.

Nothing spectacular or dramatic came to the aid of coal-mining. British mines probably trebled their output during Johnson's lifetime, but their story is singularly anonymous. In the words of a recent work, 'No flash of genius of a Crompton or a Watt could transform coal-mining. Better methods had to be slowly forged from the painful experience of common men, and only gradually did a new idea or a new device spread from pit to pit or from one coalfield to another.'[1] The ever-growing demands of London, the expansion of markets in Holland and other points across the North Sea, the call for coal for blast furnaces and engines, and the demand which sprang up in inland areas when roads and waterways made those regions accessible, all stimulated production. But if output was to be expanded, it must be by finding answers to three main questions. How could mines be freed from the menace of death by fire, gas, and water? How could more coal be hewed per pair of hands? How could the coal be moved more easily underground, to the surface, and on the surface?

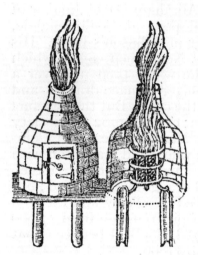

A contrivance to prevent the firing of coal or other mines. From the *Gentleman's Magazine*, vol. xxix (1759), p. 508.

Newcomen's engine helped to prevent the flooding of the deeper seams. But the deeper the mine, the more serious became the menace of choke-damp, which suffocated the miner, and fire-damp, which exploded. Choke-damp gave warning of its presence by extinguishing the miner's candle, and one might try to restore its victims in the seventeenth-century manner, which was to 'dig a hole in the earth and lay them on their bellies with their mouths in it: if that fail, fill them with good ale: but if that fail . . . conclude them desperate'. Fire-damp gave no warning signal, or hope of recovery to its victims; primitive methods of cleansing the pit by inducing explosions of the gas were of little avail, and many fiery mines had to be abandoned. Ventilation and the safety lamp made little or no headway till the nineteenth century, and this was almost equally true of mechanical methods of hewing. 'Willie Brown's iron man', invented in 1761, was a mechanical pick worked by levers, gearwheels, and a crank-handle; a horse-driven pick was also tried, as was a circular saw, but virtually nothing was accomplished to displace the time-honoured manual methods.

[1] T. S. Ashton and J. Sykes, *The Coal Industry of the Eighteenth Century* (1930), p. 12.

Only in the work of transporting the coal was any important improvement made in the eighteenth century. In the crudest mines, boys, women, and girls might carry baskets on their backs, and even climb ladders from the seam to the surface. Elsewhere the baskets were put on sledges which were dragged to the shaft by men, boys, or ponies. Parallel board tracks, on which sledges or wheeled flat carts could be run then appeared, and when iron became cheaper iron plates displaced the wood planks. About 1770 a flange was put on the inner edge of the plates, to prevent

A Reprefentation of a Coal Waggon.

the wheel from leaving the track; then the flange was transferred to the wheel and the plate became a rail, thus establishing the essential feature of the railroad. Baskets gave place to wheeled trucks which could be run on rails underground to the shaft, be hauled to the surface, and then run on rails up there. But beyond the pit-head further movement depended on the state of road, river, or sea. Road carriage of coal was possible only in dry weather until the turnpike came; river improvement on most streams was thought of in terms of coal carriage; and while sea transport of coal had produced a great fleet of ships, these were so hard to handle in bad weather that most of them were tied up when winter came.

Enthusiasts who looked at the industrial achievements of the decades when Johnson was growing old found cause for superlatives of satisfaction. These new skills, new devices, new methods of production, and new sources of national wealth were 'great and extraordinary', 'most wonderful', astonishing, unexampled, incredible, 'unparalleled in the history of the world', 'beyond the powers of calculation'. The genius of Watt, Wedgwood, and Arkwright had not merely 'counteracted the expence and folly of the American War', but had helped 'to diffuse a glory over this country unattainable by conquest or dominion'. The steam engine alone would 'produce great changes in the appearance of the civilized world'. And all these things had been done by Britons! 'Go to France', cried Arthur Young, 'and look for an Arkwright, a Wedgwood, a Darby, a Wilkinson, a Boulton, a Parker: there are no such men to be found in that Kingdom.' No longer need the country nurse the humiliating thought that Holland and France were its superiors in skill, equipment, organization, or resourcefulness. There had been a time when Englishmen rejoiced if they were able successfully to copy Dutch, French, and German methods or products. The Government had welcomed Huguenot refugees after 1685, for thereby the silk industry would gain much-needed strength and variety. Parliament gave Lombe a patent and, later, a large sum of money when he built in Derby a silk mill, copied, without acknowledgement, from Italy. London papermakers sought diligently to learn the secrets which explained the superiority of French, Dutch, and Italian paper: the East India Company tried at great expense to learn how the Indians made their rich red dyes: London calico printers were glad to copy the methods developed in Hamburg, and tin-plate makers erected flatting mills such as were used in Sweden. In cloth-finishing, refining, metallurgy, pottery, shipbuilding, and civil engineering the country had been glad to sit at the feet of the Continent, and to develop that genius which has since been defined as an infinite capacity for picking brains.

But by the middle of the century imitation has become less important than innovation. 'Few Countries', said Tucker in 1757, 'are equal, perhaps none excel, the English in the Numbers and Contrivance of their Machines to abridge Labour.' The Dutch are superior in the use of

THE MOUTH OF A COAL-PIT NEAR BROSELEY, 1788

windmills, but in the mining and metal industries 'the English are uncommonly dexterous in their Contrivance of the mechanic Powers'. Mines and furnaces have much new equipment, and the inventive ingenuity of the hardware manufacturers has already been described. In short, the men handling metals 'exhibit a Specimen of practical Mechanics scarce to be paralleled in any Part of the World'. The woollen and worsted industries lag behind, 'owing in a great measure to the mistaken Notions of the infatuated Populace, who, not being able to see further than the first Link of the Chain, consider all such Inventions as taking the Bread out of their Mouths: and therefore never fail to break out into Riots and Insurrections whenever such Things are proposed'.[1] Silk is better, for the Derby mill has been copied in several places; the inventor is trying to help the cotton and linen manufacturers 'by means of certain Engines'; and the hosiery industry has the knitting frame invented by an Englishman in the days of Elizabeth.

Had Tucker made his survey thirty years later, he would have crowed louder and longer over England's mechanical superiority. He might have recorded that even the woollen workers were now awake; he would have glowed with pleasure over the fact that Parliament had passed five laws between 1773 and 1786 to prevent the export of the new tools and machines, or of plans or models, and had forbidden the emigration of skilled artisans. He might have chuckled over the German caught in his Leeds lodgings with a model of a spinning machine all neatly packed and nailed up in a box, and pitied the unlucky cloth-maker who was to go with his family to Germany to work at £100 a year.[2] He could have told of Wedgwood's proposal that the Government open letters addressed to working-men in order to detect plans for emigration; of locked factory gates, and of Soho's complaint that Baron von Stein's attempts to discover engineering secrets were 'not agreeable to Mr. Boulton's notions of honour'.[3] Of course the legislation failed in large measure: as a last resort one could carry plans away, as Samuel Slater did when he went to America, in one's head, and thus equip a spinning factory at Pawtucket, Rhode Island. But

[1] Josiah Tucker, op. cit., pp. 20–1.
[2] *Leeds Mercury*, February 6, 1781.
[3] J. Lord, *Capital and Steam Power, 1750–1800* (1923), p. 217.

the jubilation of the writers and the efforts of the Legislature showed that England now had something which the Continent wanted in addition to wool.

Industrial growth and technological improvement were nurtured by the zest for private gain and the grant of public encouragement. Private gain could be increased in many ways, and an analysis of the motives which led to invention reveals a diversity of aims, but the same spirit. In the first place the industrialist was eager to 'abridge labour' and time, reduce the cost of wages in each unit of his product, employ women or children in place of men, speed up some process which absorbed a disproportionate amount of time or labour, displace skilled manual workers with unskilled operators, and obtain a degree of precision and accuracy of which hand labour was incapable. Thus a Scottish paper-maker in 1770 invented a rag-cutter which allowed one man to do as much work as eight had formerly done. The stress on spinning was due to the fact that many workers were required to make yarn for one weaver; one cotton loom used the yarn of four spinners, a woollen weaver kept nine or ten people busy, while Young found that in the sail-cloth industry there were '20 spinners and 2 or 3 other hands to every weaver'. The weaver was often idle for lack of yarn, especially in summer, and in 1760 the Society of Arts sought for a machine to accelerate spinning, on the ground that cloth-weavers 'find it extremely difficult in the summer season, when the spinners are at harvest work, to procure a sufficient number of hands'. Campbell tells of many new machines at work in London industries. Colour shops have hit the skilled painter by setting up horse-mills 'to grind the colours, and sell them to noblemen and gentlemen, ready mix'd, at a low price, and by the help of a few printed directions a house may be painted by any common labourer at one-third the expense it would have cost before the mystery was made public'. There are machines 'for cutting devices in Cornelians and other Stones', thanks to which 'the common heads we see on such Seals as are sold by the Jews and in Toy Shops' cost four or five shillings a dozen instead of two guineas each. Watch-makers now have engines for cutting the teeth of cogwheels, and have thus reduced the 'expense of workmanship and time to a trifle in comparison to what it was before, and brought the work to such an exactness that no hand can imitate it'.

In the second place, the way to profit lay through the ability to capture some market already supplied by others or to create some new demand. In spite of modern experience with the motor-car, rubber, wireless, and grape-fruit, we are still apt to think of economic life as one-way traffic, with demand calling for supply, and the size of the demand determining the methods of producing the supply. But supply may create demand, and the price at which the supply is offered determines the extent of the demand; and the story of cottons, pottery, and iron in the eighteenth century is better understood if we regard these commodities as goods which the customer scarcely knew he wanted or could afford until cheap production put them before him. It was shrewd foresight that made Wedgwood divide his plant into Useful and Ornamental branches. Cheap cottons would do far more than fight woollens, linen, and India. And Wilkinson, the ironmaster who built an iron bridge across the Severn, an iron barge to float on it, and an iron coffin for himself, was convinced that cheap iron and better engineering equipment would bring an Iron Age, with iron pipes, houses, roads, rails, machine-frames, and ships.

Thirdly, invention was stimulated by the hope of rewards which would come from using the new device, from collecting fees for letting others use it, or from some gift made by the State or by some society which encouraged technical progress. Leonardo da Vinci counted his chickens when he calculated that his needle-polishing machines would bring him an income equal to that of a Medici. Paul, Kay, and Watt hoped to draw large sums from those who bought licences to use their patents. Arkwright made a fortune both by using his machines in his own factories and by collecting licence fees. Parliament was willing enough to grant patent rights for fourteen years, and even in Watt's case to renew them. Manufacturers naturally resented bitterly the payment of fees and the monopoly rights of the patentee, and urged that public benefactors should present their inventions to the nation and be publicly rewarded. This idea found some favour: Lombe failed to get his silk-throwing patent renewed in 1731, but was consoled with a parliamentary grant of £14,000; and the legislature stimulated one very important piece of research when in 1713 it offered £20,000 to any man who could discover a satisfactory method of determining longitude at sea.

What Parliament did occasionally on a large scale private bodies did frequently in a less lavish manner. These bodies were the expression of that widespread interest in 'improvement' and the 'useful arts' which becomes so evident about the middle of the century. Agriculture and industry alike attracted attention, and while aristocrats, enterprising farmers, politicians, and retired tradesmen liked best to make and study experiments on the land, manufactures and commerce were not neglected. Encyclopaedias and dictionaries of science, arts, and commerce appeared: the *Gentleman's Magazine* and the *Annual Register* opened their columns to lists of patents or accounts of 'Useful Projects'; *The Wonderful Magazine* was founded in 1764 to record the new and strange. Even the poets were affected, and Dyer's valiant effort, in *The Fleece*, to write a poem on wool and woollens, was better than one might gather from Johnson's comment that 'The subject cannot be made poetical. How can a man write poetically of serges and druggets?' Those who cared to read were thus kept informed of man's advancing triumph over nature. The first balloon flights in 1781 created an enthusiastic 'air-mindedness' and led to talk of 'aerial navigation'. Dreamers played with the idea of submarines and horseless carriages: ingenious clock-makers constructed all manner of mechanical toys, including a robot which played chess. All things seemed possible: one heard of 'a very ingenious piece' of fishing mechanism in which 'one person may operate 500 hooks': one learned of a new property of oil—'when poured on the water around a ship it stills the waves'; an Italian priest had invented a machine 'to remove walls from one place to another'; an English mechanic had found 'a perpetual power that will give motion to all kinds of machinery, mills, engines, carriages, ships of war, mercantile and other vessels, lighters, craft and boats of every description': there was an electrical cure for St. Vitus Dance, and 'a composition for shaving without the use of razor, soap, or water'.

Organized encouragement found its head in the Society for the Encouragement of Arts, Manufactures, and Commerce, founded in London by a self-educated mechanic in

1754. On its membership roll were the names of lords, gentry, manufacturers, high officials, inventors, and agricultural experts. Johnson was a member, and spoke at least once at a meeting with 'a propriety, perspicuity, and energy which excited general admiration'; but he slipped quietly out of the meeting-room when the Society wished him to write one of its advertisements. The Society's aim was 'to encourage ingenuity and industry by bestowing of premiums'. It had sections devoted to agriculture, manufactures, mechanics, chemistry, the polite and liberal arts, trade and colonies. Each year it offered premiums, medals, or honorary awards to induce endeavour in all these branches. Its list for 1759 included prizes for the best samples of green and scarlet dyes, the best varnish, the best saltpetre, the largest quantity of mourning crepe made by one person, for plans of a saw-mill capable of sawing timber into useful planks, for the best paper, and the finest yarn spun from flax grown in England. In 1760 it sought a machine that would spin six threads at once: in 1765 it gave £100 to a poor country tanner who had discovered a method of tanning calfskin with oak sawdust in place of oak bark, 'which will be the means of saving a great number of oak trees'. In the 'eighties it offered rewards for a power-loom, and by 1782 had distributed about £28,000 in premiums and medals. It built up a museum of machines and models, and its publications attracted much attention. If one dare talk about the 'spirit of the age', that spirit in the mid-eighteenth century was one of insatiable curiosity; and it hovered over the head-quarters of the Society, when it was not in the Patent Office.

How was all this growing and changing economic activity organized? In what relationship did the man at the loom, the knitting frame, the kiln, or the coal face stand towards the materials and implements he used and the consumer of his product? No simple answer is possible; but if we drew up a list of every conceivable form of economic organization, from that of the independent self-sufficing jack-of-all-trades family unit to that of the large factory filled with machinery and specialized wage-earners producing for a market at the world's end, Johnson's England provided examples of every kind.

In isolated parts of the north and west, production for

personal use still retained much vitality. The family's joint efforts provided most of the food, drink, and clothing; and though this was exceptional rather than general, the non-commercial activities of rural households were many. Eden in 1797 was surprised to learn that while the poor in the south bought ready-made clothes, 'in the north almost every article of dress worn by farmers, mechanics, and labourers is manufactured at home, shoes and hats excepted. . . . Although broad cloth purchased in the shops begins now to be worn by opulent farmers and others on Sunday, yet there are many respectable persons at this day who never wore a bought pair of stockings, coat, or waistcoat in their lives'.[1] As with clothes, so with bread, cakes, beer, and vegetables. Outside the towns many, but by no means all, had the use of some piece of land, while the northern housewife combined dexterity with the needle with ability to bake a large variety of bread and cakes.

Of the forms of organization which fed the stream of trade, differences arise from the answers to the following questions: Did the producer own the tools of his craft, or did they belong to some employer or merchant? Did he own the material on which he worked, and from the sale of his product receive profit as well as wages; or was he working on another man's material for wages? He might own both tools and material, he might own the tools but not the material, or he might own neither. Did he carry out only one process, many, or all? Did he work under his own roof or under an employer's? Did he produce for an open market where he was free to sell only if the price was acceptable, or had he become virtually dependent on some merchant for orders and work?

The simplest form of industrial unit was that of the independent worker who, in Smith's words, 'has stock sufficient both to purchase the materials of his work and to maintain himself till it be completed. He is both master and workman, and enjoys the whole produce of his own labour'.[2] He was a rare type; and was becoming rarer. He could be found among the master-craftsmen and petty tradesmen of the towns; he made much of the crude earthen-

---

[1] Sir F. M. Eden, *The State of the Poor* (1797), vol. i, p. 555.
[2] Quoted by Witt Bowden, *Industrial Society in England towards the End of the Eighteenth Century* (1925), p. 245.

ware and some of the hardware; but his stronghold was the Yorkshire woollen industry. There the family firm still throve. The father went to the market weekly to buy wool, which his wife and children made into yarn; he wove the cloth, assisted by son, apprentice, or possibly journeyman, took it to the mill to be fulled, and then to his stall in the street market or his stand in the cloth-hall. There he sold it to merchant or agent, bought more wool, and returned home to repeat the process. A small piece of land attached to the house was used for gardening, grazing, and perhaps a little arable work. His equipment cost little, and it was not difficult for an ambitious man with a few pounds, a wife and some children, to set up on his own account, for if his reputation was good some wool-merchant would let him have a supply of material on credit. He could seek outside aid if his family was unable to make sufficient yarn; but the inventions of Hargreaves and Arkwright helped to free him from dependence on outsiders, for by 1780 scribbling machines were being set up in fulling mills, and the miller who fulled his piece would also scribble his wool, while Hargreaves' jenny could be set up in his home and would do the work of at least six spinning wheels. A clothier's inventory for 1779[1] values two spinning wheels at 5s., 'looms and gears' at £1 4s., a pair of worsted looms at 10s. 6d., and a spinning 'jinee' at £2 10s. The total textile equipment of this fairly large clothier, including oil cistern, cards, weigh balk, scales, and tenter-frame, was valued at only £9 12s. 6d., which was equal to the joint value of the 'spangled cow' in the barn, the clock in the house, and 'one large bibell' in the parlour. Some other occupations needed only a small outlay in equipment. Campbell in 1747 prepared a list of the 'Sums necessary to set up as Master' in the highly specialized trades of London, and reported that eight occupations needed only £5, ten could be begun with £10, twenty-five with £20, ninety with £50, and seventy-five with £100.[2]

The cost of equipment was not, however, the only consideration; had it been, many English industries might have remained in the hands of small independent producers. Let us trace the possible career of one of these small clothiers. He has the virtues or luck essential to success; he prospers,

---

[1] Inventory (MS.) of Joseph Broadbent, of Honley, near Huddersfield.
[2] R. Campbell, op. cit., pp. 331–40.

and expands his scale of operations; he takes another apprentice, employs a journeyman, then two, three, and more, and sends his yarn out to more spinners. He buys wool by the pack, he even goes to the wool counties to purchase in bulk, and brings it home to be sorted. Of his growing group of employees some come to work under his roof; others spin or weave in their own homes on wheels or looms which may be their property or his, on material which has been sent them or which they have fetched from his home—now a warehouse as well as a workshop. Eventually the master may be so busy buying, putting out, taking in, touring the wool counties for material, and the towns seeking orders for his cloth, that he has little time to spare for productive work himself. He has an agent in London, or even sets up an office there. He has become a big *entrepreneur*, a large employer, an organizer of production, and his trading activities now loom larger than his industrial interests. On his tombstone he will probably be described as a 'Merchant'. His children will see to that.

Meanwhile the merchant had not been idle. He might be content to buy what was offered in the open market. But he knew what consumers, especially those at a distance, were wanting; he had capital or knew where to get it, he could afford to buy the necessary quantities of the right kinds of raw material, and he was willing to bear the financial burden caused by the long lapse of time which stretched between the buying of those materials and their final sale as finished goods to the consumer. The longer the lanes of trade the harder it became for producer and consumer to meet and speak to each other, and the stronger the position of the middleman or series of middlemen. That strength was exerted in gaining control over production. The merchant gave orders for goods to be made according to his specifications; he provided the raw material on credit, and thus had the first claim on the goods produced; he might provide the tools; and the final processes, whether of finishing such goods as cloth, or the assembling of parts made by specialized workers, might be done in his shop. In one or other of these ways he gained control over the maker; the latter might still own the equipment, might employ journeymen and train apprentices, but the merchant had become his master.

England in 1750 was full of illustrations of the results of

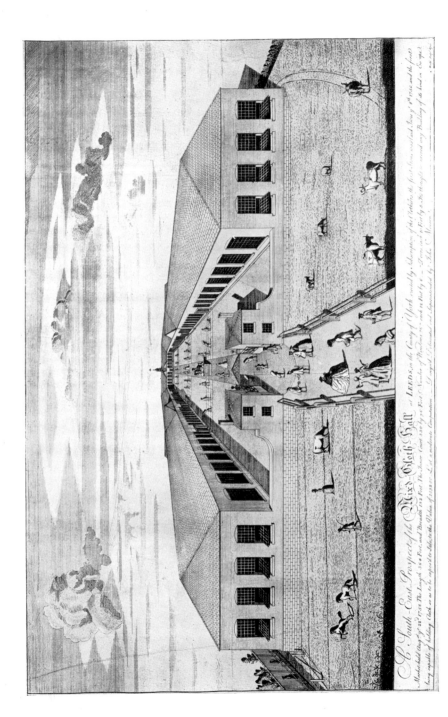

A South-East Prospect of the Mixed Cloth Hall at Leeds in the County of York

THE MIXED CLOTH HALL, LEEDS, 1758

these thrusts of the producer upward into trade and of the merchant downward to control of production. In Lancashire the men who brought in the cotton and flax and sent out the cloth supplied the initiative and material in order to be sure of getting the goods they wanted, while some small makers gradually established large putting-out connexions and blossomed forth as merchant-manufacturers. In Yorkshire the worsted industry grew up under the control of large organizers of production and sale, some woollen cloth makers had as many as twenty looms, and merchants were giving orders privately, extending their finishing plants, and putting out wool to spinners and weavers. The Sheffield cutler owned his grindstone and tools, but obtained his metal from Hull merchants who imported it from Sweden or Russia and let him have it on long credit. The key-man of the Birmingham metal-ware industry was the factor; he provided the materials, and sometimes the tools as well; he directed the production of the many different parts and supervised their assembly; sometimes he made a weekly advance of money, and he marketed the finished product. In the West of England the clothier never soiled his hands at a loom; he was a large buyer of wool, organizer, and salesman. In the hosiery industry, which grew up in the Midlands during the century at the expense of London, the metropolitan merchant sent his orders down to the hosier, who distributed material to the village families and isolated homes over a large area of Derbyshire, Nottinghamshire, and Leicestershire. Sometimes the knitter owned the frame on which he worked, but he might rent it from the hosier or from some outsider who had realized that frame-rents gave a profitable return on capital. London was full of specialized craftsmen who worked with their own tools, in their own shops or homes, for some superior who was in touch with the market and who supervised the final processes. The gold and silver lace man gave out material to about ten different kinds of workers, while goldsmiths, upholsterers, coach-makers, saddlers, and watch-makers had many dependents.

Where the burden of capital equipment was small and lay chiefly on the shoulders of the craftsman, the scale of operations of merchant or manufacturer was limited only by the size of the market he could win and the extent of his working capital. Hence, while the typical business unit of the century prefer having [the cloths] woven at their own houses'. At least three-quarters of a century was to elapse before the last hand-loom weaver in that district carried his last piece to the warehouse. But the spinning machines soon tipped the scales definitely against the domestic spinner, and the last of the big industries joined that movement towards the congregation of workers which had been evident in most of the other industries for at least two centuries.

Our picture of economic relationships is thus one of great diversity. In it we must find room to insert a thumbnail sketch of those whose business was to work, learn, and obey. Children were put to work helping their parents as soon as they were able to do any useful job. Women discharged their triple task as mother, housewife, and industrial aid. Young men were still apprenticed formally in industries where division of labour had not progressed far, where skill came only by long practice, where a trade union upheld apprenticeship, or where they hoped to become freemen of a city and masters in their trade; but where their lot was to be that of a permanent wage-earner, where proficiency came easily and quickly, or where the Statute of Apprentices of 1563 did not run, i.e. in the newer industries such as cotton, apprenticeship was optional. The Statute of 1563 was dead in many places, and dying elsewhere. Campbell frequently urges parents not to indenture their children unless they have enough money to set them up as masters later on, and mentions several occupations in which apprentices are never or rarely taken. As for the adult male worker, the laws against embezzlement of material, against truck, and against trade unions are an indication of the extent to which large numbers of men had become permanent wage-earners long before there was a single big industrial town in the country. Industrial strife was often acute, which need scarcely surprise us if the relationship between master and man was, in Tucker's words, 'much nearer to that of a Planter and Slave in our American Colonies than might be expected in such a Country as England'.[1]

Hours were long for all workers, whether master or servant. Campbell gives 6 a.m. to 8 p.m. as the normal working day for most London occupations, and though the domestic worker was in theory free to fix his own hours since he was

---

[1] Josiah Tucker, op. cit., p. 25.

paid a piece-wage, he was often at his loom or bench by 5 or 6 a.m. and did not stop, if material was available, till 8 or 9 in the evening. Industrial accidents and diseases were not uncommon. Howlett is eloquent on this point.[1] 'The collier, the clothier, the painter, the gilder, the miner, the makers of glass, the workers in iron, tin, lead, copper, while they minister to our necessities or please our tastes and fancies, are impairing their health and shortening their days.' Arts and manufactures can show as long a casualty list as war, of workers 'suffocated in mines and pits, or gradually poisoned by the noxious effluvia of metals, oils, powders, spirits, &c., used in their work, and can exhibit as mournful a scene of blinded and lame, of enfeebled, decrepit, asthmatic, consumptive wretches, panting for breath and crawling half alive upon the surface of the earth'. Campbell frequently warns parents of the hazards to health: few gilders 'live long, the Fumes of the Quicksilver affect their Nerves, and render their Lives a Burthen to them'; glaziers suffer from 'the Palsey', pewterers soon become paralytic, and refiners must have sound lungs since 'they are subject to paralytic disorders'. Wool-combers worked in an atmosphere charged with charcoal fumes, and all who worked at home lived and toiled in air laden with industrial dust, fluff, and odours, at tasks which involved monotonous repetition movements and often called for strenuous physical exertion.

It would be wrong to end this survey with the suggestion that the road to wealth, independence, power, or prestige was closed to all men who started life poor. The rewards of thrift, energy, persistence, initiative, luck, or lack of scruples were abundant, and the upper ranks of industry, commerce, finance, politics, and society were dotted with self-made men. 'Men are every day starting up from obscurity to wealth,' said Johnson. A Manchester pamphleteer, who described himself as a cobbler, declared in 1756, 'I hardly know one single instance of a large Fortune gain'd in Town but the Man who laid the Foundation of it was of very inferior Substance and a Customer of mine.' The iron-masters of the Midlands had nearly all risen from the ranks of small craftsman or petty merchant, nailer, or lock-smith, while many a City magnate who could 'undertake for

[1] *Gentleman's Magazine* (1782), vol. lii, p. 526.

supplying the State with Three or Four Millions Sterling, and raise it within the Circle of his own Acquaintances', traced his career back to an obscure provincial origin or immediate ancestry. For instance, there was Samuel Touchet, M.P., a big man in cotton, slaving, insurance, bill-broking, money-lending, and the underwriting of State loans. He tried to get a monopoly of the trade with Labrador and with Senegal, and fitted out a fleet of five armed ships to help capture Senegal from the French. His father was a Warrington pin-maker who became a successful Manchester cotton-maker and dealer. Or there was Anthony Bacon, M.P., a Manxman who went to Maryland and set up a store; he prospered and returned to England to conduct operations on a larger scale. He became a Government contractor, furnishing supplies to garrisons in Africa and the West Indies, and to the red-coats during the American Revolution. He sent negroes to America, bought ships, owned a mine in Wales, developed ironworks in Glamorganshire, and had coal-mines, fishing interests, and land in the Canadian maritime regions. He entered Parliament, possibly because he wished to be nearer the source of those fat profits which came from contracting, loan-mongering, and serving as paymaster to troops and allies abroad, but possibly, so said his enemies, in order to escape an inspection of his accounts as contractor. He died immensely rich, one of scores of men who found in London, the colonies, and India vast scope for profiteering.

For the successful manufacturer or merchant whose tastes were less spectacular and imperial, banking offered an attractive form of higher enterprise. British banking entered the eighteenth century with a well-shaped head and puny body. The Bank of England probably succeeded far beyond the dreams of its founders, and rendered a service to the public which even exceeded that given to the State. It provided a safe deposit such as few goldsmiths or scriveners could offer, and thus made hoarding unnecessary. It reduced the level of interest. Its issue of notes for £10, £15, and £20 supplied an acceptable paper currency, but the £5 note did not appear till 1794. It kept the gold coinage in better condition, and improved the operations of foreign exchange. But no one bank could serve the whole country's needs, yet the terms of the Bank's foundation forbade Parliament to create any other bank, and prohibited any corporate group of more than six persons from issuing notes. Joint-stock banking remained under this ban till the nineteenth century, and the Bank of England meanwhile established no branches in the provinces.

A large field, especially outside London, was therefore left to be tilled by private hands, and usually they were the hands of merchants, shopkeepers, or large industrialists. For their business these men might be able to use money deposited with them by neighbours who wished to put money out at interest. But their chief service lay in facilitating the circulation of the bills, promissory notes, and drafts by which internal trade payments were made until the cheque became popular and bank or government notes became safe. Outside the field of retail trade and wages payments, business was conducted on a credit basis, and its medium of exchange was a paper order or promise to pay at some future date. Every seller was also a buyer, debtor as well as creditor. As seller A he drew a bill on his debtor B, ordering payment by a certain date either to himself or to his creditor C. The debtor 'accepted' the bill and returned it to A, who posted it to C if it was drawn in C's favour, or kept it till it matured and then collected his debt. But he might wish to turn it into cash, and therefore sought for some one who would buy it from him at a discount. The cycle of payment might go the other way round, for B might take the initiative by looking for some one who had a bill for sale. This bill B bought, posted to A, who forwarded it to C, kept it till it matured, or discounted it.

This traffic in paper needed a national centre and regional sub-stations. London was the obvious national centre, and by 1700 the 'bill on London' had become the most common form of paper demand. Most men who conducted what the early nineteenth century called 'an extensive concern' either had a London house or agent or an account with some London bank or accepting house. They allowed their creditors to draw bills on them, and these were accepted on their behalf by the London financial agent; or they sent their creditor a draft drawn against the London account. To meet this drain they drew bills on their own customers and had the money paid into their London funds; if necessary they also bought bills locally and posted them to the banker. Because of the credit thus kept in London they were able, for a consideration, to aid their smaller neighbours who had payments to make in the capital or credits to be transferred therefrom; they had bills to sell, and they had spare money which could be used for discounting bills.

Gradually, therefore, the local manufacturer, merchant, or tradesman waded deeper into this stream of discount, acceptance, deposit, and loans; the merchant became merchant-banker, then banker-merchant, and finally abandoned all traffic in commodities. Some of these men descended on London when their provincial town offered nothing more to conquer. Coutts, the Edinburgh corn-dealer, turned to banking, and then to that 'noblest prospect', the high-road to England. Gurney, the Norwich worsted manufacturer, and Lloyd, the Birmingham iron-master, were two other invaders. The provincial banks which became numerous after 1750 were nearly all built on money, experience, and contacts made in industry or trade. That of Nottingham was the creation of Smith the mercer, but soon to be founder of a peerage; in Bristol a book-seller becomes banker, in Manchester a tea-merchant, in Liverpool a linen-merchant, in Leeds a grocer, in the North Riding a farmer, and so on. By 1800 there were nearly four hundred country banks, receiving deposits, issuing notes, and discounting bills.

These banks served a fourfold purpose. They facilitated commercial payments, provided loans, mobilized local capital, and offered interest to those who cared to deposit their savings. Into what other channels could those savings have gone; how else could money be put out to work? The wave of joint-stock promotion spent itself in 1720; the Bubble Act of that year forbade the establishment of companies except by charter or Act of Parliament, but the fact that there were very few applications from industrial or commercial company-promoters during the next eighty years suggests that the partnership form of organization was satisfactory where capital requirements were beyond the resources of one man's pocket. The investor was not besieged with company prospectuses till after 1820.

There was nevertheless a fairly wide range of investments even in Johnson's time. For the cautious man there was the safe return on mortgages or the profit and prestige of land-ownership; the turnpike trusts were large borrowers who

Fine Tea Coffee Chocolat Cocoa Nutts
Vermachelly Sago and all other Drugges
Sold by Page Hockett at ye
Great Mogul at Brownlow Street
end in Drury lane

'FINE TEA'
A MERCHANT'S TRADE CARD

could offer the revenue from tolls as security; and after 1760 the canal companies wanted much money. Then there were the old companies—the Bank of England, East India, Hudson's Bay, South Sea, and Africa. Finally there was the national debt, growing with every war, and the stocks of some foreign governments and companies.

The marketing facilities for investment and speculation improved steadily during the century. In the provinces the buying and selling of stocks and shares was a matter of private sale or of the auction room, but in London the stock exchange was becoming organized and those who worked in it were struggling to gain a reputation for respectability. Evicted from the Royal Exchange in 1698 because they were too numerous and noisy, the jobbers and brokers had pitched their market in Exchange Alley, with Garraway's Coffee-house at one end and Jonathan's at the other. Foreign stocks were still dealt in at the Royal Exchange, and in 1764 the newly-built Rotunda of the Bank of England became the market for British Government securities; South Sea House and East India House were also the scene of trading in the shares of those companies. But in 1762 the chief dealers formed a club at Jonathan's in order to establish some sort of control over the trade; eleven years later 'Change Alley was deserted by the club, and a signboard on which was painted 'The Stock Exchange' was placed over the door of a coffee-house in Threadneedle Street. A committee took charge, a sixpenny entrance charge was made, rules were framed, and gradually the world forgot that Johnson had defined a jobber as 'a low wretch'.

BIBLIOGRAPHY.—The best bibliographical work is J. B. WILLIAMS'S, *Guide to the Printed Materials for English Social and Economic History, 1750–1850* (2 vols., 1926). Useful select lists are found in E. POWER, *The Industrial Revolution, 1750–1850* (Economic History Society Bibliographies, No. 1, 1927), and H. L. BEALES and G. D. H. COLE, *Select List of Books on Social and Economic History, 1700–1850* (Journal of Adult Education, March 1927).

Contemporary Sources. Few of the State Papers of the eighteenth century have been edited or published; that a large mass of material is lying there waiting to be mined is made evident by the spade-work done by Miss Mann and Mr. Wadsworth for the study of Lancashire mentioned below. Local public and private MSS., such as Quarter Sessions Records, Corporation Minutes, the Boulton-Watt Collection (in the Birmingham Reference Library), and private business papers, are being increasingly studied for the light they throw on special regions and industries, and on them are based many of the monographs in the list below.

Printed material is abundant. The Statutes of the Realm, the Lords and

Commons Journals, and the Parliamentary Reports are indispensable. Some of the more important pamphlets are listed in the works of Lipson and Bowden (see below), and extracts are printed in J. SMITH, *Chronicon Rusticum-Commerciale* (2 vols., 1747). DEFOE's *Tour through the Whole Island of Great Britain* (1724–7) is now reprinted in the Everyman Library; see also his *Plan of the English Commerce* (1728) and his *Complete English Tradesman* (1726). Of YOUNG's *Tours* through the Eastern Counties (1771), the North (1771), and the Southern Counties (1768), the northern tour is the most valuable on trade and industry. See also JOSIAH TUCKER, *Instructions for Travellers* (1757). R. CAMPBELL's *The London Tradesman* (1747) is a detailed survey of all the occupations carried on in London. M. POSTLETHWAYT's *Dictionary of Trade and Commerce* (1774) and A. ANDERSON's *History of Commerce* (1764) are useful compilations; the *Gentleman's Magazine* and the *Annual Register* cover the period from 1731 and 1758 respectively. Provincial newspapers are valuable from at least 1750. ADAM SMITH's *The Wealth of Nations* is one of the best single sources for the period.

Modern Studies. The most comprehensive survey is E. LIPSON, *Economic History of England*, vols. 2 and 3 (1931). See also TRUEMAN WOOD, *Industrial England in the 18th Century* (1911); L. MOFFIT, *England on the Eve of the Industrial Revolution* (1925); W. BOWDEN, *Industrial Society in England towards the End of the 18th Century* (1925); and P. MANTOUX, *La révolution industrielle au xviiie siècle* (translated by M. Vernon, 1928). Works such as C. R. FAY, *Great Britain from Adam Smith to the Present Day* (1928); J. H. CLAPHAM, *An Economic History of Modern Britain* (1926); and L. C. A. KNOWLES, *The Industrial and Commercial Revolutions in Great Britain during the 19th Century* (4th ed., 1928), link up the eighteenth and twentieth centuries.

Of special studies, the following may be mentioned: T. S. ASHTON, *Iron and Steel in the Industrial Revolution* (1924); T. S. ASHTON and J. SYKES, *The Coal Industry in the 18th Century* (1930); A. P. WADSWORTH and J. DE L. MANN, *The Cotton Trade and Industrial Lancashire, 1600–1780* (1931); H. HEATON, *The Yorkshire Woollen and Worsted Industries* (1920); E. LIPSON, *History of the English Woollen and Worsted Industries* (1921); H. HAMILTON, *English Brass and Copper Industries to 1800* (1926); G. I. H. LLOYD, *The Cutlery Trades* (1913); V. W. BLADEN, *The Potteries in the Industrial Revolution* (in Economic Journal, Economic History Series, 1926); M. D. GEORGE, *London Life in the 18th Century* (1925); G. T. GRIFFITHS, *Population Problems in the Age of Malthus* (1926); R. B. WESTERFIELD, *Middlemen in English Business, particularly between 1660 and 1760* (1915); R. D. RICHARDS, *The Early History of Banking in England* (1929).

X

AGRICULTURE AND RURAL LIFE

By C. S. ORWIN

By Agriculture only can commerce be perpetuated; and by Agriculture alone can we live in plenty without intercourse with other nations. This, therefore, is the great art, which every government ought to protect, every proprietor of lands to practise, and every enquirer into nature to improve.— *Thoughts on Agriculture*, in *Universal Visiter* (1757).

Young *Col*. . . . has introduced the culture of turnips. . . . His intention is to provide food for his cattle in the winter. This innovation was considered by Mr. *Macsweyn* as the idle project of a young head, heated by *English* fancies; but he has now found that turnips will really grow, and that hungry sheep and cows will really eat them.—*Journey to the Western Islands* (1775).

DR. JOHNSON was a townsman both by birth and by inclination. 'No wise man will go to live in the country', he remarked when dining with Sir Joshua Reynolds, 'unless he has something to do which can be better done in the country.'[1] Nor were country dwellers any higher in his estimation than the country itself. 'Farmers, I think, are often worthless fellows. Few lords will cheat, and if they do they'll be ashamed of it; farmers cheat and are not ashamed of it; they have all the sensual vices, too, of the nobility, with cheating into the bargain.' His recorded comments on agriculture and country life are those of the typical townsman. Staying with his friend Dr. Taylor, at Ashbourne, he shows good-humoured toleration of his host's enthusiasm for farming. 'He is, in his usual way, very busy; getting a bull to his cows, and a dog to his bitches.' 'Taylor is now going to have a ram; and then, after Aries and Taurus, we shall have Gemini.'[2] He is as much interested in the deer as in the cattle, and it is the size of the bull only upon which he comments. 'The great bull has no disease but age. I hope in time to be like the great bull.' He was astonished to see polled cattle in the Hebrides, which, he says incorrectly, are a different species from the horned cattle, though they will breed together. His correspondence with Mrs. Thrale,

[1] Yet in the latter part of his life Johnson used to spend months at a time in the country.

[2] Another of his comments was upon Taylor's lack of success in breeding horses; he had had sixteen fillies without one colt—'an accident', as he observes, 'beyond all computation'.

however, seems to betray a wider interest, as when he remarks upon his host's experiments with Polish oats and Siberian barley, and the difficulties of the hay-making season; and the *Journey to the Western Isles* shows a lively concern for agricultural experiment in backward regions.

Otherwise, Johnson's consideration of rural industry is entirely academic or political. 'If corn be dear', he says, 'and butchers' meat cheap, the farmers all apply themselves to the raising of corn, till it becomes plentiful and cheap, and then butchers' meat becomes dear; so that an equality is always preserved.' This betrays a belief in the flexibility of farming far removed from reality. But if he had no innate love of his countryside and displayed no profound knowledge of the processes of farming, he had a very full appreciation of the fundamental importance of a prosperous agriculture in national life. If he held the farmers of his day in poor repute, it may be remarked that his great contemporary, John Wesley, confirmed him in his view, farmers being in his opinion 'of all the people in the kingdom the most discontented, seldom satisfied either with God or man'. But Johnson's *Further Thoughts on Agriculture* leaves no doubt as to his opinion of the political importance of the art they practised. The essay was published in *The Universal Visiter*, in March 1756, and though it does not bear Johnson's signature, it was rightly ascribed to him by Boswell 'from internal evidence'. He opens with a comment on the poor esteem in which agriculture is held by those who do not practise it. 'Nothing can more fully prove the ingratitude of mankind than the little regard which the disposers of honorary rewards have paid to Agriculture; it is treated as a subject so remote from common life by all those who do not immediately hold the plough or give fodder to the ox, that I think there is room to question whether a great part of mankind has yet been informed that life is sustained by the fruits of the earth.' He goes on to point out that it produces 'the only riches which we can call our own and of which we need not fear either deprivation or diminution'. This statement shows a remarkable appreciation of the indestructible nature of the soil, for agriculture is indeed the only industry of which it may be said that it produces wealth without destroying it. 'The field, which is this autumn laid naked by the sickle, will be covered, in the succeeding summer, by a new harvest; the grass, which the cattle are devouring, shoots up again when they have passed over it.'

He passes on to comment on the instability of a nation dependent mainly upon trade, a lesson which has not yet been learnt by this country after nearly 200 years. 'Every trading nation flourishes, while it can be said to flourish, by the courtesy of others. We cannot compel any people to buy from us or to sell to us.' Even those who do, he points out, may vary their demands and their sources of supply, and nothing we can do can stabilize our commerce with other nations. 'By Agriculture alone can we live in plenty without intercourse with other nations. This, therefore, is the great art, which every government ought to protect, every proprietor of lands to practise, and every inquirer into nature to improve.'

The *Further Thoughts* are a clear indication of the place which agriculture and country life occupied in Johnson's mind. His reaction to the rural scene was that of the townsman on a holiday. But this admitted, his analytical mind left him in no doubt as to the fundamental importance of farming in national economic life. He realized the indestructibility of the soil, the independence, both individual and national, accruing from a flourishing rural industry, and, on the other hand, the economic weakness of a nation set on trade, on the exchange of the luxuries or, at least, of the non-necessaries of living for the food and raw materials provided by the land. But he has left only one other contribution to the discussions of the agricultural problems of his day—an essay on the policy of the payment of bounties on the export of corn—and nowhere, either in his own letters or at the hands of his biographer, is he disclosed as having any of that intimate knowledge of country life which must have been common to most educated people in the days when domestic industry still flourished and the mineral resources of the country still awaited development.

Johnson seems to have accepted the prevalent land system without criticism as a natural and proper evolution. 'Land, in England, is an article of commerce. A tenant who pays his landlord his rent, thinks himself no more obliged to him than you think yourself obliged to a man in whose shop you buy a piece of goods. . . . But if you please you may let your lands cheap, and so get the value, part in money and part in homage.' This must not be taken too seriously, for elsewhere he recognizes the place of rural loyalties in the general scheme of subordination. In his day, and for more then a century after, rent without homage was virtually unknown. Land has always been a social amenity as well as an investment, and to describe it merely as 'an article of commerce' is to betray an ignorance of actual conditions which is only partially dispelled by his recognition of homage rent.

The history of farming shows it to be a process of steady evolution through the centuries, but certain periods are marked by particular activity, and the one covered by Johnson's lifetime is one of these. To appreciate the importance of the changes that it embraced, some understanding is needed of the industrial development of England at its outset, and of her agricultural organization at that time.

Briefly, it may be said that England was a country self-sufficing in all the essentials of life. With the exception of sugar, it is hardly too much to say that her import trade was entirely in luxury or semi-luxury products. The manufactured goods and raw materials which furnished the country's exports were, all of them, the products of the land, consisting mainly of wool, woollen goods, and wheat. Now, supplies of corn and wool to meet the requirements of the trade with the continent of Europe were not got from the countryside at large. On the contrary, the districts from which wheat was procured were limited to the drier counties of the eastern half of England—which alone produced a surplus beyond local requirements—and to those parts of them from which its transport to the coast could be arranged without prohibitive cost. And if the greater value of wool and the comparative ease with which it could be transported by land made it a more marketable commodity, the districts in which it was produced were even more definitely localized than those producing corn.

It follows that the great extent of rural England at the time of Johnson's birth was virtually unaffected by the country's foreign trade and, in the absence of any concentration of consuming communities, such as the growth of industrialism was subsequently to bring about, internal trade was unimportant. The countryside consisted of small communities which, owing to the difficulty of internal traffic and communication, except along the main highways, were necessarily self-sufficient in all the principal requisites of life, existing in a state of economic isolation, one from another, which was almost complete.

The organization of agriculture within these communities varied widely in different parts of the country. At the beginning of the eighteenth century, two systems of farming were to be found, which had come down with very little change from the earliest recorded times, systems which differed entirely in the conception of land utilization on which they were based. Further, there were large tracts of land in certain districts, and smaller areas in nearly all districts, which were still unreclaimed waste or woodland, unsettled by population and practically unoccupied for agricultural purposes. The wastes were situated, for the most part, on the lighter soils and in the more arid districts, such as the sandy soils of some of the midland counties, the great area of the chalk throughout the eastern, south-eastern, and southern counties, and much of the limestone stretching from the Cotswolds into Lincolnshire. The woodlands are still represented to-day by the fragments which remain of much greater forests, such as those of Wychwood, Wyre, Charnwood, Sherwood, Rockingham, Knaresborough, and many others.

Throughout the greater part of the southern, midland, northern, and eastern counties, the land other than wastes and forests was occupied mainly as ploughland and in very large fields, with a concentration of the population in villages, and little or no evidence of farm-houses and steadings built upon the land outside them. Over the rest of England, the western and south-western counties, the farming land and the settlement of population looked practically the same as it does to-day. Grassland predominated over ploughland, fields were mainly small, and the rural community, though living largely in villages and hamlets, were to be found also in homesteads scattered over the land they occupied. It must be understood that the division of the country into these two different systems is drawn very broadly, their boundaries cannot closely be defined, and by the early years of the eighteenth century there had been many invasions of the 'ploughland and big field' area by 'grassland and small field' farming. In general, however, and as a starting-

point for a consideration of farming in Johnson's time, the
division may stand.

As to the areas in which the large ploughed fields predominated, most people are aware to-day of the ancient
system of land tenure based upon communal cultivation.
The land needed for the sustenance of the village was occupied in a few large, open fields, in which the people cultivated holdings, not compact, but consisting of small strips
of land alternating with those of their neighbours, so that all
could have an equal share in the good and the less good.
Often the strips were no more than half an acre in extent,
and as such a system made the inclosure of each man's holding impossible, so all had to conform to a common course of
cropping.

The strength of the system began and ended in the idea
of equal treatment for all, upon which it was based. Its
weaknesses were manifold, but they are summed up in the
objections that no one could crop his ploughland differently
from his neighbours, for after harvest the stubbles were
thrown open to be grazed by everybody's live stock; that no
one could improve his live stock, which was subject to the
attentions of any one's bull, or any one's ram, on the common
grazings. In a word, during the thousand years from the
beginning of the Saxon occupation, during which there was
only one standard of farming and only one purpose in it,
this system worked well. But as improvements in methods
became known, as new crops became available, and as the
opportunity of farming for profit grew, so did the common
field system, with its rigid imposition on all of the standards
of the least progressive, become more and more restrictive
and out of date.

Evidence of the wide spread of common field farming, and
of its long duration, is afforded to-day in the place-names,
field-names, and surnames with which it has endowed the
language for all time. The Court farm, the Manor farm, the
Grange farm, the Hall farm, names common enough, were
the farms of the lord of the manor, most of which were consolidated and inclosed from the common fields at an early
date. Tithe farm, Rectory farm, Glebe farm, are the holdings which were attached to the rectory or vicarage, either
in olden times for the support of the parish priest, or later,
upon inclosure, as an equivalent in value to the tithe in kind

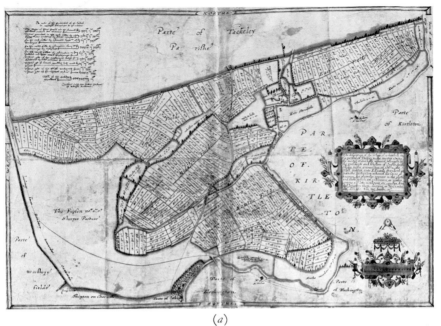

(a)

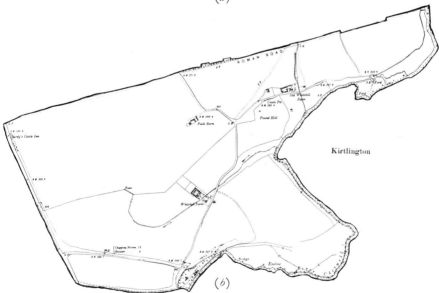

(b)

PART OF THE PARISH OF TACKLEY

(a) Before inclosure, from an old map in the possession of Corpus Christi College, Oxford, and (b) after inclosure, reproduced from the Ordnance Survey Map, with the sanction of the Controller of H.M. Stationery Office

which before had gone to the support of the parson. Long Furlong farm, Beer (i. e. Barley) Furlong farm, take their names from divisions of the open arable fields, and Cowleaze farm, Oxleaze farm, Sheepstead farm, and Commonleys farm have been created from the common pastures. The Lammas Meads and Lammas Lands, still met with here and there, were divided amongst the tenants to make their hay, and were thrown open for grazing by everybody's live stock after Lammas.

Again, the organization of the ancient manor required the services of certain people in particular capacities. The Steward and the Reeve guarded the lord's interest in the manor. The Woodward was responsible for the preservation of the timber. The Messer took charge of the harvest of the corn crops in the common fields. The Hayward removed the fences from the fields after harvest, to allow the sheep and cattle to graze. And there was another group of persons, necessary for the management of the live stock in the days when everybody's animals grazed together in common, who still live in many surnames, such as Coward, Bullard, Calvert, who tended the cows, bulls, and calves; Shepherd, Ewart, Tupper, concerned with the sheep; Swinnert and Seward, the swineherds; and lastly, the Pinder, Poynder, or Ponder, who impounded the straying stock.

The process by which the common field farms were converted into the agricultural holdings of to-day is known as the Inclosure Movement. It is impossible to assign a precise date to its beginning, and it is not entirely finished to-day, but the tendency to consolidate the scattered holdings first became pronounced about the sixteenth century. From that time onward the process went steadily forward. There was no general rule, but in one way or another, sometimes on expiration of tenancies, sometimes by purchase and consolidation, sometimes by agreement between adjacent owners, sometimes by compulsion and even by fraud—in one way or another inclosure was going slowly on. In some parts of the country all trace of common-field farming had already disappeared by Johnson's time; in other parts partial progress had been made.

At first, the thing just happened, and it is impossible, now, to know how much of the country occupied under the open-field system was inclosed by voluntary processes. But towards the end of the seventeenth century, there arose the practice of submitting agreements to inclose to the Court of Chancery for confirmation, in response to an evident need for regularizing these arrangements, and this step was quickly followed by recourse to private Acts of Parliament to authorize and to procure the inclosure of lands held in common.

Not all the inhabitants of the parish had equal rights of Common. There was the yeoman farmer with his strips of arable land in the open plough fields, his inclosures of pasture land, his meadow rights in the hayfields, and his grazing rights on the commons. But there was also a numerous other class, many of them without any land in the arable fields, or paddocks for holding stock, who had, nevertheless, either by grant or by prescription, a variety of valuable rights on the commons and wastes of the parish— the right to graze a cow, a few sheep, or some geese, the right to cut turf or gorse for fuel, and so on. It is clear that the improvements in agriculture, which were calling more and more loudly for a reform of the system of land tenure in the open fields, bore very little upon the rights enjoyed in common by the humbler members of the village community over the wastes of the manor. And so it happened that Inclosure Acts are, for the most part, of two kinds—the one passed to facilitate the re-parcelling of the arable fields by giving compact blocks of land to those who had cultivated them hitherto by scattered strips, the other passed to bring about the subdivision of the common pastures and wastes, with a view to their more intensive occupation.

The more urgent thing in the early years of the eighteenth century was the inclosure of the common arable fields, and it was not until many of them had been inclosed that, in the latter years of the eighteenth century, the growth of population and the great technical improvements in agriculture caused men to turn their attention, more and more, to the possibilities of improvement in the grass commons and wastes. To make the distinction clearer, the inclosure of the common arable fields was the first step towards improvements in the technical efficiency of farming, while the inclosure of the grass commons and wastes was the first step towards the reclamation of wild land for farming.

The obvious weakness of the system of farming which prevailed up to the beginning of the eighteenth century, by contrast with farming to-day, was its deficiency in the production of winter food for live stock. To-day, the farmer has at command crops of meadow hay, clover hay, and straw, and, for green food, mangolds, swedes, turnips, and the great variety of crops of the cabbage family. In the Middle Ages, all these green crops were unknown. So the farmer was dependent upon his meadow hay and his straw as the only winter keep for live stock, supplemented, of course, by grass in the warmer counties, and even the straw crop could not be compared in volume with straw crops to-day, for the reaping-hook left a long stubble. And so it follows that the coming of winter saw a wholesale slaughtering and salting of cattle, sheep, and pigs for the winter meat supply, and that the only live stock to survive the winter was breeding stock. Within the ruins of Old Basing House, for example, may still be seen the great brick-lined pits in which the carcases were stored, preserved in salt, and the importance of the dovecotes and the fishponds, as sources of fresh food to the inhabitants of the manor houses at this time, can be appreciated, as well as their decay in these days of plenty.

Clover, artificial grasses, and the various root crops were making their way into farming practice all through the eighteenth century. When it is remembered that under the open field farming system the stubbles were common grazing until the time for spring ploughing came round, and the fallow was common grazing all the summer, it is clear, at once, that the progressive farmer, wishing to avail himself of the new crops, would have to convince all his co-tenants in the common fields of their utility. Otherwise, his strips of clover in the barley stubble, and his strips of turnips in the fallow field would be devoured by the live stock of all the parish, and he would derive no benefit from them.

But the Inclosure Acts did more than pave the way for the new agriculture; they took account of other social reconstructions for which the times were ripe. For many centuries the Church had been partner with the farmer to the extent that she took a tithe of the produce of the soil. But the collection of the tenths must always have been troublesome and expensive, and as the art of agriculture became more complicated, so were the tithe-owner's difficulties increased. And just as there had been much voluntary inclosure of open fields before the practice of parliamentary inclosure sprang up, so there had been much compounding by farmers for payment of tithe in money before the passing of the Tithe Commutation Act, in 1836. Parson Woodforde, for example, was taking tithe in cash from his Norfolk parish some sixty years earlier. These voluntary commutations were commonly made upon inclosure, and when inclosure by statute became the rule, it was a frequent, though by no means universal, practice to extinguish tithes by providing for the tithe-owner in some other way. An allotment of land estimated to produce the value of the tithe might be made, but more generally a corn rent was substituted, by which the farmers of the parish paid a cash commutation to the tithe-owner, the amount of which fluctuated with the price of corn.

Another direction in which the Inclosure Acts were of assistance to agriculture was in the provision of roads. Owing to the difficulties of transport, a subject dealt with elsewhere in this book, the isolation of many villages was almost complete, and, in some places, not only in the winter time. Sir Thomas Bernard in 1780 speaks of Borrowdale as

a Valley, divided into small & well-cultivated Farms, occupied by the owners; who are the 'Statesmen' of Burrowdale, & live Secluded from the World in small neat Houses. . . . Insulated from the Rest of Mankind by Impracticable Mountains, equally unknowing and unknown, they have their own Chapel, their own School & their own Dialect: their Commerce consists in exchanging, with the Keswick Butchers, their Cattle for corn, which the Vale will not produce; & in bartering their Wool for Pins, Needles, & the other Productions of the fine Arts that Peddling Gipsies have to bestow—Oh Rousseau! what a Retreat was here for the Man of Nature![1]

So it is not surprising to find that by many Inclosure Acts provision is made for the construction of new roads, and that gravel pits and stone pits are designated from which the parish may derive materials, free of charge, for road repair. Under other Acts, the grazing of the roadside waste belongs not to the adjacent owner, as at Common Law, but to the parish, the profits of the grazing to be applied to the cost of road maintenance. But road improvement was slow, and at the end of the century Arthur Young and his band of agricultural surveyors, who reported on the state of rural

---

[1] *Pleasure and Pain (1780–1818)*. Edited by J. Bernard Baker (1930).

England to the newly-formed Board of Agriculture, had more, perhaps, of criticism than of praise for the highways over which they passed.

Throughout Johnson's lifetime, statutory inclosure, which had begun but slowly, proceeded with greater and greater rapidity. Its effects on the practice of farming are discussed below, but it was not until the inclosure of the commons and wastes became frequent, as distinct from the inclosure of the common arable fields, that the movement began to affect rural society. Inroads into the wastes had always been going on, as the needs of the community increased, but, excepting such spectacular tasks as the drainage of the Fens, it was not until the rapid growth of population, which began during the latter half of the eighteenth century, that organized attempts were made, on a large scale, to reclaim the less attractive lands. Earlier, social and industrial life was still centred mainly in agriculture, but it was an agriculture carried on at a low level of technical efficiency by rural communities constituted on a self-sufficing basis, most of them with practically no contacts with the outer world, and comparatively few with each other.

Granted that the practice of agriculture has been always an evolutionary process, Johnson's lifetime marks, nevertheless, the birth of modern farming. With a very little latitude, it may be said that the eighteenth century witnessed the introduction of the system of mixed farming, which, in its various manifestations, has held the field in this country right up to the present day; it marked, also, the first attempts to improve upon the primitive implements in use, for the better cultivation of the soil; the beginnings of the improvement of breeds of live stock by empirical methods—methods which all the discoveries of science have not yet superseded; the growth of leadership in agricultural improvement amongst English landlords; the foundation of State aid for agriculture; the development of the spirit of inquiry; and last, but most important of all, the change-over from subsistence farming to farming for profit.

Mixed farming is based on the theory of an interacting system of crop and meat production, by which some of the arable land produces food for man and the rest of it yields crops for sheep and cattle, pigs and poultry, the fertility of the soil being maintained by the return of animal manure to it. In a sense, it is true that this was the theory of farming in the open arable fields farmed on the three-field rotation of winter corn, spring corn, fallow, but until the introduction of clover and artificial grasses and, above all, of the turnip and its allies, the production of winter keep for live stock, on ploughland, was infinitesimal. But, with the cultivation of the new green crops, stock for slaughter could be kept on and fattened for use throughout the winter as required. Moreover, the breeding stock could be carried through the cold season in much better condition.

The effect on production was very great, for to grow good turnip crops, it was necessary thoroughly to cultivate the land both before sowing and while the crop was growing. So, in the place of the fallow in the open fields, with its crop of thistles, docks, and every sort of weed, which supplied only scant herbage in the summer months, the farmer, after inclosure, had a field which he had necessarily cultivated to free it from weed growth so as to give his turnips room. This meant, of course, that his following spring corn crops were delivered from the competition of the weeds springing from the thorough seeding which the land always had in the fallow year.

But the introduction of the root crop meant much more than this. Most of it was consumed on the land on which it grew by sheep, confined within hurdles, which ate their way across the fields. So, in addition to the thorough cleaning which the land got during the cultivation of the crop, it received an equally thorough manuring during the progress of the flock over it. Such of the roots as were pulled and carted to the yards for the better maintenance of the horned stock, served to increase the quantity of farmyard manure available for return to the ploughland. And, of course, the hay from the clover and artificial grasses made more winter keep, enabling more cattle to be wintered, more manure to be produced, and so still more fertility for the arable land. In fact, these two innovations, the cultivation and cropping of the old fallow course, and the introduction into the rotation of the new clover-and-grasses course, worked in a beneficent circle; the additional crops meant more live stock, more live stock meant more manure, more manure meant heavier crops.

The cultivation of the new crops and the break with the

old rotation began in the eastern counties. This is hardly surprising when it is remembered that the innovations were all of them introductions from the Continent, and most of the coming and going between England, France, and the Low Countries was from the Kentish and eastern counties' ports. According to Defoe, sheep and bullock feeding on turnips originated in the county of Suffolk, but the great pioneers of the new farming were Norfolk men, and it is their county and not the one in which it originated which gave its name to the new four-course rotation. This, with local modifications, eventually overran the whole of the country, and it led to an increase in production from the soil by which British farmers were able to meet the demands of the ever-growing industrial population right up to the middle of last century. It survived, unchanged in principle if reduced in practice, through the agricultural depression which marked the closing decades of the century; and it is dying very hard to-day, more than 200 years after its inception, under the stress of twentieth-century economic conditions.

Of the early pioneers, the first person to practise a rotation in which clover and turnips appeared as farm crops of whom there is record was Sir Richard Weston (1591–1652), once an exile in Flanders on account of his allegiance to the Stuart cause. He was also the pioneer of long leys, for he advocated leaving the clover down for five years before ploughing it for the wheat crop. Jethro Tull (1674–1740), to whom further reference will be made, wrought a revolution in methods of cultivation as the result of observations he had made of the tillage operations of the French vine-growers. The second Viscount Townshend (1674–1738), who spent a part of his political life in Holland, practised on his Norfolk estate much that he had learnt abroad about the cultivation of roots and clover. To 'Turnip' Townshend, in fact, is attributed the introduction of the Norfolk four-course rotation, the results of which on his own estate and during his own lifetime were only less remarkable than the incredulity with which they were received by his neighbours.

But it was not only the evolution of the new rotation which was laying the foundation of the new era in farming. The inclosure of the open fields proceeded slowly, and though the use and cultivation of the new green crops were well understood by an enterprising handful of men at the beginning of the eighteenth century, Arthur Young was still preaching from either text at the end of it. Another stimulus was given by the improvement of farm implements, heralded by the introduction of the seed-drill and the horse-hoe by Jethro Tull. Before his day, all crops were sown broadcast, a method which needed more seed and deposited it at irregular depths and irregular intervals in the soil. The result was crops which germinated, and so ripened, unevenly, crops which, from their haphazard distribution over the ground, could not be cultivated or weeded during their growth.

Now, Tull's observations of the French vine-growers' methods had led him to realize the value to the plant of the continual stirring of the soil about its roots. It killed the weeds, preserved the moisture, promoted aeration and admitted warmth, and so he set himself to produce a machine which would deposit seed in the ground at a uniform depth to ensure regular germination, in regulated quantities to prevent over-seeding, and in rows at intervals wide enough to admit of interlinear cultivation by horse and hand tools. His was not, perhaps, the first drill to be invented, but it was the first which worked. Corn or turnips were drilled in wide rows, and then the horse-hoe was kept busy between them so long as the work could be performed without injury to the tops of the growing plants.

It was many years before Tull's advocacy of the drill bore fruit, and it is not surprising that his first design of a machine relatively so complicated was found capable of much improvement directly its use became at all common. But the simplicity of the plough and other agricultural implements in general use for long ages, preserved them from any radical change in construction or design, and though improved forms appeared, here and there, from time to time, the great advance in the multiplication of new implements and the improvement of old ones following upon Jethro Tull's work, did not really begin until the end, or even after the end, of the period under review.

It is obvious, considering the conditions of land tenure and the limitations of the farmer's knowledge of technique, that the potential improvement of every process in every branch of farming at the beginning of the eighteenth century was immense. Stress has been laid upon the beneficent effects of inclosure, of the new crops and rotations, of the introduction of drill husbandry. But in no branch, perhaps, were the foundations of improvement better laid than in the live-stock industry. On fully half the country at the beginning of the century, where open field farming still persisted, sheep and cattle were maintained, in common, upon the common pastures and wastes of the parish, and any improvement of the stock under such a system was literally impossible. Food in many parishes was short even in summer, and in all places scarce during the winter. There was often no 'stint' upon the numbers which might be turned out to graze. And so the pastures were always eaten bare by excessive stocking, and the animals were stunted in their growth by continuous semi-starvation. In winter, as has been said already, no attempt was made in most places to carry anything more than the breeding stock, and these must have made rather a poor shift of it on the worn-out grazings.

Practically the whole of the sustenance for flocks and herds was derived from the common pastures and wastes. There were small grass inclosures round the village, and the tendency to fence off encroachments upon the waste was always present, but in the aggregate these did not amount to much. Sheep and cattle were not always grazed together, owing doubtless to the difference in their habits of grazing, for land closely stocked with sheep will starve a cow. The old maps of the time abound in such field-names as 'Cow-lease', 'Shepe-pasture', 'Horse-close', some of which survive to this day. But while this may have made possible a more economical use of the available pasturage, it did nothing to remove the difficulties in the way of breed improvement. All the flocks and herds of the parish mingled together, and any control of mating was obviously impossible.

Stock was pastured under the supervision of parish officers. Originally, the numbers of each class permitted to each tenant were strictly regulated, so as to prevent the evils of overgrazing and the depreciation of other men's rights. Stringent measures were also taken to deal with cattle straying from adjoining commons. Remains of the parish pounds into which trespassing stock was driven may be found to-day, and, once impounded, the removal of the animals by their owner without payment of satisfaction for damage done was an offence against common law. In many places, however, the practice of 'stinting' the commons had been unnecessary, as they were large enough and to spare, and where the right to turn out on the commons was regulated, control tended to break down. And so, by the eighteenth century it is not surprising to find frequent reference to a more or less general condition of over-stocked land and half-starved sheep and cattle.

Sheep were kept more for their wool-bearing capacity and for their usefulness on the arable land of the open fields as four-legged dung-carts, than for mutton. The demand for wool for the weavers was incessant. Defoe, in his travels, was struck constantly with the great activity of the wool industry. Penning with sheep during the summer on the fallow break of the common arable fields supplied almost the only manure that the land received during the rotation. At the beginning of the century, cattle were still in common use for draught purposes, and heavy shoulders and light quarters were appreciated more than points indicative of the butcher's beast. But, until the spread of the four-course rotation had provided the stock-breeder with food sufficient to carry his animals through the winter above the starvation point, and until the inclosure of common pastures made possible the control of breeding, no attempt at live-stock improvement could succeed. Both these conditions were being satisfied more and more as the eighteenth century went on.

Not a great deal is known about the different breeds with which the country was stocked at the opening of the period under review. As regards sheep, most districts had their own type, some of which differed very little one from another, and all of which must have been long-legged, roach-backed, hairy-woolled brutes if the descriptions of them are at all trustworthy. A broad division might be made into hill types and lowland types, the former all of them longwools, the latter including the forbears of the modern shortwools, such as the Southdown, but all of them were grass sheep, and the modern arable-land breeds were entirely unrepresented. The material upon which the improver had to work was of the worst; his opportunity, on the other hand, was immense.

Cattle types were possibly better defined. Over the midlands and west, up into Lancashire, Westmorland, and Cumberland, and southward to Dorset, the Longhorn prevailed. Except for its head it must have differed little from other local types, for in colouring and configuration Longhorns resembled the native cattle of Glamorgan and Gloucestershire, of which a few examples still remain, and it had much in common with the early Herefords. In the south of England, the red cattle, which were the forerunners of the Devon Rubies and of the modern Sussex, were to be found, and the Herefords were general along the Welsh border. Norfolk and Suffolk seem to have been unique in that they had evolved a polled breed, while over the northern and north-eastern counties the Teeswater type, from which the world-conquering modern Shorthorn is sprung, was predominant. Wales supported a black breed of its own, known in the south as the Pembrokeshire, and as Angleseys in the north.

So far as can be judged, there was no generally adopted standard of size, shape, or make for any breed. It is probable that cattle were taken in hand for improvement earlier than sheep, and the Longhorn was the first to be improved. In the middle of the eighteenth century, the Longhorn was more widespread, probably, than any other breed, and it was looked upon as the most profitable both for beef production and for cheese. The great Midland grazing district had been early inclosed, and this was the home of the Longhorn. The first-known improver of the breed was a landowner, Sir Thomas Gresley, of Drakelow, in Derbyshire, who is recorded, in 1720, as having a dairy of cows which were selected for their similarity in colour and shape. He was followed by one Webster, of Canley, in Warwickshire, who, starting with the Drakelow stock, crossed them with Cumberland and Westmorland bulls. Cumberland and Westmorland seem to have been noted in those early days for the quality of their Longhorn cattle, even as they are to-day for their Shorthorns. Webster's work served to fix the Drakelow type more firmly, and when the greatest of all the early live-stock improvers, Robert Bakewell, took up the breed, it was with some Canley heifers that he started, and at his death the Dishley herd contained the lineal descendants of one of them, 'Old Comely', calved in 1765.

Robert Bakewell was born at Dishley Grange, by Lough-borough, in 1725. As a farmer, and particularly as an improver of agricultural horses, cattle, and sheep, he made a name and a position for himself in his lifetime to which no one, landlord, yeoman, or farmer, has attained, before or since. He travelled much, to learn what he could of other people's methods, but the whole of his life was spent at Dishley, and he died there, unmarried, in 1795. His farm was visited by a constant stream of people of every class, all of whom were entertained with lavish hospitality, and it is an open question whether this enhanced the profits from the live stock he had for disposal, or whether it was responsible for the straitened circumstances in which ultimately he found himself.

Bakewell left no history of his efforts and no records of the principles which guided him in his work. On the contrary, he made a mystery of his art, and took every possible means to prevent his secrets from becoming known. Few sires were sold, most of them being let for the breeding season and returned to him. His best-known bull, 'Twopenny', was used by most of the larger breeders of the day. He brought about a great improvement in the fattening qualities of the Longhorn, though, it is said, at some sacrifice of their milking capacity, but his work proved an inspiration to others, who were able to equal and even to surpass his results.

But the Longhorn breed was not destined to survive, and Bakewell's work with sheep was his most permanent achievement, for there are probably few English breeds which do not owe the foundations of their improvement to the introduction of some of his Leicester blood. His foundation stock was the local longwool breed, though whether the Leicestershire or the Lincolnshire type is uncertain. Marshall's description of them reveals them as most unpromising material. A ram of the 'true old Leicestershire sort' was described by him, so late as 1784, as 'a something between a sheep and a goat'.[1]

In a remarkably short space of time Bakewell had improved his flock out of all knowledge. A type had been developed in which fineness of wool and aptitude to fatten were the predominant features, and the coarse bone had been reduced to an almost incredible fineness. Thus equipped, Bakewell instituted his ram-lettings, and by 1770 he was getting as much as 25 guineas for the season for his best, with an aggregate of 3,000 guineas for them all. The most

[1] William Marshall, *The Rural Economy of the Midland Counties* (1790), vol. i.

ROBERT BAKEWELL

From the painting in the possession of the Royal Agricultural Society

famous of his rams, 'Two Pounder', was once let for 800
guineas for the season.

There is no doubt that much of Bakewell's success was due
to in-breeding. When he had an animal of the type he required, he sought another of the same type to mate with it,
and if the best combination he could effect necessitated the
mating even of mother with son, father with daughter, or
brother with sister, it mattered not at all. Only in that way
was he certain of perpetuating the points he esteemed, and
in ensuring for them a prepotency of transmission to the
next generation. Herein, probably, lay his great success in
fixing the types for which he was breeding, and it may explain, also, the extraordinary rapidity with which he evolved
them, which was particularly notable in his new Leicester
sheep.

Perhaps the most famous of the old Longhorn cattle was
the bull 'Shakespeare', bred by Robert Fowler, of Little
Rollright, in Oxfordshire. 'Shakespeare' was calved in the
year 1778, and had a long career, both at Rollright and
on hire to other breeders. It is clear, from many contemporary references, that he was the outstanding bull of a
generation, and his breeding is an example of the methods
initiated by Bakewell, and followed so closely by Fowler.
His sire was Bakewell's bull 'D', who was twice a grandson
of 'Twopenny', and his dam was a daughter of 'Twopenny'.
Lawrence says that after his purchase of 'D', Robert
Fowler bred entirely from his own stock, with results that
were amply justified at the sale of the Rollright herd, after
his death, in 1791. Three of the bulls made over 200 guineas
each, one of the cows, 'Brindled Beauty', made 250 guineas
(she was by 'Shakespeare', out of 'Shakespeare's' dam), and
two more made over three figures. An average of £80 per
head was realized for bulls, cows, and calves.

Other breeders there were who carried on the Longhorn
breed in its perfection, such as Paget, of Ibstock; Prinsep,
of Croxall, of whose herd W. Pitt has left a contemporary
account in his agricultural report of Derbyshire; Richard
Astley, of Odstone Hall, Market Bosworth; the Knowleses,
Thomas and William, of Nailstone; and several more who
helped to maintain the popularity and the quality of the
Longhorn into the early years of the nineteenth century.
Nearly all of them, however, so far as is known, owed their

herd improvement to the hire of Fowler bulls or to purchases at the Rollright sale, and this carries them back to Bakewell's 'Twopenny', and so through the Canley herd, to Drakelow.

Already in the time of Bakewell and Fowler, men in the north of England were bestirring themselves to improve their native cattle, which were destined to sweep the Longhorns out of every stronghold once held by them. The Shorthorn breed, found principally in Yorkshire, Durham, and Northumberland, had a very mixed ancestry, and from time to time the Kyloe or West Highland, the Galloway, then a red breed, the Longhorn brindle, the Dutch black and white, and even the Channel Island cattle, are recorded as contributing to the make-up of the stock that was found in that part of the country in the first half of the eighteenth century. There were good farmers in the north of England; much of the land had never been farmed on the open field system, and a good deal of the rest had been early inclosed. So Bakewell had contemporaries here, such as the Culleys, Matthew and George, who were endeavouring to improve their stock, but most of them seem to have adhered to the idea that improvement could come only by the introduction of fresh blood.

It was not until Charles Colling, of Ketton, by Darlington, applied himself to the problem, that real progress was made. Born in 1751, of substantial yeomen stock long settled in the district, he worked for his father, who had taken Sir Ralph Milbanke's farm of Ketton in 1769, and at the age of thirty-one he was sent to Dishley, on the advice of his father's old friends, the Culleys, to learn what he could from Robert Bakewell. Bakewell's success with the Longhorns did nothing to weaken Colling's allegiance to the cattle of his own country. Instead of becoming a Longhorn man, he resolved to do for the Shorthorn what George Culley had failed to do, notwithstanding that after two visits to Dishley he had realized the opportunity.

Farming almost alongside of his brother Robert, also a Shorthorn man, he laid the foundation of his success by the purchase of a bull which had caught his eye in a neighbour's field on his way to church. This was 'Hubback', the ancestor of all the Shorthorns. As a matter of fact, 'Hubback' did comparatively little for Colling, for it was some years before

ROBERT FOWLER'S LONGHORNED BEAUTY

From a painting

COLLING'S SHORTHORNED HEIFER

From the engraving by Wm. Ward after the painting by T. Weaver

the lessons he had learnt from Bakewell sank in, and so 'Hubback' was sold as soon as his daughters were ready to come into the herd. An experiment, accidentally under-taken, into the comparative results of inbreeding and out-crosses, ended so conclusively in favour of the former that Colling doubted no longer. From henceforward his Short-horn herd was as closely inbred as ever were Bakewell's or Fowler's Longhorns.

An early achievement was the breeding of the famous 'Ketton Ox'. The animal was regarded as faultless, and Charles Colling kept it for exhibition. At four years of age, it weighed just over 3,000 lb., and he sold it for £149. The buyer resold it in five weeks for £250, and for the next six years, under the name of the 'Durham Ox', it travelled all over England, its weight ultimately rising to 3,800 lb. A butcher's beast to-day will average about 1,200 lb. No better way of advertising the improved breed could have been found in those days, when there were no agricultural shows and little movement amongst the agricultural popula-tion. It has been said that the Longhorn was doomed when the 'Durham Ox' set out upon its travels.

The men whose work has been noted here were the greatest of their generation; they were the outstanding representa-tives of a little band of live-stock improvers who achieved results of inestimable benefit to English farming at this time and during the early years of the following century. Other breeds, both of cattle and sheep, were taken in hand. Quart-ley and Thomas Coke were to do for the North Devons what the Colling brothers had done for the Shorthorns, and John Ellman, of Glynde, was working with success upon the unimproved Southdown sheep at the time when Bakewell was busy with his Leicesters. England has been the reservoir upon which the settlers of all the new countries of the world have drawn for cattle and sheep with which to stock them, and the success of English breeders in meeting this demand, and in enabling this country to build up the gigantic edifice of exchange of manufactured goods for food and the raw materials of industry upon which her national existence depends, may be said to have had its origins in the genius of these pioneers.

It is probable that most of the technical improvements in farming practice were the work of farmers themselves.

Stress has been laid upon the achievements of the live-stock improvers of the eighteenth century, most of whom were working farmers, because it was in this direction, perhaps, that the greatest advance was made. In many places, however, farmers were experimenting in other ways as the century went on, and the improvement of soils by chalking the heavy ones, claying the sandy ones, and manuring all of them with every kind of animal refuse was advocated. Under-drainage was begun, irrigation was practised—these and other things were due to the enterprise of yeomen or tenant farmers, working to improve their holdings in the inclosed parishes.

Nor were the landlords backward in making their contribution to progress. For every landlord was also a farmer, and his farm was the principal source of his food supply, so that his attitude towards it differed fundamentally from that adopted towards the home farm to-day, which is an amenity rather than a necessity, and a hobby rather than a commercial proposition. The reason is not far to seek, for the only occupation open to the landlords of olden times, other than the government of the country, was the development of their estates. It was an Earl of Bedford who, in the previous century, had organized the local gentry as a Company of Adventurers to drain a great part of the Fens. It was the eastern counties landlords who popularized turnips and rotation grasses, for there must have been foundation for the nickname which 'Turnip' Townshend earned. And if Coke of Norfolk was luckier than some of his contemporaries in having a biographer, there is no doubt that he did a great service to agriculture. Some of the landlords organized projects, such as inclosure and drainage, which were obviously beyond the compass of less influential and less wealthy men; others vied with their farming neighbours in the improvement of practical farming; others, again, were concerned to develop policies of estate management which should react to the general advantage. Agriculture had become fashionable. 'Farmer George' was upon the throne and the royal farms set an example in the trial of new practices, and in experiment with new ideas. Farming rivalled politics and sport as the gentleman's recreation.

Thomas Coke, of Holkham, is the best known, and rightly, of the great landlords of these times. A close friend of Charles

James Fox, he represented his county of Norfolk in Parliament for many years, but his heart was never in political life, and it was the improvement of agriculture, and particularly of his own estate, that was his first preoccupation. The estate to which he succeeded in 1776, was much of it poverty-stricken, situated as it is on a light, sandy soil in the north of Norfolk. Wheat was hardly grown, and the local sheep and cattle were poor in the extreme. Unable to renew some of his leases, he accepted the challenge and set to work to farm the land himself. He broke away from the local course of cropping, which took three consecutive corn crops, and he rested the land by keeping it under pasture for two-year periods before taking two corn crops. He introduced the practice of using marl, which substance was to be found in plenty by sinking pits, and the drifting sand which formed so much of the estate was fixed and improved. He induced Robert Bakewell to visit him, at Holkham, to teach him something of the stock-breeder's art. In short, both by inquiry and by experiment he left nothing undone which might help him in the improvement of his property, and all his great resources, which others might have employed in the pursuit of the usual pleasures of rich men, he mobilized to the same end.

The result of his enterprise was a speedy and remarkable improvement in the productivity of the estate. The enriched land grew larger and better crops; the heavier crops provided fodder for greater numbers of live stock; the heavier stocking produced more fertility for the soil. Coke's results and his enthusiasm inspired his tenants, and by granting them long leases which would secure to them returns on the outlay entailed in making similar improvements, he was able, ultimately, to stimulate them to imitate his methods. Dr. Rigby, who has left a description of the agriculture of Holkham, states that the annual rental rose from £2,200 in 1776 to £20,000 in 1816.

The question of estate development assumed a growing importance as the population increased and more and more of what had been waste lands and common grazings were inclosed for cultivation. Perhaps a large common had been parcelled out amongst those who claimed rights over it. How should the new allotment, extending, possibly, to several hundred acres, be brought under cultivation? Who should

stub the trees and bushes? Who should fence it off into
fields of convenient size and dig the drainage ditches? Who
should construct the farm-buildings and the farm-houses for
those who were to occupy it, and the cottages for those who
were to work upon it? Very little is known of the way in
which all this work was done, or of the division of the tasks
of reclamation between landlord and tenant. Much reclamation and inclosure of wastes along the borders of their farms
was done by the farmers themselves by the simple process
of putting a fence round a convenient area and stocking it
with cattle, and Edward Laurence, writing in 1727, advises
stewards to be on the look-out for encroachments such as
these, so that they may annex them for the benefit of the
landlord. But the inclosure and reclamation which went on
under statute, in the latter years of that century and well on
into the next, were better regulated. From the records that
remain, it seems that a common practice was for the landlord
to fence the land with a boundary fence, to drain it and to
divide it into fields. He also built the house and enough
buildings to accommodate the plough teams and a cow or two.
The tenant was then admitted, and it was his part of the bargain to clear the land of thorn or scrub, to lime it if necessary,
to bring under tillage such parts as were to be tilled and to
stock the remainder with cattle and sheep. To secure to him
the fruits of his labours, he had a long lease, usually holding
the farm for twenty-one years; in recognition of the unproductive character of the land in the early years, his rent
was at first nominal; to secure that he should work upon it
to improve it, the rent was to rise by stated sums at stated
intervals. The landlord, on his part, was to add more
buildings as the productivity of the farm increased and more
accommodation was needed; he was to compensate the
tenant at the end of his lease for the permanent improvement
effected by him, during his tenure, according to a schedule
attached to the lease. In fact, the lease was the instrument
by which the landlord, with his wider experience of the new
agriculture, was enabled to direct the tenant in the methods
best calculated to bring about the amelioration of the soil.
In recent years there has been common talk of 'restrictive
covenants', and farmers have succeeded in securing legislation
to make them null and void. But, in the eighteenth century
and for long after, leases were not the mechanical production

of lawyers content to copy the clauses applicable to the practice of the past generation ; rather were they prepared under the direction of landlords and their stewards from their knowledge of how to restrict bad practice and to encourage or even to compel the adoption of the best, according to the information then available. The landlord led the way, the tenant collaborated with him. Together they brought under cultivation tens of thousands of acres of hitherto unproductive soil.

The wonderful farming lands of East Lothian are the result of improvements made, under the security of nineteen-year leases, by farmers of that time, improvements which often involved carting hundreds of loads of clay on to every acre, to bind the light sandy soil. In fact, to know what the equipment of the land entailed on those who have brought it from its natural, unimproved state into the condition of well-ordered farms, is to realize how the English countryside, as it is displayed to-day, is entirely the work of men's hands, that every fraction of value it possesses attaches to it not by the bounty of Nature but by the prodigal expenditure of the labour of succeeding generations, applied to bend her to their service.

To a handful of the great landlords at this time belongs the credit of a movement from which developed the agricultural shows. After wheat, by far the most important agricultural product was wool. The British Wool Society had been launched at a great sheep-shearing festival which Sir John Sinclair, a Scottish landowner, had held at Newhall's Inn, Queensferry, in 1791. These sheep-shearings were first organized by Thomas Coke, at Holkham. They began as small gatherings of farmers whom he invited to Holkham, at the time of sheep-shearing, to express their opinions on the work upon which he was engaged. From these small beginnings they developed until as many as 600 people would assemble for a week, as his guests. Other landowners organized similar festivals, and they may be regarded as the forerunners of the agricultural shows, now such a feature of British rural life, contributing much to the encouragement of live-stock improvement, and to the dissemination of knowledge.

All through the period under review, a system of bounties on the export of corn was in operation. Corn Laws in the previous century had, at first, for their object the provision of revenue without undue interference with the cost of living. As was natural, State policy in a matter affecting the lives of the people so vitally was the subject of much controversy. Johnson's *Considerations of the Corn Laws* was written in 1766,[1] in the autumn following a bad harvest, when the consequent high price of corn had caused riots in many places. In it, he sums up the pros and cons of the bounty question from the point of view of one who is convinced of the efficacy of bounties as a stimulant to production. In effect, he thought that the policy created a reserve of corn against the needs of a rainy day. The bounty encouraged corn-growing; if harvests were plentiful the surplus was exported; if harvests were bad there was no export and, consequently, a reasonable prospect of an adequate home supply.

That, notwithstanding the bounty, there have been years of scarcity, cannot be denied. But who can regulate the seasons? In the dearest years, we owe it to the bounty that they have not been dearer. We must always suppose part of our ground sown for our own consumption, and part in hope of a foreign sale. The time sometimes comes when the product of all this land is scarcely sufficient: but if the whole be too little, how great would have been the deficiency if we had sown only that part which was designed for ourselves. . . . Plenty can only be produced by encouraging agriculture; and agriculture can be encouraged only by making it gainful.

The growing interest in agriculture culminated in 1793, when Sir John Sinclair, at the head of a group of large landowners, induced Pitt to establish a Board of Agriculture. Sinclair himself was appointed President, and Arthur Young, Secretary.

Arthur Young was already well known to his generation as an agriculturist of advanced views. The son of a parson, he was born in 1741, and, after an unsuccessful essay at farming, he made, ultimately, a supreme place for himself as a writer upon the art which he could not practise. It must be admitted, however, that during his lifetime he shared the experience of most of those who think a little ahead of their contemporaries. He met with his full share both of criticism of his views and obstruction of his plans, but there is very little in that which he advocated for the improvement

---

[1] First published in 1808.

of agriculture, both industrially and socially, which has not been justified in the light of subsequent history. His first experience of journalism had been in 1762, when at the age of twenty-one he started a monthly periodical called *The Universal Museum*. He sought, unsuccessfully, to enlist Johnson as a contributor, calling upon him when he 'was sitting by the fire so half dressed and slovenly a figure as to make me stare at him'. Ten years before the formation of the Board of Agriculture, he had begun to publish the *Annals of Agriculture*, a magazine of articles and notes upon current farming topics, which was one of the forerunners of all the agricultural journals of the nineteenth century.

The first project which engaged the Board of Agriculture was an attempt to collect the agricultural statistics of the country, based on returns from every parish, to be supplied by the clergy upon a plan which Sinclair had already adopted with success in Scotland. The scheme broke down, however, and Sinclair and Young decided upon the compilation of a report upon the state of agriculture in Britain, to be made county by county. The most able persons available were appointed to deal each with his own district, and the whole of the country was covered during the years 1793 and 1794, at a cost of about £100 a county. The quality of the Reports which they made varies considerably. Arthur Young himself made the survey of his native county, Suffolk, and also that of Sussex.

The Reports were issued in quarto form but not for general circulation. Some twenty years later, the survey was revised, for the most part by other investigators, and a public issue was made in octavo form. These two surveys afford the earliest evidence of the state of agriculture in the country as a whole, and, made as they were at a time when British farming was passing through the most important transitional stage in its history, they are of inestimable value as historical documents.

For this was the time when farming began finally to lose most of its subsistence character and to begin to produce for the market. During Johnson's lifetime, the population of the country had increased certainly by 50 per cent., and this increase was largely of consumers and not of producers of food. The extending use of machinery was bringing about the suppression of the old village industries and the concentration of a growing industrial population in the midlands and the north. This population had to be fed, and only the British farmer could feed it. Writing in 1724, Defoe records the activity of the export trade in corn to the Continent from the eastern counties ports. But during the last quarter of the century bad harvests and increase of population served to make bounties on exports inoperative, while the French wars acted as a prohibition of imports. The only problem was how to get enough food to meet the country's needs at reasonable prices.

There could be but one answer to it. The old occupied lands must be better farmed, the uncultivated wastes must be brought into use, and these things could be done only by speeding up the process of inclosure. And so, Arthur Young in his surveys and in his tours was zealous to observe the amount of inclosure, and this was his measure of the progress of farming in each district. At the same time, he urged the necessity of large-scale operations, in substitution for peasant farming, if advantage were to be taken of all that experiment and invention had to offer. To him, the social advantages of a peasant community were as nothing by contrast with the economic advantages of maximum production. Only the capitalist farmer could drain, irrigate, and marl land; he alone could afford to buy the improved breeding stock; he alone could travel the country to observe the practice of others and so to extend his own knowledge.

Statutory inclosure, alike of open arable fields and of commons and wastes, went on apace as the century drew to a close, and the spread of improved methods in cultivation, in manuring, in breeding, and in feeding increased rapidly. But it must be emphasized that rural England, as Johnson left it, had not advanced, taking it as a whole, so very far from the state in which it was at his birth. Scattered through the country, in numbers very small at first, were the Townshends, the Cokes, the Russells, who were endeavouring to spread a knowledge of the new rotations. There were the Bakewells, the Fowlers, the Ellmans, the Collings, who were giving the country improved strains of cattle and sheep. There were the Sinclairs, the Somervilles, the Youngs, the Marshalls, who were spreading the gospel of the new agriculture. But it would be entirely untrue to suggest that the great advance in knowledge made during Johnson's lifetime

ROBERT AND CHARLES COLLING

From an engraving by J. Thomson after the painting by T. Weaver

had permeated the farming industry by the time of his death. Over great areas open-field farming with all its handicaps to progress was still pursued; cattle and sheep still struggled for existence on many an unstinted common; great tracts of what to-day are fertile farm lands were still heaths, warrens, and woodlands. But the soil had been turned and the seed sown for the great harvest which the country was to reap in the Golden Age of farming that was to follow some fifty years later—a harvest which had been made possible only through the work of the pioneers of Johnson's times.

What of the people who made up rural society in the eighteenth century? The village community was self-contained to a degree that cannot be realized in these days of easy communication. The difficulties of locomotion, and even more of transport, called for the organization of the village, in most districts, as a complete economic unit, able to feed itself, to clothe itself, to provide work for its able-bodied and sustenance for its aged and infirm. In the early part of the century, conditions had changed very little from those which had obtained in Shakespeare's day, described so vividly by Lord Ernle.[1] Bread corn was grown in thousands of parishes, the inhabitants of which, to-day, are almost entirely dependent upon the produce of the prairies. The farm live stock provided all the flesh food, which must have been little enough for the humbler members of the community as the winter drew on and stocks of salted meat grew low. Clothing, from the first stage of spinning up to the fashioning of garments, was the work of the village women. They baked the bread, they brewed the beer, they salted the pig which provided winter meat, and they took their turn at seasonal labour in the fields.

The men were wholly engaged in the primary stages of the production of all the necessaries of life. They made and repaired their simple tools and worked with them in the fields, all the hours of daylight, to produce the corn and meat for food, the straw for thatch and bedding, the wool and hides for clothing. They cut brushwood or turf, from the wastes, for fuel. They made hurdles to confine their sheep, and basket-work of every kind and for every purpose. They dug stone or chalk, or they puddled clay and straw to build their cottages and cattle hovels, according to the materials which

[1] *Shakespeare's England*, vol. i, ch. xii.

their particular locality afforded; they sawed timber for the framework and boarding of barns and sheds.

The children bore a large share in the general effort. Life was precarious to an extent that can hardly be realized in days when England draws supplies from all the world, and when society has organized itself to provide for the workless, the destitute, the sick, the aged, and the very young. And so the child had to make its contribution to the common task of securing the family living. Children engaged not only in all the duties of the home, but also in the less heavy work of the fields. They scared the birds, picked the stones, tended the poultry, combed the wool, collected the rushes and dipped them in the tallow. There was very little education for the children of the labourers and small farmers. The evidence of the parish registers is that many considerable farmers could not sign their names, their humbler neighbours hardly ever. There were very few Sunday Schools, no organized amusements. Children played with shuttlecocks on Shrove Tuesday, they watched the antics of the hobbyhorse on May Day, and other festivals had their appropriate delights. Except for these occasions, work, hard work and plenty of it, was a matter of course for the children of the lower ranks of rural society.

Just as the village community itself was self-sufficient in most places, so were the families of which it was composed. But there were some tasks which even in those days fell outside the scope of every man, or called for the development of craftsmanship to a degree impossible in those who were, by necessity, Jacks of all trades. And so the villages had their complement of skilled tradesmen, the smith, the carpenter, the miller, for example, together with specialists in other crafts in the larger villages and in localities naturally favourable to them, the potter, the turner, the maltster, the weaver, the tanner, and so on.

In the districts of inclosed farms in the western and southwestern counties, holdings were small, the farmers were working farmers, and the landless labourer class was almost non-existent. The inclosed farms of the Midlands were larger, and the hired labourer more in evidence. But over the large expanse of open-field farms at the beginning of the eighteenth century there were few of the inhabitants who had not some interest in land, even though it extended to nothing more than the right to cut faggots and to graze geese on the commons, and though such slight rights rested on legal foundations even slighter. In the aggregate, farms were small, and farmers worked alongside their men.

It is not possible, here, to consider the conditions of land tenure, but it should be noted that there was a numerous class amongst the farmers, the yeomen of England, who are unrepresented in rural society to-day, unless the post-War community of owner-occupiers has taken their place. They were 'customary freeholders', that is to say, they were the absolute owners of their land subject to certain customary obligations to the lord of the manor. In the ups and downs of farming fortune of the last century or more, they have been merged, or submerged, in the tenant farmer class.

The larger villages provided examples of the middleman class, making nothing themselves but handling the goods which the community needed and could not produce, and finding a market, also, for such commodities as it produced in excess of its requirements. If Thomas Turner, the mercer, grocer, and general dealer of East Hoathly, in Sussex, is in any way typical, the middleman then, as now, was a privileged person, knowing little of the vicissitudes which are the common lot of the primary producer, and secure in his margins whatever the course of prices might be. Mr. Turner could afford to eat heavily and to drink deep, to play cards, to go to Lewes races, and to ride abroad with his wife, seemingly as his inclination took him.

Upon the part played by the Church in rural social life it is difficult to generalize. The country clergy, such as Parson Woodforde, were interested in farming their glebes, and bishops have left on record their strong belief in the moral value of agriculture. 'I love agriculture', wrote Frederick Augustus Hervey, Bishop of Derry (and seventh Earl of Bristol) to Arthur Young, 'because it makes good citizens, good husbands, good farmers, good children; because it does not leave a man time to plunder his neighbour, and because by its plenty it bereaves him of the temptation.' And Richard Watson, the Bishop of Llandaff, who had the unique distinction of being both Professor of Chemistry and Professor of Divinity, at Cambridge, has recorded that his time was 'spent partly in supporting the religion and constitutions of my Country, by seasonal

publications, and principally in building farm houses, blast-
ing rocks, inclosing wastes, making bad land good, planting
larches, etc. By such occupations I have recovered my
health, preserved my independence, set an example of a
spirited husbandry and honourably provided for my family'.

The direct interest of the clergy in the prosperity of farming was only less than that of the squires. Indeed, the
smaller squires, who formed the focus for rural society over
the greater part of the country, were themselves little else
than farmers on a larger scale than their tenants. In all the
principal needs of existence they were self-sufficient, and
the greater means at their command were applied only to the
purchase of such goods as contributed to a higher standard
of living, to the embellishment of their homes, and to the
delegation to stewards and bailiffs of the duties which their
tenants had to perform themselves. Together with some of
the clergy, they were responsible for the administration of
justice and of the Poor Law. Sport of all kinds bulked
largely in their lives. They were pleasant people, with nothing of much importance to do, but doing it according to
their lights. These led them to a rigorous insistence on social
distinctions and the privileges of class. 'It is monstrous',
wrote the Duchess of Buckingham to the Countess of
Huntingdon, of the Methodists, 'to be told that you have a
heart as sinful as the common wretches that crawl on the
earth. This is highly offensive and insulting, and I cannot
but wonder that your ladyship should relish any sentiment
so much at variance with high rank and good breeding.'

There was, however, a freedom in the intercourse between
classes in the country which is quite unknown to-day.
Where social inequality was accepted without question on
either side, fraternization was possible to an extent which
has been impossible ever since the French Revolution
exploded the idea of a predestined natural order. And so
Parson Woodforde would dine with his tailor and both could
enjoy it, while the Rev. Mr. Porter, the incumbent of East
Hoathly, could drink with the mercer and, later, pull him
naked from his bed, in the pursuit of 'innocent mirth'.
Johnson's lifelong friend Dr. Taylor, the 'King' of Ashbourne,
counted among his friends two retired innkeepers, a cheese
factor, two tanners, and a gentleman farmer; these people
were accustomed to meet at his mansion. To the extent

that such intercourse is no longer possible, society is the poorer.

The changes in the economic life of England, particularly in Johnson's later years, were sufficiently serious for large numbers of the working population. In the open-field parishes, it has been shown that the poorer members of the village community exercised rights of one kind or another on the wastes, and sometimes in the common fields, the economic value of which was out of all proportion to the monetary value of the produce they yielded, or to the rent of the land on which they were exercised. The milk of a cow, the growth of a few quarters of corn, the produce of a small flock of geese, a few score of gorse faggots, these things collectively, when taken with the few shillings earned weekly by manual labour, made up a living for the cottage dweller in the uninclosed parish. Without being sentimental about the poor man, there is ample contemporary evidence to show that whatever benefits may have accrued to the community at large from inclosure and the engrossment of farms, life for the lowest social grade in the rural community was deprived of many of its opportunities thereby.

It was necessary that all claimants to rights of any kind should formulate their claims before the Commissioners appointed to make an equitable allotment of the land comprised in the open fields and commons, upon inclosure. Many working men were unaware of the procedure and made no claim. Others were unable to substantiate rights acquired only by prescription. Even those who made good their claims and who received nominal justice were often in little better case, for of what value to a cottager was the allotment of, say, an acre of land, unfenced and possibly remote, in exchange for the right to graze a cow upon a common pasture? The rental value of the land allotted to him might well be as much as that which his share of the common pasture represented; the thing that counted was that his new holding would not serve the purpose of his former right, and his cow must go. 'Parliament may be tender of property; all I know is that I had a cow and an Act of Parliament has taken it from me.' These are the words put in the mouth of the labourer in the open-field parishes by Arthur Young, himself an advocate of inclosure and large-scale farming.

His only recourse was to sell his plot of land to a larger

allottee, and this process was not confined only to the smallest class of recipients under an inclosure award. As the eighteenth century advanced and money was being made in industry and commerce, there arose a new demand for land, and the temptation to sell overcame many of the smaller owner-occupiers. Themselves representative of the humblest class of working farmer, they drifted, naturally enough, into the labour market, and so rural England in Johnson's time witnessed the first development, on any considerable scale, of a labouring class dependent entirely upon wages and divorced from the exercise of any personal rights over the land.

> A time there was, ere England's griefs began,
> When every rood of ground maintain'd its man;
> For him light labour spread her wholesome store,
> Just gave what life required, but gave no more.

As inclosure proceeded, the class of rural society dependent solely upon wages grew; when it could not sell its labour it starved.

The problem of the maintenance of the poor was an old one even in Johnson's day. The Laws of Settlement operated in a variety of ways to increase the difficulty. Able-bodied men were reluctant to leave their place of origin in search of work, knowing that, if unsuccessful, they would be ineligible for relief. Overseers, on the other hand, would take every step to remove from the parish those likely to become chargeable, so as to escape the cost of their maintenance should this happen. Thomas Turner recounts how the vestry resolved unanimously to contribute to the extent of £40, in cash and kind, towards the purchase of a house in the parish of Waldron by one Tho. Daw,

by reason that he would then be an inhabitant of Waldron, and clear of our parish. . . . I believe it is a very prudent step in the parish, for he being a man with but one leg, and very contrary withall, and his wife being entirely deprived of that great blessing, eyesight, there is great room to suspect there would, one time or other, happen a great charge to the parish, there being a very increasing family; and I doubt the man is none of the most prudent, he having followed smuggling very much in the past, which has brought him into a trifling way of life.[1]

[1] *The Diary of Thomas Turner of East Hoathly, Sussex* (1754-65), ed. Florence Maris Turner (1925).

Lady Townshend taking her Favourite Exercise.

His Royal Highness the Prince of Wales, with a Lady of Quality, going to Ascot Races.

And the universal anxiety to escape responsibility for the
child of the unmarried mother, by passing her on to another
parish, led to much brutality in the treatment of these
unfortunate women.

Desertion was a common offence, and the advertisement
columns of the early provincial newspapers contain frequent
offers of rewards, by overseers or guardians, for the apprehension of men who had 'eloped', leaving their wives and
families chargeable to the parish. Thomas Turner describes
the return, in the custody of two men who had been sent by
the parish to fetch him, of a man who had absconded five
years before, leaving a wife and six small children who had
cost the parish upwards of £50.

Parish workhouses had been built in many places under
the authority of the Act of 1722, and persons refusing to
enter them could be denied relief in other forms. The workhouses were often farmed out to employers of labour. An
advertisement in *Jackson's Oxford Journal*, in 1791, invites
tenders from 'A Manufacturing Person to Farm the Workhouse [at Bloxham] for one year, and to maintain and Clothe
the Poor. Any Person of good Character, may, by applying
as soon as may be, to the Churchwardens and Overseers of
the said Parish, as to the conditions under which it will be
disposed of, be satisfied.' Out-relief in the parish was sometimes contracted for in the same way. Crabbe has drawn
a terrible picture in *The Village* of the destitute in the
parish poor-house.

The cost of living rose sharply after 1760, the price of
wheat, for example, showing an average increase of 35 per
cent. for the ten years 1765–74, over the average of the
previous ten years. Able-bodied men, unable to obtain work,
remained at home to secure the assistance to which their
settlement would entitle them, for, having once taken to the
road, they were driven from one parish to the next in the
attempt to pass them on before they might become chargeable. The parish registers of the century abound in records
of the burial of 'a wayfarer', 'a poor wayfaring man',
'a stranger', 'a foreigner', 'a poor man', 'a blind man',
'a lame man'—human flotsam and jetsam overtaken by
death and buried in the last parish into which they had
wandered, often without even a record of their names.

An important change in the administration of out-relief

was made by the Act of 1782 'for the Better Relief and Employment of the Poor'. By this Act, guardians were obliged to find work for a poor person applying to them for it, conveniently near to the home of the applicant; the guardians were to receive the earnings and apply them to the pauper's maintenance, any surplus being handed to him and any deficit being made up from the rates. This monstrous piece of legislation took from the able-bodied poor all personal responsibility and all incentive to a self-respecting life.

But it is clear that the agricultural labourers were not satisfied to receive their subsistence partly as a sweated wage and partly as a dole, and, in one place at least, a spark of the spirit of organization was kindled when 'the por Laberes of Feltwel parish' gave written notice that they had suffered hardship long enough, and were all determined to stop it. They asked that the harvest wage should be raised to 2s. per day. The average wage was 7s. 6d. a week without extras or perquisites. 'We shal all be sattisfied with this state, Gentelmen, and if you are not, We are all determine to proseed further in it. Gentelmen, We have prepared to make it a Generil thing in the parish both Singel & Maried, all that belong to the parish.'[1] But nearly a century was to elapse before this spark was fanned into a flame by Joseph Arch, and the first attempt was made to secure for the rural worker the benefits of organization for collective bargaining.

A word is needed on the conditions under which the rural worker was housed. Comparatively few of the cottages in use to-day were built before or during Johnson's time, though naturally localities differ in this, for survival is a question of the materials used in construction, and these were determined by the local geology in days when long transport was impossible. In the old forest districts houses were timber-framed, and they have survived in fair numbers, as in the Wealden area of Kent and Sussex and in some of the west-midland counties. In the stone districts, too, there has been much survival, of which the beautiful Cotswold villages provide magnificent examples. But in the clayland counties cottages were commonly constructed of 'mud and stud', and in these there has been a rebuilding in brick, almost complete, during the last hundred years. The inclosure of

---

[1] From an unpublished letter in the possession of Bernard Halliday, Leicester.

the open fields and the commons, and the resettlement of the land, called, also, for many new farm-houses and cottages, and the complete concentration of the population in the villages was dispersed.

Judged by modern standards, the housing of the rural working class was uniformly bad. Cottages consisting of one living-room and one bedroom, with low ceilings, small windows, and earth floor, in which large families of all ages were crowded, were common. And right at the end of Johnson's lifetime housing reformers were content to add another bedroom to separate the parents from the children, while admitting that 'it would perhaps be more decent if the boys and girls could be separated, but this would make the building too expensive, and besides, it is not so materially necessary, for the boys find employment in farm-houses at an early age'.[1]

To conclude, the period of Johnson's lifetime was one in which the stage was being set for the new scenes in the social and industrial life of rural England, and here and there parts of the pageant were being vigorously rehearsed.

The evolution of the inclosed farm from the open fields was giving that great stimulus to food production which, later, was to enable the English farmer to meet nearly all the needs of a population which doubled itself before it out-ran his capacity to feed it. It was to bring new wealth to the landowner and to the farmer, and to increase the temporal welfare of a Church maintained from the profits of the soil. But it was to upset the way of life of many of the humbler members of rural society. There could be no place for the smaller cultivators when subsistence farming gave place to production for a market which demanded all the resources both of capital and of technical skill to supply it. Nor was there to be room much longer for the labourer who had some stake in the land, which enabled him to supplement his wages with food or fuel of his own production. Farming, like manufacture, was to be industrialized; the part-time worker and his cow-gates, his goose-runs, his fuel rights, were anachronisms in an industrial age.

England was committed to a course which was to make it the only country in the world in which the most vital

---

[1] G. E. Fussell and Constance Goodman, 'The Rural Economy of England in the Eighteenth Century' (unpub.), quoting Nathaniel Kent, 1795.

industry was conducted, in the main, by hired labour. Looking back, it is difficult to see how this state of things could have been avoided. In a country where the non-agricultural population was increasing so rapidly, a strain was imposed upon home agriculture which could only be met by the fullest organization of production. But there was nothing inherent in commercial farming in its palmy days to impose hardship upon the wage labourer, for the new conditions gave returns sufficient to reward adequately all the parties to production. It was the maldistribution of profits, rather than any lack of them, which led to the change for the worse in the lot of so many of the labouring class which followed on the changes in rural economy begun in Johnson's time.

But the landless labourer, in so far as he was the victim of the industrial system in farming, has had his revenge. The rise and fall of prices mean little to the self-sufficing farmer recruited from the labouring class, but they mean everything to the capitalist farmer working to supply the market. And so, every wave of depression in agriculture, since the eighteenth century, has brought ruin to a number of the modern capitalist farmer class, and opportunity to some of the old-style labourer-farmers. The social history of farming by the system foreshadowed in Johnson's day reveals the constant rise of the rural worker, the steady invasion of the areas of capitalist agriculture by the working farmers from those districts where farming is still as much a life as an investment. If they, in their turn, become corrupted by good fortune and fall when the tide turns against them, there are always others of the class to which they once belonged waiting to fill their places.

BIBLIOGRAPHY. The principal contemporary authorities are:

ARTHUR YOUNG, *A Six Weeks Tour through the Southern Counties of England and Wales* (1768); *A Six Months Tour through the North of England* (1770); *The Farmer's Tour through the East of England* (1771); *Annals of Agriculture* (1784–1805); *On the Husbandry of three Celebrated British Farmers* (1811); WILLIAM MARSHALL, *Rural Economy of the Midland Counties* (1790); *Rural Economy of the Southern Counties* (1798); [Various Writers], *A General View of the Agriculture of the County of* [all the counties of England and Wales] *drawn up for the consideration of the Board of Agriculture and Internal Improvement* (1794); W. PITT, *General View of the Agriculture of Leicester* (1809); ROBERT DOSSIE, *Memoirs of Agriculture* (1768); EDWARD LAWRENCE, *The Duty of a Steward to his Lord* (1727); JETHRO TULL, *The Horse-hoeing Husbandry* (1733); Sir JOHN SINCLAIR, *Address to the Society for the Improvement of British Wool* (1791); JOHN LAWRENCE, *Treatise on Cattle, Sheep, Swine, &c.* (1805); EDWARD RIGBY, *Holkham and its Agriculture* (1817); OLIVER GOLD-SMITH, *The Deserted Village* (1770); DANIEL DEFOE, *A Tour through the Whole Island of Great Britain* (1724–7); Sir THOMAS BERNARD, *Pleasure and Pain* (1780–1818), (ed. J. Bernard Baker, 1930); *Autobiography of Arthur Young* (ed. M. Betham Edwards, 1898); *The Purefoy Letters, 1735–81* (ed. G. Eland, 1931); *The Diary of a Country Parson: the Reverend James Woodforde, 1758–81* (ed. John Beresford, 1924–31); *Diary of Thomas Turner of East Hoathly, Sussex (1754–65)* (ed. F. M. Turner, 1925).

The following are modern books dealing with the period:

LORD ERNLE, *English Farming Past and Present* (4th ed. 1927); E. C. K. GONNER, *Common Land and Inclosure* (1912); G. SLATER, *The English Peasantry and the Enclosure of Common Fields* (1907); W. HASBACH, *The English Agricultural Labourer* (1908); A. JOHNSON, *The Disappearance of the Small Landowner* (1909); C. S. ORWIN, *The Reclamation of Exmoor Forest* (1929); A. M. W. STIRLING, *Coke of Norfolk and his Friends* (1908); A. S. TURBERVILLE, *English Men and Manners in the Eighteenth Century* (2nd ed. 1929); E. LIPSON, *Economic History of England* (1920–31); J. L. and BARBARA HAMMOND, *The Village Labourer* (1920).

See also an article by E. DAVIES on 'The Small Landowner, 1780–1832, in the Light of the Land Tax Assessments' in the *Economic History Review* for 1927.

XI

POVERTY, CRIME, PHILANTHROPY

By J. L. AND B. HAMMOND

In the prospect of poverty, there is nothing but gloom or melancholy; the mind and body suffer together; its miseries bring no alleviation; it is a state in which every virtue is observed, and in which no conduct can avoid reproach; a state in which cheerfulness is insensibility, and dejection sullenness, of which the hardships are without honour, and the labours without reward.—*The Rambler*, No. 53.

An age which, amidst all its vices, and all its follies, has not become infamous for want of charity.—*Postscript to Landor's Essay on Milton* (1750).

When asked by a lady why he so constantly gave money to beggars, he replied with feeling, 'Madam, to enable them to beg on'.—*Memoirs of Samuel Foote*.

IN *Joseph Andrews* Fielding describes a scene in a stage coach when a man is found naked and wounded, stripped by highway robbers, in a ditch. Each passenger in turn deprecates doing anything for him until one of them, who is a lawyer, points out that suspicion and trouble may fall upon them if they leave him and he is found dead. He is then taken into the coach, but nobody will give him a coat except the postilion, who remarks with an oath that he would rather ride in his shirt all his life than suffer a fellow creature to lie in that condition. The passage ends with a characteristic stroke. 'The postilion has since been transported for robbing a hen roost.'

Anybody who had read Fielding's novels, in which insensibility to the distress of the poor is a frequent theme, would come with surprise upon a passage in Boswell's *Johnson* describing a conversation on this subject.

He said, 'the poor in England were better provided for, than in any other country of the same extent: he did not mean little Cantons, or petty Republicks. Where a great proportion of the people (said he,) are suffered to languish in helpless misery, that country must be ill policed, and wretchedly governed: a decent provision for the poor, is the true test of civilization. Gentlemen of education, he observed, were pretty much the same in all countries; the condition of the lower orders, the poor especially, was the true mark of national discrimination.'

In all ages it would be easy to find conflicting views of the social conditions of the time from truthful observers, but such divergence is specially intelligible in Johnson's age. For though a study of the actual life of the poor makes Fielding's picture seem reasonable enough, Johnson was looking at an aspect of the problem that created a great impression both at home and abroad. This was the cost of poor relief. This relief, it must be remembered, came entirely from the rates, and property is more sensible of its local than its national burdens. The cost at the opening of the century has been estimated at £400,000 and for 1750 at about £700,000. In 1776 and in 1786 Thomas Gilbert obtained official returns from the overseers which showed that the expenditure in the first of these years was just over a million and a half and in the second about two millions. These figures look modest when compared with those reached in the French war, but they seemed impressive enough at the time. During Johnson's lifetime two important Acts were passed on the subject of the Poor Law, the first in 1722, the second in 1782, and, though they differed widely in other respects, they both laid stress on the cost of poor relief. As for the impression that this expenditure made abroad, we have De Tocqueville's famous remark that in France it was the nobles, in England the poor who escaped the great burden of taxation.

To understand how it happened that the rich seemed to be bearing heavy burdens and the poor to be neglected and ill treated, it is necessary to look in turn at the Poor Laws, the Laws of Settlement, the arbitrary methods of justice, the system of punishment, and the state of the prisons.

The first thing to remember about the Poor Law in Johnson's time is that central government was in abeyance. At the beginning of the seventeenth century the Privy Council had given orders and advice to the magistrates and taken an active part in administration. In the nineteenth century a central body was set up in the Poor Law Commission, endowed with such drastic powers as to cause an agitation comparable to that excited by the Reform Bill or the Corn Laws. But in Johnson's time it was supposed that local authorities needed neither guidance nor supervision and all the problems that had occupied the Elizabethan statesmen fell upon the parish. The parish was responsible for its poor, its sick, its children and its old people, its vagrants and its idlers. Of these parishes there were no fewer than 15,000, and we can form some estimate of the size of most of them when we learn that in 1831 four-fifths had a population under 800 and nearly 7,000 had a population of under 300. For the difficult tasks thrown upon it the parish had to rely in the main on the overseer, an unsalaried officer appointed by the magistrates and acting under them.

Of all these tasks the most difficult, in respect to the demands it made on the judgement of the authorities, appeared to be that of deciding, when a poor man applied for relief, whether the overseer should give him a small pittance or try to find him work or threaten him with unpleasant consequences if he failed to find work for himself. These questions had been fiercely debated in the previous century. For some time it had been held that the right course was to find employment and make profit for the rate-payers out of it. This view still survived and it was acted upon in some cases in Johnson's time, but it had fallen into discredit. The prevailing view was put by Defoe, who argued that a pauper given employment was a vagabond given a favour at the expense of his honest neighbour, and applied by Marryott, who may be said to have introduced the workhouse test by persuading various parishes to build workhouses, not with a view to finding work but in order to drive idle men to find work for themselves.

The growing strictness of administration was reflected in the important Act of 1722 (9 George I, c. 7), passed when Johnson was a boy, which all but lasted his lifetime.[1] This Act allowed parishes to build workhouses without a special Act of Parliament, and it allowed parishes to group themselves together for this purpose. In any parish that had a workhouse, an applicant who refused 'to be lodged, kept or maintained in such house' forfeited his right to relief. Two other provisions were important. Applicants for relief had formerly been allowed to apply either to a Justice or to the overseer; the Act directed that all applications were to be made first to the overseer. This was designed to make administration stiffer. The other provision was in some respects the most important of all. The churchwardens and overseers, with the consent of the majority of the parishioners, were authorized to farm out the poor.

Farming out was a great feature of eighteenth-century

[1] i.e. till Gilbert's Act of 1782.

administration. If country gentlemen wanted roads or bridges, if towns wanted streets or sewers, a special body was set up to carry out these operations and repay itself by tolls or rates. The poor were now to be treated like roads and bridges. They were handed over in a great many places to contractors. The arrangements varied. A contractor would sometimes undertake the management of a workhouse for a fixed sum; in other cases the sum would be fixed per head. The contractor had to feed and clothe the inmates and he made what profit he could from their labour. Sometimes the parish insured itself against all liabilities, and the contractor was responsible for the sick, the insane, the aged, and the children. Sometimes special charges, such as those due to small-pox, were excluded. The contractor had, of course, every inducement to put economy before compassion, and the results of these methods inspired horror among observers of the time. 'By means of this statute', wrote John Scott, the Quaker poet, in 1773, 'the parochial managers are impowered to establish a set of petty tyrants as their substitutes, who, farming the poor at a certain price, accumulate dishonest wealth by abridging them of reasonable food, and imposing on them unreasonable labour.'[1]

A distinction must be drawn between the contracts for a fixed sum and those per head. In the former the contractor had every motive for refusing relief wherever he could, and for using the workhouse as a 'House of Terror'. But according to the second plan it was essential that there should be enough paupers to make his contract remunerative.[2] In neither case was such a contract likely to secure a well-conducted workhouse.

There was no uniformity of administration, and practice varied from place to place, and in the same place from time to time. Thus the Louth workhouse was managed for two years from 1774 by the overseers, and then let to a woollen manufacturer who ran it at a loss. Another contractor took it over, but he also found it unprofitable. Then came another spell of overseer management, and then in 1785 a contractor was found who indemnified the parish against all charges except legal expenses.[3]

---

[1] John Scott, *Observations on the Present State of the Parochial and Vagrant Poor* (1773).   [2] S. and B. Webb, *The Old Poor Law*, pp. 412 ff.
[3] Sir F. M. Eden, *State of the Poor*, vol. ii, p. 397 (1797).

A workhouse proper, whether under the management of the overseer or of a contractor, usually had a master or a matron, and a regular dietary. In addition to these there were a number of poor-houses surviving from earlier days. The poor-house was a shelter where parish paupers and casual poor might live and sleep rent free. Some of the inmates received pay from the parish, others worked for private employers. The overseers might prefer providing house-room to paying cottage rent, and they sometimes had convenient cottages for the purpose. There was no regular provision for diet; little order or discipline. We have a picture of a poor-house in Crabbe's *The Village*.

> Theirs is yon House that holds the Parish-Poor,
> Whose walls of mud scarce bear the broken door;
> There, where the putrid vapours, flagging, play,
> And the dull wheel hums doleful through the day;—
> There Children dwell who know no Parents' care;
> Parents, who know no Children's love, dwell there!
> Heart-broken Matrons on their joyless bed,
> Forsaken Wives, and Mothers never wed;
> Dejected Widows with unheeded tears,
> And crippled Age with more than childhood fears;
> The Lame, the Blind, and, far the happiest they!
> The moping Idiot and the Madman gay.

The defects of a system which threw delicate and difficult duties on small, ill-equipped local authorities made a great impression on the enlightened and compassionate people of the time. Henry Fielding gave an admirable summary of the evils of the existing Poor Law in his work, published in 1753, called a *Proposal for making an Effectual Provision for the Poor*.

Every man who hath any property, must feel the weight of that tax which is levied for the use of the Poor; and every man of any understanding must see how absurdly it is applied. So very useless, indeed is this heavy tax, and so wretched its disposition, that it is a question whether the Poor or the Rich are more dissatisfied, or have indeed, greater reason to be dissatisfied; since the plunder of the one serves so little to the real advantage of the other; for, while a million yearly is raised among the former, many of the latter are starved; many more languish in want and misery; of the rest, many are found begging or pilfering in the streets to-day, and to-morrow are locked up in gaols and bridewells.

Of all these deplorable evils we have constant experience before our eyes. The sufferings of the Poor are indeed less observed than their misdeeds; not from any want of compassion, but because they are less known; and this is the true reason why we hear them so often mentioned with abhorrence, and so seldom with pity. They starve and freeze and rot among themselves, but they beg and steal and rob among their betters.

Dissatisfaction with the system led to a continual agitation among magistrates and other public men for reform. Their proposals showed that they had put their finger on the main faults of the system, the small single Poor Law area, the mixed workhouse, and the unskilled administration of overseers who merely wanted to save the rates.

The break-up of the Poor Law was urged by a reformer, named William Hay, who persuaded the House of Commons, in 1735, to pass important resolutions in favour of establishing, in 'proper places' in each county, a workhouse to provide work for the able-bodied, a house of correction for vagrants, the idle, and the disorderly, and a hospital for the impotent, the infirm, and children. The first of these Resolutions was as follows:

That the laws in being, relating to the maintenance of the Poor of this kingdom, are defective; and notwithstanding they impose heavy burdens on parishes, yet the Poor, in most of them, are ill taken care of.

Thomas Alcock, a parson, suggested in 1752 that special provision should be made for the sick and infirm, and that the able-bodied should be set to work. Henry Fielding's proposals in 1753 were on the same lines. He wanted to set up an establishment for the county of Middlesex which should include a County House for the industrious, with separate wards for the sick and aged, and a house of correction for vagrants. Dean Tucker (1760) proposed to incorporate all parishes within a radius of about six miles from the market town into Unions. All these reformers wanted to separate the able-bodied who were willing to work from the idle; the sick from the sound. But their proposals provided for strict discipline even in the case of the industrious.

These and similar demands led in time to reform. Though a good many parish workhouses had been built under the Act of 1722, the provision which allowed parishes to combine for the building of workhouses or houses of industry had not been used to any extent. Several large workhouses of this kind were, however, built by special Act in the second half of the century under the influence of reformers like Hay or Fielding. These workhouses served large districts and were supervised by special *ad hoc* bodies, composed of magistrates, parsons, and other public men. The first house of the kind was the Nacton House of Industry, opened in March 1758, serving twenty-eight parishes in the Hundreds of Carlford and Colneis in South Suffolk. They became common in East Anglia. Unfortunately these institutions, which aimed at combining the provision of employment with improved treatment of the young, the aged, and the sick, were distrusted by the poor, and in 1765 there were serious riots in Suffolk in which the house of industry at Bulcamp was destroyed. Nor, apart from its unpopularity, was the experiment itself a success. The management of such institutions is a skilled business, and it could hardly be efficiently conducted by such a staff as the Incorporated Guardians employed. The Master or Governor, who was generally paid £40 a year, was as a rule a bankrupt farmer, or a shopkeeper, or a promoted servant or labourer,[1] assisted by doctors paid from £21 to £40 a year and a chaplain paid £25 a year.

The ideas of the reformers found expression also in the second of the two important Acts that were passed in Johnson's lifetime. This was an Act of 1782, always known as Gilbert's Act, from its author, Thomas Gilbert (1720–98), a man of great energy and public spirit, patron of Brindley's Canal schemes and an active Member of Parliament. The preamble of his Act (22 George III, c. 83) is significant, for it speaks of 'the incapacity, negligence, or misconduct of overseers' and the waste of money on 'litigations about settlements indiscretely and unadvisedly carried on'. This Act allowed parishes to join in Unions and adopt the provisions of the Act. In such places the rates were to be collected by the overseers, but the money was to be distributed by paid guardians, one for each parish, appointed by the Justices out of a list of names submitted by the parishioners. Above the paid guardian was a Visitor. The workhouse was to be reserved for the aged, the infirm, orphan children, and babies with their mothers. It was to be the business of the guardian to find employment for those who could not find it

[1] S. and B. Webb, *Statutory Authorities*, p. 135.

themselves, and to maintain them when it was found. The guardian was to receive the money earned, to supply the deficiency if it was not enough to maintain the worker, and, if it was more than enough, to give the surplus at the end of a calendar month to the person who had earned it. Few, if any, of these Unions were formed in Johnson's lifetime, though by 1834 there were 67, comprising 924 parishes.

The history of the Poor Law in Johnson's lifetime is thus the history of an experiment in strict and preventive methods followed by a reaction; the Act of 1722 representing the first phase, Gilbert's Act of 1782 the second.

The eighteenth century was not strong in statistics, and it is difficult therefore to form a general picture of the state of the country under the Poor Laws of the time. The poor man in need of relief would in some places find himself in a poor house, in others in a parish workhouse, in others in a large house of industry. In many places he would receive a small pittance, living in his own cottage; in others, again, he would be farmed out to an employer. At the beginning of the nineteenth century there were some 4,000 workhouses, that term being used to cover the village poor house, the parish workhouse, whether managed by overseer or contractor, and the big houses of industry or workhouses set up under special Acts, or Gilbert's Act.

The treatment of the poor man would thus vary from place to place, but this difference was especially marked if he was not only poor but sick. The new workhouses made an attempt to give special treatment to the sick and the insane; the madman, sometimes tied to a chain, added a peculiar element of horror to the mixed house. Liverpool, a pioneer in the eighteenth as in the nineteenth century in public health, appointed a salaried medical officer as early as 1768, and just after Johnson's death possessed four hospitals for its paupers. As a rule medical attendance was provided by contract, made with a doctor either by the overseers or by the contractor. Crabbe acted for a short time as parish doctor at Aldeburgh. A doctor named Raymond, originally appointed at a salary of 20s. a year 'to attend and supply with all necessaries in the physical, surgery, and midwifery way (fractures excepted) all the parish poor and all such as may become chargeable hereafter', had raised his terms at first to £4 and then to £20 a year. This was too much for the

Vestry, and in 1775 the parish meeting decided that 'Geo. Crabbe junr. should be employed to cure the boy Howard of the Itch, and that, whenever any of the poor shall have occasion for a surgeon, the overseers shall apply to him for that purpose'. In January 1776 he sent in his first bill for £4.[1]

There was one class of paupers, the parish apprentices, whose position was the same in all parishes. It had been the law since 1601 (the famous Act of that year was based on earlier legislation) that parish children should be bound to some occupation, the boys till the age of twenty-four, the girls till twenty-one or marriage. Till the late 'sixties of the eighteenth century, the number to be disposed of, in London at any rate, was small. After that time they afforded a more serious problem to the overseers. This increase was due to Jonas Hanway, who had settled down in 1750 to a life of philanthropy in London. As Howard later visited the prisons, so Hanway visited the workhouses for years in succession, inquiring, exhorting, and publishing the results of his investigations. Both men had a passion for accurate statistical information. The first result of Hanway's efforts was an Act passed in 1761 obliging all parishes within the Bills of Mortality to keep registers of their 'infant poor'. These Registers revealed to a House of Commons Committee who examined them in 1767 that only seven in a hundred of the children under twelve months old in 1763 survived in 1765. The second result of Hanway's activities was the Act of 1767 (7 George III, c. 39), usually known by his name, which obliged these parishes to send their children under six into the country to be boarded for not less than 2s. 6d. a week.

The treatment of these unhappy children is a dark page in eighteenth-century life. Hanway himself, who conferred on so many the doubtful benefits of survival, said 'the apprenticeship of some parish children is as great a scene of inhumanity as the suffering others to die in infancy'. The indentures had to be signed by two Justices, but this was no protection, and in practice any one who wanted unpaid drudges could obtain these children. Hanway's Act of 1767 reduced the age of freedom for boys in London from twenty-four to twenty-one, but twenty-four remained the age elsewhere till 1778. An Act of 1747 (20 George II, c. 19) had given a parish apprentice the right to complain of ill treat-

[1] René Huchon, *George Crabbe and his Times* (trans. F. Clarke, 1907), p. 64.

ment to two Justices, who could discharge him from his apprenticeship if the proof of ill usage was satisfactory, but it is impossible to picture this right being used by ignorant children such as those whose lives and deaths are vividly described in cases like the famous Metyard or Brownrigg trials.

It is generally agreed to-day that one reason why the stern Poor Law of 1834 did not cause more social disorder was the increase of employment due to the introduction of railways. There was no such escape from the stringent administration of the eighteenth century. There was less new employment, and the law of settlement checked the mobility of labour. Every person had one parish, and one parish only in which he or she had a right to relief, and it was difficult for an immigrant to establish himself, that is, to gain a settlement in another parish. An Act of 1691, amplified by one of 1697–8, had prescribed four ways in which a man could get a settlement: (1) paying the parish taxes; (2) executing a public annual office in the parish; (3) serving an apprenticeship in the parish; (4) if unmarried, being hired for a year's service in the parish. The overseers, however, with the consent of two Justices, had the right to remove within forty days any new-comer who occupied a tenement under the yearly value of £10, if they thought he was likely to become chargeable to the parish, unless he brought with him a certificate from the officers of his own parish, in which case he could not be removed till he was actually chargeable. Burn, the historian of the Poor Law, writing in 1764 described the working of this system.

The office of an overseer of the Poor, seems to be understood to be this; to keep an extraordinary look-out to prevent persons coming to inhabit without certificates, and to fly to the Justices to remove them; and if a man brings a certificate, then to caution the inhabitants not to let him a farm of £10 a year, and to take care to keep him out of all parish offices; to warn them, if they will hire *servants*, to hire them half yearly, or by the month, or by the week, or by the day, rather than by any way that shall give them a settlement; or if they do hire them for a year, then to endeavour to pick a quarrel with them before the year's end, and so to get rid of them.

It was a common practice to hire labourers for fifty-one weeks at a time to prevent them obtaining a settlement, and this was found to be legal.

We have a picture in *Joseph Andrews* of the way in which
overseers could be helped by the small village lawyers and
a resourceful Justice in their efforts to stop persons from
obtaining settlements. Lady Booby is trying to prevent the
marriage of her former servants, Andrews and Fanny. She
forbids the parson to give out the banns, but he answers that
Lawyer Scout has told him that a man who has served a
year in a parish obtains a settlement. Andrews was in this
position. She sends for Lawyer Scout. 'I am resolved (said
the lady) to have no discarded servants of mine settled here;
and so, if this be your law, I shall send to another lawyer.'
Scout said, if she sent to a hundred lawyers, not one or all of
them could alter the law. The utmost that was in the power
of a lawyer was to prevent the law's taking effect; and that
he himself could do for her ladyship as well as any other.
He points out that there is a material difference between
being settled in law and settled in fact, and that all will be
well if Lady Booby leaves the matter to him.

The laws of this land are not so vulgar, as to permit a mean fellow
to contend with one of your Ladyship's fortune. We have one sure
card, which is to carry him before Justice Frolic, who, upon hearing
your Ladyship's name, will commit him without any further questions. . . . To say truth, it is a great blessing to the country that he is
in the commission; for he hath taken several poor off our hands that
the law would never lay hold on.

In the case of Joseph Andrews the offence for which he is
sentenced is breaking off a twig (the lawyer points out that
had it been a young tree Andrews could have been hanged).
Fanny is sentenced for walking on the grass and receiving
and carrying the twig.

In real life, as in Fielding's pages, an obliging Justice,
anxious to put an undesirable person out of the parish,
would have had no difficulty in finding him guilty of some
offence against the law, and such Justices were helped by the
disreputable hangers-on who brought the legal profession
into such bad odour. 'He did not care to speak ill of any
man behind his back,' said Dr. Johnson once of a man who
had just left the company, 'but he believed the gentleman
was an *attorney*.' Smollett said of Tom Clarke in *The Adventures of Sir Launcelot Greaves* that he 'was a young fellow,
whose goodness of heart even the exercise of his profession
had not been able to corrupt. Before strangers he never

owned himself an attorney, without blushing. . . .' Fielding evidently thought his Scout a common type, and the poor were much at the mercy of what he called these 'pests of society'.

In addition to the oppressions of the Law of Settlement there was a general snare for the unfortunate in the Vagrancy Laws. A man seeking work, who could not persuade his parish to give him a certificate, or a man wishing to change his home or visit friends or relations, was in as much danger from these laws as the most hardened idler on the road. The Act of 1744 (17 George II, c. 5), one of a long series of Acts, divided offenders into three classes, the disorderly, the rogues and vagabonds, and the incorrigible rogues. The first class included all persons who threatened to run away and leave their wives and children to a parish; who unlawfully returned to a parish whence they had been legally removed; who, not having wherewith to maintain themselves, lived idle without employment and refused to work at the usual rate of wages; and beggars. For this class the punishment was hard labour in a house of correction for a period not exceeding a month. Rogues and vagabonds included persons who ran away and left their wives and children chargeable to the parish; strolling players not authorized by law; unlicensed pedlars; persons wandering about not giving a good account of themselves. For these offences a man might be publicly whipped, and sent to a house of correction until the next Quarter Sessions, and he might then be sentenced to hard labour for six months. A man who escaped, or a man who repeated the offence, was an incorrigible rogue, and might be sentenced to two years imprisonment. A third offence made him liable to transportation. We learn from a House of Commons Return of 1776 that the number of vagrants sent to houses of correction in 1772 was 2,937; in 1773, 3,243; and in 1774, 3,493.

The Poor Law system, and the Vagrancy Laws with their drastic provisions, seemed well adapted for dragooning the poor into good behaviour. Yet during the first part of the eighteenth century crime increased to an alarming extent. This was specially noticeable in London, and Henry Fielding, who became a Bow Street magistrate in 1748, found that he had to deal with organized bands of men who had 'reduced Theft and Robbery into a regular System'. The recruiting grounds of the gangs who made the streets unsafe were vividly described in his pamphlet *Enquiry into the Increase of Robbers* (1751): filthy houses in St. Giles and elsewhere, packed from cellar to garret with miserable beds for Two Penny Lodgers to whom gin was sold at 1*d*. a quartern. The inmates were in a state of desperate poverty. When two small houses of this character were emptied before Fielding's eyes of their seventy lodgers, less than one shilling was found amongst the lot, with the exception of one young woman, 'one of the prettiest Girls I have ever seen', who had recently robbed her mistress. 'That all these Wretches are not Thieves', he wrote, 'must give us either a very high Idea of their Honesty, or a very mean one of their Capacity and Courage'.

The road from poverty to crime, easy enough at any time, was made more inviting by the orgy of gin drinking to which the working classes in towns fell victims in the first half of the century. The attempt at the end of the seventeenth century to redress the balance of trade by fostering home manufactures had encouraged the production of cheap English spirits made from English corn. Ale-houses had to be licensed by the Justices, but the sale of gin was unchecked. In 1725 it was reckoned that in London, excluding the City and the Surrey side of the river, there were over 6,000 places where gin was openly sold—in one of the largest parishes every fifth house retailed it—and in addition it was to be had from street stalls and barrows, from chandlers and tobacconists, from endless garrets and cellars and back-rooms. Temptation beset the poor on every side, and they succumbed to it. 'Drunk for 1*d*., dead drunk for 2*d*., straw for nothing' was the order of the day. The amount consumed was enormous.

Gin [wrote Fielding in 1751, when he had had two years' experience as a magistrate] . . . is the principal Sustenance (if it may be so called) of more than an hundred thousand People in this Metropolis. Many of these Wretches there are, who swallow Pints of this Poison within the Twenty Four Hours; the dreadful Effects of which I have the Misfortune every Day to see, and to smell too.

Legislative attempts to end these orgies met with strong opposition from vested interests and from victims alike. In 1729 a licence costing £20 was imposed by Act of Parliament on retailers, and a duty of 2*s*. a gallon placed on cheap spirits, but the growers of wheat obtained in 1733 the repeal of this

Act, on the ground that it had discouraged sales. In 1736 a panic-stricken Parliament, brushing other considerations aside, determined to end the mania by stopping supplies. The Act of that year aimed at practical prohibition: a licence to retail was to cost £50, each gallon of spirits was to be taxed 20s. The fate of this Act, and arguments of every character for and against its repeal, are given in a House of Lords' Debate, written by Dr. Johnson, reprinted in 248 pages of Cobbett's *Parliamentary History for 1743*. Informers were busy enough at first, in hopes of obtaining their £5 reward, but they soon found that their activities led to rough handling or even to death. Johnson makes Lord Chesterfield sum up the situation: 'In a short time the people prevailed in the contest with the legislators, they intimidated information, and wearied prosecution; and were at length allowed to indulge themselves in the enjoyment of their favourite vice without any further molestation.' The Act of 1743 (16 George II, c. 8), which gave rise to this debate, attempted to check rather than to prohibit the evil. The 1736 Act was repealed; the duty of 20s. a gallon was reduced to a few pence, and the licence to retail was reduced from £50 to 20s., but was to be granted only to alehouses and taverns previously licensed by Justices of the Peace, so that distillers were no longer permitted to sell retail.

This Act had good effects, but it hit the distillers hard, and in 1747 they obtained an amending Act allowing London distillers to sell retail on payment of £5 for a licence. The result was disastrous. Fielding's *Enquiry into the Causes of the late Increase of Robbers* (1751) and Hogarth's *Gin Lane* show the condition to which London was again reduced. Bristol, Salisbury, Rochester, Manchester, and Norwich petitioned Parliament to stop the excessive drinking which caused a 'great Decay of Industry, Piety, and Virtue amongst the common People', and tended to 'the Destruction of the Commerce of this Kingdom'. As a result of these protests an Act in 1751 (24 George II, c. 40) strengthened the provisions of the 1743 Act. The duties were slightly increased, and distillers, chandlers, grocers, and keepers of jails and workhouses were expressly forbidden to retail spirits. This and subsequent Acts of the same kind checked the worst excesses, and Hanway could write cheerfully in 1759 that 'the people themselves seem at length to have discovered, that health and pleasure, food and raiment, are better than sickness and pain, want and wretchedness'.[1] It would, however, be a mistake to think of the people as sober.

Though gin drinking died down after the middle of the century crime and lawlessness continued to flourish. The eighteenth-century method of encouraging respect for the law was to make the consequences of detection in crime more terrible. If an offence grew common it must be stopped by making it capital. One thief on a gallows would terrify other thieves back into honest ways, just as a slaughtered crow hung up in a newly sown field is supposed to keep away all other crows. Curiously enough it was the humane Fielding who argued on behalf of the philosophy behind this growing severity of the criminal law. Dr. Johnson denounced it with vigour. Fielding, in his *Increase of Robbers*, attacked the growing custom of transporting, instead of executing, convicted thieves.

No man indeed of common Humanity or common Sense can think the Life of a Man and a few Shillings to be of an equal Consideration, or that the Law in punishing Theft with Death proceeds (as perhaps a private Person sometimes may) with any View to Vengeance. The Terror of the Example is the only Thing proposed, and one Man is sacrificed to the Preservation of Thousands.

To equal robbery with murder [answered Dr. Johnson in *The Rambler* (114)] is to reduce murder to robbery, to confound in common minds the gradations of iniquity, and incite the commission of a greater crime to prevent the detection of a less. If only murder were punished with death, very few robbers would stain their hands in blood; but when by the last act of cruelty no new danger is incurred, and greater security may be obtained, upon what principle shall we bid them forbear?

The alteration of the criminal code was complicated by the antiquated provisions of 'benefit of clergy'. At the end of the seventeenth century this survival of the system by which clerks were exempt from trial in a secular and handed over to an ecclesiastical court, had come to mean in practice that, though the punishment for all felony was, in theory, death, yet, in many cases, convicted felons who could read could plead 'benefit of clergy' and for sole punishment be branded in the brawn of the left hand, or whipped, and

[1] Jonas Hanway, *A Candid and Historical Account of the Hospital for the Reception of exposed and deserted young Children* (1759).

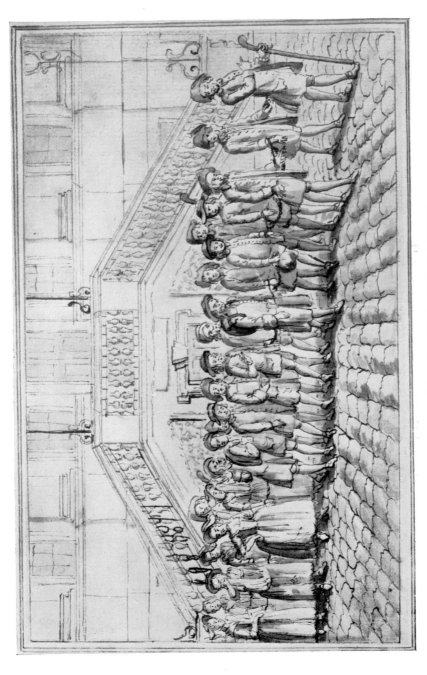

PRISONERS AT THE OLD BAILEY

From a drawing in the British Museum

possibly imprisoned for a year. There were, however, certain offences for which benefit of clergy had been abolished: treason, piracy, murder, arson, burglary, housebreaking, stealing from churches, putting in fear, highway robbery, horse stealing, stealing from the person of sums over 1s., rape, and abduction with intent to marry. Thus if you stole a horse, it made no difference if you could read or not, in both cases you were liable to the gallows; but if you stole a sheep over 1s. in value it made all the difference: a branding in one case, death or transportation in the other.

In the year 1705 (by 5 Anne, c. 6) an important change was made. Felons, even when they could not read, were allowed benefit of clergy where it still existed. The sheep stealer, literate or illiterate, could now get off with a branding or whipping and short imprisonment. But after this initial clemency in Anne's reign the rest of the century was marked by growing severity. Goldsmith described the process in Dr. Primrose's reflections in *The Vicar of Wakefield*.

Government, while it grows older, seems to acquire the moroseness of age; and, as if our property were become dearer in proportion as it increased—as if the more enormous our wealth the more extensive our fears—all our possessions are paled up with new edicts every day, and hung round with gibbets to scare every invader.

In the first place, in 1718 benefit of clergy was made less beneficial, for, by an Act in that year (4 George I, c. 11) transportation for seven years was made an alternative punishment to branding and whipping. Then the benefit of clergy itself was taken away from one offence after another. The illiterate had been given the literate's privilege; the privilege was now taken away from both alike. Thus in 1741 Parliament abolished the benefit of clergy for sheep stealing, so that the literate man was now no better off than the illiterate man had been before 1705: the gallows faced them both. This piecemeal system of taking away benefit of clergy from specific offences, or creating new offences without any benefit of clergy attached to them, reduced the criminal law to what Lecky called 'a mere sanguinary chaos', with grossly unequal penalties. The absurdities have often been quoted. To steal fruit ready gathered was a felony; to gather the fruit and steal it was only a trespass. If you were seen stealing goods from a shop, you could be transported, but if you stole them without being seen, you could be hanged.

The administration of this sanguinary chaos became itself chaotic. The normal man rebelled against the cruelties and injustices involved in carrying it out. Kind-hearted persons were reluctant to prosecute or to give evidence; kind-hearted juries refused to convict. It depended on the sensibilities of others as much as on his own guilt whether a prisoner was sentenced to death. 'They who would rejoice', wrote Johnson in the *Rambler* (114), 'at the correction of a thief, are yet shocked at the thought of destroying him. His crime shrinks to nothing, compared with his misery; and severity defeats itself by exciting pity.' Against this 'ill-judging Tenderness and Compassion' Fielding (*Increase of Robbers*) argued vigorously.

To desire to save these Wolves in Society, may arise from Benevolence; but it must be the Benevolence of a Child or a Fool, who, from Want of sufficient Reason, mistakes the true Objects of his Passion, as a Child doth when a Bugbear appears to him to be the Object of Fear. Such Tenderheartedness is indeed Barbarity, and resembles the meek Spirit of him who would not assist in blowing up his Neighbours House, to save a whole City from the Flames.

He who knows not [answered Dr. Johnson] how often rigorous laws produce total impunity, and how many crimes are concealed and forgotten for fear of hurrying the offender to that state in which there is no repentance, has conversed very little with mankind. And whatever epithets of reproach or contempt this compassion may incur from those who confound cruelty with firmness, I know not whether any wise man would wish it less powerful, or less extensive.

Suppose you were an offender, or a suspected offender, caught and committed to prison to await your trial for felony. You would at once be called on, by your fellow prisoners, to pay 'garnish' or an entrance fee, a sum varying in different prisons, and even forbidden in some. At Horsham you would have to pay 6s. 6d., at Newgate 2s. 6d. If you could not pay your clothes might have to go. '"Pay or strip" are the fatal words', says Howard. In what sort of quarters would you then find yourself? Innocent or guilty you would probably have to stay there a long time, for the jail delivery, that is the assizes, in some counties took place only once a year; at Hull it was once every three years in the 'seventies; earlier in the century the interval had been seven years.

Prisons, like workhouses, differed from place to place.

There were two main types: the common jail and the Bride-well or house of correction. In the first were included the big county jails over which the High Sheriff had partial jurisdiction, the city jails controlled by corporations, and various private jails belonging to ecclesiastical or territorial magnates. The Bridewells, which existed all over the country, were originally started in connexion with Poor Law policy for providing work for the wantonly idle, but by the middle of the century they were in most respects indistinguishable from county jails, except that they were smaller and more ruinous, and more frequently contained vagrants and minor offenders. These Bridewells were technically under the justices, who had certain powers over county jails as well, but the whole question of administration was complicated and confused, and as a matter of practice the jailer usually reigned supreme. As a rule he had no salary, or an inadequate one, and made what he could out of the prisoners.

Thanks to John Howard we have a remarkably complete picture of prison conditions towards the end of Johnson's life. This 'eccentric but truly worthy' man, as the *Annual Register* described him, started his career as a prison reformer in 1773 at the age of forty-seven. For the remaining sixteen years of his life he travelled incessantly about Great Britain and the Continent, examining all the places where criminals were confined, and placing on record clear and vivid descriptions of what he had seen and learnt.

If you were committed to one of the big county or city jails, your quarters would probably be (1) a place to sleep in, where you would be locked with some or all of your fellow prisoners from sunset till 6 or 8 in the morning, (2) a day room, and (3) if you were lucky, a court where you could get some air. The sleeping place would vary. In many jails it would be a dungeon; in some a suffocating dungeon. In one or two new jails, on the other hand, you might be given a separate cell with a bedstead, but these were exceptions, and on the whole you could count yourself fortunate if you had enough straw to lie on, and were not strung together with your fellow prisoners and chained down to the ground. Women, as a rule, were separated from men at night, except in very small prisons.

When morning came and the doors were unlocked you would meet your fellow prisoners in the day room. Often men and women were together all day, under no sort of superintendence, with results described tersely by Johnson:[1] 'The lewd inflame the lewd, the audacious harden the audacious.' Even in the larger jails there was sometimes no court for air and exercise, so that you would be shut up day and night, often with little ventilation, for the window tax, paid by the jailers, tempted them, in Howard's words, 'to stop the windows and stifle their prisoners'. In the small tumble-down prisons the courts were often too insecure to be used, for even prisoners in irons might manage to escape from them. Irons, it may be noted, often served as cheap substitutes for repairs. In the bigger jails they were also a source of revenue to the jailer, and a heavy purse meant light irons, or none at all. At Lincoln the jailer was authorized to charge a common felon 2s. 6d. a week for taking off his irons, but 'a gentleman or better sort of criminal' had to pay as much as 5s. a week.

A feeling that women should not be fettered grew up during the century, and by Howard's time the practice had died out in London, though it still survived in many places.

The food provided varied from prison to prison, but in all it was insufficient. Prisoners awaiting trial had no legal claim to food, but it was customary in most places to give them the county allowance, originally confined to convicted felons. This county allowance was occasionally a fixed amount of bread, say a pound to a pound and a half a day, but in most cases it was from a pennyworth to two pennyworth a day, so that the degree of hunger varied with the price of bread. In 1782 Howard found that the penny allowance brought in only $7\frac{1}{2}$ or 8 oz. of bread, and the famished prisoners would eat their day's food, or sometimes even their two days' food, at one meal. This meagre diet was no doubt often supplemented by gifts from relatives and friends, or from fellow members of a gang, or by charitable gifts and bequests, though felons were not such popular objects of compassion as debtors; but Howard declared emphatically that 'many criminals are half starved; such of them as at their commitment were in health, come out famished, scarce able to move, and for weeks incapable of any labour'.

Prisons varied in accommodation and food, but, with few

[1] *Idler*, No. 38, Jan. 6, 1759.

THE YARD OF THE FLEET PRISON

From Humours of the Fleet, *1749*

exceptions, they resembled each other in dirt. Noses were less sensitive then than now, but when Howard was visiting prisons in the 'seventies he found it necessary to travel on horseback owing to the offensive smell of his clothes in a post-chaise. Even his memorandum book had to be disinfected in front of the fire before it could be used. In an age when fashionable ladies used ivory back scratchers to mitigate the ravages of insects, prisons could hardly be kept free of vermin, but the unchanged straw and the dirty rags of the poorer prisoners encouraged them to breed in alarming quantities. Very seldom was any attempt made to clean the premises, or any apparatus provided for the purpose. Newcastle Newgate, where brooms and mops were provided, stands out as an exception.

In these conditions jail fever or typhus, small-pox, and the various diseases classed together as 'putrid fevers' were very active, destroying prisoners in great numbers. Johnson's conjecture that 'all the complicated horrors of a prison put an end every year to the life of one in four of those that are shut up from the common comforts of human life'[1] may be an exaggeration, but before Howard's time the ravages of jail fever were even worse, and occasionally reached the outside world. In May 1750, at the famous Black Sessions at the Old Bailey, about 100 prisoners from Newgate came for trial. The trials took place in a hall 30 feet square, packed with spectators, and the prisoners not in the dock were kept in two small rooms which had not been cleaned for many years. Of the six judges on the bench four died; of the jury and minor officials some forty died. After this disastrous sessions it was ordered that prisoners from Newgate should be washed with vinegar before trial, that not more than fifteen should come at a time, and that Newgate should also be washed with vinegar. As the *Gentleman's Magazine* remarked, 'it is well known how nasty both this and all the rest are kept'.

Howard's campaign against jail fever joined to the efforts of Mr. Popham, Member for Taunton, resulted in the passing in 1774 of the 'Gaol Distemper Act' (14 George III, c. 59). This statute, excellent on paper, required Justices to order that prisons should be cleaned, whitewashed, and ventilated; it also ordered that when it could be done

[1] *Idler*, No. 38, Jan. 6, 1759.

'conveniently' they should prevent prisoners from being kept underground. Justices were also required to order the provision in each prison of a warm and cold bath, and of separate rooms for the sick. The records of Howard's later journeys show that unfortunately the Justices in most cases paid little attention to the Act—in his polite phrase they 'overlooked' it; 'sick and dirty objects' still lay on the floor among the other prisoners, and even where baths were provided they were often tubs that were useless for felons in irons. Nor did they find it convenient to dispense with dungeons. Sometimes they even built new ones.

The Gaol Distemper Act required the Justices to appoint an experienced surgeon with a stated salary, and provision was usually made for some sort of medical attendance, the surgeon sometimes receiving a salary, sometimes sending his bill to Quarter Sessions, but it was a dangerous occupation and attendance was often perfunctory. Occasionally, however, we hear of kind-hearted medical men who visited the prisons unpaid, risking and sometimes losing their lives. Chaplains too, paid either out of the rates or from charitable bequests, were provided at most county jails. In a few cases they were friends to the prisoners, but as a rule their activities were limited to reading the service, and they counted for nothing in prison life. Perhaps Dr. Johnson was right when he said, speaking of convicts, 'Sir, one of our regular clergy will probably not impress their minds sufficiently: they should be attended by a Methodist preacher; or a Popish priest'.

If you survived till the Assizes you might have to walk ten or fifteen miles in heavy irons, for Assizes were held in a great many different towns. In some of these towns there was no regular prison, and men and women prisoners were put into makeshift quarters, close packed together, on the verge of suffocation. 'This occasions', wrote Howard, 'such *confusion and distress*, and such shrieks and outcries, as can be better conceived than described.' If, however, you were in one of the better jails you would, in accordance with the Gaol Distemper Act, be washed before you came into court, and be in a better position to protect yourself. You would need whatever wits and courage you possessed, for if your felony was a capital one (and most felonies were capital) your counsel (supposing you could afford to have one) might examine or cross-examine witnesses for you, but might not address the court on your behalf. That would be left for you to do as best you could. Fielding makes Partridge in *Tom Jones* describe the scene at a trial for horse stealing.

One thing, I own, I thought a little hard, that the prisoner's counsel was not suffered to speak for him, though he desired only to be heard one very short word; but my lord would not hearken to him, though he suffered a counsellor to talk against him for above half an hour. I thought it hard, I own, that there should be so many of them, my lord, and the court, and the jury, and the counsellors, and the witnesses, all upon one poor man, and he too in chains.

If you were discharged or acquitted before 1774, you would find that this did not necessarily lead to freedom. The fees for jailers and for sheriffs blocked the way. This scandal first roused Howard to visit other jails, when he was sheriff for Bedford in 1773. He had been horrified to see poor wretches who could not pay these demands dragged back to prison, and hoped to find a precedent for paying the fees from county rates. Next year Mr. Popham, helped by Howard's campaign, secured the passing of an Act (14 George III, c. 20) which put an end to the system in fact as well as on paper. Acquitted and discharged prisoners were to be set free at once in open court, without payment of fees to jailer or sheriff who were to be compensated for their loss, out of the rates, up to 13s. 4d. per prisoner. Pardoned felons did not come under the Act. Thus James Ward, pardoned in 1781, on condition of going to sea, was still living in prison on a pound of bread a day in 1782, for any officer who took him was faced with a bill of £3 7s. 4d. of which £1 7s. went to the Secretary of State.

Supposing that sentence of death had been passed on you, your chances of life in London were worse than elsewhere. Howard's figures show that for the twenty years before 1772 more than half of those sentenced to death in London went to the gallows, whilst in the Norfolk Circuit less than a third, and in the Midlands less than a fourth were executed.

If you were one of the unfortunates left for execution in London you would find yourself in what Fielding called the 'many Cartloads of our Fellow-creatures . . . once in six Weeks carried to Slaughter' at Tyburn, 'attended with the Compassion of the meek and tender-hearted, and with the Applause, Admiration, and Envy of all the bold and hardened'. These occasions were a recognized holiday for the London journeymen, and were regarded as a public entertainment. The Fox-North Government in 1783 abolished this spectacle, and criminals were henceforth executed outside the jail. Johnson's comment on this 'innovation' is well known. 'The publick was gratified by a procession; the criminal was supported by it. Why is all this to be swept away?'

If you were reprieved and ordered for transportation your destiny before 1776 would be America, probably Maryland or Virginia. An Act in 1718 (4 George I, c. 11) regularized a system by which a contractor took over convicted prisoners, shipped them out at his own expense, and made what he could by selling them, usually at auction, to the tobacco planters, for the term of their sentences. A grim complaint of the quality of the merchandise is quoted by Howard as made by a Bristol contractor to the Salisbury jailer in 1774: 'Sore feet prove very fatal. The mortality we met with in our last ship, if repeated in this, will so surfeit us, that we shall never take another.' Jail fever, as well as mortified toes, caused heavy losses. One contractor estimated that taking an average of seven years he lost a seventh of his cargo. From 1769 to 1776 the yearly number of felons transported averaged 960, of whom 240 were women.

This system for disposing of convicts seemed admirable to the mother country. It provided the colonists with cheap labour, and gave the convicts the chance of a fresh start in new surroundings at the end of their sentence. The colonies, however, regarded it differently. Non-criminal indentured labourers were plentiful, and Franklin protested against letting loose upon the New World the outcasts of the Old. The war with America in 1776 stopped the traffic and it was never resumed.

The problem caused in the mother country by this stoppage was acute. Jails were already overcrowded, and Justices did not welcome the idea of burdening the county funds with new prisons, and with the keep of those felons who had hitherto been taken off their hands after conviction. It must be remembered that jails were not constructed to house convicts. The majority of prisoners were got out of the way after trial. They were whipped, or burnt in the hand, or transported, or hanged; it was the prisoners awaiting trial, or the prisoners sentenced to imprisonment for misdemeanours who formed the bulk of the prison population. A solution for the problem was found in the system of the hulks, that is in housing convicted felons in old ships on the Thames and setting them to do work of public importance, such as dredging, or screening ballast for roads, or making ditches and embankments. A contractor was paid £38 a head (afterwards lowered to £27), and he undertook to feed, clothe, and lodge them, and to provide them with tools and equipment for work. The money came out of the tax-payer's pocket, and the public received the benefit of their work. This substitute for transportation was marred by horrible conditions on board, where the convicts were described by Dr. William Smith in 1776 as lying 'chained in pairs night and day except when at work in the lighters'.[1] The crowded quarters, the mouldy biscuits, that 'universal Depression of Spirits' noted by their overseer made them easy victims to jail fever, and out of 632 prisoners 176 died between August 1776 and March 1778. After that, under pressure from Howard and a Parliamentary Committee on the subject, the physical conditions were improved. New hulks were started at Portsmouth in 1786, and though the system was introduced as a temporary expedient, it lasted for eighty-two years. A melancholy commentary on the hope expressed in the original Act establishing the hulks, that 'Care and Correction' might reclaim the inmates from their evil courses, is given in a Report on them in 1812. The convicts, says this Report, 'must be expected to return into society with more depraved habits and dispositions, than those with which they went into confinement'.

Whilst transportation was in abeyance an attempt was made to put some of Howard's reforming ideas into force. By the 'Penitentiary Act' of 1779 (19 George III, c. 74) two prisons were to be built, one for 600 men, the other for 300 women, where offenders could undergo 'solitary Imprisonment, accompanied by well-regulated Labour and religious Instruction'. Solitary imprisonment did not mean what is now understood by solitary confinement. Each prisoner was to have a separate cell, but he would mix with others at work, at Divine Service, at meals and airings. Howard, indeed, was said by Whitbread to have expressed

[1] *State of the Gaols in London, Westminster, &c.* (1776).

his horror of solitary confinement. But this scheme got no farther than the Statute Book. The 'supervisors', of whom Howard was one, could not agree on a site. Bentham's new scheme for a 'Panopticon' diverted the attention of reformers later, and meanwhile the acute problem of what to do with the surplus convicts, not provided for by the hulks, had been solved by the reintroduction of transportation. Attempts to send convicts again to the tobacco plantations were resisted by the United States. British America and the West Indies refused to take any shiploads. Finally, after an abortive attempt to dispose of them in Africa, Australia and the adjacent islands were fixed on as a suitable home. The first shipload arrived at Botany Bay in January 1788.

There was another set of prisoners, the debtors, not kept in irons nor liable to be sent to the hulks, or overseas, or to the gallows, of whom Howard could, nevertheless, say that some of them 'are the most pitiable objects in our jails'. The gross cruelty, amounting to deliberate torture, revealed in the London debtors prisons by Oglethorpe's Committee in 1728 and 1729 was a thing of the past in Howard's day, but debtors were still at the mercy of jailers who counted on getting their living out of them. Most common jails housed both debtors and felons; occasionally the debtors and felons were together by day, as in the prison to which the Vicar of Wakefield was sent, but in most there were separate quarters for debtors, the 'masterside' where those lived who could afford to pay for rooms; the 'commonside' where the poorer prisoners found some sort of accommodation, usually free, though if a prisoner wished to lie on anything softer than the floor he generally had to pay for it. Dr. William Smith, who had an intimate professional knowledge of London prisons, described the commonside quarters as 'places much more unhealthy and not much cleaner than a pigstye'.[1]

Sometimes debtors were housed in prisons by themselves: those queer communities like the Fleet or the Marshalsea, or the King's Bench prison of which a vivid description is given in Smollett's *Adventures of Sir Launcelot Greaves*. Smollett's description of the fight between two prisoners loses its air of exaggeration when we read in Dr. William Smith: 'At present they are left to settle their disputes as they can. . . .

[1] *State of the Gaols in London, Westminster, &c.*

None, perhaps, are murdered; but I have seen them covered with bruises, and other marks of violence, even to the loss of their eyes.'

Debtors had no legal claim to be fed, though in about half the prisons the county allowance of bread was provided them. Where no allowance was made they had to depend on relatives or friends, or the charity of passers-by. Dr. Johnson describes how, when passing under one of the gates of the city he was 'struck with horror by a rueful cry, which summoned me *to remember the poor debtors*'.[1] Sometimes they would sell small objects they had made, out of a window. Fortunately poor debtors were a favourite object of compassion, and the charitable often left them legacies, though these by no means always reached the proper recipients.

Eighteenth-century literature is full of descriptions of sudden arrests for debt, from Richardson's description of Clarissa in the Spunging House, 'a horrid hole of a house', downwards, but nowhere is there a more pathetic picture than that given by Howard of the debtors at Durham sitting with nothing to do in two small damp unhealthy rooms which they were never allowed to leave except occasionally for chapel, 'eating boiled bread and water . . . the only nourishment some had lived upon for near a twelvemonth' and complaining of 'that great nuisance of bugs': a pest from which debtors and felons suffered alike.

The position of debtors was an admitted scandal in the eighteenth century. The law presumed that every man was solvent and gave a creditor the power of putting his debtor in prison, though not of distraining on his goods. The creditor in fact could inflict a life sentence on his debtor. For sums under 40s. it is true there were special methods of procedure before what were called 'Courts of Conscience', small local courts set up in various districts by special Acts, with powers of imprisonment for limited periods only, such as three months, but for anything over 40s. there was no term set to the time the debtor might spend in prison, where he was heaping up fresh debts in addition to his original one. Dr. Johnson published a powerful indictment of the system in 1758 and 1759 in *The Idler* (22 and 38):

The confinement . . . of any man in the sloth and darkness of a prison, is a loss to the nation, and no gain to the creditor. For of the

[1] *Idler*, No. 22, Sept. 16, 1758.

multitudes who are pining in those cells of misery, a very small part is suspected of any fraudulent act by which they retain what belongs to others. The rest are imprisoned by the wantonness of pride, the malignity of revenge, or the acrimony of disappointed expectation.

The result of this and other protests was the passing in 1759 of what was called the 'Lords' Act' (32 George II, c. 28), an Act which made permanent provisions which had previously been embodied in temporary Acts to which little attention was paid. By this Act a prisoner who owed less than £100 could make a statement on oath of his estate and effects, the court could then assign these to the creditor and discharge the prisoner, unless, and the 'unless' is important, the creditor, or one of the creditors, insisted on the prisoner being detained in prison. If the creditor insisted, he was bound henceforth to pay the debtor his 'groats', that is a groat or 4*d*. a day. The Act had little effect.[1] What Burke denounced in 1780 as 'the arbitrary discretion of a private, nay interested, and irritated, individual' continued to keep the debtor in prison, and to obtain the 'groats' was an expensive process which few prisoners could afford. Out of over a thousand debtors in prisons outside London, Howard found only twelve who had obtained this allowance.

When prisons became overcrowded, the legislature from time to time emptied them by temporary insolvent Acts, by which debtors could deliver up their possessions and obtain freedom, whether their creditors liked it or not.

The difficulty of forming a picture of the condition of the poor in Johnson's lifetime which would be universally true, a difficulty illustrated by the contrast with which this chapter opens, becomes steadily more manifest as the survey proceeds. There are two main causes. In the first place there is no uniformity of administration. Custom and practice differ from place to place according to the temper or views of persons of local influence. Observers of equal authority thus give quite different conclusions on such a question as the effects of the Laws of Settlement. Adam Smith wrote in 1776: 'There is scarce a poor man in England, of forty years of age, I will venture to say, who has not, in some part of his life, felt himself most cruelly oppressed by this ill contrived law of settlements.' Eden replied that though there were

---

[1] The Thatched House Society (see *infra*, p. 331) helped to make it effective by extracting the 'groats' from the creditor.

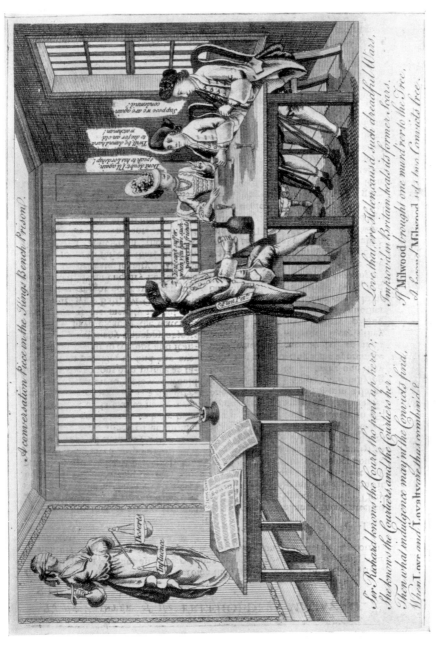

A ROOM IN THE FLEET PRISON

From Humours of the Fleet, *1749*

cases of vexatious removal, the laws of settlement were not administered in this way everywhere. Richard Burn and William Hay thought the laws oppressive. One of the resolutions passed by the House of Commons in 1735, at the instance of William Hay, spoke of the laws of settlement and vagrancy as 'vexatious to the Poor, and of little advantage to the Public'. John Howlett, a public-spirited and most intelligent parson, thought their effect slight and unimportant. In his parish 40 out of 240 families of mechanics and labourers were strangers. It is indeed obvious that a Law of Settlement so stringent could not have been administered in its full severity everywhere without putting an intolerable strain on the resources of the parishes. Moreover, the system was tempered by a practice that grew up of issuing travelling passes. These were permits given by Justices to poor travellers. Burn, who thought that the Law of Settlement was harsh, thought this method of alleviating it pernicious. How commonly such passes were given is not known. But, whatever the exceptions, the Laws of Settlement were undoubtedly a genuine hardship to all classes of poor people in some places and to some classes in all places.

There is a second cause of difficulty in reaching conclusions about the actual suffering of the poor. When we look at the drastic character of the penal laws, and remember the reputation of the time for violent manners, we are astonished by the small number of persons in prison at any moment. Howard found in 1776 that there were 4,084 prisoners in England and Wales (1,696 of these were in London), of whom 2,437 were debtors. This was a smaller proportion of the population than was in prison during most of the nineteenth century. The reason of course is that just as the country had too little in the way of government, so it had too little in the way of police. Order depended in the towns on beadles, special constables, and night watchmen with rattles, and in the villages on a few unpaid constables. Fielding in *Amelia* describes the London watchmen,

who, being to guard our streets by night from thieves and robbers, an office which at least requires strength of body, are chosen out of those poor old decrepit people who are from their want of bodily strength rendered incapable of getting a livelihood by work. . . If the poor old fellows should run away from such enemies, no one I think can wonder, unless it be that they were able to make their escape.

Special rewards were offered to stimulate capture and prosecution, in the hope that such incentives would supply the place of an organized police force. In general the law-breaker, whether vagrant or bandit, whether victim or culprit, reaped the advantages of that inefficiency of government which had helped to produce him. There was, however, one significant exception. Fielding's novels describe the zeal and industry with which the magistrates punished poaching. In 1770 Parliament passed the first of a series of Game Laws which became fiercer and fiercer in the generation that followed. The statistics show that in the next generation the Game Laws were carried out much more thoroughly than any others; the convictions for poaching assumed a larger and larger share in the volume of crime. The explanation is obvious. The Justices were specially interested in enforcing these laws, and they had a police for this purpose in their gamekeepers.

A society unable, owing to its lack of police, to secure respect for the law by enforcing it, turned for a remedy to the stiffening of the penal code and to harsher and harsher treatment of vagrants and beggars. The Plymouth Guardians, for example, obtained power in 1759 compulsorily to ship vagrants on board any vessel that would take them. The Exeter Guardians in 1774 obtained power to imprison for twelve months with hard labour any rogue, vagabond, sturdy beggar, or idle and disorderly person. In the attempt to put down vagrancy, one of the great evils of the time, statesmen drew the net so widely as to leave it to the discretion of magistrate or constable to punish or not any man or woman who fell into misfortune, or had no powerful patron. Under such a system a great many people who break the law escape punishment, but a great many who are guiltless of crime suffer for their poverty.

We have now to consider another aspect of the social history of the time: the effort of philanthropy to remove or mitigate suffering.

It has often been remarked of the eighteenth century that it was strong in men of character and genius, and weak in institutions and machinery. In such a society it would be natural to expect abuses and suffering, and to expect also a demand for remedies, and efforts to awaken public indignation. We can judge what a change came over the English conscience in Johnson's lifetime, when we remember that the clause which gave England the lion's share in the Slave Trade was regarded as one of the prizes of the Treaty of Utrecht, signed when he was a child (1713), and that before his death the Slave Trade was the object of a powerful, and all but victorious, agitation. That conscience, directed by Granville Sharp and Wilberforce against the Slave Trade, and by Burke and Fox against misgovernment in India, was not indifferent to the suffering to be found in English prisons, or English workhouses, or in the daily life of a people whose institutions had not kept pace with social change. A glance merely at the extracts quoted in this chapter would show how many a parson and magistrate spent his days debating remedies and denouncing wrongs. When we consider how strong a sense of distress and responsibility is to be found in the literature of the time, from Fielding to Adam Smith, from Smollett to Burke, from Goldsmith to Johnson, it is not surprising that the two schools that were to play so large a part in civilizing English life were born at this time. The humanitarian school was represented by Sir William Meredith, a Rockingham Whig, who tried to soften the penal law in the spirit of Romilly, and men like Fox, Burke, and Sheridan; the Evangelical by Wesley, Thornton, Hannah More, and Wilberforce.

John Brown (1715–66), a parson and a writer of note, who published in 1757 an *Estimate of the Manners and Principles of the Times*, spoke of the liberality of the English people to the miserable and friendless as characteristic of the national spirit of humanity. Apart from the building of hospitals and infirmaries in most of the large towns, a subject which falls outside this chapter, the compassion of the time led to the establishment of the Foundling Hospital, the Magdalene Hospital, the Marine Society, and the Thatched House Society.

The project of a Foundling Hospital was originally suggested by some merchants in 1708, but it was objected that such a hospital 'might seem to encourage vice by making too easy a provision for illegitimate children'. A little later the plan was taken up by a man of character and vigour, Thomas Coram, a sea captain (1668–1751), who, after settling in Massachusetts as a shipbuilder, returned to England in 1711. Coram threw himself at once into public enterprises, proposing a scheme, which was later adopted, for settling unemployed artisans in Nova Scotia. He started his campaign for a Foundling Hospital by persuading twenty-one aristocratic ladies to sign a manifesto, in which they undertook to support such a hospital if the King would grant a charter. 'Names like these', says Pugh, after giving his list of Duchesses, 'could not fail of succeeding.'[1] The Charter was granted in 1739, and the Hospital built. The King gave two thousand pounds, and another thousand towards establishing a preacher. Handel gave an organ, and the score of *The Messiah*, besides directing musical performances at which over ten thousand pounds were collected. Hogarth gave a picture, and subscriptions flowed in. 'Such was the zeal which influenced the minds of persons for this favourite object, that perhaps no institution merely of a charitable nature was ever so munificently supported.'[2]

In 1756 Parliament gave a grant, on condition that all children brought to the Hospital should be taken in. This led to a great increase both in the admissions, and in the death-rate. Between 1756 and 1760, when it became plain to Parliament that this was a bad system, nearly 15,000 children were admitted, of whom only 4,400 lived to be apprenticed. Parliament, having given in all £570,000, ceased to make grants after 1771, and the Hospital became again a private charity. Indiscriminate admission had ceased in 1760, and the death-rate had fallen.

In the year of Coram's death, Johnson published an appeal for prostitutes. 'It cannot be doubted but that numbers follow this dreadful course of life, with shame, horror, and regret; but, where can they hope for refuge? *The world is not their friend, nor the world's law.*'[3] In 1758 Sir John Fielding and others supported his plea, and Robert Dingley published a *Proposal for establishing a place of Reception for penitent Prostitutes*. Jonas Hanway supported him with a pamphlet; a committee was formed and a hospital built. Hanway gave active help, making inquiries into similar institutions in Rome, Naples, Seville, and Amsterdam. By 1786, 2,400 women had been admitted, of whom more than 1,500 had been reconciled to their friends or placed

---

[1] John Pugh, *Remarkable Occurrences in the Life of Jonas Hanway Esq.* (1787), p. 159.
[2] Ibid., p. 161. [3] *Rambler*, No. 107 (26 March, 1751).

out in service. Hanway also started a hospital for venereal diseases, but this did not prosper.

The sufferings of debtors led to the establishment, in 1772, of the Society for the Discharge and Relief of Persons imprisoned for small Debts, commonly known as the Thatched House Society. The most active member was James Neild (1774–1814), a jeweller, who acted as Treasurer of the Society, and afterwards made a reputation as a critic of the prison system. His work, *The State of the Prisons in England, Scotland, and Wales*, published after Johnson's death, proved of great value to Romilly, Bennet, and Peel in the later campaign for reform. The President of the Thatched House Society was Lord Romney, the Vice-Presidents, Lord Beauchamp, Lord Chief Baron Smythe, Mr. Justice Nares, and the well-known Evangelical philanthropist, James Thornton. The special purpose of the Society was indicated by a rule 'that such debtors shall have the Preference as are most aged, or infirm, or have the largest families unprovided for, are the most likely to be useful to the community, and appear to have lost their liberty by unavoidable misfortune, at least not by Fraud, Vice, or Extravagance'. Each petitioner had to name two respectable housekeepers as vouchers for his integrity, sobriety, and industry. By 1792, when evidence about the Society was given to a Parliamentary Committee on Imprisonment for Debt, nearly £30,000 had been spent, and 12,590 prisoners had been released. Two-thirds were manufacturers or labourers. The Society every year obtained their 'groats' for about 150 other debtors whom they could not release.

Of the philanthropists of the time three are especially interesting: James Oglethorpe (1696–1785), Jonas Hanway (1712–86), and John Howard (1726?–90).

Oglethorpe, who served as a young man in Prince Eugene's army, entered Parliament in 1722. His attention was drawn to the condition of the debtors' prisons by the fate of a friend who died of small-pox in the Fleet. The scandalous state of these prisons had been exposed as early as 1691, but nothing had been done. Oglethorpe was more fortunate, for he persuaded Parliament to inquire first into the condition of the Fleet and the Marshalsea, and then into that of other prisons. His Committee proved an effective body, and terrible revelations followed. Oglethorpe, having secured some improvement by new regulations, set himself to provide a refuge for liberated debtors in the New World. He was the founder and the first Governor of the colony of Georgia, and he showed himself well ahead of his day by forbidding his colonists to import slaves. He saw military service both in America, where he gained success, and at home, in the Jacobite Rebellion, where he was less fortunate. He is most generally known to-day from Pope's couplet:

> One driven by strong benevolence of soul
> Shall fly, like Oglethorpe, from pole to pole.

Georgia became a home of the Moravian sect, and when Oglethorpe returned to England he carried a Bill through Parliament, exempting Moravians from the obligation to bear arms or take an oath. He was one of the earliest of Johnson's admirers, and in his old age he makes agreeable appearances in the pages of Boswell, arguing against luxury, defending duelling, criticizing the power of Parliament, or telling anecdotes drawn from his adventurous life. Boswell said of him that his benevolence of soul continued unabated to the end, though he had been treated with a neglect that might have made him cold and callous.

Jonas Hanway, like Oglethorpe, came into public life at home after adventure abroad. After an apprenticeship in a merchant's office in Lisbon, he accepted the offer of a partnership in the house of a merchant, Robert Dingley, in St. Petersburg. He arrived there, in 1743, at an interesting moment. An enterprising seaman, named Elton, had offered to visit Persia with a view to introducing Russian trade, but after a successful journey, and some adventures, he had deserted his Russian employers, to take service under a usurping Shah, as 'superintendent of the Persian coast of the Caspian'. The merchants were looking for somebody to take his place. Hanway volunteered, and he started a few months later on travels that engaged him two years, with a caravan of thirty-seven bales of English cloth. It was a journey full of perils, but he returned unhurt, though he had come into a revolution at Astrabad, been attacked by pirates in the Caspian, and laid up with fever. In 1750 he left Russia, and made his home in London. He was especially interested in the protection of children. With the help of Sir John Fielding and others, he founded the Marine Society for training poor boys for the sea, and he anticipated Bennet and Shaftesbury in calling attention to the cruelties suffered by climbing boys. Of all his various tasks, the one that occupied him most was that of rescuing pauper children. He prepared himself by visiting poor-houses and foundling hospitals, first in France and Holland, and then at home. His experience as a Governor of the Foundling Hospital in London increased his anxiety to help parish children, and led him to secure the two Acts of 1761 and 1767 already described. Hanway braved the derision of the London streets by carrying an umbrella, and the wrath of Johnson by attacking the 'pernicious custom of tea drinking'. The vast collection of pamphlets that Hanway left behind him showed the vigour and the range of his philanthropy.

John Howard, originally apprenticed as a grocer, found himself, on his father's death, a young man of independent means. He married his first wife, who was an elderly woman, in gratitude for her care of him during a nervous illness. She did not live long, and after her death he was taken prisoner, when sailing for Portugal, by a French privateer. He and his fellow travellers suffered great hardships in a French jail. He was sent to England on parole, secured an exchange for himself, and release for his fellow victims. He married a second time, settled at Cardington in Bedford, built model cottages and a village school, and found himself in 1773 High Sheriff for the County. His experience in that office gave new purpose to his life, and he devoted himself, till his death, to prison reform. Although a delicate man, he travelled over 50,000 miles, visiting almost every country in Europe, and putting himself deliberately in contact with disease. He spent £30,000, and he published a series of editions of his famous work, *The State of the Prisons in England and Wales*. He died of camp fever at Kershon, on the shores of the Black Sea, when investigating the conditions of a sick Russian army.

When Johnson died, the philanthropists had not made a deep impression on the abuses of the time. The reformers who tried to make the Poor Law more humane and efficient had suffered sharp disappointments in practice. Sympathy with debtors found expression rather in organized charity than in change of system. The penal law could not be re-organized until the English people had an effective police, and for that they had to wait another half century. If we read Howard's pages, written thirty years after Oglethorpe's Committee had reported on the Fleet and Marshalsea, we may ask ourselves what had come of Oglethorpe's efforts; if we read the descriptions of English prisons given by Mrs. Fry or Fowell Buxton, thirty years after Howard's death, we may ask ourselves what it was that Howard accomplished by his life of self-sacrifice and peril. The positive achievements of these men, and of men like them, may seem inconsiderable, and the nation they had begun to educate was thrown back with violence in the panic spread by the French Revolution. But a disparaging view would be a short-sighted view. Few reformers live to see the full triumph of their efforts, and most of them die thinking of their work as wasted. The test comes afterwards. We can see to-day that Oglethorpe's Committee may be regarded as the predecessor of the Committees that were guided and used by Romilly and Henry Grey Bennet with such effect a century later; that Hanway, pleading for the pauper apprentice, prepared the way for the work of Robert Owen and the first Sir Robert Peel; that Howard's passion for systematic investigation taught the nation to learn later from the Reports and Returns that served the purposes of Sadler, Ashley, and Fielden. Of these early philanthropists we may say that, if they could not save the eighteenth century by their energy, they helped to save the nineteenth by their example.

BIBLIOGRAPHY.—For the Poor Laws the chief contemporary authorities are Rev. RICHARD BURN's *The History of the Poor Laws* (1764); THOMAS RUGGLES' *The History of the Poor, their Rights, Duties, and the Laws respecting them, in a series of letters* (2 vols., 1793); and Sir FREDERICK MORTON EDEN's *The State of the Poor* (3 vols., 1797). The first volume contains a history of the Poor from the Conquest down to the end of the eighteenth century including an account of 'the various Plans proposed and adopted' for their Relief. The other volumes contain detailed Parochial Reports. HENRY FIELDING's *Proposal for making an Effectual Provision for the Poor* (1753) contains much valuable information. JOHN PUGH's *Remarkable Occurrences in the Life of Jonas Hanway Esq.* (1787) gives an account of Hanway's work for parish children as well as of his other activities.

Of modern books on the subject the three most important are: SIDNEY and BEATRICE WEBB's *English Poor Law History*, Part I: *The Old Poor Law*; the same authors' *Statutory Authorities*; and DOROTHY MARSHALL's *The English Poor in the Eighteenth Century* (1926). Sir GEORGE NICHOLLS's *History of the English Poor Law* (2 vols., 1854) also contains a good deal of information.

For Crime and the Penal Code the best contemporary authorities are HENRY FIELDING's *Enquiry into the Causes of the late Increase of Robbers &c. with some Proposals for Remedying this Growing Evil* (1751), which gives a valuable description of the underworld; Sir SAMUEL ROMILLY's *Observations on a late Publication entitled Thoughts on Executive Justice* (1786); the same author's *Observations on the Criminal Law of England* (1810); and P. COLQUHOUN's *Treatise on the Police of the Metropolis* (1796). Among modern authorities are Sir J. F. STEPHEN's *History of Criminal Law of England* (3 vols., 1883) and W. E. H. LECKY's *History of England in the Eighteenth Century*, vol. ii, chap. 4, and vol. vii, chap. 21.

About Prisons there is a considerable literature. Chief among contemporary authorities stands JOHN HOWARD's *The State of the Prisons in England and Wales* (first edition published 1777, third edition, 1784). WILLIAM SMITH's (M.D.) *State of the Gaols in London, Westminster, and Borough of Southwark* (1776) also gives valuable information. JAMES NEILD's *State of the Prisons in England, Scotland, and Wales* (1812) is a later book modelled on Howard's. Of Parliamentary Committees on the subject the following are the most important: Report of Committee on Act of 1776, giving important evidence, including Howard's, about the system of Hulks, see *House of Commons Journals*, April 15, 1778. Report of Committee on 1784 Act about Transportation, see *House of Commons Journals*, May 9, 1785. Report of House of Commons Select Committee on Transportation, 1837–8, giving a history of transportation. Of the state of the London debtors' prisons in Johnson's early days a full and horrifying account is given in the Reports of Oglethorpe's Committee into Gaols, 1728 and 1729. These are contained in *House of Commons Journals*, vol. xxi, especially pp. 274 ff., 376 ff., and 576 ff. (There is a printer's error running through this volume. The second half of each year is dated as belonging to the succeeding year.) About Debtors in general the clearest account of the law in the eighteenth century is contained in the Parliamentary Committee into Imprisonment for Debt, see *House of Commons Journals*, April 2, 1792. Among modern books a comprehensive one is SIDNEY and BEATRICE WEBB's *English Prisons under Local Government*, which gives an historical account of prison administration from the seventeenth to the twentieth century, with references to the main authorities. E. I. MACCORMAC's *White Servitude in Maryland* (1904, Johns Hopkins University Studies) gives an interesting account of transportation from the American point of view.

Much general information on the subject of this chapter is contained in contemporary novels. GOLDSMITH's *The Vicar of Wakefield*; SMOLLETT's *Adventures of Sir Launcelot Greaves*; and FIELDING's *Tom Jones, Joseph Andrews*, and *Amelia* are specially important. Amongst modern works the most valuable for detailed and documented information on several of the subjects in this chapter, especially gin drinking and parish apprentices, is M. DOROTHY GEORGE's *London Life in the XVIIIth Century* (1925).

XII

MANNERS, MEALS, AND DOMESTIC PASTIMES

By DOROTHY MARSHALL

Every man of any education would rather be called a rascal, than accused of deficiency in the graces.—*Life of Johnson* (May 1776).

A man seldom thinks with more earnestness of anything than he does of his dinner; and if he cannot get that well dressed, he should be suspected of inaccuracy in other things.—PIOZZI, *Anecdotes*.

I could write a better book of cookery than has ever yet been written; it should be a book upon philosophical principles.—*Life of Johnson* (15 April 1778).

THE period of Dr. Johnson's life was one in which great changes of manners took place, and there is some ground for considering that the eighteenth century first saw the adoption in England of a definite code of social politeness. In the earlier part of the century verbal refinement was disregarded, even among those people who had received the education of a gentleman and who were in a financial position to sustain the rôle and mix with good society. At a time when general conversation was interlarded with oaths, improprieties, and profanities, Defoe railed vehemently but uselessly against the general practice of swearing. But when the Queen herself, on the passage of the Civil List, could send a message to Sir Robert Walpole to the effect that 'the fat bitch' had forgiven him, protests were vain. When the change came it sprang from an impulse within society and from an appreciation of the graces of social refinement, which is so clearly mirrored in Lord Chesterfield's letters. Here the foundation of true politeness is placed on a modern basis; good manners are shown to be formalized consideration for other people. For this reason much that Chesterfield wrote is true not only for his own generation but for any civilized society. Parts of his letters, however, have the further interest of foreshadowing the languid, affected gentleman of the latter part of the century. Good manners are becoming not so much the negative avoidance of grossness as the cultivation of elegance. In a letter written to his son in 1751 he begged him to apply himself diligently to the precepts of his dancing master.

Desire him [he wrote] to teach you every genteel attitude, that the human body can be put into; let him make you go in and out of his room frequently, and present yourself to him, as if he were by turns different persons; such as a minister, a lady, a superior, an equal, an inferior, etc. Learn to sit genteelly in different companies, to loll genteelly, and with good manners, in those companies where you are authorised to be free: and to sit up respectfully where the same freedom is not allowable. Learn even to compose your countenance occasionally to the respectful, the cheerful, and the insinuating. Take particular care that the motions of your hands and arms be easy and graceful, for the genteelness of a man consists more in them than in anything else, especially in his dancing.

Though his son failed to profit by the advice so given and remained to the end of his life 'an awkward fellow', there were others who graduated successfully in the school of foppery, often without that foundation of true manners which Chesterfield advocated so persistently. Miss Burney's novels provide illustrations of this growth of affectation. One young man reduced Evelina to a mingled state of merriment and embarrassment by his airs in requesting her to dance.

Bowing almost to the ground, with a sort of a swing, and waving his hands with the greatest conceit, after a short and silly pause, he said, 'Madam, may I presume?' and stopt offering to take my hand. I drew it back but could scarce forebear laughing. 'Allow me, Madam,' continued he, affectedly breaking off every half moment, 'the honour and happiness—if I am not so unhappy as to address you too late—to have the happiness and honour——.'

In spite, however, of so genteel a use of his hands he failed to attain the 'honour and happiness' to which he aspired, and it was only later that Evelina discovered that she had committed the unpardonable rudeness of accepting a second partner after rejecting the first. By the time *Cecilia* was written such affectation of manners had been carried by one set to ridiculous excess. Thus Miss Larolles could declare of Mr. Meadows:

Why, he's the very head of the ton. There's nothing in the world so fashionable as taking no notice of things, and never seeing people, and saying nothing at all, and never hearing a word, and not knowing one's own acquaintance, and always finding fault; all the ton do so, and I assure you, as to Mr. Meadows, he's so excessively courted by everybody, that if he does but say a syllable, he thinks its such an immense favour, you've no idea.[1]

Such elegant behaviour was of necessity confined to the few who had the time and lack of intelligence to practise it. Among people of sense it was ridiculed; among the lower middle class it was either disregarded or vulgarized. Nevertheless it was a sign of the very real improvement which affected even those members of the lower classes who came into contact with polite society. By the middle of the century the light comedy, *High Life below Stairs*, portrayed the servant as having manners as fine as his master, while Mrs. Thrale, in one of her letters, gives the following instance of the general improvement of manners:

I was reading the 'Spectator' to Sophy while my maid papered my curls yester-morning, it was the 3rd vol. 217, where the man complains of an indelicate mistress, who said on some occasion that her stomach ach'd, and lamented how her teeth had got a seed between them. The woman that dressed me was so astonished at this grossness, though common enough in Addison's time one sees, that she cried out, 'Well Madam! surely that could never have been a lady who used expressions like those'.

Indeed so susceptible had the polite female of the period become that when in 1773 Mr. Rishton read *The Faërie Queene* aloud to his wife and sister-in-law he won their approval by being 'extremely delicate, omitting whatever, to the poet's great disgrace, has crept in that is improper for a woman's ear'. A further illustration of this artificial delicacy is to be seen in the stilted use of the third person as a means of expressing respectful courtesy, a convention which rarely allowed a gentleman to use the second person when addressing a lady of his acquaintance.

These improvements and refinements were in the main confined to the polite world and to those who attended to its wants. Even in London, where the lower middle classes had frequent opportunities of observing the conduct of their betters, both the utter lack of the rudiments of polish which Evelina found in the Branghtons, and the parody of it, which so 'incommodated' her in Mr. Smith, were rather

---

[1] Johnson, who had an ingrained objection to coarseness and would not allow swearing in his company, also had a hearty contempt for affectation. 'Never', he said to 'Queeney' Thrale, 'delight yourself with the dignity of silence or the superiority of inattention.'

THE PANTHEON, 1772

From the mezzotint by R. Earlom after the painting by C. Brandoin

typical than uncommon, though among this class was also to be found much good sense and quiet decent behaviour. As for the labouring poor, the mob and rabble of eighteenth-century writers, their manners in London and the country alike were rude, insolent, and boorish. No foreigner came to England without registering this complaint; in London to look like a Frenchman was often enough to give rise to boos and jeers. In the country districts every stranger was suspect. Moritz could frequently find no inn that would accommodate a foreign traveller who came on foot, and he would certainly not have endorsed Johnson's dictum that at a tavern 'you are sure you are welcome: and the more noise you make, the more trouble you give, the more good things you call for, the welcomer you are. No servants will attend you with the alacrity which waiters do, who are incited by the prospect of an immediate reward in proportion as they please. No, Sir, there is nothing that has yet been contrived by man, by which so much happiness is produced as by a good tavern or inn.' But many English travellers were little better pleased by rural England than Moritz had been. Hannah More and Wesley alike describe a barbarous people, while, as William Hutton[1] was passing through Market Bosworth, the villagers set their dogs on him merely because he was a stranger. Nor, in many cases, were their social superiors capable of elevating these isolated communities. The local squire, unless he belonged to that grade of society which visited London regularly, was in his instincts as great a boor as they, though his greater wealth had once procured for him the elements of an education which still enabled him, with the aid of the clerk of the peace, to discharge his responsibilities as a Justice and to play some part in local life. As one writer declared, 'He spends that part of the day, in which he is not on horse-back, at table, in smoking and getting drunk . . . he is naturally a very dull animal'. Le Blanc was of the opinion that 'the country people in England, to say nothing more, are very clownish and unpolished; and the clergy in the country, are not much more agreeable company. These honest gentlemen are never easy but in each other's company; and commonly had rather smoak at the steward's table, than dine at the master's.'

Such strictures, passed by London writers and men of culture, though in the main accurate, may yet be far from fair. Among the rural population there was often to be found a simplicity of manners which, though lacking in polish, was far from being devoid of dignity. Thus Crabbe described the manner of life of his great-uncle Mr. Tovell, a man of some education, having been to a Mercantile school, who was in the latter half of the century farming his own estate of about £800 a year:

On entering the house, there was nothing at first sight to remind one of the farm:—a spacious hall, paved with black and white marble, at one extremity a very handsome drawingroom, and the other a fine old staircase of black oak, polished until it was as slippery as ice, and having a chime clock and a barrel organ on its landing place. But this drawingroom, a corresponding dining parlour, and a handsome sleeping apartment upstairs were all tabooed ground, and made use of on great and solemn occasions only. . . . At all other times the family and their visitors lived entirely in the old fashioned kitchen along with the servants. My great-uncle occupied an arm-chair, or, in attacks of the gout, a couch on one side of the large open chimney. Mrs. Tovell sat at a small table, on which, in the evening, stood one small candle, in an iron candlestick, plying her needle by the feeble glimmer, surrounded by her maids, all busy at the same employments; but in winter a noble block of wood, sometimes the whole circumference of a pollard, threw its comfortable warmth and cheerful blaze over the whole apartment. . . . If the sacred apartments had not been opened, the family dined on this wise:—the heads seated in the kitchen at an old table; the farm men standing in the adjourning scullery, door open—the female servants at a side table, called a bouter:—with the principals, at the table, perchance some travelling rat catcher, a tinker, a farrier, or an occasional gardener in his shirt sleeves, his face probably streaming with perspiration.

This peep of rural England, though neither vulgar nor gross, is very far removed from the elegancy of the 'ton'. Yet one was as characteristic as the other of the closing period of Johnson's life.

The ordinary English home of the period appears to have been well run despite the lack of everything that could be described as modern conveniences. The difficulties in pro-curing water were not allowed to stand in the way of cleanli-ness, and our prowess in this direction impressed foreigners favourably. In 1726 de Saussure wrote:

The amount of water English people employ is inconceivable,

especially for the cleaning of their houses. Though they are not slaves to cleanliness, like the Dutch, still they are very remarkable for this virtue. Not a week passes by but well kept houses are washed twice in the seven days and that from top to bottom; and even every morning most kitchens, staircases and entrances are scrubbed. All furniture, and especially all kitchen utensils, are kept with the greatest cleanliness. Even the large hammers and the locks on the door are rubbed and shine brightly.

This excessive cleanliness he found extended not only to the houses but to the people also, for in another place he noted, 'English women and men are very clean: not a day passes by without their washing their hands, arms, faces, necks and throats in cold water, and that in winter as well as in summer'. In 1747 Kalm, and again in 1772 Grosley, also commented on the neatness and order of the average London house.

That this excellence was achieved through the efficiency of the eighteenth-century servant is a suggestion which no contemporary would have entertained for a minute. In no other century but our own was so much time and energy expended in complaining about the servants. Nor were complaints confined to the women; bachelors and husbands alike wrote indignant letters to the press, while to a literary hack in search of a subject the wickedness of servants was an unfailing blessing. These laments were surprisingly modern in tone; wages were too high and yet went on rising, maids were perpetually changing their places and if you dared so much as to correct them they departed, there being, as one of them told Defoe, more places than parish churches in England. In addition to these sins, since the women did not wear uniform, maids dressed themselves as fine as their mistresses, spending all their money upon their backs instead of saving providently for old age so as to escape the poor-house. Nor was it always easy to obtain good servants in the country. In 1771 Mrs. Delany wrote to a friend, 'I doubt very much whether you will get a servant that has been used to London that will sit down quietly in the country; there seems to be a universal dissipation of manners from the highest to the lowest, and the cook I gave an account of, who was a most desirable servant, said she could not live in the country, it was so melancholy', while Mrs. Purefoy, as her letters show, found a chronic difficulty in getting and keeping maids. Moreover, footmen and livery servants gave endless trouble, not only to their masters but to the public at large; they were saucy and insolent in the streets, they made a rowdy element at the theatre, they lounged outside the Houses of Parliament, making rude comments on the passers-by, and above all they demanded scandalous 'vails', or tips, from their master's guests.

The demanding of vails was one of the minor social evils of the century and one that seriously affected domestic life. This exaction was not confined to guests staying in the house but was enforced even though the entertainment received had been no more than a single dinner. Nor was it confined to the servants of the wealthy, though they were the most remorseless in their quest, standing in a formal line to speed the parting guest and extract from him the expected largess, so that it was commonly reckoned that to dine at the best houses cost anything from ten shillings to a guinea or two, according to the rank of the master. Even the servants of the professional and middle classes took their toll of visitors. Grosley noted with surprise that his landlady's sister always gave a shilling to the maid when she dined with the family, and Parson Woodforde regularly dispensed vails among his neighbours' servants. In the last two decades of the century, shame at the comments of foreign visitors and a recognition of the inconvenience of the system led to a determined campaign against the practice, so that by the time of Johnson's death the worst abuses were being checked, though other complaints against servants went on without diminution. Partly because English servants were considered difficult to manage there was a vogue for employing foreigners and in particular negroes. This fashion was not confined to the upper ranks of society; Johnson's personal man-servant, Francis, was a negro.

What contemporaries wrote and said about their servant problem was only half the truth. The perfect servant is a myth of history, to be discovered in the 'good old days' but never in any period under investigation, and eighteenth-century servants could make out a good case against the conditions in which they lived. Houses were inconveniently built and the domestic quarters were bad. In the bigger houses, though there might be a servants' hall, the men slept in the cellars and the maids in the attic, while in the smaller houses accommodation was still less adequate. We find mention of a kitchen which 'had no outlet but into the shop on the one hand and into the sitting room of the family on the other; and no light but through a window borrowed from the shop. This gloomy chamber was the residence of the family's maid-servant'. Servants had no recognized right to any free time or to holidays and were for ever at the beck and call of the mistress. In addition the work was hard. Mrs. Purefoy when engaging a cook-maid wrote:

She must milk 3 or 4 cows & understand how to manage that Dairy, & know how to boyll and roast ffowlls & butchers' meatt. Wee wash once a month, she & the washerwoman wash all but the small linnen & next day she & the washerwoman wash the Buck [i.e. a large quantity, usually of the coarser kind]. She helps the other maid wash the rooms when they are done, she makes the Garrett beds & cleans them & cleans ye great stairs & scours all the Irons & scours the Pewter in use, & wc have a woman to help when 't is all done. There is very good time to do all this provided she is a servant, & when she has done her work she sits down to spin.

Is it any wonder that servants dawdled over messages or left their places in search of change? Yet despite these inconveniences of service good places were eagerly sought and the better class of servants was recruited from many sources, serving-women in particular often coming from the homes of the poorer country clergy. Nor was there any such stigma as tends to be attached to domestic service to-day. Partly because social distinctions were so rigidly drawn there was a good deal of actual familiarity between master and man, between a mistress and her maid, a familiarity which often scandalized foreigners, who considered the English much amiss in this respect.

Though the eighteenth century resembled our own in being harassed by a servant problem, yet the customs and arrangements of its daily life were very dissimilar. The day was divided much more after the method now followed on the Continent. Dinner was the chief meal, though towards the end of the century another, supper, was added. Breakfast was only a light repast, so much so that Evelina doubted whether it could be counted as a meal at all, and many Dissenters, though normally so precise in their performance of the obligation to ask a blessing and return thanks, often omitted the ceremony at breakfast, which usually consisted of no more than tea and rolls, bread and butter, or sometimes toast in winter. Yet though so slight a meal, breakfast was not taken by the majority of people until the day had well begun. Writing in 1768, Fanny Burney described the daily routine as follows: 'We live here, generally speaking, in a very regular way.—we breakfast always at 10, and rise as much before that as we please—we dine precisely at 2, drink tea about 6—and sup exactly at 9.' The time before breakfast was occupied in various ways. Fanny herself, when in the country, walked for an hour in the fields, starting out between six and seven, but when in London she was never able to indulge herself 'in this delightful manner' because of the danger of footpads and robbers. In towns the time was more formally employed. Calls were often made before breakfast, and at Bath the whole business of drinking the waters or bathing took place then. This late hour for breakfast made it possible to invest the meal with a certain amount of ceremony, and breakfast parties, particularly in the earlier part of the century, were common. In 1743 there were comments in *The Gentleman's Magazine* on the habit of public breakfast parties, the most popular places being Ranelagh, Ruckholt near Stratford, Marylebone Gardens, and Cox's at the Green Man, Dulwich. Sometimes such parties consumed the greater part of the morning; Bubb Dodington noted with pleasure in his diary,

The Princess of Wales and Lady Augusta attended by Lady Middlesex and Mr. Breton did Mrs. Dodington and me the honour of breakfasting with us. After breakfast, we walked all round my gardens: we came in, and they went into all the rooms, except the common dining parlour: when we were coming down stairs, I told their Royal Highness, that there was one room, which I had forgotten to show them; they desired to see it and found a cold collation (for it was near three o'clock).

The morning was considered to extend until dinner-time, so that Moritz in 1782 noted that it was 'usual to walk out in a sort of negligèe, or morning-dress, your hair not dressed, but merely rolled up in rollers, and in a frock and boots'. The tendency was for the hour of dinner to become later and later, particularly in fashionable circles, causing Moritz to remark that 'the farther you go from the Court, into the City, the more regular and domestic the people become'. In the first part of the century, even in good society, the normal

'REFRESHMENT AT ST. JAMES'S'

After a drawing by G. T. Stubbs

time for dinner was two or sometimes three o'clock, and for that part of the population which was engaged in business these hours prevailed during most of the century. The Burneys, living in the country, dined, as we have seen, at two, the London business men at three after the Change was shut. But in the polite world four and even five was considered correct, so that Evelina remarked with country-bred surprise, 'We never dine till the day is almost over'.

Dinner being the chief meal of the day was in society an affair of formality. De Saussure observed that 'an Englishman's table is remarkably clean, the linen is very white, the plate shines brightly, and knives and forks are changed surprisingly often, that is to say, every time a plate is removed. When everybody has done eating, the table is cleared, the cloth even being removed, and a bottle of wine with a glass for each guest is placed on the table'. The custom by which the ladies retired as soon as the wine appeared seemed to him one of scant courtesy, as indeed it did to other foreign visitors. Le Blanc remarked that the men showed as much pleasure on their withdrawal as ever schoolboys did in the absence of their master. Once the men were left alone the solemn business of toasts began. This was a very exact ceremony, the master of the house calling upon the assembled company in turn and in accordance with the laws of precedence to propose a toast. Such toasts might be personal or political; a young fop anxious to gain a reputation for gallantry would name a reigning beauty, a disappointed politician would drink confusion to a prominent minister. But whatever the toast was it had to be drunk equally and by all; to abstain was an affront to the company, and even to mix water with the wine was considered to require an apology.

When at length the toasts were finished and the pipes of tobacco smoked the gentlemen rejoined the ladies and tea was served. The ceremony of drinking tea also frequently preceded evening parties and private dances. Indeed it would appear that when the eighteenth-century lady lacked an occupation she took tea, for alike in the home, at public places of amusement such as Ranelagh, and while taking the waters at Bath, the consumption of tea went on steadily. In this respect Johnson was a hardened offender, for when the company wished to retire to bed he would call for dishes of tea to delay their leaving. The habit of drinking tea on social occasions was one that he warmly favoured, as Boswell noted when he wrote, 'We talked of an evening society for conversation at a house in town of which we were all members', but of which Johnson said 'It will never do, Sir. There is nothing served about there, neither tea, nor coffee, nor lemonade, nor anything whatever, and depend upon it, Sir, a man does not love to go to a place from whence he comes out exactly as he went in'. In less polite society and within the family circle, by the latter part of the century, tea was becoming not so much an excuse for conversation as a light meal to bridge the gap between an early dinner and a late supper.

Suppers developed considerably in importance as the century progressed. In 1726 de Saussure observed sadly: 'There is no supper. If you wish to eat or drink in the evening you can do so, but supper is not considered a necessary meal.' By the close of Johnson's life this was no longer true for most people, though his fondness for a heavy meal led the Streatham circle to have a 'late and great dinner', followed by a supper of biscuits, toast, and water. In society suppers were becoming elaborate and taking place later and later in the evening. To sup at two in the morning was now a normal feature of a private ball. In 1777 Horace Walpole wrote,

Silly dissipation rather increases and without an object. The present folly is late hours. Everybody tries to be particular by being too late; and, as everybody tries it, nobody is so. It is the fashion now to go to Ranelagh two hours after it is over. You may not believe this, but it is literal. The music ends at ten; the company go at twelve. Lord Derby's cook lately gave him warning. The man owned he liked his place, but said he should be killed by dressing suppers at three in the morning.

Even in middle-class families supper had become a necessity. The Burneys supped at nine; so did Thomas Wright Hill, whose people were bakers, a quiet unpretentious family. In the country districts supper parties were popular and the guest who came to dine usually stopped to sup and returned in the small hours of the morning. Thus in 1779 Parson Woodforde 'at one o'clock took a ride to Lyng and dined, spent the afternoon, supped, and spent the evening and stayed till after 2 this morning'.

MR. AND MRS. THRALE ENTERTAINING DR. JOHNSON TO TEA AT RICHMOND

From the painting by J. Zoffany in the possession of the Earl of Durham

Both at dinner and supper heavy meals were taken to counterbalance a breakfast of rolls and a slight tea, and a list of the dishes served helps to explain the broad and comfortable faces so often seen in eighteenth-century portraits. Foreigners then, as now, disapproved of our dietary. It was said of us in 1727 that 'English people are large eaters; they prefer meat to bread, some people scarcely touching the latter'. The same observer also reported that they 'consume a great deal of butter, and they do not know how to prepare fish and vegetables except with this ingredient melted . . . no vegetables are eaten except with meat, and then always put under the roast or boiled meat'. The picture drawn by Moritz at the end of the century was substantially the same when he made the complaint, echoed by so many strangers forced to endure the culinary efforts of English landladies, 'For an English dinner, to such lodgers as I am, generally consists of a piece of half-boiled, or half-roasted meat; and a few cabbage leaves boiled in plain water; on which they pour a sauce made of flour and butter'. 'This, I assure you,' he added bitterly, 'is the usual method of dressing vegetables in England,' while he declared that, unless you stipulated how many cups were to be made with the half ounce, instead of coffee all you got was 'a prodigious quantity of brown water'. On the other hand, he was prepared to concede that our wheaten bread, butter, and Cheshire cheese were excellent, making up for many deficiencies.

Even contemporaries realized that the country squire was a particularly gross feeder. Of him it was said: 'He eats nothing but salt beef, cold mutton, cabbage, carrots and pudding, which last is his favourite dish; and that which is heaviest he likes best. His drink is ale, coarse Portugal wine and now and then a little of the strongest brandy.' The statement that we were by preference a nation of meat-eaters is substantiated by the many accounts which have survived of actual meals consumed, but it is perhaps comforting for our national esteem to find that the list is not entirely confined to beef and mutton and that it is to some extent balanced by the popularity of fish, oysters in particular being much prized. Dr. Johnson's own taste was for the heavy and the rich, though luckily for his constitution he was also devoted to fruit. Mrs. Thrale's account, based on long experience, of the delicacies which he principally favoured included

a leg of pork, boiled till it dropped from the bone, a veal pye with plums and sugar, or the outside cut of a salt buttock of beef, . . . with regard to drink, his liking was for the strongest, as it was not the flavour, but the effect he sought for, and professed to desire, and [she adds] when first I knew him, he used to pour capillaire into his Port wine. For the last twelve years, however, he left off all fer-mented liquors. To make himself some amends indeed, he took his chocolate liberally, pouring in large quantities of cream, or even melted butter; and was so fond of fruit, that though he usually eat seven or eight large peaches of a morning before breakfast began, and treated them with proportionate attention after dinner again, yet I have heard him protest that he never had quite as much as he wished of wall fruit, except once in his life, and that was when we were all together at Ombersley, the seat of my Lord Sandys.

Such a recital makes it easier to appreciate why the Streatham circle were content with biscuits and toast and water when supper time came round!

Many less famous men were equally devoted to the pleasures of the table. Parson Woodforde rarely entered up the events of the day without adding a critical account of his meals, whether he was entertaining guests at home or dining abroad. We read of a fine pike roasted for dinner, 'with a Pudding in his Belly', on which he makes the appreciative comment, 'and very good it was indeed'. Another dinner consisted of a leg of mutton with caper sauce, a pig's face, a neck of pork roasted with gooseberries, and a plum pudding. Mutton appeared frequently; thus on another occasion there was a roast leg of mutton and a baked pudding for the first course, followed by a roast duck, a meat pie, eggs, and tarts, while for supper there were a brace of partridges, some cold tongue, 'Potatoes in Shells', and more tarts. Other delicacies which appeared sometimes were roast swan, which the worthy parson considered 'good eating with sweet sauce', and Parmesan cheese which produced the comment, 'which I eat very heartily and like it exceedingly'. Among the sweets in addition to tarts, orange and apple pudding, sillabubs and jelly were favourite dishes.

This impressive picture of solid comfort which eighteenth-century fare provides must be greatly modified by the reflection that it related only to one section of the people.

The great mass of the labouring poor had to be content with much simpler food. It is not easy to draw a general picture of their condition, which varied in different parts of the country according to wages and prices. Foreigners were generally impressed by the high standard of the food of the London manufacturers and labourers, and in the provinces it seems clear that the mass of the people benefited by the prosperity of the country and that the general standard of living was rising slowly until checked by the high prices caused by the American war. Though the North was still unaffected, in the southern counties pure wheat bread was displacing the old coarse varieties of barley and rye, much to the scandal of social reformers. Also, luxuries like tea and sugar were rapidly passing into common use, though in an adulterated form. During his tour of the southern counties Arthur Young asked a small farmer, 'What is the employment of the labourers' wives and children? Drinking tea he replied'; and added Young disapprovingly, 'I cannot but remark that I found the custom almost universal'. This 'growth of luxury among the poor', to quote contemporaries, met with almost universal censure, but not all the weight of social disapproval nor yet the pressure of rising prices was successful in weaning the southern labourer from his white bread or his wife from her thin and watery tea. The other chief elements in the labourers' diet were butter and cheese and, once or twice a week, meat. Circumstances differed from place to place and from family to family. Where it was possible to keep a cow on the common, or a pig, it was easier to supplement the budget and attain a more varied menu, though the south country labourer was in most places hampered by the fact that the shortage of fuel, and often the inadequacy of his cottage, made domestic cooking difficult, if not impossible, and threw him back on the resources of a public bakery. Some knowledge of prices makes it easier to attempt to reconstruct a budget. In 1771 in the course of one of his tours Young declared that the average price for bread was $1\frac{1}{4}d.$ a pound, butter was $6d.$, butcher's meat $3d.$, and cheese the same, but that these figures fluctuated according to the distance from the capital. At this time the average for rent per year was £1 8s. 2d., and for firing £1 3s. 11d. There were the expenses of clothes and other necessities also to be provided out of a wage which varied from an average of 5s. 8d. in the extreme north, where prices also were lower, to about 7s. 6d. in most parts of the country. It is obvious, therefore, that though his earnings may have been augmented by his family and by pickings from the common, if the country was not inclosed, or perquisites from the farmer who employed him, yet the labourer who could eat his fill of even the plainest and least varied food, must count himself fortunate. The manufacturer in the provinces generally found himself in rather better circumstances than the labourer, and his food was therefore more generous and varied, particularly in the article of meat.

Heavy drinking was common in all classes of society. De Saussure, when commenting on the excessive use of water in the cause of cleanliness, seemed surprised that people drank so little of it! Small beer was the usual drink of everday life, but the first half of the century was disfigured by an appalling growth in the consumption of spirits.

Apart from this dangerous growth in the use of spirits, drinking was the customary accompaniment of every ceremony. Thus, when the farmers came to pay their tithe Parson Woodforde recorded that he gave them 'Wine, Punch and Ale as much as they pleased', adding, 'they drank of wine 6 Bottles, of Rum 1 gallon and a half, and I know not what ale', after which comes the not surprising statement, 'we had many droll songs from some of them'. Le Blanc criticized adversely the custom which made it correct etiquette for the visiting servant to be made as drunk as his master, just, he added pathetically, when he was most needed. Moritz found that it was considered discourteous, even in the humblest inn, not to drink to the health of the assembled company, and everywhere the ceremony of toasting offered a polite excuse for tippling. In Thomas Turner's diary, written in 1754, there are a series of good resolutions which, as subsequent entries showed, were too often broken. The writer was a small shopkeeper of a religious turn of mind, very conscious of his own failings, and the standard which he set himself provides an interesting sidelight as to what was considered harmless and moderate drinking. 'If I am at home, or in company abroad, I will never drink more than four glasses of strong beer: one to toast the King's health, the second to the Royal Family, the third to all friends, and the fourth to the pleasure of the company. If there is either wine or punch, never upon any terms of perswasion to drink more than eight glasses, each glass to hold no more than half a quarter of a pint.' A few entries will show how the prevailing vice proved too much for this programme of retrenchment and reform. Once he came home, 'I may say, quite sober, considering the house we was at', but he had to confess to having 'I believe, contracted a slight impediment in my speech, occasioned by the fumes of the liquor operating too furiously on my brain'. Another evening was even more disastrous, for he was forced to admit, 'after supper our behaviour was far from that of serious harmless mirth, it was downright obstreperious, mixed with a great deal of folly and stupidity. Our diversion was dancing or jumping about, without a violin or any musick, singing of foolish healths, and drinking all the time as fast as it could well be poured down; and the parson of the parish was one among the mixed multitude. About three o'clock,' he observed piously, 'finding myself to have had as much liquor as would do me good, I slipt away unobserved.' Mrs. Turner remained at the rowdy party and only returned home, escorted by a servant, at ten minutes past five! Accounts of such drinking bouts could easily be multiplied. Horace Walpole, writing in 1741, described how after a ball 'Lincoln, Lord Holderness, Lord Robert Sutton, young Churchill, and a dozen more, grew jolly, stayed till seven in the morning and drank thirty-two bottles', while, after the end of another party, 'the rest of the company finish'd the entertainment with pelting the mob in Pall Mall with bottles and glasses'. Even those who did not get drunk themselves showed a kindly tolerance to those who did, as when in 1781 Parson Woodforde wrote in his diary: 'Poor John Bowles died this morning about 10 o'clock, hope he is departed out of this Life for a better one. Poor man, he killed himself by drinking so much spirits.'

With so much eating and drinking there is little wonder that the head of the house was frequently called upon to provide remedies for physical ills and that the women spent some portion of their time concocting simples and draughts in their still-rooms and kitchens. Just as Parson Woodforde noted the things he ate and drank, so he also recorded the aches and pains of his household and the treatment that was followed. Over-eating was surely the cause of the trouble when he wrote, 'Nancy and myself being rather out of spirits and ill last night, took a dose of Rhubarb each last night and this morning we were both brave'. It was a remedy they frequently followed and it rarely failed to have the desired effect of making them both 'brave' next morning. Other remedies were more drastic, for when the small servant-lad Jack had a touch of the ague this was the course of procedure: 'I gave him a dram of gin at the beginning of the fit and pushed him headlong into one of my Ponds and ordered him to bed immediately and he was better after it and had nothing of the cold fit after but was very hot.' He was sufficiently enlightened in 1776 to have his servants inoculated for small-pox, and observed with satisfaction that they 'took their salts very well this morning and drank well of Water Gruel', and that later they had for dinner 'Norfolk dumplings and Vinegar Sauce and Potatoes also, and they eat very hearty'. Despite the fertility of his ideas in prescribing remedies, no apparent harm was done either to himself, his niece, or his 'folk'.

When the cures were of no avail and death followed, then the mourners both honoured the dead and comforted their grief by a lavish funeral display so that Le Blanc observed that 'the care the English take of all particulars of their burial, would make one believe, that they find more pleasure in dying than living'. Hatchments were hung on the front of the house and cards of invitation, adorned with all the trappings of grief, skulls, skeletons, coffins, and gravestones, were issued by the undertakers. Women, known as 'Wakers', sat up with the dead, and emblems of mourning were freely distributed to friends and servants. In memory of the departed, mourners were presented with mourning rings, some of which were of a considerable value. The pall-bearers were given black silk hatbands and black gloves and servants in attendance received the same. The parson who performed the service was also presented with a hat-band and gloves in addition to his fee, which varied with the rank of the corpse and the generosity of the relatives. The following account of a funeral in 1782 comes from the Parson's diary: 'Before we went to the Church there was Chocolate and Toast and Cake with red Wine and white. At half past 11 o'clock we went to Church with the Corpse in the following Procession. The Corpse first in a Hearse and a Pair of Horses, then followed six Chaises . . . The Underbearers and Servants all in Hatbands black closed the Procession and a fine handsome appearance the whole Procession made.' When the service was over the party returned to the house, where they were once again regaled with cake and dried toast, chocolate, and wine, so that the rector observed: 'It was as decent, neat, handsome Funeral as I ever saw.' It was a very poor and mean funeral which was not followed by two or three coaches, as among the smaller tradesmen and shopkeepers class the rest of the family were prepared to make considerable sacrifices for this end. Even among the labouring poor burial clubs were common, and at pauper funerals, at least in the rural parishes, it was customary to toll the bell and provide beer for the bearers of the coffin.

Weddings were normally managed with much less ceremony. In part this was due to the fact that until the passing of Hardwicke's Marriage Act in 1753 the regulations governing their solemnization were very lax. But even after the necessity for the banns to be published and the marriage to take place in church, owing to fashionable female delicacy a public marriage was regarded as an ordeal to be avoided by a well brought up young lady and licences for the old-fashioned private weddings were frequently obtained. Thus, writing in 1759, Horace Walpole described his niece's wedding, declaring: 'It was as sensible a wedding as ever was. There was neither form nor indecency, both which generally meet on such occasions. They were married at my brother's in Pall Mall, just before dinner, by Mr. Keppel; the company my brother, Mrs. Keppel, Lady Elizabeth Keppel, Lady Betty de Waldegrave and I; the Earl and new Countess got into their post chaise at eight o'clock, and went to Navestock alone, where they stay till Saturday night.' Honeymoons, in the modern sense, were not yet an accepted convention; hence the remark that the pair departed that night alone, for sometimes it happened that the newly married couple were accompanied by a relation or a friend. If the wedding was followed by a ball the bride and bridegroom were supposed to open it, and frequently the newly married pair either remained at home, or went immediately to the bridegroom's house, or even paid a short visit to friends. The first convenient Sunday after her marriage the bride made her public appearance at church, an occasion of social importance rivalling that of the wedding.

By the middle of the century the practice of public weddings was gaining ground, to the horror of persons of conservative tastes who felt that female delicacy was being sadly outraged. One such public wedding is described in Fanny Burney's early Diary.

The walk that leads up to the church was crowded almost incredibly, a prodigious mob indeed! I'm sure I trembled for the bride. Oh what a *gauntlet* for any woman of delicacy to run! Mr. Bagg handed the bride and her company out of their coach, and then Mr. Case took her hand and led her to the church door and the bridegroom follow'd handing Mrs. Case. . . . I declare my heart ach'd to think how terrible the poor Bride's feelings must be to walk by such crowds, the occasion in itself so awful. How little does it need the addition of that frightful mob! . . . Well of all things in the world I don't suppose anything can be so dreadful as a public wedding——my stars, [she added eloquently] I should never be able to support it.

This was in 1768, and the conversation which took place in the Burney household afterwards showed that her feelings were generally shared.[1]

Foreigners considered the English a melancholy race, and Lord Chesterfield impressed it upon his son that to laugh was an excess unworthy of a gentleman. Yet, despite this depressing picture the amusements of the time were many and various. Gambling was common to all places and classes, so that Le Blanc observed, 'that there is not a more common saying in the English tongue than "ten to one such a thing is true"'. Sometimes it was the sheer love of gambling that led to the making of bets of every kind, while almost every sport and pastime of the age depended on it for additional excitement, so that it runs like a red thread through eighteenth-century life. Games of chance, such as hazard, were inordinately popular and drew the young bloods of the Town to the clubs like moths round a candle. Nor was it only the young men who were affected; the Duke of Cumberland was a great gambler, and the women were as bad as the men. In 1761 Horace Walpole wrote, 'In less than two hours t'other night, the Duke of Cumberland lost four hundred and fifty pounds at Loo, Miss Pelham won three hundred, and I, the rest'. Beside the losses of Charles Fox and his

[1] Cf. *infra*, pp. 404–5.

friends such sums would have appeared small. In 1770 Walpole wrote in disgust that the gaming was 'worthy the decline of our Empire, or Commonwealth, which you please. The young men of the age lose five, ten, fifteen thousand pounds in an evening' at White's. 'Lord Stavordale, not one and twenty, lost eleven thousand there, last Tuesday, but recovered it by one great hand at hazard: he swore a great oath—Now, if I had been playing *deep*, I might have won millions.' Making extravagant and often absurd wagers was nearly as popular as card-playing, as the betting book in which they were recorded at White's still testifies. Even the Government exploited the universal craze for gambling by raising state lotteries, which were patronized by all classes of society. Though circumstances differed widely, each class gambled to the limit of its income and beyond, and on cards, on horses, on cocks, on dogs, the lord and the labourer alike staked more than they could afford to lose.

The home and centre of social pleasure was found in London. Here, for the learned, literary and intellectual circles flourished and the pleasures of conversation were most freely enjoyed. Here were the shops where dandified mercers' assistants tempted the ladies with their silks or explained the latest details of the mode. Here too were the public spectacles to be enjoyed and all the amusements offered by Ranelagh, Vauxhall, and such fashionable places of assembly. In addition there were private parties and balls, while for the men, if such entertainment began to pall, there were the coffee-houses, where they could retire from the tittle-tattle of the tea-table, and the clubs, full of members equally ready to gamble and drink. It was little wonder, then, that the polite world considered an occasional visit to London not only its chief amusement but even a prime necessity. Consequently those who could afford it came up for varying periods, staying either in their own town houses or, in the majority of cases, occupying the 'genteel lodgings', which, since visits were of some duration, took the place of the modern hotel. After London the inland spas and the rapidly expanding watering-places were favourite centres of social life, each of which developed its own characteristics.

Yet large as London and Bath loom in the literature of the time the majority of people had to be content with such social amenities as the nearest county town could provide.

That the society of such places was cramped, narrow, and provincial is extremely probable. Fanny Burney had nothing but hard words for the average country town when in 1768 she wrote: 'A City or a village are the only places which I think can be comfortable, for a County Town, I think has all the bad qualities without one of the good ones, of both.' Yet others who were less exacting found pleasure enough in the gaieties of the nearest considerable town. By the second half of the century most of these had a theatre or hall of some kind where public performances could be given, and here for a few weeks every year would come a company of strolling players such as the troop which Dr. Johnson found in Lichfield when he visited it in 1776. On such occasions people came in from the neighbouring villages, as when Parson Woodforde took Sister Clark, Nancy, and Sam to the play at Norwich. 'The Play was Hamlet and the Entertainment the Camp.' 'The Play', he pronounced, 'was very well but the other like a Puppet Show, fit only for children.' Norwich also boasted of public gardens where on another occasion the Parson heard a 'sad Concert' and then revived his drooping spirits with a display of fireworks, which, he added, were 'very good and worth the money'. These gardens were patronized by a very mixed collection of people, and he expressed mild disapproval at the 'prodigious' number of common girls arrayed in their finery.

Dancing was a favourite amusement, and on varied pretexts, such as the local horse-races or the celebration of a British victory, balls were organized at the principal inn. In 1767 the town of Ansford, copying the fashion set by London, arranged a Masquerade Ball, which, though it might have failed to satisfy the more exacting taste of the capital, could nevertheless be described as 'very elegant'. The music was provided by four violins, a base viol, a taber and pipe, a hautboy, and a French horn.[1] Another less ambitious affair, held at the same inn, was deemed worthy of being considered a 'very genteel Hop'. Balls, both public and private, followed the fashions set by London and Bath and were conducted with much formality. They were opened by a minuet, in which the dancers had an opportunity of showing the elegance of their breeding, for to dance with dignity and grace

[1] For further particulars about Masquerades, see *infra*, pp. 402–4.

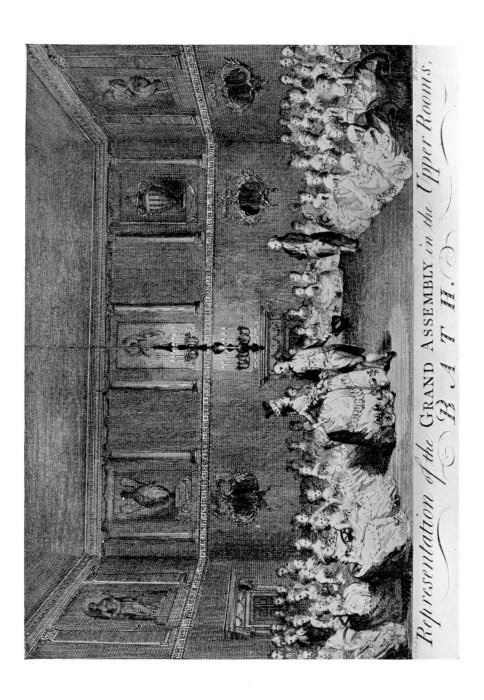

Representation of the GRAND ASSEMBLY *in the* Upper Rooms, BATH.

was part of every polite education. Then came country dances, which enjoyed a high degree of popularity and offered considerable variety as the top couple in turn 'called the dance', and could therefore within limits select which they pleased. The usage as to partners varied; the normal custom was for the same couple to dance the entire evening together, but in some places, particularly on the more friendly and informal occasions, partners were changed every two dances. To leave a dance in the middle, or, having gone down the dance, to retire without going up it again, was to be guilty of bad manners to the whole company and to show oneself a person of very inferior breeding; a rule which, since country dances were strenuous affairs, Miss Burney found hard to bear. The hour of supper varied from twelve to two and sometimes the company indulged in a little music before the dancing was resumed. Then while waiting for their carriages in the early morning, they were generally refreshed with tea and coffee. Etiquette further demanded that next morning the gentleman should call to inquire after his partner's health, or at the very least send his servant.

Many of the most popular amusements were inseparably connected with the activities of country life, but for the less energetic members of the community, or when the weather made out-door sport impossible, there were other methods of passing the time, neither so exacting nor so exhausting. The vogue for novels and the increase in newspapers and periodicals showed that reading was not neglected; in the country the local carrier brought the books of the day and the papers from the nearest town, while country letter-writers eagerly inquired as to the latest literary news or ordered recent pamphlets from their bookseller, as when Henry Purefoy wrote for 'The Disadvantages of the Married State or the Artifices & foibles of the fair Sex such as in Musick Dancing Dresse Equipage Desire of Ofspring &c considered & the Single Life plainly proved preferable to that of Marriage'. Women employed much of their time about the house or in doing fine needlework, an activity which met with Dr. Johnson's high approval. But the perusal of any eighteenth-century diary carries the conviction that visiting and gossip were the favourite occupations, despite the fact that the country roads were so bad. For example, Mrs. Purefoy could visit her more distant relations only when the moon was full; and entries like the following were a commonplace:

We dined at Mrs. Churchill's; coming from thence, about six o'clock, from a causeway too narrow, in Mrs. Churchill's meadow, called their private road, the coach was overturned into a wet ditch; the company, particularly the gentlemen, were very wet, and if there had been a foot more of water, they must all have been suffocated. We were obliged to return to the house and played at cards till daylight.

When it was impossible to visit, amusement had to be contrived at home, and, where numbers permitted it, private theatricals were a favourite diversion. But for domestic, as well as social, occasions, cards were the invariable and invaluable stand-by. Brag, picquet, quadrille, basset, loo, commerce, and wisk were all played, though each had its special vogue. Thus Lady Mary Montagu wrote in 1749: 'Your new fashioned game of brag was the genteel amusement when I was a girl; crimp succeeded to that, and basset and hazard employed the town when I left it to go to Constantinople. At my return, I found them all at commerce, which gave place to quadrille, and that to whist; but the rage of play has been ever the same, and will be so among the idle of both sexes.' Wisk, or whist, swept the town about 1742 so that Horace Walpole, who called it a universal opium, wrote in December: 'I have not yet learnt to play, but find I wait in vain for its being left off.' In the latter part of the century commerce was still being played by the fashionable world, as it afforded opportunities for high stakes, there being on occasion as much as 1,000 guineas in the pool, the lowest hand giving 10 guineas each deal, while at hazard, chief of gambling games, fortunes were won and lost at a single sitting. In the country both quadrille and loo remained popular games for winter evenings, and though the element of gambling was rarely absent (for Dr. Johnson, in gravely stating that he and his friends never played for money at Oxford,[1] was a notable exception), yet the stakes could be, and were, adapted to slender purses. When Parson Woodforde and Nancy played, it was seldom that more than sixpence changed hands and commerce was played with a pool of a shilling apiece. In addition to cards other

---

[1] Johnson's game at Oxford was draughts. He never learnt any card game, which in later life he said he regretted. Boswell's favourite game was Brag.

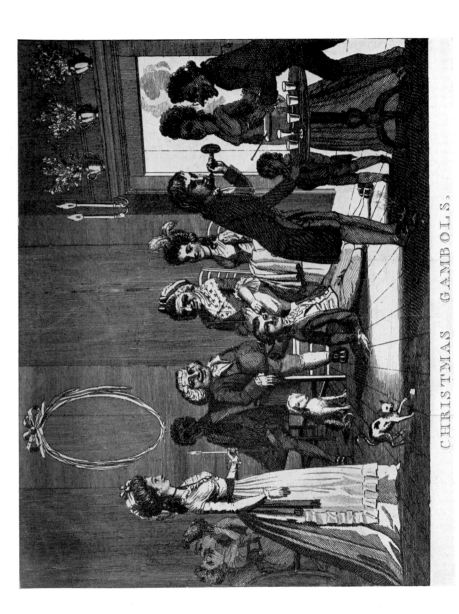

CHRISTMAS GAMBOLS.

From the Wit's Magazine, *1784*

indoor games such as draughts and billiards were also popular.

There was, however, another side to this picture of an amusement-loving, gambling people. Sunday was strictly kept by many sections of the community. Even his landlady's small son reproved Moritz for singing on the Sabbath, and de Saussure reported that card playing was forbidden, though he added that the prohibition was not observed in the highest circles. Among those who could afford to indulge themselves not all did so; no description of eighteenth-century social life would be complete without some reference to the sober lives led both by members of the older Dissenting bodies and by the new followers of Wesley. Sunday was observed with fanatical strictness. Thomas Wright Hill, when recalling the memories of his youth, describes the day as starting with breakfast taken at eight in a darkened room, for the shutters were only opened at the top, followed by extempore prayer. Nine o'clock found the children with their father at the meeting-house, where service lasted until eleven. On the return his father would read aloud to the family from Henry's *Expositions*, a ponderous book in six volumes, and, cushions having been dealt out to mitigate the hardness of the floor, which was uncarpeted, more prayers followed. Meat was seldom eaten on Sunday and then always cold in order to avoid a breach of the commandments, so that the dinner 'rarely consisted of anything more or less than a boiled pudding; sometimes made savoury with suet, sometimes with dried currants; sometimes of small bread boiled whole, and rendered palatable by a compound sauce'. A second service at one o'clock was attended by the mistress and maid also, and then came the one brief relaxation of the day when his father smoked his pipe and told the children scripture stories. When they were older they were allowed to employ this respite in reading the Apocrypha. From five to six was occupied by a third service, slightly enlivened by hymns, after which the children retired to their mother's room to repeat the catechism and hymns, an exercise followed by an exhortation from her on moral behaviour. Then, at last, came a much desired and deserved piece of plum cake, at once a reward for past good conduct and a bribe for its continuance, while his father read another sermon, which was followed by a long extempore prayer.

'When the prayer of Sunday night was concluded,' wrote Hill in later days, 'my feelings I was used to compare with those of Christian when his burden was miraculously unstrapped and fell from his back. This conclusion would occur about nine o'clock. The family then took a cheerful supper, and thoughts of religion were suspended for a time.' The example of such a family, which was typical of many of the well-to-do tradesmen in the smaller towns, adds yet another strand to the variety of eighteenth-century life, a strand moreover which owing to its sombre colour is apt to be unnoticed among the brighter threads, but yet strengthened the whole fabric of the national life.

Such were the manners and amusements of Dr. Johnson's England—masquerades and theatres, visiting and gossip, betting and cards, weddings and funerals, and mighty eating and drinking. There is in the picture none of the drabness of monotony. The scene shifts rapidly from the discussions of literary circles to the ball and the race-course, from the sober-minded Wesleyan to the foul-mouthed hunting squire. It was a period in which refinement of manner was only too often accompanied by brutality of behaviour. In it are to be found the richness and vigour, the generosity combined with intolerance, that, mirrored in the personality of Johnson, make him so peculiarly the embodiment of his age. To picture him against the background of any other century is unthinkable; he belongs inevitably and completely to the eighteenth.

BIBLIOGRAPHY.—The main original authorities for the manners, food, and amusements of the eighteenth century are memoirs, diaries, correspondence, travels through England, fiction, and contemporary periodicals. Particularly useful for the life of the upper classes are FANNY BURNEY's *Diary and Letters*; MRS. DELANY's *Autobiography and Correspondence*; BUBB DODINGTON's *Diary*; the Diary of the first Duchess of Northumberland, extracts from which have been published as *The Diaries of a Duchess* (edited J. Greig, 1926); and the Letters of Horace Walpole, Lord Chesterfield, Lady Mary Wortley Montagu, and Lady Sarah Lennox (edited by the Countess of Ilchester and Lord Stavordale, 2 vols., 1902). Rural society is well illustrated by *The Diary of a Country Parson* (edited by J. Beresford, 1926–30), by COLE's *Blecheley Diary* (edited by F. G. Stokes, 1932), and by *The Purefoy Letters 1735–81* (edited by G. Eland, 1931). A picture of the social background of the tradesman can be found in THOMAS TURNER's *Diary* (edited by F. M. Turner, 1925), which, though brief and chiefly concerned with his spiritual progress, has some interesting details, and in the *Remains of . . . Thomas Wright Hill*. That of the artisan is supplied by WILLIAM HUTTON's *Autobiography*, and that of the footman by JOHN MACDONALD's *Travels* (edited by J. Beresford, 1927).

Accounts of travels through England are often illuminating. Important among these are C. DE SAUSSURE's *A Foreign View of England in the reigns of George I & II* (1902); LE BLANC's *Letters on the English and French Nations* (Eng. trans., 2 vols., 1747); VOLTAIRE's *Letters concerning the English Nation*; KALM's *Visit to England* (1748, Eng. trans., 1892), which, though his main interest was in the practical details of agriculture, devotes considerable space to London; P. J. GROSLEY, *A Tour to London, or New Observations on the English* (1772, trans. T. Nugent); and C. MORITZ, *Travels through various parts of England in 1782* (in vol. ii of Pinkerton's *Collections of . . . Voyages and Travels 1808–14*; reprinted, edited by P. E. Matheson, in the Oxford Miscellany series, 1924); ARTHUR YOUNG's *Tour through the Southern Counties* (1768), *Tour throught he North of England* (1770); and *The Farmer's Tour through the East of England* (1771) are also useful for details of wages and prices.

These authorities should be supplemented by the novels of FIELDING, SMOLLET, BURNEY, and GOLDSMITH, and by contemporary periodicals, such as *The Gentleman's Magazine*. The *Newgate Calendar* often contains vivid details of low life. Useful modern accounts are to be found in LECKY's *History of England*, chapters v and xxi, *Social England* (edited by H. D. Trail), W. C. SYDNEY's *England and the English in the Eighteenth Century*, and A. S. TURBERVILLE's *English Men and Manners in the Eighteenth Century*.

XIII

SPORTS AND GAMES

By E. D. CUMING

Triflers may make or find any thing a trifle, but since it is the great character-istick of a wise man to see events in their causes, to obviate consequences, and ascertain contingencies, your Lordship will think nothing a trifle by which the mind is inured to caution, foresight, and circumspection.—*Dedication to* PAYNE'S *Game of Draughts* (1756).

I have now learned (said he), by hunting, to perceive, that it is no diversion at all, nor ever takes a man out of himself for a moment . . . It is very strange, and very melancholy, that the paucity of human pleasures should persuade us ever to call hunting one of them. He was however proud to be amongst the sportsmen; and I think no praise ever went so close to his heart, as when Mr. Hamilton called out one day upon Brighthelmstone Downs, Why Johnson rides as well, for ought I see, as the most illiterate fellow in England.—MRS. PIOZZI, *Anecdotes.*

A fighting cock has a nobleness of resolution.—*Life of Johnson* (1 April 1775).

RACING in Johnson's day was a sport very different from that we know; meetings were held on any open ground or common to which every one had access; the owners of horses entered for a race provided the money to make the prize, which usually amounted to 50 guineas; a meeting consisted of a single race which was run in heats in order to spin out the proceedings, and perhaps a match or two arranged between individual owners.[1] The system of heats, now forgotten, in practice meant that the race was run twice, thrice, or even four times over, the winner being the horse that won most heats. In order to weed out those horses which were hope-lessly beaten the 'Distance Post' was placed 240 yards from the winning post, and any horse which had not passed the former when the winner reached the latter was 'distanced', and could not start in subsequent heats. As races might be of any length up to four miles, three heats meant running twelve miles at short intervals on the same day; in regard to this, however, it is to be remembered that horses in pre-railway times were bred less for speed than staying power, and efforts that would be impossible to a modern thorough-bred were well within the compass of the eighteenth-century horse. The most important races then were the Royal

[1] De Rochefoucauld gives an admirable account of English sport, and especially of horse-racing. See *A Frenchman in England, 1784*, pp. 52–76.

A RACECOURSE

Plates instituted by William III and increased in number by his successors; these, worth 100 guineas each, were established with the object of encouraging horses of a serviceable stamp as then understood, i.e. able to carry weight over a long distance. In 1751, to take a representative year, fourteen of these Plates were given in England; ten for 6-year-old horses carrying 12 stone, the race to be four miles, three heats; one Plate for 5-year-olds, weight 10 stone, 2-mile heats; two for 5-year-old mares, weight 10 stone, a single 4-mile heat; and the other for 4-year-olds, weight 9 stone, 2½-mile heats. These conditions were altered in 1773, one heat being substituted for three; but there seems always to have been a certain latitude in the matter of both distances and weight. Races for hunters had been run at Ascot as early as 1722, but these were not officially recognized until 1762, when 'Qualifications for a Hunter' were prescribed. Selling stakes had brief vogue during our period; in these the winning horse might be claimed by any one who chose to pay for it a sum equal to that of the stake won: thus, if a horse won a £50 purse the owner was bound to part with it if required for £50. Such races do not appear to have been popular; they soon went out of fashion, to be revived in another form in the next century. The Royal Plates survived until 1886, though they had long ceased to fulfil their purpose and their importance had been eclipsed by the numerous stakes of far greater value made possible by gate-money.

The sport was carried on in very slipshod fashion; horses were untrained; courses were ill-kept; jockeys were incompetent;[1] what rules existed were enforced with laxity; and the crowd was turbulent. That the standard of riding was low is no matter for surprise when crossing and jostling were permissible 'if no agreement to the contrary'; and overmuch weight need not be attached to the rule providing for such a contingency as a rider falling from his horse, when he might be knocked out of his saddle by a rival. In such case any bystander might catch and mount the horse thus left riderless and finish the race. It may be remarked that we have a similar rule in modern steeplechasing.

[1] English jockeys were more competent than French jockeys, however. See, for example, the details of a horse-race in France, witnessed by Johnson and Mrs. Thrale, which they both record. See *Johnsonian Miscellanies* (ed. G. B. Hill, 2 vols., 1897), vol. ii, p. 289; *The French Journals of Mrs. Thrale and Dr. Johnson* (ed. Tyson and Guppy, 1932), p. 98.

An eighteenth-century race in which crossing and jostling were allowed can be pictured: the heat started by beat of drum, ensued what was less a contest of speed than a running fight among the jockeys who, 'whip and kick, and attempt to unhorse each other, by entwining their legs! I well remember a fellow . . . who was accustomed to boast of the execution he had formerly done with the but end of his whip, and of the eyes and teeth he had beat out!'[1]

Another source of information supplies the scene at a finish. Thus George Morland, the famous painter, wrote to his friend Philip Dawe in 1785: premising that he had 'commenced new business of jockey to the races', he proceeds to tell how, having lost the first heat, 'a mob of horsemen then gathered round, telling me I could not ride, which is always the way if you lose the heat; they began at last to use their whips'.[2]

Nor was the jockey better used if he won. Morland adds: 'At Margate races I was very near being killed. I won the heat so completely that the other horses were half a mile behind, upon which near 400 sailors, smugglers, fishermen, &c., set upon me with sticks, stones, waggoner's whips, fists, &c., and one man . . . took me by the thigh and pulled me off the horse.'[2]

About the year 1792, crossing and jostling, always forbidden in the Royal Plates, were barred *failing* agreement to the contrary, thus reversing the old rule; but a very great deal remained to be done when Lord George Bentinck took in hand the gigantic task of purifying the Turf in the eighteen-thirties and forties.

The Thoroughbred at this time averaged only 14 hands 1 inch in height, and of course had in it much of the Eastern blood derived from imported sires. Thoroughbreds were not numerous; in 1752 sixty such stallions stood for service in all England; anything on four legs might be entered and flogged over a course. If riders maltreated their rivals they maltreated their unfortunate mounts as freely; there is in the *Gentleman's Magazine* of 1758 a protest against the excessive misuse of whip and spur in race-riding; and fifty years later Lawrence, in the work before quoted, declaimed against the brutality of riders.

---

[1] John Lawrence, *History and Delineation of the Horse* (1809), p. 249.
[2] Sir Walter Gilbey, 1st Bt., and E. D. Cuming, *George Morland, His Life and Works* (1907), pp. 46, 47.

The Legislature, sensible of the benefit racing properly conducted would confer upon the then vital industry of horse-breeding, sought to put down meetings of low class by an Act of 1740 (13 Geo. II, c. 19). This prescribed the weights to be carried by horses of from 13 to 15 hands (the extremes), and forbade prizes of less than £50 at any meeting save those at Newmarket and Black Hambleton, endowed races being also excepted; these measures aimed at the exclusion of 'small and weak horses'. Incidentally the Act glanced at the misconduct of the crowd: with a frankness incompatible with a wide franchise qualification it declared its anxiety to remove 'all temptation from the lower class of people who constantly attend these races to the great loss of time and labour, and whose behaviour still calls for stricter regulation to curb their licentiousness and correct their manners'. In which praiseworthy aim, as Morland shows, it achieved small success. This law, in so far as it dealt with weights to be carried, was repealed in 1745.

With all its defects and shortcomings this was an epoch-making period on the Turf: it saw the advent of the great sires who laid the foundations of the modern thoroughbred —Matchem, foaled 1746; Herod, 1758; Eclipse, 1764; High-flyer, 1774, among others. Jockeys worthy of the name appeared—John Singleton, Samuel Chifney, and, in 1783, Frank Buckle, to mention the best.

Toward the end of our period the classic races were established—the St. Leger in 1776, the Oaks in 1779, and the Derby in 1780. The Jockey Club was founded about 1750, according to Mr. Robert Black,[1] and three years later was 'in activity' at Newmarket; though those activities did not embrace the sorely needed control of racing until a later day. The government of the Club seems to have become complete twenty or twenty-five years afterwards; the immediate object of the founders was to secure at Newmarket a place of their own immune from the intrusion of ruffians and black-legs. The rule of the Club may be dated from about 1773, the year in which Mr. James Weatherby was appointed Keeper of The Match-Book, and publication of his *Racing Calendar* began in succession to the less complete calendars compiled by Heber, Pond, and others since the early years of the century. No provision was made for the convenience of the

[1] *The Jockey Club and Its Founders* (1891), p. 10.

general public, and it is difficult to determine the date of erection of the first Stand for spectators willing to pay for such accommodation. The earliest proof of the existence of one known to me occurs in the title of a picture by Peter Tilleman: his 'View of a Horse Match on the Long Course from The Starting Post to the Stand' was painted in 1728.

HUNTING. The stag had lost pride of place in the eighteenth century; the decline of stag-hunting seems to be reflected in the introduction of that travesty of the real thing, carted deer hunting, about the year 1728. 'Hunting' at this time meant essentially the chase of the hare: a sport within the reach of all, hares being numerous—in some districts too numerous to please the farmer—and packs of harriers being maintained by country gentlemen all over the country; or opportunities of sport might be afforded by 'trencher-fed' packs which consist of hounds, one, a couple or more, kept by farmers, and brought together on appointed days.

The merits of fox-hunting were realized in the north of England more than a hundred years before they were appreciated in the south; but by this time a few packs—the Old Charlton in Sussex and Mr. Fownes's in Dorsetshire—were leading the way, stooping to fox, and fox only. Broadly speaking, the change from hare to fox came about by degrees; packs which had hunted hare were entered to fox and hunted either indifferently, renouncing chase of the former altogether as time passed. There was jealousy between hare-hunter and fox-hunter: thus Mr. John Gardiner in 1750: 'Twenty in the field after a Hare, my Lord, find more Delight and sincere Enjoyment, than *one* in twenty in a Fox Chace. . . . but for the *name* of Fox-hunting, a Man might as well mount at his Stable-Door, and determine to gallop twenty miles on End into another County.'[1]

Thirty years later appeared Beckford's classic, and perhaps we discern the retort of the fox-hunter in the author's remark: 'If I could have persuaded myself to ride on the turnpike road to the three-mile stone and back again, I should have thought I had had no need of a pack of harriers.'[2]

Though the superiority of fox-hunting had become ap-

---

[1] John S. Gardiner, *The Art and the Pleasures of Hare Hunting* (1750), p. 2.
[2] Peter Beckford, *Thoughts on Hunting* (1781), Letter x.

BRUSHING INTO COVER

From an engraving after the painting by James Seymour (1702–52)

parent to those who preferred a gallop in the wake of
hounds to watching harriers work out the devious line of a
hare,[1] the number of harrier packs greatly exceeded that of
foxhounds, and continued to do so until the nineteenth
century was far advanced. A Table of Hunts in the *New
Sporting Magazine* of 1835–6 shows 138 of the former to 101
of the latter. The change from hare to fox was slow; this
was due, partly at least, to scarcity of foxes; we have
abundant proof of the shortage in the existence of 'Fox-
courts' wherein 'bagmen' were kept, and in the extensive
importations from the Continent.

The foxhound was lacking in some respects; his nose had
not acquired the fine discrimination careful breeding subsequently developed, and he was unable to distinguish
between the scent of the hunted fox and that of another
which might get up. It was Beckford who said that when
hounds could tell the difference between one fox and another
the sport 'would then be perfect'.

Neither horse nor hound was as fast as its modern descen-
dant: Nimrod (Chas. Jas. Apperley) writes of the half-bred
nag of the eighteenth century as a 'delightful animal to ride',
and capable, at the pace he was required to go, of living with
hounds for some hours, taking his fences well and safely to
the last.[2] As a matter of fact the eighteenth-century hunter,
in the south of England at all events, was not required to do
much jumping; fences of all kinds were far fewer in those days
than they became after the Inclosure Acts of George III,
and the horse was not asked to jump all the fences that
came in his way; the average follower of hounds had not a
firm seat in the saddle across country, and in the exercise of
a wise discretion his habit was to dismount when he came to
a jump of which he did not like the look and lead his mount
over. Hence a run took much less out of the horse; William
Somerville, the poet, used to pull out his favourite Old Ball
three times a week. Thrice a fortnight makes a hunter's
work nowadays.

Hounds being slow it was necessary to take the quarry at
a disadvantage; hence the system of starting at dawn to find

---

[1] Ladies sometimes rode to hounds. It will be remembered that the whole
of the Vicar of Wakefield's family 'on fine days rode a-hunting', and that
Sophia Western damaged her nose as the result of a fall from her horse.
[2] *The Chase, The Road and The Turf* (Sir Herbert Maxwell's ed., 1898), p. 10.

a fox before he had digested his night's meal and was in fair running trim.

The career of Mr. Hugo Meynell, who succeeded Mr. Thos. Boothby as Master of the Quorn in 1753, and held office till 1800, of itself stamps this period as noteworthy. Such were the services rendered by him to the sport that the 'Meynellian Science' and 'Fox-hunting' are interchangeable terms.

OTTER-HUNTING. Somerville's poem (1735), less familiar than the oft-quoted lines on fox-hunting, is the best account we have of this sport in his day—if it may be called 'sport' at all, when the unlucky beast was pursued with hounds, nets, and spears in such wise that his chance of escape was slender. In parts of the country rewards were paid for the destruction of otters as inimical to fish life; so perhaps we may regard eighteenth-century otter-hunting as a congenial method of decimating a pest.

COURSING was forbidden to those who did not possess the property qualifications laid down in the Act of 1671 (22–3 Car. II, c. 2, s. 5), but the law was very generally ignored. William Taplin[1] affirms that thousands of dogs were kept by gipsies, labourers and mendicants, whereby hares were persecuted; and we need not doubt that farmers paid little attention to the prohibition. Public coursing meetings were held under the Duke of Norfolk's Rules which dated back to the time of Elizabeth; and at these, except in Berkshire, only matches were run. The modern system came into vogue in that county about 1750, and we find it described as a 'growing diversion' in 1776. After the establishment of the first Coursing Clubs—the Swaffham, Norfolk, in 1776; the Ashdown Park, Berkshire, in 1780; and the Malton, Yorkshire, in 1781—the modern system made progress. Those three, with Lancashire and Hertfordshire, were great coursing counties. In some counties the sport was hardly known.

The fourth Earl of Orford,[2] founder of the Swaffham Club, is held the 'father' of English coursing.

SHOOTING. All the old statutes for the protection of game from the days of James I were still in force; under these only the possessor of specified property qualifications might take or kill deer, hares, pheasants, partridges, and rabbits; in the current phrase such were 'within the Game Act'. By this

---

[1] *Observations on the Present State of The Game in England* (1772), pp. 29–30.
[2] George Walpole, third earl of the second creation.

Ginger Red

Birchin Yellow

FIGHTING COCKS
From engravings in the Sporting Magazine, *1792*

CZARINA and MARIA.

COURSING
From the engraving by J. Scott after the painting by S. Gilpin

time the gun had to a very great extent usurped the place of the hawk, firearms having undergone improvements which made for convenience. The old match-lock, with barrel 5 feet or 5½ feet long, had been superseded by the flintlock, with a 3½ foot barrel; the mountings preferably of brass to obviate rust. These were changes for the better, but the gun was by no means perfect, regarded even by contemporary standards; it was less reliable than any one with regard for the integrity of his fingers could wish; *vide* the advice that the front of the guard should be a stop for the grip of the left hand; so that if the barrel burst the hand was less liable to injury.[1]

With such a weapon men began to shoot birds on the wing; indeed, had taken another step forward, striving to pick a single bird from the risen covey, whereas aforetime they 'blazed into the brown'. The sportsman seems to have missed that single bird more often than he killed it, but that is only what might be expected of inexperience. 'Partridge shooting', says George Edie, 'is generally esteemed the genteelest and best sport we have'.[2] Two methods of pursuing the genteelest sport were in vogue—walking up the birds with dogs, and that of the stalking horse, for which latter some old jade past work was employed, or, in default, a dummy contrived of straw and canvas carried by the sportsman, and behind which he crept as near his game as he might.

Double-barrelled guns existed but were regarded askance. Some men, Colonel Thornton, for example, did not like them; that famous sportsman has left on record his opinion that 'all double barrels are trifles, rather knicknacks than useful.'[3] Others, like Mr. John Holt of Tottenham, who died in 1831 at the age of eighty-five, 'would have scorned to use a double-barrel', considering it unsportsmanlike.[4]

A very favourite way of taking partridges was with the net: the dog having shown the birds, the man, or men, unrolled the net and cautiously drew it over them; when, the covey thus secured, the birds could be selected at will; for 'if you shall let go the old cock and hen it will not only be to act like a *Gentleman* but a means to increase your

[1] Symonds (or Symond ?), *A Treatise of Field Diversions* (1776), p. 149.
[2] *The Art of English Shooting* (1777), p. 14.
[3] *A Sporting Tour* (Sir Herbert Maxwell's ed., 1898), p. 176.
[4] *Sporting Magazine*, vol. lxxxv, 1831, p. 201.

pastime.'[1] Pleasing combination of appeal to the nobler instincts with that to material interests! Another advantage of netting was that 'one bird netted by day is worth five shot ones';[2] which suggests that the latter were apt to be mangled. Again, netting had 'this singular pride that it can entertain ladies without the least Imputation of Indecorum';[3] which seems to draw a nice distinction between shooting a bird and wringing its neck.

Pheasant shooting, it is to be inferred, was less popular (or less genteel?) than partridge shooting; it was far more fatiguing 'owing to the bushes, briars, &c., of the woods.'[4] Beaters were not employed; a team of from two to four brace of spaniels routed up the birds, the guns, not more than three or four, following 30 or 40 yards apart. While the spaniel was used with the net and for pheasant shooting, the setter was the dog most generally employed in partridge and grouse-shooting; pointers had been introduced from Spain early in the century, but appear to have gained but slowly in favour over the 'setting dog' which had been the sportsman's companion for 200 years. Edie considered the pointer the better dog of the two, and doubtless there were those who agreed with him.

Grouse-shooting was confined to dwellers in the northern counties; we do not learn much about it from contemporary writers other than Colonel Thornton; and his experience, gained as it was in Scotland, falls without our purview. The Rev. W. B. Daniel comments briefly upon the sport which then was enjoyed only by owners of moors and their friends:

Upon the hills, where a *horse* can travel, this is a noble diversion; to be undertaken otherwise, demands constant and hard labour, for the Shooter is, during the course of the day, *ascending*, that is, if he finds a *brood* on the top of one eminence, they will sweep over the valley, until they reach the summit of another, up which the Sportsman has to climb.[5]

Wildfowl might be shot swimming, or on the wing, the latter being the better plan. Wildfowling, however, was little practised by gentlemen 'owing to the several disagreeable circumstances attending.'[6] (Our ancestors, it seems,

---

[1] Nicolas Cox, *The Gentleman's Recreation* (4th ed., 1687), Fowling, p. 45.
[2] Symonds (or Symond?), p. 144. [3] Ibid., p. 105.
[4] Edie, p. 18.
[5] *Rural Sports* (1801), vol. ii, p. 418. [6] Edie, p. 25.

SHOOTING IN 1769

From the painting by George Stubbs

were not such stout fellows as we were taught.) Pigeons,
fieldfares, and starlings might be shot sitting; of the last-
named Edie says twenty-five or even thirty might be bagged
at one shot; which, let us hope, is meant rather as a tribute
to the plenty of starlings than as an unworthy temptation
to the gunner.

The stricter school held it unsportsmanlike to shoot hares:

> Let the Courser and the Huntsman share
> Their just and proper Title to the Hare.[1]

The preference for a partridge netted *by day* will have been
noticed: this may be a covert allusion to the prevalence of
poaching at night. The London market was supplied by
poachers; an innkeeper told Taplin that he had purchased
as many as 125 hares at a time to send to London. Farmers,
who could not, by reason of deficient qualification, shoot
openly, employed the net and snare; Taplin says he never
in the season visited a farmer whose pantry did not contain
a hare or two and a few brace of birds. The writers of the
time have little to tell us about gamekeepers, and what they
do say is to their discredit; they were 'the worst of poachers,
taking one brace for their master and two for themselves';
they were 'a set of abusive rascals and a disgrace to the
family that employed them'; and their masters were blamed
for allowing them to carry guns.

ANGLING. The appliances of the angler in those days left
more to the skill of the man than does our more elaborate
tackle. The rod, usually home-made, consisted of two or
three carefully straightened and seasoned twigs spliced
together; the line was of horse-hair, preferably from the tail
of a young stallion, tapering from the rod's tip to which it
was tied, to a single hair at the hook. For bait fishing, a line
the length of the rod was recommended; for the fly, one
twice or thrice that length; and with such a tool the fisher-
man killed his trout, dace, grayling, and other small fish.
Hooks dressed on silkworm gut were approved; we find
such gut advertised as 'a new article' in 1760, though there
is mention of it in 1724. For salmon ('a gentle fish but cumbrous to take', as old Mascall feelingly observed) and pike,
a rod with wire rings and a reel to carry 30 yards of line were

[1] Abraham Markland; *Pteryplegia; or The Art of Shooting Flying* (1727),
p. 20.

used. Silk lines were known but disliked as being liable to rot; waterproofing was an invention of much later date.

Every modern form of angling was practised; also some now condemned as poaching. So with baits; there were no restrictions; the eyes and spawn of fish were held legitimate lures, as were cow's brains and pastes of strange composition, some of which were rendered more attractive by the application of oil of ivy and other unguents. The fly-fishing season lasted from April or May till September or October, and some experts allotted special flies to each month, though the wiser, or more painstaking, of the fraternity would, with his landing net catch a fly on the water and forthwith sit down and tie one like it. 'Dibbing', now known as 'Dapping', was a favourite method; trolling was confined to pike; the float and leger were in vogue for ground fishing and the trimmer was employed on lakes and meres.

Various enactments protected stews and ponds. Salmon and sea-trout were the only fish of interest to the angler for which a close season was prescribed; other freshwater fish might be taken all the year round and in any stream not on private property. Only the enthusiast fished when it was raining, if we may draw an inference from the advice to use fly during a shower 'if you are inclined to stand it'.

Cock-fighting was *the* diversion of the age, as it had been for centuries past and was to be for near a century to come. All classes indulged in it from the peer who bred his Blackreds, Duckwings, Piles, or what not, by the thousand, to the humblest villager who had his 'shakebag'. There is no more convincing proof of the universality of cocking than the number of expressions derived therefrom which have passed into current phraseology—'pit against', 'clean pair of heels', 'cut out for', 'scoot', to mention a few. County fought county, town fought town, village fought village; peer and gentleman fought among themselves, and ploughman fought cowherd. The stake or prize ranged from 1,000 guineas at one end of the scale to a fat pig at the other. Spurs, steel and silver, had been introduced about the end of the seventeenth century and quickly came into general use among well-to-do cockers; they were expensive—in 1698 the Duke of Rutland paid £3 for six pairs[1]—hence the humbler sort continued

[1] Hist. MSS. Comm., *Duke of Rutland's MSS. at Belvoir Castle*, vol. iv, p. 557.

FISHING

From The Art of Angling *by R. Brookes, 1766*

to prepare their birds for battle by sharpening the beak and natural spurs with a knife. Race meetings were great occasions for cocking; they brought together men from all the country round, thus offering an unrivalled opportunity for a main: to take an example at random, in 1751: 'At Epsom, on the 14th of May and following Days (being the Time of the Races) Mr. *Bennet senr.* fought Mr. *Howell,* shewing forty-one cocks on each Side, for six Guineas a Battle and an Hundred the Main.'

A main might consist of any odd number of cocks from seven upwards; forty-one was a very usual showing; the object being that one competitor should win a majority of the battles. There were mains of various kinds: a 'long' main lasted four days or more; a 'short' one two or three days. Then there was the 'Welsh' Main fought out on the same system as modern coursing, the winner of each battle being pitted against a fellow winner. In a 'Battle Royal' a number of cocks were pitted together and suffered to fight one another as seemed good to them. Different sorts of spurs were in use —'long heels', 2 to $2\frac{1}{2}$ inches long; 'short heels' $1\frac{1}{2}$ inches long; 'sickle', 'lance', and 'penknife' spurs; but the one most in use was the simple spur like a stout needle curved, long or short. The results of important mains were regularly published in the *Racing Calendar*, as also were particulars of forthcoming events.

The Rules and Orders for Cocking framed during the reign of Charles II were still in force, but the old method of matching birds by measurement had now given place to matching by weight; and in duly organized mains they were matched to an ounce. A graphic description of cocking is given by a French visitor to England in a letter dated February 23, 1728:

The animals used are of a particular breed; they are large but short-legged birds, their feathers are scarce, they have no crests to speak of, and are very ugly to look at. . . . The stage on which they fight is round and small. One of the cocks is released, and struts about proudly for a few seconds. He is then caught up, and his enemy appears. When the bets are made, one of the cocks is placed on either end of the stage; they are armed with silver spurs, and immediately rush at each other and fight furiously. It is surprising to see the ardour, the strength, and courage of these little animals, for they rarely give up till one of them is dead . . . the noise is terrible, and it is impossible to hear yourself speak unless you shout . . . Cocks will sometimes fight a whole hour before one or the other is victorious.[1]

With regard to that first remark: the cock 'cut out for battle' was certainly no beauty, but M. de Saussure evidently did not know that the comb and wattles had been cut off as soon as the sex of the young bird was recognized, or that the neck feathers from head to shoulders were clipped, the tail cut to the rump and the wing feathers cut 'slope-wise' to sharp points, to prepare the cock for the pit. He writes as though the lack of plumage and comb were natural.

Country folk carried on the sport with little regard for Rules and Orders; a patron of the village public-house would come in with a bag containing his cock and offer to pit it against that of any one present; a friend might take him up, fetch his own bird, and each man shook out his champion on the floor; hence the term 'shake-bag', formerly 'turn-poke'. Organized cockings often took place in the village churchyard, more particularly on church festivals. There were indoor and outdoor pits; some of the latter still exist in their original shape—an amphitheatre, seats cut in the turf rising in tiers round the central plot whereon the battle took place. Space forbids reference to the many superstitions surrounding the cockpit, but mention may be made of the rural practice of putting gamefowls' eggs in a magpie's nest to be hatched; the magpie being the special protégé of the Evil One, it was thought that chicks so hatched were the fiercer. Inconsistently enough, the cocker who swept dust from the Communion Table and sprinkled it on the pit felt assured that evil influences had been thereby dispelled and the best bird (his own, naturally) must win.

COCK-THROWING and GOOSE-RIDING were 'diversions' in favour with the proletariat. The former was properly a Shrove Tuesday institution; its devotees, however, were not strict about the occasion. It was a brutal business, but in spite of efforts to put an end to it, cock-throwing survived until the end of the eighteenth century.

Some unfortunate bird, usually one trained by its owner to dodge a missile, was tied by the leg with a length of cord to a peg, and for twopence any one might have three throws with a broomstick from a distance of 22 yards. If the thrower

[1] César de Saussure, *A Foreign View of England in the Reigns of George I and George II* (1902), pp. 280–2.

COCK PIT ROYAL. 1796.

knocked the cock over and could run in and seize it before it
rose the bird was his. The well-trained victim became
clever in evading the stick, and thus was a source of profit to
the owner. The street was often the scene chosen, and then
cock-throwing ranked as a nuisance; in 1759 the lieges of
Newbury lodged an objection to cock-throwing in the street.
Goose-riding does not appear to have been peculiar to any
season or festival: the bird with neck well greased was hung
by the legs to a bough or to a rope stretched between two
poles, and the competitors, riding at speed beneath, tried
to pull off the head.

BULL-BAITING was very popular. The bullward, or bullard,
led his beast about the country, stopping at any town or
village to enlist the patronage of local 'bull-hankers'. The
animal was fastened by a rope or chain to a stake, and any
one who cared to pay a shilling might set his dog at him.
Bull-hankers sometimes carried long staves with which to
break the fall of a dog when tossed—a frequent happening.
Near the stake was dug a hole of size sufficient to admit the
bull's muzzle, the experienced dog always trying to seize
that most tender part of the anatomy. The condition of
such a bull was pitiable; continually baited, his head and
neck were covered with scars, and wounds part-healed and
new. The Stamford and Tutbury Bull-runnings were
peculiar to those towns; the former was less objectionable
than bull-baiting; the latter was abominably cruel. The
Stamford institution endured until 1840, when respectable
rate-payers raised effective objection to it—on account of
the expense. It was costing £300 a year to bring in troops to
reinforce the local police and keep rowdyism within bounds.

BULL-RACING was popular; when cattle were used for
draught, trials of speed naturally grew therefrom; any bull,
bullock, or cow might be entered, and the race often took
place in the street. That at Lyndhurst was celebrated; it
was run over a two-mile course, and in heats.

BADGER-BAITING was another sport (save the mark!) to
which the age was addicted. The yard of a public-house was
commonly the venue; here, in a hole dug for the purpose, a
stake was fixed and the badger being secured thereto by a chain
passed *through* his tail, dogs were set on him. The jaws and
teeth of the badger being exceptionally strong, he might
maim or kill half a dozen dogs before he succumbed himself.

FALCONRY was now far advanced in its decline, ousted by the gun. True, the Royal Mews was still maintained by George II, and his son Frederick, Prince of Wales, used to fly his hawks on Epsom Downs; but those who indulged in this oldest of sports were few. Establishment of the Falconers' Club in 1770 is indicative of endeavour to keep it alive. In 1781 the club counted fifty-six members; these held a meeting every year at some chosen spot, Alconbury Hill in Huntingdonshire being a favourite resort by reason of the many kites still to be found in the locality. Hawking was always the sport of the rich man; a falcon to be properly 'manned' must be ever on the fist of him who flies her, hence a professional falconer who devoted all his time to his charges was indispensable. The gun, as already said, did much to make an end of falconry, and the increase of hedges, walls, &c., brought about by Inclosure Acts, contributed to the same result, providing cover for the quarry when the falcon stooped.

PUGILISM, as carried on until this time, has been described as 'downright slaughtering'; and, to say truth, introduction of scientific methods did little to improve it. To Jack Broughton, who succeeded Tom Pipes as Champion of England in 1740, is due credit for what was at least an attempt to redeem the Noble Art from reproach. In 1743 Broughton framed the first Rules for prize-fighting, and sought to elevate boxing to a science at the Academy he opened in the Haymarket four years later. A wise man, he thoughtfully provided his pupils with 'mufflers', later known as boxing-gloves—'that would effectually secure them from the inconveniency of black eyes, broken jaws, and bloody noses'. 'Inconveniency' applied to a broken jaw seems an understatement, but let that pass. Broughton's well-meant efforts were not generally appreciated, nor was his example everywhere followed, for fighting in booths at fairs and kindred resorts continued in all its savagery. In 1749 boxing and cudgel play at Southwark Fair were suppressed as a public nuisance, such a pitch of barbarity had they reached; and we need not suppose that Southwark was worse than other places.

The pugilist who fought his way to fame usually became the protégé of some peer who took interest in the Ring; such a patron found the money for a prize-fight and backed his

'BROUGHTON AND SLACK IN THE MEMORABLE BATTLE, AT THE AMPHITHEATRE, ON
TUESDAY, APRIL 10: 1750'

man: thus, the Duke of Cumberland was the patron and backer of Broughton for several years until, on April 10, 1750, that hero was defeated by Jack Slack in a fight which lasted only fourteen minutes; a blow between the eyes blinded Broughton and thus brought the battle to an end. The defeat of his protégé and consequent loss of his bets, said to amount to some thousand pounds, caused the Duke to withdraw his support; a step which compelled Broughton to close his academy, and withdraw from the Ring. Ten years later the Duke bestowed his patronage on Slack, who won the championship in 1750, backing him for £100 against Bill Stevens, the champion of 1760. From 1761 to 1783 the championship was in a very unsettled state, several men holding it in turn; and so matters continued till the appearance of Tom Johnson, a corn-porter, whose defeat of Jarvis in 1783 brought him into notice. Johnson, whose real name is said to have been Jackling, was a man of very unusual strength; he could take up a sack of corn and swing it round his head; also he possessed great courage; and to these advantages he added 'most minute attention to Art'; in other words, displayed science; and thus it came about that he defeated every man who came against him during the 1780's, his opponents including Bill Warr, Michael Ryan, Bill Darts, who had held the championship for six years from 1765, and Peter Corcoran, who claimed it in 1771, but whose title to the honour for some reason was considered doubtful. Johnson held the championship for eleven years from 1783. Another famous pugilist was George Taylor, Champion in 1734. This man fought numerous battles before he entered the ring against Tom Faulkener at St. Albans in 1758; he had lost an eye in a former fight, and after an hour and seventeen minutes a blow from Faulkener closed the other; thus blinded he had to accept defeat. It would seem that he sustained other injuries not suspected at the time, for he died three months afterwards. Men were sometimes so badly punished that it was necessary to support them from the ring.[1]

For many years prize-fights were brought off on the ground, a rope holding, or intended to hold, off the crowd; but fights

---

[1] Dr. Johnson's uncle Andrew was not only a bookseller but a notable boxer, who kept the ring in Smithfield for a whole year without being defeated. See Mrs. Piozzi's *Anecdotes of Samuel Johnson* (1786), p. 5.

were too often marred by the misconduct of onlookers; backers of the man who seemed to be losing would force their way into the ring and with kicks and blows strive to disable his opponent. Hence the introduction of a stage raised 6 feet or more above the ground. Johnson's fight with Bill Warr at Oakhampton, Berkshire, in 1787 took place on such a stage.

Displays of boxing were common attractions at the country fairs; a professional would go the round of these, advertising by handbills his readiness to meet the local talent; and it is very improbable that such bouts were conducted with any regard for rules.

CUDGEL PLAY was also to be seen at the fairs; the weapon was a stout stick with basket-handguard; he who first drew blood from his adversary's head won the bout. There is no better description of cudgel play, though at a much later date, than that in *Tom Brown's Schooldays*.

WRESTLING was a popular exercise, especially in counties where a particular style had been evolved. The wrestlers of Cornwall and Devon were the most celebrated; after them those of Cumberland and Westmorland; then the Norfolk and Bedfordshire men. Other districts adopted one or other of these styles; thus, Sir Thomas Parkyns of Bunny Park, Notts, was an enthusiast who organized an annual wrestling meeting in his park, the Cornish style being favoured. Sir Thomas died in 1741, but the meeting was regularly held for many years afterwards.

CRICKET underwent important changes. In its very early days the game was confined to the humbler classes, and perhaps we see in the method of scoring—cutting notches on a stick—evidence of illiteracy; but in Johnson's time men of all classes were playing, and exciting adverse comment by so doing: says one such critic: 'Noblemen, gentlemen and clergy have certainly a right to divert themselves in what manner they think fit, nor do I dispute their privilege of making butchers, cobblers or tinkers their companions . . .'[1]

Cricket then had little in common with the modern game beyond the fact that the stumps were placed 22 yards apart. These were only two and 1 foot high; whether they were set 2 feet apart or less is an open question, but space between them was left for the 'popping' or 'block' hole. Into this

[1] *The British Champion*, of Sept. 8, 1743.

CRICKET AT MOULSEY HURST

From the painting by Richard Wilson

the striker had to put the end of his bat before the wicket-keeper could 'pop' the ball into it; if the ball was in first the striker was out. The bat was curved like an old-fashioned dinner knife; bowling was fast and along the ground as the low wicket required.

When the upper ranks of society adopted the game a match drew large crowds of spectators; the scribe above-mentioned regarded this with a jaundiced eye; he doubted whether the nobility and gentry had 'the right to invite thousands of people to be spectators of their agility at the expense of their duty and honesty'. How the honesty of the crowd was involved he omits to say, but possibly in his law-abiding mind was thought of the Act of 1711 (9 Anne, c. 19), which forbade the playing of any game for a stake exceeding £10; and as cricket was not specifically mentioned matches were always played for money; though the ultra-cautious kept on the safe side of the law by making the stake a guinea, or more, 'per man'.

The Hambledon Club which played on Broad Ha'penny Down in Hampshire would claim priority of age; but the late Mr. Philip Norman assigns the honour to Kent, showing that cricket was played at Maidstone before 1640.[1] The score in the first recorded match—that between the Gentlemen of Sevenoaks against the Gentlemen of London in July 1734 has not been preserved; we have that of the Kent v. All England in 1746—Kent 111 runs to the 110 of All England. The latter team consisted of players from Middlesex, Sussex, and Surrey; to which counties, with Hampshire (not re-presented in this game), cricket was then confined. This match took place on the Artillery Ground, Finsbury. The Prince of Wales and the Duke of Cumberland were among the spectators. The *British Champion* critic must have been horrified by the composition of the Kent team: Lord John Sackville was a member of the eleven, and his captain was Rumney, the head gardener at Knowle.

The London, or Artillery, Club compiled the first code of laws; this was revised in 1755, in 1774, and again in 1788. Lillywhite,[2] writing in 1862, says the Laws were 'not very extensive nor clearly defined until about a century ago; which doubtless refers to the revision of 1774, when radical

[1] *Scores and Annals of the West Kent Cricket Club* (1897), p. 1.
[2] *Cricket Scores and Biographies, 1746–1826.*

changes were made. Noteworthy among these was the abolition of the 'popping hole', greatly, we may surmise, to the relief of wicket-keepers, for painful collisions between eager digits and equally eager bat's-end must have been frequent. A third stump was added, and the height raised to 22 inches; and to get a man out it was necessary to put the wicket down. The increased height of the wicket compelled adoption of a new bat, and thus it came about that the straight blade supplanted the curved. Also the style of bowling changed. In a word, to quote the Rev. John Mytton,[1] 'Cricket now began to assume that truly skilful and scientific character which it now possesses.'

The dissolution of the Hambledon Club in 1790 produced far-reaching results; the dispersal of its members about the country was instrumental in spreading knowledge of cricket; and by the end of the century it had become the National Game.

FOOTBALL was played in various forms, none of which bore any resemblance to Rugby or Association. The commonest was that noticed by M. Misson at the end of the seventeenth century: 'En Hyver le *Football* est une exercise utile et charmante,' he tells us—but we may as well have his praise in English: 'It is a ball of leather as big as one's head filled with air: this is kicked about the streets by any who can get at it; there is nothing of science about it.'[2]

In Cumberland until about 1760 or 1770 there existed an old custom of barring out the schoolmaster on certain occasions; who, if he could not get in, proposed terms; these always included permission for a football match and a cocking. The sides for the game were composed of boys from the parishes lying east and west of the school, and the game began in the churchyard. Utility and charm did not distinguish football as everywhere played; Derby, for instance, was the scene of a periodical contest between parishes, and 'the play was very rough'.[3] Camp Ball, a form

---

[1] *Gentleman's Magazine*, July 1833, p. 43.

[2] *Mémoires et Observations* (1698), p. 255.

[3] This shrove-tide football continued to be played at Derby till 1846; it is still played, with great gusto, at Ashbourne every Shrove Tuesday and Ash Wednesday. The game starts at 2 p.m. and does not cease until a goal has been scored, even if that should not occur till midnight. Men, women, and children take part in the game, and all classes, including the gentry, used to do so. The sides are 'upwards' and 'downwards', the former being those who live to the north of the stream which flows east and west through the

of the game peculiar to East Anglia, would hardly have won commendation even from that indulgent Frenchman; an old writer has described it as 'a friendlie kind of fight'. Large numbers of men took part, the game (or fight) lasted all day and, friendliness notwithstanding, was fruitful of casualties; so fruitful that connexion may be discerned between camp ball and that rule of the East Wretham Friendly Society, founded 1784, which denied any weekly allowance to the member who sustained hurt or disablement by, *inter alia*, football or wrestling.[1]

ARCHERY, which had gone out of fashion except in Lancashire and Cheshire, was revived during the latter years of the century by the efforts of Sir Ashton Lever of Leicester House, who induced others to join in formation of the Toxophilites in 1780, the Duke of Bedford taking office as President. The movement spread rapidly; other societies or clubs were formed, and 'Bow-meetings' became the rage, ladies taking a prominent part. Such was the popularity of archery by 1792 that the *Sporting Magazine* made it the subject of an illustrated article in the second monthly number.

BOWLS, which under James I's Declaration of Lawful Sports had been 'at all times prohibited to the meaner sort of people', had for years been popular with all classes, that prohibition being entirely ignored. Very many country inns possessed bowling greens, and at the other end of the social scale the green was a feature of innumerable country house gardens.

TENNIS, RACKETS, AND FIVES may be considered together,

centre of the town—it does not matter how many yards, miles, or hundreds of miles it may be—and the latter those who live to the south of the stream, again without restriction of distance. The game is started by the 'throwing up' of the ball by some one who is specially invited for the occasion, and who is hoisted on to the shoulders of the crowd for the purpose. The ball is of stout leather stuffed with cork shavings, the outside painted red, white, and blue, and pictorially decorated. The field of play is anywhere the crowd chooses, even private property not being immune, but the stream itself is a favourite venue, if only because it affords an opportunity of paying off old scores with a ducking. There is little or no kicking of the ball, which is propelled backwards and forwards by the sheer weight of the massed players. The goals are three miles apart, each being the shutter of a mill-wheel, and to score a goal it is necessary for a player to swim the mill-pond through the narrow archway of the sluice and to touch the mill-wheel with the ball.

These particulars are kindly supplied by Dr. E. A. Sadler of Ashbourne.

[1] *Annals of Agriculture*, vol. xix, p. 266.

the second and third owing their origin to the first, of which it has been said that it takes a lifetime to learn the rules. Their intricacies, however, did not deter Royalty; Charles Fitzroy, afterwards Fitzroy-Scudamore, was Master of the Royal Tennis Courts from 1728 to 1762. Requiring a specially designed court, tennis was a game practically confined to the wealthy and leisured classes, though courts open to the public existed in London, which enjoyed no very good reputation, haunted as they were by sharpers. In the later decades of the century a professional player, Pilet, or Pillet, by name, travelled the country giving lessons. RACKETS, played with tennis rackets, came into fashion about 1749; and, we may assume, won favour by reason of its greater simplicity. FIVES, played with the hand against any convenient wall, was followed by Bat-fives, played with an implement roughly resembling a tennis racket. These two games had so much in common during their early days that it is hard to distinguish between them. Fives was not adopted by our public schools until well on in the nineteenth century.

Sports, more especially racing and hunting, offered a remunerative field to the eighteenth-century artist; there were painters who found that it paid better to do the likeness of a gentleman's racehorse than that of the gentleman's wife; is it not recorded that when George Stubbs, R.A. (1724–1806), was receiving 100 guineas for the portrait of a racehorse Sir Joshua Reynolds' fee for a three-quarter length of a lady was 70 guineas? From the time of John Wootton (c. 1685–1765) painters of varying degrees of merit sought Newmarket, among them John Sartorius (c. 1700?–80?), James Seymour (1702–52), who was one of the best among Stubbs' contemporaries, and Sawrey Gilpin, R.A. (1733–1807), either to make the head-quarters of the Turf their home or to spend years there. The fact that artists, like other men, must earn a living explains why equine portraits predominate so largely over racing scenes; owners commissioned the former, whereas there was no assured market for the latter. In Hunting, the case was reversed; for one likeness of a hunter we find fifty hunting scenes such as those painted by John Boultbee (1747–1812) or Philip Reinagle, R.A. (1749–1833). Shooting received far less artistic attention, though that universal genius Stubbs painted a few shooting works, as also did George Morland (1763–1804). Angling made small appeal to the eighteenth-century painter; indeed it may fairly be said that it furnished the excuse for a landscape.

BIBLIOGRAPHY.—*Racing Calendar; Statutes of the Realm.* T. A. COOK, *History of The English Turf* (3 vols., 1905); The Earl of March, *Records of the Old Charlton Hunt* (1910); DAVID BROWN & W. F. LAMONBY, *Greyhound Studbook* (vol. iii, 1882 *et seq.*); Col. PETER HAWKER, *Instructions to Young Sportsmen* (1814); ROBT. NOBBES, *The Compleat Troller* (1681 & 1790); CHAS. BOWLKER, *The Art of Angling* (1788); Sir W. GILBEY, 1st Bt., *Sport in The Olden Time, Cock-fighting* (1912); SALVIN & BRODRICK, *Falconry in the British Isles* (1855); PIERCE EGAN, *Boxiana* (1828–9); J. WILLIAMS, *New Articles of Cricket* (1774); JOHN NYREN, *Young Cricketer's Tutor* (1833); T. ROBERTS, *The English Bowman* (1801); J. SPENNS & JULIAN MARSHALL, *Tennis, Rackets, Fives* (1890).

J. STRUTT, *Sports and Pastimes of the People of England* (1801); DELABERE P. BLAINE, *Encyclopaedia of Rural Sports* (2nd ed. 1852); Sir WALTER GILBEY, 1st Bt., *Animal Painters of England* (3 vols., 1899 and 1911).

XIV

COSTUME

By TALBOT HUGHES

Sir, were I to have anything fine, it should be very fine. Were I to wear a ring, it should not be a bauble, but a stone of great value. Were I to wear a laced or embroidered waistcoat, it should be very rich.—*Tour to the Hebrides* (27 Oct. 1773).

You little creatures should never wear those sort of clothes however; they are unsuitable in every way. What! have not all insects gay colours?—MRS. PIOZZI, *Anecdotes*.

THE character of the great Samuel Johnson himself was reflected in his attire by his habitual choice of plainly-cut garments in which the extravagant styles of current fashions were never discernible. His loose figure and awkward gait were scarcely calculated to set off fine fashions. Incessant absorption of the mind was probably also in part responsible for his usual carelessness about dress, and it is said that on one occasion his appearance was so slovenly that he was mistaken for a watchman and presented with a shilling. Although, like every one else, he donned black on solemn occasions such as funerals, he usually kept to the sombre brown tones seen in his portraits. But for his visit to Paris in 1755, he spent £30 on a new suit and a new Bourgeois wig; and on one other occasion at least he appears to have broken his rule. At Drury Lane, on the production of his tragedy, *Irene*, he wore a gay scarlet waistcoat with rich gold lace, a gold-laced hat, and a handsome Paris wig. It seems, indeed, from his own confession, that he was by no means at ease in this attire; but no doubt he had felt constrained to mark in this way the importance of what he regarded as the crowning event in his career. His action was quite in consonance with the sentiments he once expressed on the subject to Boswell. 'Fine clothes', he explained, 'are good only as they supply the want of other means of procuring respect.'

Boswell suggests that the warming acquaintance of his wealthy friends, the Thrales, inspired him with a little more interest in his appearance. He even enlivened his coat with metal buttons, but there is ample evidence that buckles, both at the knees and shoe-latchets, were neglected, as on the occasion when he was visited by Madame de Boufflers. He

Taste A-La-Mode, as in the Year 1735,
being the Contrast to the Year 1745

Taste A-La-Mode, 1745

FASHIONS OF 1735 AND 1745
After the paintings by L. P. Boitard

showed his decided antipathy to anything he considered exaggerated in style when he was induced to buy a pair of larger shoe-buckles, for he would have none of the grotesquely large ones that had just come into fashion. When visiting, Dr. Johnson would perhaps smarten up his appearance with a neckcloth, but on less formal occasions his neckbands and even his wristbands were frequently left unbuttoned. His wigs also appear to have had scant attention. Bennet Langton saw him in a little dark wig that scarcely covered his head, and, when Boswell was first introduced to him in 1763, he wore a little old shrivelled unpowdered wig perched on the top of his head. The portrait of Johnson at the National Portrait Gallery shows a suit of warm brown, rather full in cut and with long buttonholes. The sleeve-cuffs are not of the large type then in fashion and have no buttons. His travelling-costume on the journey to the Hebrides is seen in the print by T. Trotter. It is of ordinary character, a very large pocket being the only remarkable feature.

In an account of the costume worn in Samuel Johnson's time it must be borne in mind that most of the contemporary descriptions represent the more extravagant styles of the fops and smart people, and that, although these attracted many of the middle class who sought to follow fashion, the average male citizen retained the plain clothes of the mid-eighteenth century, with but slight variations, right to the end of the eighties. The chief changes in style were shorter coats with narrower skirts, tighter sleeves with smaller cuffs, pocket flaps square instead of curved to a centre, and higher collars with lapels and double-breasted fronts. Fashions, according to a contemporary observer, commenced at St. James's, made rapid progress to the Inns of Court, and then declined in the East. Two prints of the Mall by Boitard exhibit the contrast between the fashions of the year 1735 and those of ten years later. In the earlier print the hats of both sexes are small, ladies' dresses are short, and male coats and waistcoats long. The print of 1745 shows hoops at their widest extent with dresses almost touching the ground, while the male garments are considerably shortened.

Before the middle of the century costume decoration and embroidery were heavy and showy in design, and the colour schemes were chiefly strong, even gaudy—yellows, oranges, scarlets, strong blues, violets, dull slates, and pinks. Most of the lighter tones were also decided, though some of the ground-mixtures were greys, dove-colours, and lilacs, which gave a softer quality to the masses. Taste aimed at richness of effect, heightened with tinsels or gold and silver trimmings. The coats and waistcoats of the men were heavily ornamented with gold and silver or worked in chenille or floral embroidery. Heavy fringe often garnished the bottom of waistcoats.

Most of the fashions emanated from Paris, especially after the Peace of Aix-la-Chapelle in 1748, when travelling on the Continent once more became possible. The sacque dress was what the French called the *robe de chambre*. The hooped skirt was also of French origin, as was the cloak with hood known as the Capuchin, which in these days when intrigue was so prevalent was often used as the receptacle for *billets doux*. French wigs were a speciality in fine construction, and the extravagant modes in lace sets and treble ruffles were fostered by the French lace trade. From France also came many of the brocades, sword-knots, buckles, and other accessories sold to the English *beau monde* at enhanced prices, though many of these articles were actually produced in Spitalfields and passed off on the English fops as the latest modes from Paris. The various beautiful materials made at Spitalfields included lutestrings, alamodes, brocades, satins, paduasoys, and ducapes, besides black velvets and silks for the scarves, manteaux, and hoods, which were indispensable to the wardrobe of every lady of fashion.

In the 'sixties taste grew more refined, and the gaudy decorations and violent colour schemes of feminine attire gave place to lighter designs and more subtle colours. Dresses of silk in quiet hues of peach, lavender, and pearly-grey were delicately enriched with graceful sprays or striped designs which lent more elegance to the simpler styles. Lutestrings and shot silks with frail gauze trimmings, full lawn kerchiefs or fine lace at the neck, and treble lace ruffles, together with the style of the bandeau, high cap, and feathers, so long as they were in reasonable proportions, heightened the stateliness of the general effect and made this one of the most beautiful periods in the history of costume.

Extravagance was never at such a height as in the seventies, when a writer remarks: 'The jewels that are worn not only at Court but even at the East side of the Temple

CAPTAIN JOHN AUGUSTUS HERVEY TAKING LEAVE OF HIS FAMILY

From the painting by J. Zoffany in the possession of the Marquess of Bristol

would surpass belief, and no woman could refuse a ten pound tax for Old England who would carry ten thousand pounds in diamonds on her head, neck, and stomacher.' But we also learn that the demi-reps and coquettes disported themselves in dresses just as gorgeous as those worn in politer circles, and that many of the shop assistants and servants, who did not scruple to borrow their mistresses' attire, frequented the places of amusement, so that it was often difficult to tell by mere appearances who were the distinguished people—except by their manner and bearing. This difficulty is partly explained by the fact that many dressed in the second-hand clothes of their betters. Business in old clothes and fripperies was very profitable, and valets and maids added considerably to their salaries by this means.

The year 1780 was one of domestic retrenchment in order to raise supplies for the hostilities against France and Spain; but expenditure on fashion is hard to reduce, and the accounts of costly painted satins, gauze trimmings, and jewelled head-dressings for full dress still continue. A writer gives an example of an attempt at retrenchment on the part of two ladies of his acquaintance who boasted of having purchased simple nightgowns instead of the dressed sacques in which they had hitherto always appeared. It must be remembered that the term 'nightgown' did not in those days denote the garment so named nowadays; Dr. Johnson's *Dictionary* defines it as an undress-gown worn in the evening. The bed-gown was the eighteenth-century equivalent of the modern nightgown or nightdress.

Gentlemen's suits followed the same fashions in elegance of style.[1] The rococo ornamentation in gold on coats and waistcoats was abandoned in favour of borders of graceful trailing flowers mingled with gold thread and metal or glass sequins of various colours matching the materials. Colour schemes were brilliant—there were, for example, suits of shot silk in plum colour and in blue or green checked with fire tones—and the cut of clothes was brought to a fine art in shapely fitting. The seventeenth-century fashion of coats with buttons to the bottom of the skirt was still to be seen— according to prints—up to about 1736. These coats were cut

---

[1] Some idea of the cost of men's clothes may be derived from Sir James Prior's *Life of Goldsmith* (2 vols., 1837), vol. ii, p. 232, where Goldsmith's tailor's bill is reproduced.

rather low at the neck, the pockets being set correspondingly low. Coat-seams braided with rich lace—another survival from the previous century—continued to be favoured by men of elegance as late as 1750, and large sleeve-cuffs of rich brocade to match the waistcoat were frequently seen. The ample cuffs which developed until they covered the elbows between 1740 and 1750 were held by four, five, or six buttons; another cuff was formed by a long sleeve increased in width in its lower half, which was slit open at the side, the ends being turned up and buttoned back to form the cuff, though it was frequently worn without reversing the cuff. This was the last stage of a seventeenth-century style, as was the vertical pocket, still occasionally seen in coats, overcoats, and jackets as late as the 'seventies. The next style of coat was not so generous in shape and had a turnover collar sometimes of velvet.

The number of buttons varied according to the size of braids and enrichment from eight to twelve, finishing at the waist in line with the top of the pocket, which had five decorative buttons—a reminder of past usefulness, as they seldom fastened the flap. The later type of coat, in the 'seventies, with long narrow skirts and tighter sleeves and cuffs developed a higher collar and large angular lapels; others had a double-breasted front, cut back at the waist. The waistcoat of this period also had lapels which were often worn outside the coat. Waistcoats tended to be considerably shortened until finally the lower part finished straight across the waist.

The decorative braidings to buttons and buttonholes known as 'frogs' were matched in effect and frequently finished with small tassels or rosettes. The grouping of buttons and braids in sets of twos and threes was yet another survival from Stuart times. Buttons were a great feature of eighteenth-century costume and were often very costly ornaments. They were made in gold, silver, and bronze gilt richly chased, sometimes of repoussé work, or enamelled and set with precious stones or fine paste. A print displaying the dazzling appearance of a fop adorned with Birmingham buttons of cut steel was issued in 1778. With the extravagant modes of the 'seventies buttons of large dimensions appeared on the coats of the Macaroni,[1] some being

[1] The term Macaroni does not indicate one particular style of dress, but extremes in various styles affected by men of fashion in this period.

STEEL BUTTONS | *Coup de Bouton*

decorated with pictures and mottoes. Others were embellished with coloured tinsels, and buttons of blue paste and silvered glass decorated many waistcoats.

The waistcoat was worn freely opened to expose the lace ends of the tie and the shirt of fine linen, and writers of this period deride certain elderly beaux who wore the open waistcoat even in winter, thereby pretending to a hardiness they did not possess, for they were well padded with flannel beneath. This fashion was confined to the wealthier classes, and humbler folk were content to hide their coarse shirts with false frilled fronts and half-sleeves of better linen.

The male shirt-sleeve was gathered at the wrist to a band on which plain or lace ruffles were tacked; the breast-opening was also set with a frill or lace in the 'forties, and the neckband was widened to form a collar which later appeared above the stock or linen binding.

The long lawn tie bound round the throat, brought forward and tied, with the end tucked into the waistcoat, was the fashion in the earlier part of Johnson's life, and was worn by many elderly men and by Johnson himself until his death. The ends were either plain or set with fine lace, and in the 'forties smart men sometimes caught up one end through a large buttonhole of the coat. Stocks were a later development, and were usually of white linen. The first mention of a coloured stock—a mulberry coloured stock worn by a Macaroni dandy—is made in 1775.

The breeches worn at the beginning of this period were fastened by three buttons showing at the waist and three hidden in the fly, while the knees were fastened at the sides with from three to six buttons. In front of either hip was a pocket with buttoned flap. These details are shown by very few prints, but one of the actor Woodward, dated 1753, gives a good and clear example of male costume at this time. The later breeches had no pocket-flaps, as the front was made into one piece, fastened to the waist with a central button and one at each corner. Gold fobs with watch or seals hung from the breeches-pocket, where at first they were hidden by the long waistcoats; but when the Macaroni curtailed the length of this garment to a straight-across form he turned the fob to attractive account by wearing two—one on each side—long and loaded with seals which jingled and knocked together in harmony with his dandified steps.

When buckles and clasps replaced the ribbon and lace ties for fastening the breeches at the knees about 1693 the gilded youths who started the change had been termed 'vain coxcombs', but when in 1780 the bucks of the period attempted to revive the old fashion by wearing rosettes at the knees they in turn met with derision and the craze was short lived. The highwayman dandy, Jack Rann, wore sixteen strings at his knees to denote the number of his imprisonments.

Stockings were generally worn rolled over the knee before 1745 and had decorated clocks which became less defined as the century progressed, especially when striped and spotted stockings became fashionable. Red was a favourite colour for stockings about 1735, while yellow was the modish shade in 1760. At all important functions, however, white silk stockings were invariably worn.

Square-toed shoes lasted from the beginning of the century until the 'thirties when round toes became general, and the side quarters and high squared front were lowered. The term 'square toes', applied to old-fashioned people, dates from this time. Scarlet heels and narrow latchets with small buckles were worn until the middle of the century. Later, heels became almost flat, while the front instep was gradually lowered in a rounded form until it only just showed above the buckles, which gradually increased in size and width until in 1772 they almost covered the front of the foot. Some of these were described as 'German Artois buckles of the largest dimensions with knobs'. After 1791 buckles were no longer required for the new type of man's shoe, while the lady's shoes had no latchets. The despairing buckle-makers petitioned George III to aid their dying industry, but his efforts to re-popularize the fashion were all in vain. Jack-boots and boots with brown tops were used for riding throughout the century, the only change being in the depth of the tops, which in dandy examples came nearly to the ankle in the 'eighties. Half-boots without tops were also seen in the 'seventies, some being curved up at the front, others at the back.

The hat normally worn during the greater part of Johnson's life was three-cornered in shape. Usually made of beaver and costing about two guineas, it was tilted at an angle, and scope was left to individual taste in cock, bows,

THE DRUMMOND FAMILY

From the painting by J. Zoffany in the possession of Mr. George H. Drummond

tassels, and ties that held the sides to the crown. Leaders of
taste often devised loops of their own contrivance, which set
the fashion to a wide circle of acquaintances, and some
dandies of the late 'seventies had their hat-brims braided up
to a large button in the centre of the crown. Before the
middle of the century well-dressed men wore the inside of
the brim set with white feathers, and throughout the period
rosettes, cockades, and favours of various kinds were worn
to flaunt political opinions or to mark special occasions.
Whigs displayed an orange cockade, while Tories wore white
roses, rue, thyme, or rosemary, or a spray of oak tied with
green ribbons. Fashion made no change in the three-cornered
hats except that of altering their dimensions, but this it
carried to extremes. In 1750 the small type then in vogue
was derisively called the 'little skimming dish hat', and
critics declared that it not only did not cover the head, but
was made of such flimsy materials that it did not even provide protection from the weather. One such small hat was
known as the 'Nivernois' from the Duke of that name who
was one of the signatories to the Treaty of Aix-la-Chapelle.
Hats afterwards went to the opposite extreme, so that the
faces of their wearers almost disappeared beneath them. In
the 'seventies little round hats with small brims were introduced, and their size soon increased, while the flat top
gradually rose higher, till eventually they developed into
the favourite hat of the 'eighties. In the summer of 1781
white hats were introduced with the recommendation that
they were cooler in the sun; but two years later they had
disappeared.

The types of wig worn during the course of the eighteenth
century were almost innumerable with their many variations in foretops, frontlets, and tails, and the latitude allowed
by fashion in the arrangement of curls or half-curls. In
Johnson's boyhood the monstrous periwig of Queen Anne's
reign was reduced to a modified size in the full-bottomed
wigs which were worn by the older men through the first
half of the century; but the lighter bag-wig with the sides
pressed forward in front of the ears came to stay in the
reign of George II, when large bags and huge bows with a
black ribbon brought round the neck became the fashion.
Up to 1740 natural hair caught with a bow at the back and
curled at the sides was usually worn by ordinary gentlefolk,

but in the politer circles powder now became essential.
About 1770 blue powder was introduced, and reddish powder
about seven years later.

Short pigtail-perukes made their appearance about 1746,
but the pigtails soon hung almost to the waist, being plaited
and bound with ribbon. Some were stiffened and others
curved outwards giving an eccentric resemblance to a mon-
key's tail; the lesser pigtails, long or curly, prevailed for a
long time with elderly men. Another innovation in the
'forties was the club-wig, the tail of which was folded into a
flat loop bound or fastened in the middle with a clasp. The
Macaronis favoured wigs of this type, increasing them to
extravagant dimensions and twisting them in amusing ways:
a Tyburn-top wig with a small round hat is mentioned as a
mode of the Macaroni in 1776. Leaders of eccentric taste
in the seventies wore the front of the wig, called the foretop,
increased in height to absurd proportions. Such wigs were
often 'frenched' or 'trenched'. The three-tailed wig was
also in use at the same time, but the most popular forms
were the short bob, the triple bob, the major bob, and the
frizzed bob or grizzle wig.

The removal of wigs at home necessitated some covering,
since many of those who wore them regularly had their
heads shaven. Loose caps with folded brims and top tassels
were made in every material from plain linen, like the one
shown in Romney's portrait of Cowper, to the gorgeous silks
and velvets to be seen in many portraits of notable men.

In this age of formal manners when it was usual for noblemen to wear the insignia of their orders with ordinary dress
and in public places, swords continued to be a conspicuous
and often costly accessory to male attire, their hilts being
richly chiselled and even enamelled and jewelled. It is true
that men of fashion began to discard the sword with informal dress from about 1730, but it was not completely
banished till the year 1780, when a man of pleasure notes
with regret that 'the sword is abolished except for full-
dress and military'. As swords passed out of use sword-
sticks became increasingly useful, for the ill-lit streets were
frequented by many ruffians, some disguised as beggars,
others as disabled seamen with wooden legs or arms which
suddenly acted as clubs, others again as link-men who would
suddenly extinguish their light and attack their passenger.

1771   1773

1778   1778

MILLINERY AND HAIR-DRESSING
From the Town and Country Magazine

1780

1780

1777

1780

MILLINERY AND HAIR-DRESSING
From the Town and Country Magazine

The walking-sticks of the eighteenth century were usually about waist-high and furnished with handles of precious workmanship, in ivory with a design in silver pins, or repoussé work in silver or gold sometimes further embellished with enamel, or of china made at various English factories. The favourite cane was malacca, varnished or unvarnished, and nearly all sticks were fitted with a carrying-cord passed through a hole about six inches down and garnished with tassels at the end. Tall, elegant canes were fashionable for both sexes and continued in favour during the whole of Johnson's life, though many startling changes were introduced by the 'extreme fellows', and we read in 1731: 'Polite young gentlemen at the Court end of town now carry large oaken sticks with great heads and ugly faces carved on them.' There was also a competition between a stick as high as a leaping-pole and a yard of varnished cane 'scraped taper' and bound at one end with wax thread; the latter was called a switch and was carried under the arm. About ten years later the Macaronis created a new fashion by plaiting the cords round their sticks and finishing the ends with tassels nearly as big as those of window curtains.

Umbrellas were first introduced into England in the late seventeenth century. They are referred to in Swift's *Tale of a Tub* (1704),[1] and in his *Description of a City Shower*, which appeared in the *Tatler* of October 1710; also in Gay's *Trivia* (1716). In 1714 we read that certain coxcombs of Lincoln's Inn were laughed at for borrowing the large umbrella from Wall's Coffee-house; but, although we know that they must have been used quite early in the century by women as a protection not against the sun but the rain, and although they gradually came into use in trades requiring protection from the weather, they do not appear to have been generally adopted before 1777, when several satirical prints were published showing large umbrellas carried by footmen accompanying ladies, and also by men of the upper and lower classes. The early umbrellas were made of waxed silk or taffeta.

The eighteenth century was remarkable for a series of extraordinary fashions adopted by the young bloods who were the leaders in eccentricity of dress. One fop of 1747 wears a huge laced hat fiercely cocked at the corners with

[1] The form of the word here is umbrell*o*.

3 E

an enormous bow on the left side, a long black wig-ribbon tied in front of the neck with straggling ends, a double-breasted coat with the skirts stiffened out with buckram, stockings folded over the knees, long shoe-latchets standing outwards, and his sword dangling crosswise at the back. One of the idiosyncrasies of bucks and beaux was to wear their handkerchiefs hanging from their pockets,[1] and some of them even went to the length of carrying muffs. In 1737 they had adopted a taste for carelessness in attire, wearing long, loose coats called 'wrap-rascals', with laced hats and long whips to imitate stage-coachmen. Others wore black caps and jackets like those of grooms or jockeys, and spurred boots which they deliberately kept dirty.[2] Macaronis, the 'fellows of savoir vivre', or the 'Petits Maîtres' revived the mode of untidy clothes and careless manners. In their endeavour to live up to the sobriquet of 'The Slovens' they wore their hats uncocked with the brims flopping, their breeches were left unbuckled at the knees, their coiffure was ruffled, and sometimes they even left papillots (curl-papers) in their hair.

The taste for slovenliness was only a passing phase; at other times the Macaroni would run to the opposite extreme in elegance and foppery. One Macaroni appeared in the Assembly Rooms in a shot-silk coat, pink satin waistcoat, and breeches covered with silver net, white stockings with pink clocks, and pink satin shoes with large pearl buckles. His hair was dressed remarkably high and stuck full of pearl pins. Striped, spotted, or chequered materials were preferred for the chief Macaroni garments, which included long coats like banjans (dressing-gowns) with pockets set low in the skirts. Other Macaroni fashions included eccentric short jackets worn with little round hats with or without brims, and loose breeches described as Dutchmen's. Their elevated wigs were likened to Dutch skittle bowls, while their huge clubs of twisted hair at the back were known as door-

---

[1] Fine lace handkerchiefs were chiefly used for show. Those meant for practical use were apt to be discoloured with snuff. The practice of blowing the nose with the fingers was frequent even in the highest circles.

[2] In this period it was not uncommon for a nobleman to don a jockey-suit and ride his own horse in a race. The eccentric Lord Ferrers on being brought to London for his execution for murder in 1760 was dressed like a jockey in a close-fitting riding frock and jacket, with spurred boots. He chose, however, to be hanged in his wedding-suit, and the hangman used the silken rope to which his rank entitled him.

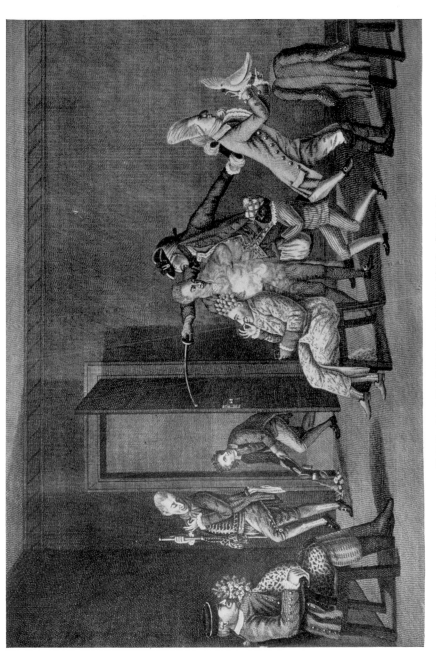

THE MACARONI DRESSING ROOM

From the engraving by Charles White, 1772

knockers. In 1780 many of these young coxcombs affected
a military air, adopting a blue coat with brass buttons and
a red collar, and in the following year there was a craze for
velvet coats in 'couleur de puce' after the French taste.
Then followed suits as tight as could be tailored and decorated with frogs, tassels, braids, and buttons of unusual size.
Breeches grew tighter and tighter. 'The Isis Macaroni'
depicted in a print wears very tight trousers split up the
calves and provided with side-pockets. As trousers did not
come into use till Wellington introduced them into the Army
in 1808, these fops might claim to have initiated the later
universal garment, though it is true that before this sailors
wore loose breeches to the calves. A print of a fishing-party
by Bunbury, dated 1791, also shows a youth in long trousers
guiding the punt. Many of these young men used cosmetics
and lipsalve, while their patches vied with those of the
ladies, and huge posies were fastened to their coats. Their
hair or their wig was set with perfumed pomades, and their
clothes were saturated with scent.

At formal gatherings ladies and gentlemen were expected
to appear in what was known as full dress. During the first
half of the century the full-dress costume for ladies consisted
of a bodice and an elaborate skirt. The bodice was of a
corset type and was frequently made on the stays with a
round, low neck.[1] It could be laced either in front or at the
back. In the former case, the lacing was either covered with
a stomacher or was itself made a decorative feature by
means of bows or jewelled ornaments; in the latter, the
decoration was embroidered on the front section of the
material. Two types of cuff were used on the elbow-sleeve:
the earlier long narrow cuff caught at the front with a bow
or clasp, and the single, double, or treble fan-shaped cuff
gathered to a ruche and usually set with a bow. Both types
had two or three lace ruffles. Later came a tight-fitting
gathered or pleated cuff for the elbow. Sleeves of the types
already mentioned were worn with the full-dress corset-
bodice, but others had sleeves of a different light material

[1] The long stiff corset worn in the eighteenth century was made of strong
linen stiffened with whalebone or cane and laced at the back or front, the
lower end of the bones being turned or set with pads or tabs to support the
band of the petticoat or panniers. In the earlier half of the century corsets
were often richly decorated or covered with fine brocade or other material and
worn as a bodice by women of all classes.

gathered in sections by ribbons or clasps, or drawn to
bows on the side. They could also be made in several falls
of lace.

Later in the century full dress assumed so many forms,
and fashions changed so rapidly, that it is impossible to do
more than note a few examples which reveal the catholicity
of contemporary taste. A ball-dress is described as an
Italian gown of muslin and silver over a lilac petticoat with
a small hoop; another as a Seffino gown with large hoops,
small tippets raised with wire, and ruffles in four falls; yet
a third as a French polonaise of white satin painted with
wreaths of flowers over a large hooped skirt, the bodice set
with Vandyke cuffs and large treble ruffles. A Rubens
handkerchief was tucked in the neck.

The sacque dress was introduced in the reign of George II.
This was made with a single pleat falling from the shoulders,
the back-portion being divided into two sets of box-pleats
meeting in the centre and caught only at the back of the
shoulders, the rest falling into graceful folds. The front
edges were set with rich purfling, ruching, or a band of
embroidery or silk of another colour increasing in width
towards the bottom. Later the back-pleats were narrowed
and held more closely to the figure until they gradually
dwindled into a tight-fitting bodice, only dividing at the
waist. The sacque was held by a canvas bodice laced at the
back, the fronts being set with the dress material, laced
together across the stays, and covered with a rich stomacher
or ruching and bows. A full skirt was worn with this dress,
the front portion being decorated with flounces or ruched
designs of a scroll or curved character. These dresses could
be looped up with under-ties, and later, in the 'sixties, took
the form of the polonaise gown.

On less formal occasions half-dress could be worn. An
example of this was the long Rutland gown with Turkish
sleeves and a hood, worn in 1779; the favourite colours were
Circassian white, ruby, blue, and brown. A satin negligée,
a loose open gown introduced about 1751, is described as
having elk trimmings and ruffle cuffs. Fête gowns profusely
long and festooned on the left side over puckered coats of
silver gauze or painted Indian tiffin bordered with silver
blonde are also mentioned. Among dishabilles worn in the
house were a short German gown with light sleeves and a

pink Persian coat, a Circassian dress with short apron and small hoop, a short polonaise with deep flounced petticoats, and an aurora-coloured jacket with a short petticoat to match.

Ladies' riding costumes in the eighteenth century were made in the richest materials, sometimes trimmed and lined with fur, and they often had the addition of a short cape or tasselled hood which fell from the shoulders and buttoned behind. These riding-habits became masculine in cut and were modelled on the male coat and waistcoat. The Duchess of Bedford's[1] riding-dress, which consisted of a double-breasted blue coat faced with white, a full skirt, high cravat, and three-cornered hat, is said to have inspired the original design for naval uniform. Boswell mentions the Duchess of Devonshire wearing a costume of military cut in the early 'eighties. Masculine fashions were, indeed, widely adopted, not only for riding-dresses and sports, when ladies joined in the sport of partridge, duck, and pheasant shooting, and wore long coats with capes and sleeve-cuffs buttoned at the sides, but even on more ordinary occasions.

The most notable innovation in female costume during the reign of George I was the expansion of the skirt by hoops. According to one account the hooped petticoat was invented in France when the war broke out in the reign of Queen Anne, while another, with less likelihood, accredits this revival of the farthingale to a Mrs. Scully who died in 1717. Hoops reached their widest circumference of about nine yards between 1735 and 1740, beating the French hoops by some two yards. The construction of the hoop is shown in Hogarth's engraving 'High Life', which also indicates how they were raised at the sides when their wearer was seated in a sedan-chair or carriage. In George II's reign, when hoops decreased in circumference, the width at the hips was increased by side panniers. Satires on the 'Cork rumps'— the back panniers worn about 1776—seem to indicate that they were suggested by a life-saving apparatus invented by Lady Grosvenor when warned against the perils of the Water Regatta.

It is rather surprising to read of a prudish father in those times of coquetry and intrigue becoming enraged because the tailor arrived with a pair of white dimity breeches for his daughter, who explained that she wore them because of the

[1] Diana Spencer, wife of the fourth Duke.

high leaps she was obliged to make in dancing the cotillion. We also read of a lady of the *demi-monde* taking her dancing-lessons in nothing but her drawers and practising in her under-petticoat. As these two satirical comments on drawers were made by writers in 1781 we may conclude that the breeches underwear for ladies had at last arrived with the more masculine styles of dress.

The shorter garter with a side rosette or bow was chiefly worn by ladies under the knee, but other garters were made of gay ribbon or woven silk nearly a yard long. These were often embellished with the owner's name, an amorous motto, or sentimental designs—a fashion also adopted with the velvet bracelets which were fashionable in the 'eighties. Garters appear, however, to have been put to other uses, for we read of a lady hanging herself with their aid, and the poet Cowper would also have succeeded in ending his life had not his scarlet garters given way.

Aprons of silk or satin, with two pockets or without pockets, varied in size according to fashion or to the fullness of the skirt. Embroidered with floral designs in silver or coloured silks and having a scalloped edge set with silver or gilt lace, they were in use with full dress up to the 'sixties when they became lighter in decoration. A crescent apron is mentioned in the 'seventies. There were, besides, muslin aprons of exquisite drawn work embroidered with flowers and birds. The white embroidery of this period has rarely, if ever, been surpassed. Check aprons are frequently mentioned with the working class.

Ladies' pockets, which were pear-shaped with a vertical opening at the upper part, were mostly made in linen handsomely embroidered, for, though they were usually worn in pairs on a band round the waist under the skirt, they showed when the skirt was tucked at the hips, two being depicted in the print 'A Masquerade at the Pantheon' by C. White.

The common purse of the period was a leather bag with ties, but there was a more elegant form in silver thread and in the stocking-purse closed by two rings with a compartment at either end. These purses were knitted or meshed in coloured designs of silk and beads and were finished at the ends with decorative tassels. Ladies also had beautiful purses specially decorated for their card games.

Mrs Rudd

Drawn from the Life, Sep.r 16, 1775

From the Town and Country Magazine, *1775*

Gloves were mostly of elbow-length and fitted rather loosely at the wrist; the more elegant ones were embroidered with trailing flowers in silver, gold, or coloured threads, sometimes with the addition of small tufts at the knuckles. Silk mittens were much worn. Some were made with a semicircular piece at the top, by which the fingers could be covered, but this was usually turned back to show a coloured lining, often embroidered. Other varieties were mittens of black or white lace and gloves in crochet. Chicken-skin gloves are mentioned about 1770 as being worn at night. For riding the long leather glove was worn with a short-sleeved jacket, but when the more masculine coats with long sleeves came in during the 'seventies a glove with a gauntlet was adopted. Small muffs of fur or rich materials were carried in winter, and these became huge creations in the 'eighties.

Up to 1750 ladies' shoes had many features in common with their male counterparts, high heels, often of red leather, high sides, square fronts, and smallish buckles. They usually had very pointed toes which turned up slightly. Some of the earlier shoes were decorated with a broad lace down the front, but they were chiefly made in rich brocades or embroidered silk or satin. In the 'seventies, with a round or less pointed toe, heels took a spindle form and larger buckles covered the foot. Thereafter there was a change in favour of lower heels, a pointed instep, and the revival of the pointed toe. In the 'eighties buckles were gradually replaced by rosettes and bows, though those who could afford to do so still wore diamond buckles in full dress. The mule or half-shoes and slippers were used in the house.

The most popular hat for ladies in the first half of this century was of straw with a wide brim and a small shallow crown; it was generally worn over a small muslin cap with latchets of lace. When the male hats increased in size the ladies wore their hats with wide drooping brims in sympathy. About 1745 a hat with a steeple crown like that associated with witches was in vogue. Caps included the small mob cap and French caps with fan-like sides and large gauze wings behind. The latter were worn surmounting the 'high-cap coiffure', and eventually developed to such dimensions that they almost hid the profile with six pleatings to the face. Bandeaux of silk and gauze were twisted in the hair, and turbans embellished with pearls, jewels, or paste ornaments and set with front-bows or feathers became the mode in the later 'seventies when the coiffure spread at the top sides to receive the massed erection of flowers and feathers. About 1780 Italian caps of crêpe or puckered blonde gauze with flat lappets were fashionable. Lappets were often made of stamped or painted tiffin. Many hats were looped at one side with jewelled rosettes, some being held on both sides and set with black and white feathers. Large plain satin hats especially in black with large puckered caps with wide wings were much in favour. The Spencer hat, created by Lady Charlotte Spencer and worn without a cap, was fashionable for a while, but soon gave place to the Cumberland bonnet made of the finest black lace mingled with ruby ribbon. A little tall-crowned hat with five bands and a feather is noted as being worn with a riding-dress.

Hoods were worn throughout the century. One of the most notable was the calash, said to have been invented by the Duchess of Bedford about 1776. This was a fold-up hood of black silk gathered on four or five diminishing semicircles of whalebone or cane, with a short frill at the back and ribbon ties. Its chief use was to afford protection from sun or wind. One satirical print published in 1777 shows a lady raising her calash by means of a block and pulley: another derides both the calash and the parasol, which also appeared about this time. In its earliest form the latter consisted of a small sun umbrella at the head of a long slender cane, and the fancy for hats with very wide brims was attributed to the trouble of carrying a little sun umbrella in the pocket.

The calash appears to have been adapted from the stiff black hoods worn by women of the lower classes. They were simple in form, with a stiffened frilled edge: two women in a crowd are seen wearing them in a print of 1743 called 'Christmas Gambols'. The calash was not the only mode derived from the common people, for another very fashionable form of head-gear was started by a lady of doubtful virtue who appeared at Ranelagh in a cap designed from the covering worn by the market-women of Covent Garden. This consisted of a binding of gauze, spider-net, catgut, or Leicester web, folded about the head, crossed beneath the chin, and pinned behind, the ends hanging down like pigeons' tails.

Though French fashions usually reigned in England, we learn that in 1714 two English ladies succeeded in banishing the Parisian mode of high powdered coiffure by appearing with a simple low head-dress without powder. But when the French *beau monde* adopted the simpler mode of hair-dressing London took to powder again and gradually evolved the high head-dress which was eventually to reach such fantastic proportions. For the first half of the century the coiffure remained fairly simple in form. The hair was drawn up into small curls, and in some cases curls hung down at the back. Flowers, pearls, and jewelled trinkets were freely used to adorn the hair, and later a bandeau or ribbon was entwined in it. In the sixties powder came into fashion again, and during the next decade the head-dress steadily grew in size and elaboration. In 1772 one writer states: 'Hair-dressing has arrived at such a pitch of ridicule that the very mop squeezers employ friseurs at least once a week to dress their hair *à la Grecque* with three drop locks and a bit of turnover in imitation of their betters.' In 1779 the extreme coiffure surmounted by feathers drew satirical advice to the 'walking steeples' to avoid the chandeliers whose lighted candles might demolish their combustible heads! So lofty had these head-dresses become that it was seriously suggested that the tops of carriages and sedan-chairs should be raised. Numerous complaints were made in the magazines of the time about the difficulty experienced by theatre-goers in catching a glimpse of the stage when their view was liable to be obstructed by enormous heads of hair, sometimes even heightened by large hats tilted over the front of the coiffure. It was, indeed, just about this time that the fashion over-reached itself; for in the early part of 1780 an article by 'A Matron' in *The Lady's Magazine* draws attention to the diminution in the use of powder, pomatum, and the wool cushions on which these elaborate coiffures were constructed. It appears to have been on the occasion of the Queen's birthday in this year that the first effective blow against these preposterous erections was struck. The ladies of the Court then lowered them by one third, but the middle classes were unable to conform to this change quite so quickly. As the height was reduced, the coiffure became wider and rounder in form with a few dropping curls caught behind the neck by a large bow. Powder of reddish and grey hues took the place of white.[1]

[1] The value of a head of hair used in the making of fine wigs was often

Cosmetics were of course essential to the toilet of the lady of fashion. Almond paste was used for bleaching the hands and arms, and Italian washes, such as Mrs. Bailey's 'Eau de Fleurs de Venise', were used for the face. Specialists in pomades, paints, lipsalves, enamels, perfumes, and powders drove a thriving trade. Some beauties carried the care of their complexion to great lengths. One bridegroom complained that his bride preserved her beauty at night by sleeping with her hair in a greasy net and a bundle of flannel as large as a turban round her head, while her arms were encased in perfumed gloves; and an outraged husband in 1773 made a similar complaint on marrying a beauty who enveloped her whole head and face except her nose to take care of her eyes and prevent wrinkles, and swaddled her body in bedgowns and petticoats.

Dress-etiquette for the audience at the theatre was fairly strict, and a description of the costumes which were de rigueur at the performances of the Opera at the King's Theatre, Haymarket, in 1779, is full of interest. Gentlemen in the pit and boxes were expected to wear either full dress or at least French frocks with swords. The head was to be uncovered with a bag-wig. In the first gallery 'a gentle déshabillé' was required, but in the upper gallery no great attention was paid to dress, since most gentlemen went there incognito. The etiquette for the Oratorio at the same theatre was similar. At the ordinary playhouses half-dress at least, with the hair or wig dressed 'chapeau bas', was expected of those frequenting the lower boxes, and for a man to appear with his hat on in the front or side boxes bespoke him as ill-bred and ignorant of 'the Ton'. In other parts of the house every one could dress as he pleased.

Few gentlemen went in full dress to Ranelagh or Vauxhall, but a half-dress was usually worn, and it was not considered good form for any one to appear in boots. All gentlemen wore their hats. At the masquerades and ridottos held at the King's Theatre all had to appear masked, either in characteristic dresses or in dominos. The gentlemen usually wore their masks till supper-time, and then unmasked for the

considerable, and girls frequently offered their hair at the various markets and fairs. One Oxford lass sold her hair to a Strand chapman in 1700 for sixty pounds. This was a high price, for the Countess of Suffolk did not get more than twenty for hers in 1715. An elderly lady's head of white hair fetched fifty pounds in 1720.

THE BATTLE OF UMBRELLAS.

From an engraving of 1784

rest of the night. Ladies seldom unmasked unless they were among the number of the 'Impures'. As the ridottos took place in Lent the greatest decorum was observed and ladies of easy virtue were excluded. Only people of rank and fashion attended, and it was customary to appear in black full dress whether the Court was in mourning or not.

Masquerades came into vogue during the third quarter of the century, but fell into disrepute with the polite company early in the eighties, as they had degenerated into riot, debauch, and inebriety. Parties of friends would often attend the masquerades in specially dressed groups. Here would be seen an Indian chief with his squaws, there a Turkish Pasha surrounded by his harem. One party of four consisted of a keeper with his dancing bear, a lame fiddler, and an attendant who played excellently on the saltbox. An abbess was followed by several nuns, 'devotees of Venus elegantly dressed, supported with the greatest art of make-up'. The religious habit was a favourite garb: an observer remarks of a certain lady, who appeared as a Spanish nun, that had Mrs. Potiphar been so enchanting Joseph would not have been recorded as insensible and his garment would never have been rent. Some of these costumes did not err on the side of reverence: one female mask dressed partly as a man with a woman's head-dress surmounted by a huge clerical hat called herself 'La Fille de l'Archevêque'. Live animals were sometimes introduced into these assemblies; ladies appeared as country wenches with a live chicken, a duck, or a goose, and others brought their dogs, monkeys, and parrots.

A famous masquerade given by the Savoir Vivre Club at the Pantheon in 1775 was attended by fourteen thousand masks, and in the following year sixteen thousand masks attended the fête given jointly by the Savoir Vivre, Almack's, Boodle's, Sanderson's, and the Thatched House Clubs. A great many Turkish costumes were worn on this occasion, the turbans being adorned with wonderful jewels. A certain Lady Villars in a Polish costume is said to have had fifty thousand pounds worth of jewels on her.

A print of the Pantheon in 1773 by C. White exhibits the type and cut of many amusing costumes and shows the large Pantomime heads which were a feature of the entertainment. Ladies frequently went dressed as men and vice versa: a

Mrs. Tomlinson appeared as a Councillor, a Mr. Dawes as a cook-maid, and a Captain Rice as a Billingsgate fish-wife. We are told that the most distinguished Belles went clad 'en homme', often as Macaroni dandies. The favourite costumes included heathen deities, virgins of the sun, popes, devils, jesters, Scotsmen with bagpipes, Macaronis, harlequins and columbines, Quakers, ballad-singers, Blue-coat boys, parish girls, procurers, quack-doctors, and tallow-chandlers. Among the more intriguing characters were May-day sweeps, Billy Buttons, and Teddy Dolls, St. David in large top-boots mounted on a goat, a Spanish character called 'La Fiera en Mascherata', a squire groom with a four-pound saddle at his side, a Georgian hoity-toity, and a King of the Antipodes who is said to have waved his galagaskins in the air as a lesson to monarchs to wear the breeches. There was a curious fancy for double masks: one lady was Elizabethan on one side and in the prevailing mode on the other, a second was a decrepit old woman on one side and a pretty young girl on the other, while a third was smartly dressed in front and ragged behind.

Sir Joshua Reynolds contented himself with a simple domino when he appeared at masquerades, but Goldsmith was seen on two occasions wearing old English dresses. Though there is no evidence that the great Dr. Johnson himself ever took part in a masquerade, Boswell was certainly swept into the craze. His usual sober brown clothes were exchanged for a plain robe over a shirt of flowered brocade, his hair rolled high with a simple bandeau entwined in its folds. At the Stratford Pageant in 1769 he assumed the rôle of a dashing Corsican brigand-chief, but a picture of him in this dress produces a rather tame effect in spite of the gun slung over his back and the pair of heavy pistols thrust in his belt. He wears a short jacket with a badge over the heart, a plain waistcoat, leather breeches tied at the knees, buttoned gaiters, and a round high-crowned hat with a feather and the motto 'Viva la Libertà'. In his hand he carries a tall stick, the top of which is curiously twisted like a snake.

Fashionable weddings were attended in full dress, the men wearing laced frocks with swords and white waistcoats and gloves. The conventional attire for a bride as we know it to-day had already been fixed—the dress of white silk or satin with a train, the long veil, and the orange-blossoms in the hair. The bride of the lower classes contented herself with the best white dress she could afford and wore a light veil over her head or hat. The bridegroom wore white gloves and a white bow in his hat.[1] The parade of mourning at eighteenth-century funerals was exceedingly interesting. The corpse itself was dressed in perfumed woollen cerecloth, linen being prohibited except on payment of a heavy fine, though we read that the corpse of Nance Oldfield, the actress, was richly adorned with lace. The clergyman clad in canonical vestments led the procession, and the mourners of both sexes followed in pairs, arm in arm. When the deceased was a young woman, six young men with white hatbands and gloves were chosen to act as pall-bearers, while six young women dressed in white attended the corpse of a young man. At the funerals of married persons and infants white scarves, hatbands, and gloves were presented to the mourners, but this custom was not so frequently seen after the 'eighties. The mortuary cloths could be hired, the richest costing from five to six crowns. Palls were of black velvet or cloth edged with a white silk or linen band about a foot wide. If the deceased was a bachelor, a maid, or a woman who had died in childbirth a large white pall was used, which half-covered the six coffin-bearers, who were provided with black or white gloves and black crêpe hatbands.

[1] Cf. supra, pp. 353–4.

BIBLIOGRAPHY.—The author's account is based on many years' experience in collecting costumes and on the following sources of information:
The original works of WILLIAM HOGARTH; Old English Costume, a Collection of Stage-dresses, etc.; F. W. FAIRHOLT, Costume in England (1885); D. C. CALTHORP, English Costume (1907); MRS. C. ASHDOWN, British Costume (1910); T. T. OSSERHYN, Costume in the time of George II (1845); F. M. KELLY and R. SWABE, Historic Costume (1925); TALBOT HUGHES, Dress Design (1911); J. R. PLANCHÉ, Cyclopaedia of costume; Plocacosmos or the whole art of Hairdressing by the hairdresser Stewart, 1782; Autobiography of Mrs. Delany; S. BRINTON, The 18th Century in English Caricature (1904); 'GEORGE PASTON', Social Caricature in the 18th century (1905). Also the contemporary magazines: The Gentleman's Magazine, The Lady's Magazine, The Review, The Spectator, The St. James Gazette, and especially The Town and Country Magazine, in which many types of wigs and head-dresses are illustrated. Books on miniatures are also valuable in this respect.
The chief collections of costume are to be found at the Victoria and Albert Museum, the London Museum, and the museums at Nottingham and Hastings.

PRINTED IN
GREAT BRITAIN
AT THE
UNIVERSITY PRESS
OXFORD
BY
JOHN JOHNSON
PRINTER
TO THE
UNIVERSITY